Sebastian Berg
Intellectual Radicalism after 1989

Political Science | Volume 32

to my friends

Sebastian Berg (Dr. habil.) teaches Social and Cultural Studies of Anglophone Societies at Ruhr University Bochum. His research interests include the history and politics of »the Left«, social movements, and environmentalism.

Sebastian Berg

Intellectual Radicalism after 1989

Crisis and Re-orientation in the British and the American Left

[transcript]

Further: Habilitation, Faculty of Philosophy, Chemnitz University of Technology, 2012.

This work is licensed under the
Creative Commons Attribution-NonCommercial-NoDerivs 3.0 (BY-NC-ND)
which means that the text may be used for non-commercial purposes, provided credit is given to the author.
For details go to http://creativecommons.org/licenses/by-nc-nd/3.0/.

All rights reserved. No part of this book may be reprinted or reproduced or utilized in any form or by any electronic, mechanical, or other means, now known or hereafter invented, including photocopying and recording, or in any information storage or retrieval system, without permission in writing from the publisher.

© 2016 transcript Verlag, Bielefeld
Cover layout: Kordula Röckenhaus, Bielefeld
Printed in Germany
Print-ISBN 978-3-8376-3418-1
PDF-ISBN 978-3-8394-3418-5

Table of Contents

I. Introduction: the Paradox of 1989 | 7

II. Analysing the Impact of 1989 on the British and the American Intellectual Left | 21
1. 1989/91 and the Prospects of Socialism: Options for a Theoretical Debate of the Left on Strategies and Agencies | 21
1.1. The Intellectuals' Core Ideas of Democratic Socialism | 23
1.2. Social Democracy as a Model and Social Democratic Parties as Agents of Change? | 26
1.3. Post-Marxism as a Re-formulation of, or a Departure from, Socialist Strategies for Change? | 36
2. A Short History of the British and the American Intellectual Left and the Journals Analysed | 45
2.1. The Many British New Lefts | 45
2.2. *New Left Review* and *Socialist Register* | 51
2.3. Two Generations of the American Intellectual Left | 60
2.4. *Dissent* and *Monthly Review* | 65
2.5. Similarites and Differences among the British and the American Lefts | 73

III. Crisis and Re-orientation: Evidence from the Journals | 77
1. The Moment of 1989: Emotional Responses to the Collapse of the Eastern Bloc | 77
2. Assessments of State Socialism | 90
3. The State of Theory | 131
3.1. Marxism | 131
3.2. The Retrieval of Classics from the Radical and Socialist Traditions | 172
3.3. Marxism and Radicalism | 187
4. Out of the Impasse: the Search for Models | 190
4.1. Dimensions of Democratic Socialism | 190
4.2. Market Socialism – a Promising Project? | 231
4.3. Sweden and Other Dreamlands | 242

4.4.	Europe: Capitalist Club or Site of Struggle and Project for the Left?	250	
4.5.	Locating Socialism	260	
5.	Re-starting History: Agency and Strategy	263	

IV. Between Radical Critique and Moderate Recommendations? | 309

1.	Between Social Democracy and post-Marxism?	310	
1.1.	Democratic Socialism and Social Democracy	310	
1.2.	Neo-Marxism and Post-Marxism	312	
2.	British and American or Anglo-American Re-orientations?	314	
3.	Outlook and Conclusion	316	

V. Bibliography | 321

VI. Acknowledgements | 339

VII. Detailed Table of Contents | 341

I. Introduction
The Paradox of 1989

In 1991, Robin Blackburn, then editor of *New Left Review*, argued in a long article with the title "Fin de Siècle: Socialism after the Crash", that "today's moribund 'Great Power Communism' is not a spectre stalking the globe but an unhappy spirit, begging to be laid to rest" (1991: 5). Although he conceded that "for Marxists, to disclaim any responsibility whatever for the October Revolution and the state which issued from it would be wrong" (ibid: 9), he believed in the possibility of a new beginning for radical and Marxist social theory – especially if theorists not only considered the Eastern Bloc's lack of democratic structures, but analysed its economic problems and failures as well. About one year later, the American political philosopher and editor of the left-wing journal *Dissent*, Michael Walzer, seemed more sceptical:

We are in a period of uncertainty and confusion. The collapse of communism ought to open new opportunities for the democratic left, but its immediate effect has been to raise questions about many leftist (not only communist) orthodoxies: about the 'direction' of history, the role of state planning in the economy, the value and effectiveness of the market, the future of nationalism, and so on. (1992: 466)

Again three years later, American cultural sociologist Jeffrey C. Alexander observed in the pages of *New Left Review* that the events of 1989 had to be understood as a 'new transition': "It is the transition from communism to capitalism, a phrase that seems oxymoronic even to our chastened ears. The sense of world-historical transformation remains, but the straight line of history seems to be running in reverse" (1995: 65). Calling his article "Modern, Anti, Post and Neo", Alexander described how North Atlantic intellectuals had come full circle, arriving again at a world of ideas quite similar to what he defined as the modernism of the 1950s.[1] Towards the end of the decade, the British political scientist Andrew Gamble wrote an introduction to a compilation of reflections on Marxism's future role within the social sciences. As a title, he chose the question: "Why bother with Marxism?" and explained:

Nothing quite as cataclysmic however has occurred before in the history of Marxism as the collapse of communism in Eastern Europe and the Soviet Union between 1989 and 1991. Its significance for Marxism must not be underrated. Despite the ossification of Marxism as a doctrine in the Soviet Union, and the open repudiation of the Soviet system by Marxists in other parts of the world, the extent to which in the previous seventy years the meaning of Marxism and of socialism had become inextricably bound up with the fate of the Soviet Union had not been fully appreciated. (1999: 1)

Gamble saw two alternatives, neither of which appeared attractive to him: Marxism could either continue to exist in isolation and as a former shadow of itself or else merge with the intellectual mainstream. He pleaded for keeping at least some core elements of Marxism – especially the formulation of critical questions on the origins, character and developments of economic and social relations (ibid: 4). Finally, the Swedish sociologist Göran Therborn diagnosed in an article "After Dialectics. Radical Social Theory in a Post-Communist World", published in *New Left Review* in early 2007, that a post-1945 and – according to him – especially post-1968, Western Marxist triangle had been disentangled: social theory as the combination of historical social science, philosophy of dialectics and a working-class poli-

---

[1] Alexander's version of modernism borrows from modernisation theory. This theory held a hegemonic position within the social sciences from the 1940s to the 1960s. Modernisation theorists worked under the assumption that societies were coherently organized systems, traditional or modern, developing through evolutionary processes towards individualism, secularism, capitalism, democracy (cf. 1995: 67-68).

tics aiming at the overthrow of the existing order (cf. 2007: 69). In particular, the politically revolutionary third dimension had disappeared as a result of the historical defeats of Western European social democracy in the 1970s and 1980s, the intellectual challenges of postmodernism and poststructuralism, and the collapse of the Eastern Bloc. According to Therborn, the European Marxist and socialist left was more seriously affected than the traditionally weaker, more sober and geographically farther removed American one (cf. ibid: 99-100). However, with regard to both, two decades after the events of 1989/91, the collapse of the Eastern Bloc and slightly later of the Soviet Union is still often characterised as a last stumbling block for a tired and disillusioned Western Marxist left, old as well as new.[2]

This constitutes a paradox because Western Marxism in most of its shades had for a long time distanced itself from really existing socialism. The paradox was characterised by the British political theorist Norman Geras as "a tendency, amongst people who have thought, insisted, for years that the Soviet and Eastern European regimes were not a genuine embodiment or product of Marxist belief, to wonder if the entire tradition is not now bankrupted by their wreckage – as though the ideas and values of Marxism were then, after all, wrapped up in these regimes, as before they were said not to be." (1990: 32) Especially in Britain, numerous studies have been published over the last approximately fifteen years which diagnose, deplore and criticise the end of Marxism as an intellectual-political project. They come up with a variety of explanations for what was, in their eyes, an improper ending. Even more surprising than the diversity of the reasons suggested – some of which seem contradictory – is the empirical

---

2   The distinction of old and new left is widely used in Britain and North America. The 'old left' which developed in the late nineteenth and early twentieth century, stood for a more traditional version of socialism with the emancipation of the working class as the central goal, changes in the economic order as the means with which to achieve it, and socialist or working-class parties and the labour movements as the agents which fight for it. The new left, which emerged in the 1960s and 1970s, aimed at liberating people from various types of structural oppression such as, for example, racism, sexism, or imperialism. The new left identifies civil rights groups, pressure groups, grassroots organisations, and non-governmental organisations as the major agents of change – ideally united in a 'rainbow coalition'.

base on which they are founded. With the exception of Paul Newman's study on Ralph Miliband[3] (2002), they concentrate either on the journal *New Left Review* or on the individual often seen as its mastermind – Perry Anderson[4] (Achcar 2000; Blackledge 2000; Blackledge 2002; Blackledge 2004; Elliott 1998; Sprinker 1993; Thompson 2001; Thompson 2007). They elaborate on Anderson's "Olympianism" (Elliott 1998), "Deutscherism" (Blackledge 2004, Elliott 1998), and his and *New Left Review*'s "historical pessimism" (Blackledge 2002, Thompson 2007), the journal's over-reliance on short-lived social movements, its distrust of the British working class and its too rosy picture of Third Worldism. Most important for the paradox of 1989, the pessimism resulting from the events is interpreted as the logical consequence of what Gregory Elliott called the 'Deutscherite' perspective (1998). At its core was the perception, ascribed to Isaac Deutscher, of the U.S.S.R. and its allies as non-capitalist and, furthermore, post-capitalist societies, despite their shortcomings (to be explained with the Soviet Union's backward economy and hostile environment) (cf. van der Linden 2007: 139-146).[5] Deutscher was convinced that eventually these deficiencies would be corrected:

Stalinism has exhausted its historical function. Like every other great revolution, the Russian revolution has made ruthless use of force and violence to bring into being a new social order and to ensure its survival. An old-established regime relies for its continuance on the force of social custom. A revolutionary order creates new custom by force. Only when its material framework has been firmly set and consolidated can it rely on its own inherent vitality; then it frees itself from the terror that formerly safeguarded it. (1953: 164)

---

3   Ralph Miliband, 1924-1994, Marxist political scientist, taught at London School of Economics and the University of Leeds, co-founded *Socialist Register* with John Saville in 1964.

4   Perry Anderson, born 1938, from 1962 editor of *New Left Review* for almost 20 years, became editor again in 2000 and stayed on until the end of 2003; he left Britain in the 1980s to take up a post as professor of history and sociology at UCLA and is seen by many observers as the leading figure in *New Left Review*.

5   For a short summary of Deutscher's perspective, see Marcel van der Linden, *Western Marxism and the Soviet Union. A Survey of Critical Theories and Debates Since 1917* (Leiden: Brill, 2007), pp. 139-146.

As Thompson pointed out, according to Deutscher's perspective the principal achievement of the October Revolution, namely the abolition of private property, had in fact never been reversed and thus the Soviet Union stood in the revolutionary tradition of 1917 (cf. 2007: 33). It was at least 'one step further' than the capitalist West. Hence, change towards a version of socialism worth the name *could* be implemented from above (cf. Elliott 1998: 30). However, there was no guarantee that it would, and the Cold-War climate diminished the likelihood of this to happen (cf. Thompson 2007: 33). Still, it remained more probable than a socialist transformation in the West, realised through working-class struggle – especially at a time when the working class was declining in absolute numbers and also becoming ever more fragmented (cf. Anderson 1992: 279-375). According to Paul Blackledge, "this transposition of the extrinsic history of the class struggle from the point of production to the global arena of the Cold War effectively tied his [Perry Anderson's; S.B.] vision of socialism to the fate of the Soviet Union" (2004: 99). For those who thought like Anderson, socialist agency, or at least the possibility of movement towards socialism, rested with the Soviet Union, and some of them saw the Gorbachev era as a delayed vindication of Deutscher's thesis.

Important as Anderson indubitably is for the history of the Anglophone intellectual left in the second half of the twentieth century, the question arises in how far studies focusing on him suffice as analyses of the problems that 1989 caused for certain strands of Marxist and socialist thinking. Can the Deutscher-based explanation help us to understand the intellectual left's tiredness and confusion after 1989 beyond the specific cases of Anderson and perhaps *New Left Review*? Reducing – at least implicitly – the history of a non-aligned, heterogeneous intellectual left to a journal (even if it admittedly calls itself the 'flagship of the intellectual left') and further narrowing down this journal to the ideas of Perry Anderson, Robin Blackburn[6], and – for its earlier phase – Tom Nairn[7], entails the danger of substi-

---

6 Robin Blackburn, born 1940, member of *New Left Review*'s editorial board since 1962 and editor from 1981 to 1999, played an active role in British student protests in 1968, close long-term cooperation with Anderson, professor of sociology at the University of Essex.

7 Tom Nairn, born 1932, member of *New Left Review*'s editorial board from the early 1960s until the late 1980s, co-formulated the Anderson-Nairn thesis,

tuting accusations of individuals 'selling out' their former political convictions for thorough analysis. Many more Marxist and leftwing intellectuals than those writing in the pages of *New Left Review* had deeply ambivalent feelings about the changes of 1989 though they had, with Norman Geras, declared again and again – at least since 1956 – that the Soviet Union and the Eastern Bloc did not represent their idea of socialism.

A major methodological problem for an approach focusing less narrowly on individuals and their political biographies lies in the question of who belongs to the 'intellectual left' and points to a difficulty that always arises once one sets out to investigate the ideas of collectives that are more amorphous than, say, political parties or interest groups. I try to come to grips with this problem through developing a comparative approach based on a clearly defined corpus of sources: political-academic journals. They were chosen because researchers of intellectuals generally agree that journals form important nodal points around which intellectuals assemble (cf. Bock 1998: 41). This study embarks on a comprehensive analysis of the relevant material in four such publications. Two of them, *New Left Review* and *Socialist Register*, were British in origin while the other two, *Dissent* and *Monthly Review*, had U.S.-American roots, and all tried to produce social theory with political surplus value. With its comparative focus, thus, the study does not only analyse the similarities and differences between the journals, but also the possible variance between British and North American intellectuals. The analysis covers those articles in which authors tried to make sense of recent developments within the five years from January 1990 to December 1994. Although these publications did not represent the British and American intellectual left as a whole, they played important roles within its debates.[8] Moreover, although discussions did not end in 1994, the time frame is deliberately chosen: five years are short enough to allow for a

---

claiming that Britain's archaic political culture had to be explained with its proto-bourgeois revolution and a later alliance of aristocracy and bourgeoisie; he fell out with the editorial board due to different perceptions of nationalism, professor of nationalism and cultural diversity at Royal Melbourne Institute of Technology.

8 This selection of journals allows for a consideration of many of those thinkers (and their intellectual environment) whose work is discussed by Alexander and Therborn.

detailed reading and long enough to explore longer-term trends. Further, these five years form a period of crisis in the Gramscian sense: the old had died but the new could not yet be born. Arguably, the new came to life from the mid-1990s onwards when intellectuals embarked on critiques of globalisation, opposition to the incremental acceptance of war – legitimised through the UN – as a means of 'solving' geo-political conflicts and scepticism over centre-left and social democratic parties' return to governmental power on supposedly neo-liberal platforms.[9] With this methodological design, the study complements the existing historical-biographical long-term accounts with a comparative analysis of networks or collectives of intellectuals.

There are strong arguments for choosing these publications as cases for a comparative study. Some are formal: the journals stand out: with birth years between 1949 and 1964, and uninterrupted activity since, through longevity and a high degree of personal continuity among editors and contributors. With Irving Howe[10], Paul Sweezy[11], Perry Anderson and Ralph Miliband, respectively, the character and perspective of each periodical was shaped by one particularly influential, long-serving editor – two of them British and two citizens of the United States, though certainly none of the journals can be seen as a mere brainchild of its head editor.[12] All stand for a

---

9   *Socialist Register* debated globalisation already from 1992 onwards. But as a topic that occupied the minds of a large number of political economists, globalisation critique developed from the mid-1990s.

10 Irving Howe, 1920-1993, literary scholar and political activists, belonged to the 'New York Intellectuals', disapproved of the move of many of his contemporaries from Trotskyism to Neo-Conservatism and embraced a loosely defined 'democratic socialism', became co-founder, with Lewis Coser, of *Dissent* in 1954.

11 Paul Sweezy, 1910-2004, Marxist economist, academic and New Deal administrator, co-founder, with Leo Huberman, of *Monthly Review* in 1949, became well-known for his work on 'monopoly capitalism'.

12 There are numerous discussions on editorial politics and mechanisms of decision making in *New Left Review*. The tenor is that Perry Anderson has played (and still plays) an extremely important role in its life, even at times when he was not the official editor, as in the early 1990s. Anderson's role was discussed by Paul Blackledge (2004), Lin Chun (1996), Dennis Dworkin (1997), Gregory

genre of writing that integrates essayistic elements into academic articles. Further reasons for this selection of journals lie in their content and political outlook. Since they were founded during the early Cold War, most of those individuals setting them up belonged to a generation of leftwing intellectuals born in the 1910s and 1920s and politically socialised in the interwar years and the Second World War. During that time, it was difficult to unambiguously define one's position vis-à-vis the Soviet Union – which stood for Stalinist violence but also for a decisive contribution to the defeat of Nazism. Whereas it seemed often impossible then to square the circle of expressing solidarity with both the U.S.S.R. and with workers' interests on a global scale, after the war it became increasingly difficult to react adequately to the developing block confrontation. With different approaches, each of the journals tried to find a democratic-socialist position, a 'third way' or 'third space' that was neither uncritically pro-communist nor dogmatically anti-communist. They subscribed to a socialist and – with the partial exception of *Dissent* – Marxist ecumenism. Having started their political activities in the orbit of radical-left organisations, the U.S. intellectuals associated with *Dissent* and *Monthly Review* had already broken with Moscow in the 1930s or 1940s or had always been broad-minded Marxists rather than 'party soldiers' (cf. Diggins 1992: 152). In Britain, they broke free from the Communist Party in 1956. The four journals saw themselves as critically allied primarily to the labour, peace and civil rights movements in their respective countries (as well as internationally) and, in some cases – as deliberately following popular-front traditions in coalition building – in a critical dialogue with the major political parties of the centre-left. Further, the contributors represented a specific intellectual type: they were neither closely associated with parties nor, although sympathetic, intimately allied with radical movements. They became the first generation of an academic left which – to a large degree – substituted 'theoretical practice' for in-

---

Elliott (1998) and Michael Kenny (1995). None of the other journals' internal lives have attracted comparable interest. Perhaps they were run more smoothly (*Socialist Register*, for example, did not work with an editorial committee before Ralph Miliband's death in 1994), yet apparently *New Left Review* is also an exceptional case. The other publications are less frequently used as reference points for making statements about one's own political position – a role that, to me as a foreign observer, seems quite evident in the case of New Left Review.

volvement in political struggles.[13] Still, they saw themselves as 'organic intellectuals'. Having preceded the student New Left of the late 1960s, all the journals sympathised with the student protests but also disagreed on certain points. Nevertheless, they provided important orientation for the younger new-left generation of 1968. Several student activists of the late 1960s later joined their editorial boards or contributed articles. In the changing political and academic climate of the 1970s and 1980s, the journals expressed scepticism of (post-)Marxist revisionism and of neo-Trotskyite approaches. They became severe critics of the rising neoliberalism and did not follow many progressives' turn towards post-structuralism and deconstruction. Instead, they kept their faith in historical-materialist and political economic explanations. From their early days, the journals acknowledged each other, followed each others' debates, and criticised each other – at times rather heavily.[14] Finally, most writers in the journals shared the view that – despite all the differences they saw between their ideas of socialism and the version that had been realised in Eastern Europe and the Soviet Union – a self-critical debate was unavoidable.

A comparative analysis of these journals' articles faces two difficulties: first, it is almost impossible to find journals that can be considered as 'real' equivalents – not only because of the specificities of the political-cultural settings in which the publications try to make themselves read, but also because it is of all things the relative uniqueness of a periodical that makes it successful and worth reading. The journals in question differ from each other in their respective versions of Marxism and socialism, in the breadth of political opinion that is tolerated within their pages and in many further

---

13 This distinguished the journals from others, such as *Marxism Today* and *International Socialism* in Britain or *The Nation* and *New Politics* in the USA, which either moved, as a consequence of embracing Marxist revisionism, closer to centre-left parties, or, because of a different understanding of the relation of structure and agency, claimed to have a more intimate link to the radical left sections of labour and social movements.

14 It should be noted that several contributors published in more than one journal – for example, Daniel Singer in *Socialist Register* and *Monthly Review*, Norman Geras in *New Left Review* and *Socialist Register*, Cornel West in *Monthly Review* and *Dissent*, Ralph Miliband in *New Left Review*, *Socialist Register* and *Monthly Review*.

respects: different levels of theoretical abstraction and fields of empirical focus, varying prestige in the academic world, and wider popular versus narrower academic recruitment areas of contributors and implied readerships. They are marked by conceptual specificities such as *New Left Review*'s short-lived sympathies for Mao and Althusser in the 1970s, a leftwing, critical Zionism among post-Trotskyist *Dissenters*, Miliband's theory of the capitalist state shining through the pages of *Socialist Register*, or Sweezy's theory of capitalist development visible in those of *Monthly Review*. Nevertheless, all of them solicit articles rather than simply inviting contributions and all of them try to reach a readership spectrum from the left wings of the respective centre-left parties in Britain and the United States to the many groups of the radical left. The second difficulty arises from the limitations of a purely contrastive comparison. It can certainly identify differences, similarities and analogies in the intellectual reactions to 1989. However, it is an insufficient tool when it comes to explaining the paradox described in the beginning of this introduction. Such an explanation requires hypothesising and subsequent hypotheses-testing via comparison and contextualization.

For left intellectuals writing in the journals, the events of 1989/91 constituted a turning point. The Eastern Bloc – whether post-capitalist or not – had domesticated Western capitalism because it was perceived in the West as a systemic alternative to capitalism. This fuction was left vacant with the Eastern Bloc's demise. Neither the labour movements of the West nor the societies and states of the South could be counted on as suitable substitutes. Hence, the future was likely to suffer from the imposition of a more brutal, 'liberated' capitalism. In so far, the years 1989/91 constituted a turning point. However, the texts published in the journals reacted not only to these political, but to discursive shifts. At the time, Dick Flacks suggested that "[t]o make social theory is frequently to attempt to make history" (1991: 3). The intellectual left saw themselves engaged in a struggle about discursive power. Did they still have chances to influence political discourse on issues such as the reasons of the failure of state socialism, the designing of alternative futures beyond capitalism as it existed in the last decade of the 20th century?[15] Furthermore, writers asked themselves in how far the events of

---

15 The problem of finding the adequate term for the political and economic systems of the states of the Eastern Bloc has caused considerable debate among the

1989 marked a caesura that required a rethinking of key components of the critical social theory and political analysis they had produced. Did Marxist and socialist concepts still prove to be useful for explaining historical developments and formulating political goals and strategies? It seems that, at least for most, Marxism still provided an analytical toolkit when it came to explaining social phenomena and developments of the past and of the present. For the design of concrete goals and practical political strategies, however, many writers moved towards post-Marxism and social democracy. Without systemic alternative, it became next to impossible for the Marxists and socialists in focus here to formulate a fundamental political disagreement with social democrats and post-Marxists. In this sense, 1989/91 became an ending, which put intellectuals in a state of existential crisis. As a general tendency, this can be observed in all the journals investigated. Nevertheless, one has to ask whether this embrace of post-Marxist or social democratic positions was shared to the same extent by British and American texts and by the two different generations, which were represented among the contributors and editorial committees – one politically socialised with the experience of the Great Depression, the rise of fascism, the popular front, and the Second World War, the other in the context of welfare capitalism, the Cold War and the Vietnam War. Shortly, what follows is a theoretically-informed comparison, elaborating in how far two generations of Anglo-American intellectuals' reactions entail an adoption of social democratic and post-Marxist assumptions, principles, goals and strategies.

This study looks into a large sample of articles from different angles. It uses a method that could be called 'deconstructive': it investigates lines of argument in regard to the question of their position on, for example, the deficiencies of state socialism (Part III, Chapter 2) or the core values of democratic socialism (Part III, Capter 4.1). Considering the narrative intention of the texts, it nevertheless reads them with questions in mind that are in many cases different from the questions the writers addressed in their articles and from the purposes their texts served. After introducing the Marxist-inspired democratic socialism, for which the journals claimed to stand as well as social democracy and post-Marxism, Section III will first

---

left in the West. I use the term 'state socialism' to confess agnosticism with regard to these debates rather than to take a position within them. For an overview of the discussions see van der Linden 2007.

analyse articles and passages which were almost emotional – expressing thoughts ranging from elation to grief and sorrow over the events of 1989. These represent the most personal attempts at coming to terms with the historical break. The Section then goes on to investigate more analytical reflections. Writers tried to establish what had actually happened in 1989/91 and why it had happened. Many of the contributions asked in how far the Western side should be held responsible for the implosion of the Eastern Bloc through stifling its potential to develop. Would the history of the state socialist systems have been different without the 'competition' from the 'West' and without the arms race? These articles often contained implicit normative comparisons. The systems of the Eastern Bloc had their deficiencies – but were these more serious than the shortcomings of the systems of the capitalist West? The following chapter discusses the future status of socialist theory. If Therborn's earlier mentioned diagnosis that the Marxist triangle had been broken was correct, what would remain of Marxism? Was Marxism simply an overrated theory, a system of thought that had been granted the stature of an intellectual giant which was now eventually cut to size?[16] Which elements should be retained as kernels of a socialist theory and politics? What was their relationship to other social theories? If Blackburn's perception, also mentioned earlier, was right that Marxism had to accept responsibility for developments in the Eastern Bloc – what would this mean for radical social theory? In how far should Marxists and socialists accept the allegation that a logical connection existed between the holistic claim of Marxist theory and the authoritarian excesses of Stalinism? Should socialists look for alternative ideas and strategies from within and beyond the socialist traditions? Which looked most promising? The following chapter starts out from numerous writers' agreement that one of the

---

16 To understand Marxism as a 'system of thought' implies granting it a privileged position in explanations of historical phenomena. Rather than seeing it as one analytical approach among many, employing Marxism as a system of thought rests on the assumption that its explanatory validity – and superiority to other theories – is self-evident or proven. Different from this approach is the use of Marxism as a 'spirit of critique', which means to evaluate historical phenomena from a distinctive normative position. Rather than claiming its explanatory superiority, employing Marxism as a spirit of critique rests on the assumption of its evident ethical legitimacy.

most serious mistakes of Marxists had been their reluctance to engage in utopian thinking. What direction could such creative thinking take to start designing scenarios for an emancipatory politics? In this context, contributors spent much time reflecting on the concept of democratic socialism. Most of them admitted that a lack of democracy had constituted the biggest stumbling block for movement towards a socialist society in political terms. However, the implosion was interpreted not just as the consequence of political inadequacies; economic problems played an equally important role – most seriously the incapability of the Eastern Bloc's economic system – based on centralised top-down planning – to satisfy the needs of its own citizens. Consequently, contributors engaged in the debates on the potentially beneficial role of markets as distributive mechanisms in general, and of possible structures of market socialism more specifically. Thirdly, within this search for alternatives, really-existing models were also investigated: these could include socialist systems considered as working more humanely or more efficiently than those of the Eastern Bloc, while also extending to capitalist systems which had most successfully reconciled the search for profit with a welfarist social policy. The final chapter of Section III deals with the problem of how to achieve political change. Which parts of the world, which classes or collectives within a given society could one imagine as revolutionary or transformative agents? What was the role of the capitalist state and its institutions such as elections, governments and parliaments? Would political change be organised from above, struggled for from below or would it require double pressure from both sides? In this context, the question of the necessity of a revolution could not be ignored. Did it still make sense to envisage a violent rupture, a revolution in the traditional sense, as a prerequisite and a promising starting point for the implementation of a socialist project? In addition, intellectuals had to think about their own role within an emancipatory strategy. Could they function as a transformative vanguard? Or was their task more low-key – did they have to feed the political public with critical social theory? Which were the groups they should try to reach: political parties, trade unions, social movements? Via contrastive comparison of articles and passages within contributions, Section III shows a near-universal agreement among radical intellectuals that a great deal of new thinking was necessary though there was a high degree of disagreement as to what direction it should take.

The final part (Section IV) takes the comparison a step further by asking whether these new directions in socialist thinking need to be understood as intellectual moves towards social democracy, post-Marxism, or both. To this end, the section discusses what the empirical findings in Section III mean for central elements of traditional Marxism and socialism: it tries, for example, to identify intellectuals' positions on the logic of historical development, on the necessity of a qualitative break with capitalism and on the privileged role of the working class in emancipatory struggles and it juxtaposes these with the perspectives of social democracy and post-Marxism. What can be learned from this comparison is – among other things – that old distinctions of revolutionary socialists on the one hand and reformist social democrats on the other and of historical-materialist Marxists on the one hand and postmodern post-Marxists on the other have lost most of their relevance for radical intellectuals in both Britain and the United States. The section continues with a summary of the British-U.S. comparison and concludes by reflecting on the longer-term consequences of the events of 1989/91 for the intellectual left as a political and discursive community.

The argument to come follows a strictly symmetrical structure: each topic's treatment is analysed for each journal individually, followed by a short comparison. This allows the book to be read in different ways: most readers will probably be interested in specific topics. They can read the relevant chapters or subchapters in Part III in detail. Alternatively, they can focus on the contrastive comparison at the end of each chapter. Others might want to learn how the individual journals deal with and debate the historical conjuncture and turning point. They can use the relevant sections in each of the chapters and ignore the others. This structure proves useful for different categories of implied readers, even though it betrays the study's origin as a habilitation thesis.

II. Analysing the Impact of 1989 on the British and the American Intellectual Left

1. 1989/91 AND THE PROSPECTS OF SOCIALISM: OPTIONS FOR A THEORETICAL DEBATE OF THE LEFT ON STRATEGIES AND AGENCIES

Socialists who wanted to remain socialists and continue to work for an alternative to capitalism had three major options for reacting to the collapse of the Eastern Bloc. For one, they could, of course, simply argue that it did not affect them at all. The societies of Eastern Europe had never represented Western socialists' version of socialism or they did not even deserve to be called socialist at all. Their deformations were the outcomes of Stalinism and Stalin's unrealistic concept of building 'socialism in one country'. The states could not have been reformed from within without collapsing under their internal contradictions and conflicts. This position was taken by many on the left who were organised in, or sympathised with, the 'Trotskyist' movement – in Britain, for example, members of the *Socialist Workers Party*, or readers of and contributors to the political-academic journal *International Socialism*.[1] British intellectuals such as Tony Cliff, Alex Callinicos, and Colin Barker belonged to those who argued it was business as usual for socialists. As the introduction has shown, those who did not belong to these *Fourth-International* circles tended to feel more affected. Two

---

1 The *Socialist Workers Party*, formerly known as *International Socialists*, is the strongest among Britain's several Trotskyist parties. For details see Callaghan 1984, 1987.

alternatives for reacting to the events of 1989/1991 seemed to suggest themselves. Reading the collapse of the East as the final declaration of political bankruptcy of Marxism-Leninism, socialists could turn to its main rival: social democracy. Although social democracy historically counts as the origin of both Marxism-Leninism and a gradual, reformist or transformative approach towards the building of socialism, such attempts at moving towards social democracy caused considerable unease. Traditionally, socialists had regarded social democrats as traitors who had made their peace with capitalism and abandoned internationalism. To label someone a social democrat was often understood (and generally meant) as an insult. As a second option, socialists could also embrace post-Marxism. This seemed to offer a possible way forward especially for those who saw the collapse of the Eastern Bloc as a crisis of Marxism in general. Again, such a move caused problems. Although post-Marxists claimed to keep what was worth keeping from the Marxist tradition, Marxists – and other more traditionally-minded socialists – accused them of having given up on a whole range of realist, materialist, and modern paradigms of thinking about the social world and of having taken up too many elements of postmodern and post-structuralist thinking. Therefore, post-Marxists were also viewed with hostility rather than as a collective worth joining.

If, however, the observations made by Walzer, Alexander and Therborn which I quoted in the introduction were correct, socialist intellectuals had, as a consequence of 1989, taken over much more from social democratic and post-Marxist ideas than most of them would have liked to admit. For some, such an acknowledgement would have diminished the status of Marxism, which would accordingly no longer function as the sole system of reference for their political analyses and self-identification. For others, their reluctance might have been caused by intra-left dynamics of distinction and factionalism, separatism or even sectarianism. I will come back to these questions in the concluding part of this study. First however, the analysis needs to establish whether such an appropriation of social democratic or post-Marxist ideas did really occur – perhaps disguised by different terminology.

The remainder of this chapter outlines how to test this thesis and how to formulate answers to these questions in a differentiated way. It starts with general characterisations of, shortly, the basic principles of the socialist intellectuals close to this study's journals[2] and then, a bit more in detail, social democracy and post-Marxism. The next chapter provides a general characterisation of the intellectual groups, of the historical context in which they developed and of the journals in focus.

1.1. The Intellectuals' Core Ideas of Democratic Socialism

Defining even the *basic* principles shared by the intellectuals contributing to the journals constitutes a challenge. The difficulty results from multiple factors which include not only the differences in tasks, goals and self-perceptions between the British and the American left, and the range of pluralism to which all of the journals subscribed, but also from the long distances and numerous roads which intellectual socialists and neo-Marxists had travelled from traditional Marxism and socialism (cf. Anderson 1976; Anderson 1980; Buhle 1991; Panitch 2001). Consequently, to draw a sketch of prototypical socialist positions as they were widely shared by contributors in the late 1980s and early 1990s constitutes a risky endeavour. The following characteristics should hence be understood as key words which intellectuals used as points of reflective departure and fleshed out in different ways rather than as facets of a comprehensive and unanimously shared programme. However, what radical intellectuals indeed shared at the time was the conviction that precisely this orientation towards certain key words and principles – to a certain explanatory paradigm – distinguished them from other intellectuals who understood themselves as, for example, liberal, neo-Conservative, communitarian, social-democratic, or post-modern.

Socialist intellectuals shared the notion that the organisation of economic life in capitalism depended on the existence of different classes. In turn, the emancipation of one of them, the working class, which was forced to

---

2   This outline is deliberately kept short. More information on the specific versions of socialist thought circulated and debated in the British and the American intellectual left in general and in the four journals in particular over the second half of the twentieth century will be provided in the historical overview (Chapter II.3).

sell its labour power to reproduce itself constituted socialists' most important goal. Ideally, the classless society of socialism should replace the classed society of capitalism. This substitution required a radical shift in power structures, which should be achieved, in traditional versions of socialism, by a revolution – the overthrow of the existing economic and political order. The necessity of revolution followed from the perception that the institutions of the capitalist state tended to act in the interests of capitalism. Although crude notions of the state as the 'executive committee of the bourgeoisie' had long been corrected by sophisticated state theories, radical and socialist intellectuals retained the perception that states were not neutral but mirrored and often reinforced power differentials in society. Radical redistributions of power – the concept of revolution had also been thoroughly debated and starkly modified – would become a realistic option only once the part of the population which had an objective interest in it – the working class – had become sufficiently large and consequently powerful. Hence moves towards socialism were most likely to occur, or at least seemed most promising, in the most advanced – namely the highly industrialised and wealthy – societies. A successful revolution would result in the socialisation of ownership of at least a considerable part of the industrial and service sectors. Proper economic development would then require planning since a socialist economy's guiding principle would no longer be the extraction of profit, but instead the satisfaction of a society's needs. The identification of such needs required democratic structures and institutions of decision making that were not limited to familiar forms of parliamentary democracy but extended to the economic and the social spheres. Socialist democracy would thus include public works councils and mechanisms for popular planning at all levels and in all important areas of public life.

At a more theoretical level, socialist intellectuals were convinced that their approaches to economic, social and political change amounted to more than just a political programme or vision that could either succeed or fail. They observed long-term historical trends which seemed to vindicate their belief that once a certain stage of capitalist development was reached, its substitution by something different would necessarily become possible, likely, or even unavoidable. This chance for superseding capitalism would arise when capitalism had lost the capacity to solve its inherent contradictions. This approach to history was intimately linked with the principles of dialectics – the contradictions themselves would provoke or initiate processes through which to solve them. The most fundamental contradictions – those which directly affected people's abilities to survive and maintain themselves – usually emerged in the economic sphere. According to the principles of materialism, economic realities prominently influenced all other spheres of social life. Hence without first amending the hierarchical and exploitative structures in the economic sphere, one would stand only a limited chance of exacting a lasting change on hierarchical social relations in, for example, the political or the cultural spheres.

This framework calling for the interpretation of and intervention into historical-political developments was related to many different levels of social organisation – from the private and micro-sociological to the global. And although socialism's goal was working-class emancipation worldwide, national states played a prominent role for socialist intellectuals as they constituted the arena where most power struggles were fought and where social relations and the unequal access to political power were institutionalised. Nevertheless, in the twentieth century especially, this focus on the national state was complemented by a global perspective, which tried to establish how mechanisms of economic imperialism worked on an international scale.[3]

Over the decades, numerous tendencies and schools of thought have emerged which have tried to refine all the elements presented in this rough sketch in several ways. Generally, these attempts at fine-tuning took the direction of replacing more apodictic and determinist conceptions with more circumspect and open ones. Still, even if socialist intellectuals accepted ideas that, for example, the abolition of a hierarchical class system would not automatically end the oppression of women by men, or that, under conditions of parliamentary democracy, roads to socialism might exist which would differ from a narrow concept of a revolutionary overthrow of the existing order, they would still contend that without putting an end to class exploitation, equality between women and men remained impossible and that meaningful democracy required a much more equal distribution of

---

3 In this context, the works of a number of social scientists became widely discussed and were subsumed under labels such as dependency theory and world system theory. Some representatives of these theories (for example, Samir Amin, Giovanni Arrighi, or Immanuel Wallerstein) contributed to the journals discussed in this study.

power in society. Hence, in the second half of the twentieth century, radical and socialist intellectuals retained such a set of core assumptions whose consideration was indispensable for any fruitful reflection on democratic socialism. In this sense, socialism continued to be influenced by Marxism and continued to constitute a system of thought.

1.2. Social Democracy as a Model and Social Democratic Parties as Agents of Change?

Social democracy is a Western and specifically a North Western European phenomenon. Social democratic parties and governments have considerably influenced the political, social and economic landscapes of Germany, Britain, Austria, the Netherlands, Belgium, Scandinavia and later, to a certain extent, also France. Though a real equivalent to social democracy does not exist in North America – a phenomenon that has occupied the reflections of scholars from Werner Sombart to Göran Therborn – it shares a great deal with strands of American liberalism in terms of ideas and practical policy. It even seems as if Democratic policy, from the New Deal via the uneasy embrace of 'post-materialist' issues to the Clinton-style 'New Democratic' 'third way', has often preceded, and provided a model for social democrats.

Social democracy's roots lie in the labour and socialist movements which developed from the mid-19th century onwards, to whose demands it intended to give a political voice: "Social democratic policy crucially links politics with needs and material interests. What is more, political preferences flow from interest, and interests have a collective, as well as an individual, basis" (Krieger 1999: 17). Since the times of Eduard Bernstein, social democrats have accepted parliamentary democracy. They set out to start a transformation of the economic order. Hence, they followed a gradualist logic of social change, legitimised through majority support, which would give moral authority to ballot-box or parliamentary socialism.[4] Opinions differed and changed over time as to whether socialism could only be *started* within capitalism or whether it could also be *completed* within it. In any case, mass support was required for, on the one hand, winning majorities. On the other hand, for many social democrats mass support of a more

---

4   For the problematics of parliamentary socialism see Miliband 1962, Przeworski 1985, Panitch & Leys 1997.

activist kind counted as a necessary prerequisite for moves towards socialism. Important as parliamentary work was, it would be more effective if accompanied and reinforced by extra-parliamentary pressure, especially in the work place. Otherwise, power differences in society – linked with the ownership of the means of production – were likely to disadvantage working-class interests against those with more political leverage. In Britain, where the Labour Party was established – and for most of its history predominantly financed – by the trade unions, it became common to speak of the industrial and the political wing of the labour movement.

Social democrats' idea of socialism was first of all pragmatic and aimed at improving the living conditions of the working class. For some, this was social democracy's whole purpose, while others interpreted this approach as part of a Gramscian 'war of position' over hegemony in society. As Przeworski argued, capitalism was not necessarily irrational but offered chances to practice a limited functional socialism (cf. 1993: 836). However, for a long time, a rhetorical commitment to some tenets of Marxism was maintained – the West German and Austrian social democratic parties dropped the declared goal of the socialisation of the means of production in the late 1950s, the British Labour Party kept it until 1995. In this sense, social democracy constituted a "hybrid political tradition of socialism and liberalism" (Padgett & Paterson 1991: 1) and pursued a reformist or transformative rather than a revolutionary strategy. As long as they propagated some type of socialism, they generally understood it as a socialisation of (parts of) the means of production. However from as early as the 1920s onwards, this position stood at loggerheads with the 'politics of compromise' which social democrats actually pursued – in their own view for good reason:

They find the courage to explain to the working class that it is better to be exploited than to create a situation which contains the risk of turning against them. They refuse to stake their fortunes on a worsening of the crisis. They offer compromise; they maintain and defend it. (Przeworski 1985: 46)

On the national level, their first spells of government were far from impressive. Shaken by sharp controversy with the Leninists in the recent past and also by the tragic abandonment of a commitment to internationalism on the eve of the First World War, when in power in the 1920s, they remained fiscally orthodox and administered 'pragmatically' over the many crises of the difficult interwar years. There were, however, important and socially ambitious activities – such as Poplarism– on the level of the local state.[5] At the national level, the turning point came with Keynesianism. It provided a route for leaving fiscal orthodoxy behind while leaving large parts of the capitalist logic and structures in place. With Keynesianism, it seemed possible to achieve more equality in society and to improve the living conditions of working-class people without disturbing the supposed positive sides of capitalist economic dynamics. It could be embraced by those who accepted capitalism for the time being, but also by those who subscribed to the ideal of 'collective sovereignty', the creation of democratic procedures by which people could change institutions and decide over the allocation and distribution of resources. All this seemed easy and relatively uncontroversial so long as growth could be stimulated and distributive policies did not necessarily amount to a zero-sum game.

The Keynes-inspired 25 years between the late 1940s and the oil crisis of 1973 became social democracy's golden age. While Keynesianism and governmental economic planning had already been applied earlier in Sweden and in the United States of the New Deal years, after the end of the Second World War, a whole group of – comparatively wealthy – countries created mixed economies, in which key industries were either transferred to national or publicly controlled ownership. In the early period, planning played a prominent role though it lost importance in most countries after only a few years. Przeworski's 'functional socialism' took the shape of welfare states which provided universal services of widely varying generosity in order to enhance social security and material equality. The gap between the richest and the poorest sections of the population became nar-

---

5 The East London borough of Poplar became famous for its early attempts at creating a local welfare state from below. The Labour-led council insisted on paying adequate levels of poor relief and refused to cut municipal workers' wages in the 1920s. They demanded a fairer distribution of rate revenue within London, meaning a transfer of money from richer to poorer boroughs and were sentenced to jail for passing 'illegal' budgets. Eventually they succeeded in setting up a new system of basic welfare support in the city. Similar struggles took place in Westham, Chester-le-Street and Bedwelty (cf. Lansley, Goss & Wolmar 1989: 2).

rower. However, as already mentioned, Keynesian welfare capitalism depended on economic growth, a constantly high demand for goods and services, and a balanced increase in wages and productivity. Growth-dependent welfarism became the most acceptable egalitarian doctrine for most West Europeans and North Americans in a world split into a 'free West' and a 'communist East'. Even most conservative and Christian-democratic parties subscribed to this doctrine, though controversy persisted over its details and its political purpose.

At this stage, it seemed as if *reformist* social democracy had irrevocably won over *transformative* social democracy – a fundamental change in social relations, even if to be achieved gradually, seemed off the agenda. Although the leading British theorist of 'revisionism', Anthony Crosland, suggested as late as 1963 "to replace competitive social relations by fellowship and class solidarity, and the motive of personal profit by a more altruistic and other-regarding motive", social change was restricted to attitudinal issues (1963: 56). In his influential book, *The Future of Socialism,* Crosland had outlined a version of a social democratic society in an age of affluence which he considered to be almost completely realised in Britain: a certain degree of economic democracy had been achieved, a democracy of consumers had emerged, and class differences had become much less visible. Residues of poverty and social problems remained, but could be solved by technocratic solutions such as via reforms in the education system. Crosland anticipated that post-materialist quality-of-life issues would become more important and eventually also lead to democratisation in the field of cultural life. Similar views were expressed in the new programmes of the German and Austrian social democratic parties (although still as goals to be realised rather than already attained) and also by North America based economists such as Joseph Schumpeter (1954) and John Kenneth Galbraith (1958). In sum, social democrats had made their peace with capitalism, embraced liberal democracy, restricted themselves to rectifying the most glaring anachronistic and residual injustices and inequalities. Nevertheless, frequency of use of the term 'socialism' varied in different political cultures and depended on the perceived pressure among social democrats to distance themselves from anything that could be turned into associating their parties with those of Eastern Bloc states. With working-class people participating in consumption and becoming culturally less distinguishable from members of the middle class, it also became less advisable to retain class-struggle rhetoric for domestic-electoral reasons. Extending their appeal to the new and secularised middle classes, social democratic parties tended to reinvent themselves as what Otto Kirchheimer had called "catch-all parties" (cf. 1990[1966]). This idea of social cohesion and class collaboration found its institutional expression in corporatism – concerted fine-tuning and global steering of economic development by government, trade unions, and federated employers' organisations, all subscribing to scientific methods for technological modernisation. Padgett and Paterson argue that with these vaguely defined ideas, social democracy achieved a hegemonic position in Northern European political discourse, but this discourse, according to them, was ideologically empty (cf. 1991: 38).

In several countries, Britain among them, revisionism did not go uncontested. Left wingers were critical, maintaining that the goal of social equality had been translated into equal opportunities to participate in consumption and economic reform into rationalisation (cf. Padgett & Paterson 1991: 37-38). While before the late 1960s or early 1970s the left within social democracy was generally weak, it then profited from two developments: on the one hand, the Keynesian model of accumulation ran into difficulties and seemed to have reached its limits. Economic growth and increases in productivity slowed down. As a consequence, distributive struggles reappeared and – as they usually did, according to Panitch – also reappeared within social democratic parties (cf. 1988: 357). On the other hand, with activists from the late-1960s New Left, a new radical, 'post-materialist', section of the middle class joined parties of the centre-left. They criticised the narrow 'economic rationality' of welfare capitalism which was supposedly responsible for killing people's creativity, exploiting third-world societies, threatening the environment, leading murderous wars, and reproducing social divisions along the lines of class, ethnicity, and gender. As alternatives, they propagated grassroots democracy and people's empowerment, throughout society and within the parties themselves. New distributive struggles and new-left ideas met in reflections and experiments like '*autogestion*' in France, the shop stewards movement, the *Institute of Workers Control*, and the Labour Party's *Alternative Economic Strategy* in Britain, or the 'Meidner plan' (the incremental transformation of companies into workers cooperatives) in Sweden. Based on varieties of neo-Marxist analyses of monopoly capitalism, these social democrats started thinking about qualitative growth, market socialism, rainbow coalitions, and workers' co-determination.[6] On the national level, these initiatives soon ran into difficulties – in Britain in the late 1970s, in France and Sweden in the early 1980s. The social democratic New Left lacked a strategy for how to deal with the powerful resistance by financial institutions and the business world. On the local level they were more successful: in Britain the 'New Urban Left' and their 'local socialism' experimented for some time with grassroots democracy and at least partly and temporarily managed to unite different groups of the population against Thatcherite policies. Occasionally, activists were able to introduce elements of grassroots democracy in the parties themselves at both local and national levels.

Eventually however, the new-left momentum was lost. First, many former Keynesian revisionists made their peace with monetarism or neoliberalism. Padgett and Paterson see this as "a natural evolution of revisionist social democracy in a period of recession – the ideology of growth management became one of crisis management" (1991: 50). Secondly, parts of the New Left adapted to the 'new realism' as well. They continued to pursue their projects of socio-cultural liberation and emancipation, but disentangled them from a general critique of the – by now much leaner – capitalist welfare state. 'New realism' implied an acceptance of the structural changes which governments of the right had introduced in Britain, the United States, and Germany in the 1980s; it meant the turn to some vaguely nationalist project of modernisation in France; and it evoked moves towards the European Community in Sweden. No one within social democracy came up with comprehensive alternatives to the by now firmly established neo-liberal regime of accumulation. Whereas the revisionists of the 1950s had changed social democratic parties from class-based to catch-all organisations, the new realists of the 1980s and 1990s transformed them from centre-left into centrist ones.[7] Social democracy's new programmatic openness – characterised as flexibility by its supporters and as vagueness by its opponents – was compensated for through 'charismatic leadership' and

---

6   In many cases, invitations to workers to participate in decision making on economic policy followed a double rationale of empowering them while simultaneously persuading them to accept wage increases which were only moderate – an attempt at tackling what many politicians identified as the main problem of the 1970s: rising inflation.

7   Scandinavia was, to a certain degree, the exception to this trend.

increasing reliance on political marketing strategies. Still, in many societies new parties and organisations emerged to occupy the space on the left vacated by social democracy – the perspective that it remained necessary to seriously reform or even transform capitalism.

The claim that there never was socialism in America (meaning Anglo-America and especially the United States) is, of course, incorrect. That socialist and social democratic parties never attained the level of mass support on which they could rely in large parts of Europe is another matter.[8] A number of explanations exist for this difference: in areas of the United States where socialist tendencies mustered some political strength, they faced massive persecution and suppression. The 'Red Scare' and the years of McCarthyism constitute only two tips of an anti-socialist iceberg. Further, as an immigrant country with a moving frontier, expansion of territory for settlement acted as a safety valve against unrest due to social inequalities. Moving elsewhere – as an individual – proved an attractive alternative to collective political pressure. Even if this chance constituted a myth rather than reality for poor working-class people, the idea of geographical mobility helped to maintain social tranquillity in the United Sates (cf. Howe 1985). Still, U.S. society harnessed the idea of equality. Although this was first of all understood as an individual's equal right to be 'free', it also had a collective dimension. Groups excluded from the equal right to be free, demanded inclusion into this category *as groups*. Unlike in Europe, where people organized via social class lines, since the era of Jacksonian democracy, in the United States these groups were very often ethnic, as immigration societies are likely to invite solidarity and collectivism along ethnic lines.[9] It stands that many of the ideas, ideals, interests and demands expressed in and around social democracy in Europe, were expressed within the broad framework of American liberalism. Standing generally for a progressive political orientation, from the late 19th century onwards, liberals

---

8   For detailed histories of the American left see: Aronovitz 1996, Buhle 1991, Diggins 1992, Weinstein 2004.

9   Göran Therborn argued that the European route through the twentieth century was characterised by class conflicts fought along the lines of sophisticated ideologies. The North-American path, on the other hand, consisted of conflicts about exclusion and demands for inclusion which very often activated ethnic identifications and solidarities (cf. 2000: 19-20).

predominantly clustered around the Democratic Party even though for a long time the Republican Party also had a liberal wing.

The overlap of socialist, social democratic and liberal values is not surprising. All grew from the same roots – the Enlightenment and the bourgeois revolutions from the late 18th to the mid-19th century. Both revolutionary socialists and gradualist social democrats considered themselves to be those thinkers who took liberalism more seriously than anyone else. They aimed at developing the material and economic base upon which liberalism could prosper: social equality. American liberals differed from revolutionary socialists in so far as they did not consider themselves as revolutionaries. They saw the United States as a post-revolutionary polity in which politicians should rely on the institutions created through this revolution. Liberals did not conceive of themselves as transformers but as reformers, though one could argue that they changed the role of institutions and the scope of governmental activity at least as much as social democrats. Even so, these changes followed a rationale of compromise rather than confrontation to an even stronger degree than in the case of social democrats.

Since the last third of the 19th century, liberalism in the United States had a social, caring dimension. With the Social Gospel Movement and with the liberal Republicans, activists and politicians engaged in attempts to resolve social hardship and create a common good. They believed in good-faith efforts, careful and sensitive administration, and in the application of scientific methods (as did many social democrats – for example the British Fabians of the early 20th century and the technocratic modernisers of the Wilson cabinets during the 1960s). To a certain extent, the Populist movement of the late 19th century also embraced social liberalism, though they stood for a mixture of radical, liberal, and deeply conservative ideas. Historians distinguish three major periods of U.S. social liberalism in the 20th century: the 'progressive era' of the early years, the New Deal of the 1930s and the 'Great Society' efforts of the 1960s. Each of these phases expanded the boundaries of governmental activity and weakened (though did not kill) anti-statist sentiment. In the first period, Theodore Roosevelt propagated a centrally-planned, state supervised economy, in the name of a 'New Nationalism'. Here, the power of corporations and monopolies ('trusts'), which were perceived as threats to American freedoms, was curtailed. At the time, people disagreed about strategies. Some, like Roosevelt, believed that large corporations could be effectively steered into serving the interests of the U.S. population. Others, like Woodrow Wilson, were more sceptical and suggested to disaggregate them. Both strands developed ideas for a corporatist, associational democratic economy. However, liberalism lost influence after the First World War and flourished in a modified form only with the beginning of the second important period in the 1930.

This time, the problems consisted of a banking system that collapsed under its own irresponsibility, which resulted in a sudden explosion of unemployment and poverty. The consequent Great Depression required more comprehensive economic interventionism. During the New Deal era, a whole range of strategies were tested. Large-scale planning in the private sector was accompanied by the disentangling of trusts and the foundation of large public sector institutions for economic reconstruction and modernisation (the Tennessee Valley Authority is probably the best-known example). The New Deal increasingly relied on Keynesian approaches to fiscal policy, which proved to be the least controversial within the framework of a traditionally anti-statist political culture. Still, the newly created planning jobs in the large New Deal administration attracted many American radicals. Hence, during these years, social liberalism had a small left-wing minority of declared transformers.[10] The turn to Keynesianism and the consequent identification of under-consumption as the source of economic crises, the cooptation of labour unions to corporatist decision making (quite a radical innovation in U.S. politics) and later the beginning of the Cold War all contributed to a consensus which was in many respects similar to the post-war consensus in several countries of Western Europe. Expanding consumption through fiscal policies seemed the most suitable strategy for alleviating poverty and scarcity and for guaranteeing economic growth. Restricting the state's interventionist role to fiscal policy could square the circle of working for a fairer and more equal society while taking into account public antipathy to state intrusion, associated with the 'totalitarian' systems of government in the U.S.S.R. and Nazi-Germany.

By the 1950s, this type of social liberalism had achieved – despite occasional backlashes – the status of a hegemonic doctrine in the United States, even if the social dimension was neither legitimised via social democratic

---

10 Some of them later belonged to the early contributors to *Monthly Review*.

rhetoric nor comparable in scope to the emerging welfare states in Britain and Germany, let alone Scandinavia. Cheryl Greenberg characterises the consensus as "protection of individual rights within a capitalist framework of growth sustained by fiscal policies" (2001: 67). This settlement was also accepted by the Republican administrations of Eisenhower and Nixon, just as Conservatives and Christian Democrats were involved in administering the "golden age of social democracy" on the other side of the Atlantic. In much the same way that Crosland celebrated the socialism of affluence, writers like Lionel Trilling (*The Liberal Imagination*, 1950) and Louis Hartz (*The Liberal Tradition*, 1955) wrote about a post-ideological era in which social liberalism was triumphant. The liberals' idea of politics as statecraft and economic-technocratic expertise meant that they remained – in the era of the early Cold War – deeply sceptical about politics as ideological struggle, mass political action and grassroots self-empowerment. Hence liberals' relationship with the Civil Rights Movement was ambivalent, and in the activist 1960s liberalism's hegemony became increasingly corrosive. The limits of the social liberal imagination prohibited an understanding of issues like racism as structural deficiencies of U.S. society. The thought ran that such problems should be treated as incidents of individual prejudice.

In the third period, the substitution of a more active liberalism for the cautious liberalism of the 1950s, following from Johnson's Great Society programme, fell prey to the rising costs of the Vietnam tragedy and the escalating ideological battle over the Cold War. Johnson's "war on poverty" was interpreted by some liberals as the introduction of socialism by stealth, while others criticised the war in South East Asia as liberalism's moral bankruptcy. Hence the centre-left of U.S. politics, symbolised by the New Deal Coalition which had given the Democrats comfortable majorities in Washington for a long time, disintegrated from the mid-1960s onwards. In the Democratic Party, a search for the soul of liberalism began, which first caused a move to the left – culminating in the candidacy of George McGovern for the 1972 Presidential elections. McGovern campaigned on a platform which included many new-left demands and which mirrored the increased influence of grassroots activists on democratic programmes. After their candidate lost heavily, the Democrats went through a long process of reorientation, in the face of the U.S. economy's being confronted with heavy competition from Japan and Western Europe, the oil crisis and inflation, a weakened currency and rising unemployment figures. Like

European social democrats, liberals in the United States did not know how to react to the failure of the Keynesian model of welfare capitalism, which was based on continuing economic growth and rising productivity. The Carter administration embodied this confusion, Ronald Reagan suggested that government was part of the problem rather than its solution, and when Bill Clinton became the first Democratic President after more than a decade, he declared the era of big government to be over, further lending credence to Reagan's diagnosis. Thus by the early 1990s, similar to social democrats in Western Europe, liberal political opinion in North America had embraced central tenets of the neo-liberal world view and accepted its accumulation regime. Like social democracy, social liberalism seemed a spent force: the ways forward were third ways.

Thus by the late 1980s, social democracy and social liberalism seemed to be in serious trouble when asked to define the core of their political project. Still, ideas of regulating capitalism in order to make it beneficial for all members of society had long been propagated. Hence the ideas of reformist social democracy, social liberalism and welfare capitalism had become deeply ingrained into the political cultures of West European and North American societies. A certain level of equality was still seen by many as a valuable political goal. The traditional social democratic project of a strong state, capable of creating an egalitarian society in material and social terms could still serve as the political vision for an intellectual left.

1.3. Post-Marxism as a Re-formulation of, or a Departure from, Socialist Strategies for Change?

While social democracy's history began in the 19th century, the term post-Marxism appeared only recently, although some theorists argue that the body of thought it describes is as old as Marxism itself. Post-Marxism developed – under this name – as reaction to a Marxism seen as being in a serious crisis, both intellectually and politically. In order to understand post-Marxism, one must historicise it, just as it has itself done with Marxism. Post-Marxism constitutes a part of a leftwing intellectual movement which reacted to the neo-liberal onslaught of the 1980s and focused in particular on its cultural and identity politics. It tried to recapture and use the individualism of the New Left for an innovative left project, individualism which had been partly demonised and partly appropriated by Thatcherite Conservatism and by Reagan and sections of the U.S. right. Post-Marxism starts out from the proposition that the only chance to resolve an allegedly fundamental crisis in Marxism consists of a root-and-branch renewal, one which should preserve what is worth keeping from Marxism and leave behind everything else. According to Stuart Sim, not even the core of Marxist theory is retained. Post-Marxists only rescue some elements – picked at random in acts of intellectual quarrying – from "the collapse of Marxism as a global cultural and political force in the later twentieth century, and reorient them to take on a new meaning within a rapidly changing cultural climate" (2000: 1). For post-Marxists, Marxism found itself in crisis not only through the events of 1989, but also because it had discredited itself through lending legitimacy to the exclusive power of state bureaucracies in the Eastern Bloc:[11]

Post-Marxists dislike the control aspects of Marxism (particularly as exercised at party level), totalising theories in general, the deification of Marx, and subordination of the individual to the system that communism demands. They favour pluralism, difference, scepticism towards authority, political spontaneity, and the cause of the new social movements. (Sim 2000: 3)

Assuming a link between Marxism's totalising tendencies as a system of thought and the suppression of criticism in the states of the Eastern Bloc, post-Marxists regard it as *one* framework of thought among many; it does not have all the answers (cf. Gamble 1999: 7).

The label 'post-Marxism' is used in two different ways. On the one hand, it serves as an umbrella term for all those who developed more and more doubts about the scientific validity and political usability of Marxism. In such a wide sense, the label might even include neo-conservatives, such

---

11 This opinion was not only shared among post-Marxists of course. Robin Blackburn's statement which opened the introduction to this study was in agreement with this perspective. Still, Blackburn would most likely not have described himself as a post-Marxist. *New Left Review*, however, was sufficiently interested in post-Marxism to publish a debate between the leading proponents of post-Marxism at the time, Ernesto Laclau and Chantal Mouffe, and the Marxist Norman Geras, a member of the journal's editorial board, in its pages (cf. Geras 1987; Laclau & Mouffe 1987).

as the American Irving Kristol, who started their political odysseys as Trotskyists. According to Andrew Gamble, the term post-Marxism might be applied to a spectrum of theorists who do not know anymore whether to assign Marxism the status of a science, a discourse, or a critique (cf. 1999: 5). In a narrower sense, however, the term is closely associated with the work of Ernesto Laclau and Chantal Mouffe and especially their controversial book *Hegemony and Socialist Strategy* (1986). The authors argue that there is a fundamental difference between *post*-Marxists who have left Marxism completely behind and post-*Marxists* who are concerned with a 'radical' reformulation of the Marxist project or 'spirit'. Their relationship to Marxism is similar to that of postmodernists to modernism, or of poststructuralists to structuralism. It is a relationship of consideration but at the same time of moving beyond. Marxism is historicised as part of the enlightenment tradition whereas post-Marxism borrows heavily from postmodern and poststructuralist theories (cf. Daly 1999: 63).

Used in the wider, umbrella sense, post-Marxism has a long pedigree. Some commentators go so far as to suggest that Marx himself was the first post-Marxist. They point to contradictions in his work regarding the relationship of structure and agency. Wherever he emphasises agency over the laws of historical materialism and economic development (which he formulates elsewhere), he already prepares the path for one of post-Marxism's central claims: the dominance of historical contingency, of human activity and (political) activism, in shaping historical processes and the subordinate or negligible role of a teleological determinism. The discrepancies between the prognoses of Marx, Engels and others and actual historical developments in the twentieth century led to a considerable number of reflections on this topic of contingency and determinism, structure and agency. According to Perry Anderson (1976), the whole story of 'Western Marxism' in the first half of the twentieth century should be understood as intellectual attempts to come to terms with unexpected – and, for leftists, far from promising – developments, which undermined Marxists' original historical optimism. The most important milestone in re-conceptualising the contingency-versus-determinism problematic in the first half of the 20th century was contributed by Antonio Gramsci in his reflections on hegemony. With the identification of ideologically hegemonic power blocs across social classes, he thought to have found the reason which explained capitalism's failure to collapse. Later, Louis Althusser added the concepts of overdetermination and relative autonomy to shift the balance even further from determinism towards contingency. Other theorists questioned further central tenets of traditional Marxism or, more precisely, their relevance under twentieth century conditions. André Gorz and Herbert Marcuse both doubted the indispensable role of the working class for revolutionary change. Rudolf Bahro pointed to Marxism's blindness with regard to the natural limits impairing its vision of a post-capitalist society of plenty. In Britain, Stuart Hall and other thinkers close to the journal *Marxism Today* synthesised many of these issues into considerations on how the left should react to the unexpected popularity of the Thatcherite project – also among working-class people.

Post-Marxism in the narrow sense stemmed from these British reformulations. It is closely linked, as Sim points out, not only with poststructuralist thinking but with second-wave feminism. Often however, post-Marxists emphasise their difference from the poststructuralist mainstream. To some extent, they distance themselves from the latter's radical anti-foundationalism and anti-universalism. Instead they stick to specific emancipatory projects and to a normative dimension of political theory. They understand discursive operations as struggles rather than games and retain some aspects of cultural materialism (cf. Frankfurter Arbeitskreis für politische Theorie und Philosophie 2004: 17-21). Along with poststructuralism, they share the conviction that what counts as reality is constructed in the discursive sphere and that therefore exchanges within it are of utmost importance. Laclau and Mouffe's title, *Hegemony and Socialist Strategy*, implies that they try to design a discursive project with which to argue for both socialism and what they call 'radical democracy': a plethora of open-ended and indeterminate struggles for human emancipation.

What are the main elements of such a post-Marxist project? Unsurprisingly, there is no general agreement. It seems, however, that post-Marxists understand their considerations on social and political issues as a *critique* rather than a holistic theory or an ideology. They emphasise their position's self-reflexivity and its openness to criticism. The reluctance to take criticism seriously had put traditional Marxism on the track of authoritarianism. Many post-Marxists still see the critique of political economy, Marx's analysis of the capitalist system, as useful and some would suggest it to be Marxism's most important achievement. Still, they remain unconvinced that all history is the history of class struggles, not even in 'the last instance'. Instead, they observe the co-existence of numerous struggles fought along the lines of people's different identifications. Neither the outcome of these struggles nor the emergence of new ones can be predicted. Post-Marxists are less concerned about the 'grand narrative' of the class struggle *per se,* than poststructuralists. Rather, they direct their criticism to essentialist conclusions drawn from it. Unlike traditional Marxists, they maintain that other types of struggle are not of secondary status in comparison to the class struggle and that not all struggles can be referred back to class antagonisms. The class struggle is neither superior to other forms of social conflict, nor is it inevitable.

Indeed, many attempts to explain historical change exclusively by quasi-automatic mechanisms – where the relations of production become antagonistic to the production process and hence create social conflict – have been proven wrong, both frequently and in many parts of the world. Even if one saw the analysis of the transformation from feudalism to capitalism as correct, this would be of limited use for prognoses on future developments of capitalism. Post-Marxists concede that Marxism itself has produced various reflections on this issue, but, as already mentioned, the "logic of necessity" has very often clashed with the "logic of contingency" (cf. Daly 1999: 64). According to Glyn Daly, these logics are incompatible but have produced a creative tension and thus contributed to Marxism's intellectual advances over time (ibid). For post-Marxists, the tension has been resolved by abandoning any remnants of the 'logic of necessity'. Consequently, they cannot envisage an end of history and argue against all kinds of eschatologies – to use André Gorz's phrase – of which Marxism is one. Instead, post-Marxists suggest that all emancipatory movements and projects need to – and will – seek power. Thus the future is only imaginable as an unbroken sequence of power struggles between emancipatory movements and counter-movements. Power struggles will be permanent.

This position assigns a central role to politics as the political process must not be reduced to being a mere epiphenomenon of economic relations. Post-Marxists unambiguously bid farewell to the base-superstructure model, even to its refined Althusserian variety of articulations in dominance and the determining power of the economic in the last instance.[12] The post-

---

12 Althusser himself had argued that the moment of the last instance never came and should be understood as an abstraction (cf. Sim 2000: 19).

Marxist understanding of the political is discursive rather than economic. According to Daly, Laclau and Mouffe

> have affirmed that nothing can be identified outside the constitutive process itself and that all identity, order and objectivity must be considered as fully discursive: that is as phenomena which are wholly the result of articulatory and political (power) practices and which are ultimately prone to other articulatory practices. (1999: 64)

Post-Marxists observe an incremental return of the political from early on in the intellectual history of Marxism, symbolised again, above all in Gramsci's introduction of the hegemony concept. However, whereas for Gramsci different economically defined classes allied with each other and fought each other over political hegemony, post-Marxists see also these fighting and allying groups as discursively constructed. Hence it becomes impossible to predict which groups might in which ways create themselves to act politically and it would be a futile exercise to risk prognoses about the political debates and fault lines of the future. For many post-Marxists, involvement in these fluid processes and intervention into the construction and negotiation of identities through formulating political values and demands has become the primary task of radical intellectuals.

Traditional Marxism worked with dialectical methods. This implied the existence of identifiable fixed opposites and of processes through which the interaction of these creates a new third. Post-Marxists disagreed with such assumptions for two reasons. Firstly, they followed a poststructuralist, Lacanian logic of the discursive construction of objects and identities. These acquire meaning only in relation to each other and hence cannot be understood as clear opposites. With this assumption, the very base for a dialectical dynamics ceases to exist. Secondly, post-Marxists regard the idea that a new 'third', a synthesis, would be created 'automatically' in a dialectical process as dangerous. Unlike traditional Marxists, they do not believe that the outcomes of political struggles would necessarily be 'progressive'. Solutions to specific problems and controversies, strategies for overcoming differentials of power and wealth would not merely suggest themselves. Instead, such measures require planning and creative thinking. Thus it is important to overcome Marxists' traditional hesitance to imagine a socialist society: post-Marxists consider it a necessary task to design the structures, institutions and workings of a 'new' society and to reflect on strategies for how to attract people to these models.

In terms of people, it has already been mentioned that the working class is not conceived of as the primary revolutionary actor. Thus attracting support is not synonymous with convincing the working class. Not all post-Marxists bid an unqualified farewell to the working class but – especially in the political climate of Britain and the United States during the 1980s – they have learned to see working-class people as heterogeneous in their political outlook and a considerable number of them as conservative.[13] Of course, this deliberate un-privileging of the working class echoes the notion that social relations are characterised by manifold and fluid contradictions and conflicts in society which cannot be traced back merely to the 'master' narrative of the conflict between exploiters and exploited. Post-Marxists point to a whole range of issues which have developed, marking them as nodal points around which political identifications are created. They also expect new points of identification to arise in the future:

[T]he historical expansion of emancipatory discourses (especially post 1968), combined with the critical Marxist identification of the increased dislocatory effects of capitalism, reveals a proliferation of the sites of antagonism which present new challenges to the social order and which go way beyond traditional questions of how we produce or consume. (Daly 1999: 81)

In this context, post-Marxists take note of an increasing individualism which has replaced the old working-class collectivism. Political struggles, initiated first and foremost by new social movements, are much more about the right to be different and to be accepted as being different than about equality in the traditional, material sense. People demand space and respect for expressing themselves. The political goal of these demands consists of giving individuals the power over their own lives – as Gorz has expressed it

---

13 This was the core of Stuart Hall's controversial interventions during the 1980s in which he characterised Thatcherism as an authoritarian-populist project which profited from working-class resentment and exploited working people's unease with Labour's traditional left programme – supported by many on the intellectual left – and their selling of a ticket on the welfare-state past. For the debate on Hall's interpretation see Hall 1988; Jessop et al. 1988.

(cf. Sim 2000: 8). On the one hand, such a politics represents the 'postmodern condition' of culturally fragmented and individualised societies. On the other, post-Marxists interpret it as a reaction to capitalism's penetration of all areas of life.

It follows from this approach that the traditional Marxist conception of revolution has run its course. An obviously plural radical politics can only be imagined as a plethora of different emancipatory struggles. Even if these might lead to limited 'revolutions' (in the sense of qualitative leaps) in particular areas of social life, they need to follow certain standards of behaviour. The most important is to accept formal democratic procedures. Political actors might struggle for hegemony, but they would not be free to choose their strategies. Post-Marxists have made their peace with parliamentary democracy and its formal rules. Laclau and Mouffe remain convinced that the left is nevertheless distinguishable from the liberal political mainstream of the time: "The task of the Left therefore cannot be to renounce liberal-democratic ideology, but on the contrary, to deepen and expand it in the direction of a radical and plural democracy." (1986: 348) Claiming that they take concepts such as 'liberty', 'equality', 'justice' and 'democracy' more seriously than their opponents, post-Marxists suggest a decentralisation of politics and an expansion of grassroots democracy. Another writer often characterised as a leading post-Marxist, Paul Hirst, spent much time reflecting on the workings of what he called "associative democracy" (cf. 1994). The radicalism of this approach lies in the idea that decentralisation changes power structures (and consequently power relations) in society and thus paves the way for a continuous process of democratisation. Such a process would be a 'permanent' democratic revolution or a permanent process of reform – not in a teleological, linear or dialectical sense but simply because each solution to a particular problem or deficiency, each satisfaction of specific demands is likely to create new problems. Post-Marxists call these 'dislocatory effects'. Such a dynamics of change should not be confused with the traditional Marxist narrative of historical progress since it is completely open; it is by no means sure that the left will succeed (though decentralisation might put it into a stronger position) and it will have to defend everything it has successfully introduced.

Post-Marxists' utopian idea is moderate. Historically, the establishment of socialist structures has proved difficult. The practice of setting-up authoritarian regimes in order to introduce socialism has discredited itself.

Social democratically inspired capitalist welfare states, with their top-down model of service provision, have also proven incapable of responding to many of the more recent emancipatory demands and unable to defend themselves against neo-liberal onslaughts. These failures do not testify to the meaninglessness of the democratic state and its institutions in capitalism. Post-Marxists agree that parliamentary work must be accompanied and reinforced by extra-parliamentary pressure in order to succeed. In the long run, associations within civil society, decentralised decision making structures and a dense network of locally organised self-help and pressure groups will probably take over many parliamentary and governmental tasks. Post-Marxists ideal scenario consists of a snowball effect of continuous democratisation and emancipation. Yet they are still aware that the snowball might be stopped or driven uphill (cf. Sim 2000: 26). With such a conception, post-Marxists move close to communitarianist models. What distinguishes them from communitarianists is their pronounced awareness of power differences and hierarchies in society. However, like communitarianists, they tacitly assume that all groups will stick to certain standards, conventions and ethics regarding political debate and decision making procedures, even if doing so means having to accept unwelcome outcomes.

Just like social democrats, post-Marxists implicitly take the nation-state as their most important frame of reference. Marxism's anti-imperialist internationalism has been replaced by an acceptance of the capitalist world system which again can only be changed incrementally (cf. Petras 1998). Post-Marxists are aware of the debates on global governance and they seem to see a chance for adapting their associational model to the global sphere. They envisage a worldwide civil society composed of transnational social movements and non-governmental organisations, which become increasingly involved in geopolitical confrontations and ideally transform them into discursive struggles over global justice and the emancipation of the poor and oppressed all over the world.

By the late 1980s, post-Marxism was advertised as a possible way out of the political and ideological impasse traditional socialist politics seemed incapable of finding. It retained many elements of the emancipatory spirit of a libertarian Marxism – enriched by the issues raised by the social movements of the late 1960s and 1970s – and tried to formulate a new political project on this base. It took seriously the criticisms of Marxism's 'grand narrative' or 'meta-narrative' status and the 'totalising tendencies' that followed from them. It constituted a radical project whose main emphasis was less on egalitarianism and more on self-emancipation, grassroots democracy and the vision of a society composed of loosely associated communities. Such a project could certainly become attractive for left intellectuals.

2. A Short History of the British and the American Intellectual Left and the Journals Analysed

2.1. The Many British New Lefts

The British Left was formed by a very differentiated and rich political tradition. At its centre has always been the elaborate interrelated structure of the Labour Party and the trade union movement. These unions both preceded and helped to set the party up, thereby inscribing themselves in its texture and politics. Additionally, the left founded a number of organisations and other movements, such as the Communist Party of Great Britain (influential in a couple of trade unions), a variety of competing Trotskyist groups, various currents of leftwing nationalism in Scotland, Wales, and Northern Ireland, a social movement radicalism with – already in the 1950s – a sizeable peace movement, and several strands of radical (including Marxist) intellectual thought.[1] The latter was comprised of a number of individuals who tried to set up a New Left as a "movement of ideas" from 1956 onwards (New Left Review 1960: 2). For its initiators, the necessity of such a New Left, which borrowed its name and some of its strategies from the French *Nouvelle Gauche*, followed from the Communist Party's unwillingness to critically engage with its own history of Stalinism and from the Gaitskellite Labour Party's perceived adaptation to capitalism. The New Left formed on the one hand as a backward looking alliance, echoing the *Left Clubs* of the 1930s. However, on the other, it addressed issues of the time and stood in close contact with the *Campaign for Nuclear Disarmament*. These and other actions demonstrated the group's commitment to making socialism relevant for an era characterised by widespread

---

[1] For a comprehensive history of the British left see Callaghan (1987).

private material prosperity, hidden inequalities, the decline of the old industrial centres, the changing relationship between state and economy, the 'pluralisation of social identities', and the threat of nuclear annihilation (cf. Kenny: 1995: 5). Its reflections extended into four different directions: towards socialist humanism (associated with E. P. Thompson and, later, the *Socialist Register*), culturalism (represented by Raymond Williams and, from 1964 onward, the *Centre for Contemporary Cultural Studies*), structural Marxism (imported from 1963 onwards by *New Left Review*) and the movement for workers control (personified within the New Left by Ken Coates and later institutionalised with the *Institute of Workers Control*) (cf. Chun 1996: 194).

The New Left developed from two different roots and both set up periodicals – *New Reasoner* and *University and Left Review*. The former was launched in 1956 after a long era of self-censorship among the Communist Historians Group (most of whose members were based in Northern England), which came to an end with the crushing of the revolt in Budapest.[2] The latter was founded after a number of Oxford and London students called attention to the persistence of British imperialism in the same year. For Gregory Elliott, these originss defined the New Left's approach: "The product of the European moment of 1956, the British New Left at the outset had sought to bridge the mutually injurious gulf between 'theory' and 'practice', culture and politics, intellectuals and workers, socialist milieu and labourist organization" (1998: 7). Both wings shared a number of characteristics, but also differed in many respects. Both were committed to the *Campagin for Nuclear Disarmament* (CND) and "positive neutralism" (a strategy for British foreign policy that implied distancing Britain from super-power politics, creating its own foreign policy and collaborating with other, especially unaligned, countries) and opposed the "pathology of anti-

---

2   The relationship between the Communist Historians Group and the leadership of the CPGB had been contentious for a long time. The historians avoided topics too close to recent politics and concentrated on the change from feudalism to capitalism in Britain. Relations became even more fraught when E. P. Thompson and John Saville started publishing *The Reasoner* as a journal for party intellectuals urging a self-critical assessment of the CPGB's Stalinist period. For a detailed account on the *Communist Historians Group* see Dworkin 1997: 10-44 and Woodhams 2001.

communism" (Samuel 1989: 49). However, they regarded the Communist Party as "dogmatically theoretical" and the Labour Party as "narrowly empirical" (ibid: 43). Thus, they emphasised the establishment of "a political milieu that was neither Communist nor Labour, an alternative space on the map of the Left" (Dworkin 1997: 66). They wanted their alternative to constitute a "third way" between both Eastern and Western military blocs, and between Communism and social democracy, consistent with the 'socialist humanism' mentioned above. At its core was a strong belief in the possibility of grassroots-level human – and working-class – agency (cf. Sedgwick 1976: 137). Beyond this optimistic central tenet, they formed a pluralist group. Dorothy Thompson, one of the movement's activists, explained:

The Left movement which grew up around the journals and clubs in the fifties and sixties was a coalition of people with varied religious and philosophical belief systems who were united around the political concept of a non-aligned European movement which would work out socialist policies independently of superpower influence and control. Not only did they not represent a single ideological position, they were by no means united in their definition of socialism – only perhaps by the negative qualities of disillusion with Soviet-style communism and West-European, especially British, social democracy. (1996: 94)

For finding likeminded people, they looked not only to the French New Left, but also to the United States. *Dissent* provided both inspiration and contributions to the British journal. The American sociologist C. Wright Mills's "Letter to the New Left" was printed in the first issue of *New Left Review* in 1960 and for some even hailed the American *Dissent* as *Universities and Left Review*'s "sister publication" (Samuel 1989: 44). The British New Left was in its majority loosely Marxist, but more attracted by Marx's early writings, more focussed on the 'humanist' than on the 'determinist' aspects, and more interested in 'alienation' (and later in 'hegemony') than in 'exploitation'. Like others (and despite their commitment to a third space), they all struggled with the question of how to relate to the Labour Party – a problem that became increasingly urgent when one division of the New Left supported the tiny Fife Socialist League in the 1959 election while others stayed with the Labour Party.[3] Generally, the New Left sought contact with the anti-revisionist left wing of the Labour Party (cf. ibid: 50).[4]

The most important difference between the two sections of the New Left was generational. While it has become common to distinguish between the first and the second New Left (the second consisting of those who edited *New Left Review* from 1963 onwards – Perry Anderson, Robin Blackburn, Tom Nairn, etc.), the first was already trans-generational: members were born either shortly after the First or shortly before the Second World War.[5] Though this is not much in terms of age difference, it explains the two groups' divergent political perspectives in terms of fundamentally different experiences: depression, fascism, and army life for the older group; affluence, Cold War, and university life for the younger. While the older generation wanted to revive the British socialist traditions studied in the Communist Historians Group, the younger hoped to develop new ones that took the conditions of the post-war welfare state society into consideration. According to Raphael Samuel, the younger generation wanted the movement to take "as its starting point the spirit of youth" (1989: 44). For a short time, from 1956 to 1962, the New Left indeed became a movement, with a well-known café in London as its base, and, at its peak, 45 clubs with 3,000 paying members all over the country. However, the clubs declined soon afterwards, as several political manoeuvres led to tactical disagreements within the peace movement: the Labour Party first adopted unilateralism in 1960 and renounced it only one year later. In addition, Harold Wilson's succession of Hugh Gaitskell as party leader promised the perceived chance of a leftward move by the Labour Party

In 1962, another New Left group, commonly known as the 'Second New Left' formed around Perry Anderson. It accused both generations of the prior group of populism, empiricism, and nationalism. The conflict

---

3 Some New Leftists, like Mervyn Jones and, for a time, Raymond Williams, became members of the Labour Party.

4 Also Peter Sedgwick observed a political-strategic overlap between New Left and Labour Left, because both tried to combine utopianism and *realpolitik* (cf. 1976: 135-7)

5 Detailed accounts of the developments, debates and conflicts between the different generations of the New Left have been provided by Chun (1996) and Kenny (1995).

between the two groups was, according to authors such as Sassoon (1981) or Thompson (2001), more about style and terminology than about substance – both stood at the time for similar versions of a radical reformism.[6] The fight has often been presented as a showdown between E. P. Thompson and Perry Anderson – a perspective that ignores the amicable relationships and mutual respect between many of the others involved.[7] The main difference was that the second New Left took a politically more detached position and became occupied with 'theoretical practice', starting a programme of importing and familiarising themselves and others with continental European Marxist theory. All three sections of the New Left were involved in initiating far-reaching and original critical approaches towards British politics, society, history, and culture. These were institutionalised and expressed not only in the two periodicals discussed below, but also in many other new foundations of the time.

The relationship between this pre-1968 New Left and the student radicals was not always easy. The activists ignored the first New Left's *May Day Manifesto*, written by Raymond Williams, which intended to revive the original New Left as a response to the negative experience of the Wilson governments (cf. Chun 1996: 155-6). Some New Leftists, such as Ralph Miliband, John Saville, Stuart Hall, and many in the group around Anderson, supported the students, while others, like Thompson, considered the 1968 revolt as being outside the rational revolutionary tradition (ibid: 168-

---

6 Lin Chun argues that they developed into different directions – for example, on the question of how to define revolutionary change: whereas for the Thompsonian first New Left revolutionary upheaval was the exception and piecemeal change the historical norm, Anderson believed that the revolution was a necessity in capitalist democracies due to their repressive tendencies. Miliband was convinced that revolutions were under certain conditions but not always necessary – and recommended to analyse in detail the power structures within concrete societies and the openings they offered (cf. 1996: 227-8).

7 Obviously, Thompson and Anderson enjoyed emphasising the bellicose character of the disputes and their personal roles within them – see Thompson's *The Poverty of Theory* (1978) and Anderson's *Arguments within English Marxism* (1980).

9).[8] In a further parallel to the United States, several of the leading student activists, for example the former *Black Dwarf* editors Tariq Ali and Sheila Rowbotham, later joined the editorial boards of the pre-1968 journals. The 1970s tuned out to be a very creative, but at the same time complicated, decade for the British left, with the emergence of new social movements, self-experiments of grassroots groups, the rise of radical trade unionism, the development of a strong left within the Labour Party, while all these innovations became overshadowed by economic crisis and decline. Furthermore, a turn from neo-Marxism to poststructuralism could be observed on the left of British academic life. It affected formerly Marxist publications such as the periodical *Economy and Society*, and academic disciplines, especially Cultural Studies. This development was prepared, welcomed and supported by a minority of the pre-1968 New Left. However, a debate about socialism continued, both in the two journals introduced below, and also in other publications such as *Capital and Class*, *New Socialist* (sponsored by the Labour Party), or the 'Eurocommunist' *Marxism Today*. By the end of the 1970s, the feeling of crisis came to dominate left analyses – as could be seen in the study *Policing the Crisis*, edited by members of the Centre for Contemporary Cultural Studies (1978), and Eric Hobsbawm's "The Forward March of Labour Halted?" (1978). Intellectuals disagreed on the merits and practicality of the Bennite Labour Left's isolationist economic strategy, the world view and the future of the British working class, the correct position towards European integration, and the sense of modernising the British *ancién regime* as a way of changing power relations in society. With the consolidation of Thatcherism (or, to put it differently, after a series of catastrophic defeats for the British left from the isolation of the Labour Left via the Falklands war and failed protests against rate-capping by leftwing local councils to the miners strike), they began to analyse its make-up and the conditions of its relative success and debated what these would mean for future socialist strategies (cf. Hall 1988; Jessop et al. 1988). The New Left's original idea of combining theory and practice was revived in the establishment of the short-lived *Socialist Society* and later the *Chesterfield Conferences*.

---

8   The Anderson team disagreed, however, on the issue of 'red bases' at the universities (cf. Sassoon 1981: 248).

The multiple British New Lefts had contributed immensely to opening up new ways of left theorising in Britain. Thus, for a considerable time, they arguably reached their goal of acting as a 'movement of ideas' (although they only became a 'real' political movement for a short historical moment in the late 1950s and early 1960s and did not solve all the questions they had formulated for themselves – for example, on the relationship of the intellectual left to the *Labour Party*, or the requirements of a socialist strategy in an age of widespread but selective affluence). The events of 1989, then, affected an intellectual left that had become pluralized, increasingly detached from political movements and parties, and nervous about the unexpected persistence of Thatcherism and its radical reorganisation of large areas of public life.

2.2. *New Left Review* and *Socialist Register*

New Left Review

The number of scholarly contributions to the history of *New Left Review* testifies to its crucial importance for the British – and as several writers would claim, for the international – intellectual left (cf. Blackledge 2000, 2002, 2004, Chun 1996, Elliott 1998, Meiksins Wood 1995, Sassoon 1981, Thompson 2001, 2007). Its central role is also underlined by the impressive number of articles by 'leading thinkers' from around the world published in its pages – the journal's website proudly mentions 32 names that include Giovanni Arrighi, Pierre Bourdieu, Nancy Fraser, Jürgen Habermas, Fredrik Jameson, Göran Therborn, and Slavoj Zizek, among others (cf. New Left Review 2002: 1). However, the history of the journal is not easy to tell. First, the *New Left Review* is rather reluctant to speak about its own past, and Robin Blackburn's overview of its developmental stages on the website is correspondingly short. It also becomes difficult to balance the personal and the political in its internal conflicts and, moreover, to discern the 'voice' of Perry Anderson, often regarded as the journal's intellectual head, from those of the endeavour as a whole.[9] Finally, the *New Left Review*'s (and Anderson's) position has traditionally functioned as a political com-

---

9 Whereas the other journals had two editors for most of the time, Anderson acted as *New Left Review*'s sole editor from 1963 to 1982, cooperating with an editorial committee of varying size.

pass; positioning oneself in relation to *New Left Review* (and to Anderson), has always served the purpose of making a point about one's own political perspective – more than would be the case with most other publications. Gilbert Achcar is in so far correct when calling the journal, despite its commitment to a plurality of positions, the "chief organ" of the New Left (2000: 138).

One of the magazine's peculiarities is its three birth years: 1956, 1960, and 1963. The first witnessed the foundation of its two predecessors, *New Reasoner* and *Universities and Left Review*. Both works were committed to producing a populist, activist, anti-elitist publication for the New Left movement. While they merged in 1960, the editors and the resulting *New Left Review* remained dedicated to these themes. Later a new group including Perry Anderson, Robin Blackburn, and Tom Nairn took charge of the journal, leading Dennis Dworkin to make the claim that Anderson had literally bought the journal through paying its debts (1997: 77). Under this new leadership, it changed course: "*New Left Review* adopted without apology a high intellectual style and undertook a substantial and demanding work of theoretical renewal, the political and theoretical rationale for which they soon explained in cogent and solid statements of position." (Rustin 1985: 49).[10] Hence, 1963 constituted a watershed both in terms of the purpose which the journal was supposed to fulfil as well as in terms of the personnel to carry it out. Upon the arrival of the new group, the old editorial collective left to concentrate on other types of activity or set up *Socialist Register* as an alternative to *New Left Review*. Despite the overhaul, there are nevertheless lines of continuity with the pre-Anderson *Review*: most importantly, according to Fred Inglis, a particular neo-Gramscian humanism and a permanent elaboration of Gramsci's concept of 'hegemony' (cf. 1996: 91). This connection helps to explain why many activists from the first New Left did not stop publishing in the pages of *New Left Review*.

At the core of *New Left Review*'s new direction was a programme of theory import which should provide an end to the perceived insularity of the Brit-

---

10 Whether this renewal was a takeover, as E. P. Thompson claimed, or the rescuing action for a project to be deserted by its founders, as Anderson recounted it, is not relevant here. For a slightly more detached and hence perhaps more reliable view on the change see Williams 1979: 364-66.

ish left's intellectual life. This new perspective tied in, first, with a feature that Peter Sedgwick called "Olympianism", a remote, global perspective resulting from personal research interests (1976: 148). To this end, Elliott quotes a critic who claims that Anderson's oeuvre covered historical developments from 800 BC until last week (cf. 1998: XI). The new direction also related to a number of additional theoretical assumptions: the baseline of the journal's understanding of Marxism was that it constituted a method combining historical and structural analysis of economic and social change. Thus a Marxist approach had to employ a macro- and long-term perspective. This approach bore the danger of forcing an analysis in too unspecific in perspective, as was diagnosed by Duncan Thompson. He explains that *New Left Review* in the mid-1980s built, for example, its evaluation of the political situation in Europe on analyses of the major left parties but ignored the newer, smaller anti-capitalist ones (cf. Thompson 2001: 29). A second characteristic feature was the Deutscherite reading of the Cold War as a struggle between a post-capitalist Eastern bloc and a capitalist West. Finally, *New Left Review* popularised a view of British historical development that became known as the Anderson-Nairn thesis. Criticized by Thompson as over-abstract (and thus 'anti-humanist'), the thesis claimed that the British left's political achievements and theoretical perspectives were harmed by the consequences of a premature bourgeois revolution.[11] Anderson and Nairn saw utilitarianism and Fabianism as its intellectual corollaries and criticised the lack of a powerful revolutionary left tradition. Theory import became a necessary precondition for a radicalisation of the British labour movement, and intellectual engagement with leftwing theory took precedence over articles on working-class history and contemporary political struggles in Britain. The *New Left Review* collective ambitiously attempted to deconstruct the whole construction of Britain's bourgeois

---

11 This premature revolution resulted, according to the thesis, in an alliance between the middle class and the aristocracy, isolated the working class (that in other revolutions had liaised with the bourgeoisie) and left the emerging labour movement with a 'corporate' class consciousness, making it, in the words of Michael Sprinker, at the same time "antagonistic but effectively deferential", thus demanding their share of and stake in society rather than its transformation (1993: 101). For details of the debate on Anderson and Nairn's thesis see Anderson 1980.

intellectual culture.[12] Surprisingly, this perspective was accompanied by an emphasis on technicist large-scale solutions not too different from those recommended within the traditions criticised. With this approach, Wood contested that the journal was in danger of falling prey to intellectual substitutionism:

> If there is an epochal rupture in the evolution of the Western left since 1956, it occurs at the point when a section of the left intelligentsia stopped thinking of themselves as an ally in popular struggles, or even as a vanguard, or even as a critic from the philosophical sidelines, the point at which people stopped thinking of themselves, to use Miliband's formula, as intellectuals *of* an emancipatory movement, and started to think of themselves as intellectuals *for* that movement, or, to put it more strongly, when they started thinking of themselves as the movement itself. (1995: 34-5)

While *New Left Review* could (at least somewhat) legitimately be accused of this type of elitism, it has certainly never been sectarian. It followed an increasingly ecumenical approach to theory which allowed for contributions far beyond (its own versions of) Marxism. It remained unclear where this tolerance ended – that is why, for example, it proved impossible to transform the journal into a 'feminist and socialist' publication (as tried in the early 1980s by a group of socialist feminists who had been invited to the editorial committee), or why the debate on whether democratic progress in the Eastern Bloc would make possible a revival of revolutionary socialism in the West led to a collective exodus of a number of editors. In general, however, in the 1980s *New Left Review* became more open to postmodern positions than *Dissent, Monthly Review*, and *Socialist Register*, and more open to liberal ones than the latter two, even if Robin Blackburn, the editor from 1982 onwards, claimed that the journal distanced itself from the populism, relativism, and identity politics of the broader (post-) New Left (cf. New Left Review 2002: 4). According to Donald Sassoon, the price of

---

12 The most explicit example of this demolition work might be Perry Anderson's all-round critique of intellectual life and theory production in Britain to be found in "Components of the National Culture" (Anderson 1992). 25 years later, Anderson stuck to the essence of his critique but regretted several of its bombastic formulations (1992: Acknowledgements).

this ecumenical perspective and the coverage of topics from philosophy to international relations, from aesthetics to Third World issues was that the journal became a cultural rather than a political project; it provided food for thought but did not act as a political rallying point (cf. 1981: 20). On the positive side, this shift enabled the journal to become a location for important debates within the left – the best-known examples include the controversy between Nicos Poulantzas and Ralph Miliband over the capitalist state in the 1970s and that already mentioned between Stuart Hall and Kevin Bonnett and colleagues over the essentials of Thatcherism in the 1980s (cf. Poulantzas 1969, 1976; Miliband 1970, 1973; Hall 1988; Jessop et al. 1988). Occasionally, coverage changed in surprising ways: whereas the magazine remained far aloof of British industrial militancy in the crisis-ridden 1970s – to a degree that Geoff Hodgson called it the "lost sheep of the British labour movement" (quoted in Thompson 2001: 25) – they developed interest in the changing Labour Party of the early 1980s and published contributions of some of its left-wingers, such as Tony Benn, Eric Heffer, and Ken Livingstone (Benn & Heffer 1986; Livingstone 1983). *New Left Review* never hesitated to take positions different from the mainstream of the British left – for example, on the question of the importance of constitutional reform or European unification: since 1972, when Tom Nairn's article "The European Problem" was published in *New Left Review* 75, they regarded integration into Europe as an "alternative road to socialism", while in the 1980s they supported the demands for constitutional reform by the group Charter 88 (Davidson 1999: 3). Its ecumenical eclecticism extended to sporadic discussions of Third World themes, which were treated less systematically than in *Monthly Review*.

The key to understanding *New Left Review*'s theoretical development lies in its changing approaches to reform and revolution in the West. It started out with a proto-Eurocommunist phase from the early 1960s until 1968, followed by a revolutionary phase continuing until the late 1970s, at first Maoist and then inspired by the student protests, and later Trotskyist and critical of Western Marxism, finally the journal reached a 'post-revolutionary' phase starting in the early 1980s in which a new interest in labour politics became visible. For Duncan Thompson, this "reanchorage was also, at least implicitly, a recognition that the *Review*'s search since 1968 for an answer to the strategic questions facing a new left politics in the West within the canon of classical revolutionary Marxism had proved unavailing" (2001: 26).[13] It did not give up its belief – and in this respect sharply disagreed with *Marxism Today* – in a *potentially* anti-capitalist, though not necessarily revolutionary, working class as an agent of political transformation. When the democratic reform process began in the U.S.S.R., *New Left Review* hoped for the possibility of socialist advance in the West once more. Tariq Ali commented in 1988: "Many of us who remain socialists in the West are beginning to regard the Soviet Union once again as a country of hope" (quoted in Thompson 2001: 30). When viewed through a Deutscherite lens, and from a position still detached from domestic developments in Britain, the collapse of the Eastern Bloc seemed thus catastrophic.

Many judged *New Left Review* in the late 1980s to be a journal of 'intellectual pessimism', and accused it of ultra-theory accompanied by political eclecticism and negligence of working-class struggle.[14] Its strengths and achievements, however, are undisputed. It made continental European Marxist theory available in Britain and arguably opened up many of the theoretical routes subsequently travelled by the post-1968 left and the new social movements, provided thorough, though selective, coverage of world affairs, and offered space for a non-sectarian discussion of strategies for political change.

Socialist Register

The founding of the annual *Socialist Register* was a reaction to the changes within *New Left Review* in 1962/63. Ralph Miliband (who was of comparable importance to *Socialist Register* as Perry Anderson was to *New Left Review*) had, from the beginning, expressed scepticism about the merger of *New Reasoner* (to whose editorial group he belonged) and *Universities and Left Review*. The value and importance of *New Reasoner* for Miliband consisted not only of its particular concept of non-dogmatic, originally dissident, Communism, but also of its climate of 'comradely discussion' which strongly appealed to him as a socialist academic who had given up

---

13 Again, it is difficult to decide, in how far this judgment is applicable to the contributors as a whole, to the editorial committee, or just to Perry Anderson.
14 This allegation was made by, for example, Ellen Meiksins Wood. It was also the reason for her to move on to the editorship of *Monthly Review* (cf. Monthly Review 1999: 75).

on the Labour Left and worked as an isolated Marxist at the *London School of Economics*. In his opinion, the split from *New Left Review* was provoked more by differences of style and journalistic philosophy than by theoretical substance. Unlike E. P. Thompson, whom he unsuccessfully tried to attract as co-editor to *Socialist Register* beside John Saville, Miliband did not feel personal animosity with the new editors of *New Left Review*. Instead, he highly appreciated several of their analyses and shared their interest in Marxism. However, he criticised their reluctance to test their theoretical hypotheses through empirical studies (cf. Newman 2002: 113-20).

The annual publication set up by Saville and Miliband was meant to be a 'survey of movements and ideas', as its subtitle in the early years suggested, and was committed to the revival of a 'theoretical Marxism' that was neither reduced to the base-superstructure simplifications of official dogma nor uncritical towards the structural Marxisms that would be soon to emerge. Miliband's concern with political power in capitalist societies was central to the publication, as were the related questions of socialist agency and strategy (cf. Newman 2002: 350). Most authors, though not sharing a political line in the strict sense, saw themselves to the left of social democracy, as committed to a non-sectarian socialism, and many to Marxism. They were convinced, with Miliband, that institutional power checks would still be necessary in a socialist state and remained critical of the Communist world, but nevertheless still unsupportive of anti-Communists. It could be argued that *Socialist Register* was less concerned with the downside of the Eastern Bloc than *New Reasoner* had been, due to the latter's traumatic break with the British *Communist Party*. In 1960, Miliband explained his attitude towards the U.S.S.R. in a letter to Dorothy Thompson with the following words:

The real point is whether the kind of society they [the U.S.S.R.; SB] are creating looks like approximating something we think is socialism and whether in the development of socialism in the world they are or are not a hopeful, indeed the most hopeful factor. On both counts my answer is yes, with all the qualifications, hesitations and this and what you will. (quoted in Kozak 2006: no pages).[15]

---

15 Obviously, his opinion has changed over the years. Directly after the collapse in 1989 he spoke of an "awful perversion of socialism" and of "oligarchical collectivist regimes" (cf. Newman 2002: 308).

Socialist Register intended to design and pursue a more concrete strategy than those arguing for a vaguely defined 'socialist humanism' and thus tried to base their work, which they regarded as an exercise in "sustained socialist education", on the notion of 'socialist democracy' (Panitch 1995: 12). To realise this concept, Socialist Register hoped to build counter discourses and structures in both state and civil society (ibid: 14). The annual took pride in its internationalism (different, as Kozak suggests, from New Left Review's 'Third Worldism' [2006]) which owed a great deal to the polyglot Belgian-Jewish refugee Miliband and to his close links with the editors of Monthly Review who facilitated contacts to writers from the Latin-American left. One of the publication's most distinguishing features was its comprehensive coverage of developments in Britain and especially in the Labour Party. *Socialist Register* popularised what among political scientists and activists became known as the Miliband-Coates thesis: the dilemma of the left lay in the Labour Party's centrality for working-class politics and the unresolved problem of how to push its leadership towards more radical positions (cf. Panitch 1995: 11).

'Critique' served as the key word for *Socialist Register*'s approach and work. It focused on a wide variety of issues: changes in contemporary capitalism, Western and especially American imperialism, left wing parties (especially in Western Europe), Communist regimes, and Marxist theory. Yet coverage also extended to labour history, grassroots struggles, battles of the *Labour Party*'s left and independence movements in the Third World. Compared to *New Left Review*, the annual was characterised by a consistency in outlook and topics, although it took up several new issues over the years. For example, it paid increasing attention to the internationalisation of capital and the consequences this would have for socialist strategy. The annual's pick of contributors became more international and less British as well: in the 1980s, Canadian editor Leo Panitch with close British links first accompanied the two British editors and later replaced John Saville.

The *Register*'s primary concern lay in political changes rather than in theoretical debates. Thus it developed an interest in, but remained sceptical about, the student unrest of 1968 and the activities of guerrilla movements, both of which seemed to reveal the limits of voluntarism.[16] Nevertheless writers took up several of the issues central to the New Left agenda and tried to give them a socialist twist. Thus, for example, they called for a socialist women's movement separate from bourgeois feminism.[17] With this sensitivity to political changes, it is not surprising that they were deeply concerned about the offensives of a changed right in the late 1970s, about the 'crisis of the left' in the 1980s and about the 'revisionist left's (including many theoreticians') attack on the Bennite Left in the Labour Party. The latter points were denounced as a "retreat of the intellectuals" (Miliband 1994a: 16). In these times of new right hegemony, the Gorbachev reforms were welcomed by the great majority of contributors. Michael Newman even assumes that the general feeling of retreat and despair led Miliband to overemphasise the chances of the experiments in the U.S.S.R. (2002: 311).

Unlike the *New Left Review*'s Olympian detachment, the *Register* was committed to a down-to-earth non-sectarian political involvement. The perhaps most serious weakness of this philosophy was the narrow focus on critique which, as Miliband conceded shortly before his death, led to a neglect of reflections on a utopian social order for the future and on creative thought about the ways to get there:

There are many people on the Left who would say that the answer should be 'nothing much can be done until the revolution, save preparing for it'; but even if this were to be taken as realistic, 'preparing for it' would still involve a series of struggles over specific issues, with a clear indication of what was being struggled for, and without resort to incantation. (Miliband 1994a: 6).

Miliband, always extremely critical of his own work as well as of the articles published in *Socialist Register*, listed a number of topics which the annual had not sufficiently considered: Northern Ireland, the Isra-

---

16 Tariq Ali, one of the leading figures of the 1968 student protests, conceded ten years later in an article for *Socialist Register* that for him the most important lesson of the events was that socialism would be achieved with the consent of the mass of working people or not at all (cf. Miliband 1994: 5).
17 Marion Kozak remarks that the *Register*'s old-left editors were unsure how to relate to debates about the politics of feminism (2006: no pages).

el/Palestine conflict, science, mass communication, and literature and the arts (cf. 1994: 18). However, its focus on political core themes made it, according to Perry Anderson, a sympathetic observer of the weaknesses and inconsistencies of the more ecumenical and eclectic *New Left Review* (cf. Newman 2002: 346). Its original anti-anti-Communist outlook, however, meant that it was forced into reflecting very seriously about its future purpose after the fall of the Eastern European Communist regimes in 1989.

2.3. Two Generations of the American Intellectual Left

Before the emergence of student radicalism in the 1960s, the intellectual left in the United States consisted of two strands which formed important parts of the 'Old Left' that had developed in the 1920s and 1930s.[18][19] The first had their roots in the Popular Front of the 1930s and combined members of the U.S. Communist Party (CP) with New Deal leftists and radical intellectuals.[20] The great majority of intellectuals had never been members of the CP, but were, in the words of John P. Diggins, vague "Marxists of the heart" (1992: 152). Paul Buhle also emphasises that many of the intellectuals were more attracted to the politically broader appeal of the Popular Front and the left wing of the New Deal Coalition than to the narrower CP

---

18 The predecessor to the intellectual wing of the old left was the 'lyrical left' of the first two decades of the twentieth century – which was less concerned with political questions in a narrow sense but experminented with new aesthetic forms of expression and bohemian lifestyles. In this sense, it could be interpreted as a 'proto-New Left'.

19 Andrei S. Markovits distinguishes between an orthodox (until 1968) and a heterodox period (after 1968) within the history of the European and the American Left after 1945. The first one is characterized by a conflict between the Communist and the social democratic left, the second by the New Left and the intellectualisation of leftwing thinking (2005). It seems a bit problematic to apply this model to either the American Left (with its weak social democratic current to whose numbers, however, the former Trotskyist New York intellectuals might be counted) or the British Left (where a New Left emerged as early as 1956).

20 In 1935, Stalin had called for a "popular front" of all liberal and progressive forces to contain the fascist powers (cf. Wald 1987: 129).

(cf. 1991: 198). The second group consisted of Trotskyists, many of whom had their roots in the New York intellectual scene (cf. Wald 1987). Their numbers were considerably smaller than those of the first group (the CP alone had about 80,000 members in 1945 and large groups of sympathizers), but nevertheless they had considerable shop-floor influence. While the immediate post-war time was one of optimism for many on the left, the climate changed in 1948 due to the disastrous Wallace presidential campaign and the damaging dynamic of the emerging Cold War.[21] Persecution intensified, and the question of how to position oneself in the conflict between the Western and the Eastern bloc became increasingly important. As a result of these circumstances – and due to dwindling ethnic solidarities in an era of sub-urbanisation – the CP became ever more isolated and lost its hegemonic role within the American left, a process that only intensified after the party's break with the New Deal Coalition in 1950. Independent Marxist intellectuals, who had supported the Popular Front and the New Deal Coalition, started looking for ways out of this impasse. In this context, Paul Sweezy and Leo Huberman founded the magazine *Monthly Review* in 1949.[22]

Like elsewhere, in the United States Trotskyism was split. However, all Trotskyists opposed the Popular Front and contested participation in a war between 'imperialist powers'. For many of them, especially for Trotskyist intellectuals confronted with working-class apathy which allowed anti-Trotskyist purges within the trade unions, vanguardist ideas changed into a mood of desperation and intellectual activity took the shape of a "melancholy critique of mass delusion" (Buhle 1991: 206). The danger of self-annihilation had replaced the promise of self-emancipation. They rejected the optimistic Marxist notion that human activity mirrored the progressive movement of history (cf. Diggins 1992: 161). They all felt and expressed hostility towards the U.S.S.R. in the Cold War. They disagreed, however, as to how far this enmity should go. Some became uncritical supporters of the Truman and Eisenhower administrations, collaborated with Joseph

---

21 The CP was involved in setting up a third party, called Progressive Party, as whose candidate Henry Wallace run in the 1948 presidential election. He ended with only 2.4 per cent of the vote (cf. Isserman 1993: 6-7).
22 Leo Huberman, 1903-1968, social scientist, journalist and author, taught at Columbia University.

McCarthy, wrote for *Partisan Review*, and participated in the anti-Communist *Congress for Cultural Freedom*. A minority preferred a position that Maurice Isserman coined the "second-and-a-half camp" in the Cold War – no position of equidistance between the superpowers, but nevertheless one which was also critical towards the United States (cf. 1993: 105). This stance was taken by Irving Howe, Stanley Plastrik, Manny Geltmann and Lewis Coser, the founders of the magazine *Dissent* in 1954.[23]

Post-Trotskyists, like those close to *Dissent,* and Marxists, such as the founders of *Monthly Review*, did not have much in common, and Howe, for example, accused the editors of the latter journal to be "authoritarians of the left" (quoted in Wald 1987: 328).[24] However, they shared the view that the times looked far from promising for radical change in the United States. The emergence of the Civil Rights Movement in the South in the mid-fifties surprised both groups. This was a new type of radicalism, which many observers regarded as 'domestic American' and that altered the world view of left intellectuals. Up to this time, these intellectuals had assumed that their role was to act *for* the interests of African Americans rather than to be taught new strategies of political activism *by* them. At the same time, other intellectual and political activities began to aggregate into something that Paul Buhle called a "proto-New Left" (1991: 216). Shifts in this direction included a revival of pacifism at the University of Wisconsin, Madison, the protests of the "student wing" of the Civil Rights Movement (above all, the Student Non-Violent Coordinating Committee; SNCC) and the reflections of a number of writers whose background was different from both, the CP and the New York intellectual scene. Such authors include William Appleman Williams (a revisionist historian, questioning the United States' 'inno-

---

23 Lewis Coser, 1913-2003, born in Germany, political sociologist and conflict theorist taught at various U.S. universities, second long-term editor of *Dissent* beside Irving Howe.

24 Paul Sweezy was one of a total of 88 signers of an "Open Letter to American Liberals" in which they criticised the "American Committee For the Defense of Leon Trotsky" which held an inquiry into the charges formulated against Trotsky in the Moscow show trials in the late 1930s. Many American socialists and liberals declared sympathy for Stalin's popular front strategy and feared a weakening of the efforts to contain Fascism. Chaired by John Dewey, the committee cleared Trotsky of all allegations (cf. Wald 1987: 128-139).

cence' in the emergence of the Cold War) who founded the journal *Studies on the Left* in 1959 and was also based at the University of Wisconsin; C. Wright Mills (a Texas-born sociologist, influenced by existentialism); C.L.R. James (a heterodox Trotskyist); and F. E. Matthiesen (a cultural critic who, through a financial gift, had made the setting-up of *Monthly Review* possible). Michael Harrington also fits the list: his studies about poverty in the 'affluent' United States (published as *The Other America* in 1963) became widely read and debated. The term proto-New Left is an adequate characterisation of these people as they shared a number of assumptions which became central for the American New Left of the 1960s: the need to abolish economistic Marxism, to break with the idea of the state as the vehicle for organising a transition to socialism, to transcend now-old and – as they argued – irrelevant distinctions (between idealists and materialists or Communists and Trotskyists)(cf. Aronowitz 1996: 17).

The "real" New Left, as a student movement and – despite a certain fashionable anti-intellectualism – as an intellectual affair, appeared with the *Students for a Democratic Society*'s (SDS) *Port Huron Statement* of 1963 and the *Free Speech Movement* at Berkeley.[25] The New Left, as Paul Buhle put it, used the experiences of the Old Left and started where the latter had stopped: with the 'race' question and with curiosity towards the political implications of popular culture (cf. 1991: 256). For the New Left, the "poverty of abundance" had replaced the "abundance of poverty" that characterised the world of the Old Left (cf. Diggins 1992: 232). Diggins also emphasised that the New Left radicalised itself on the basis of its experiences, whereas the Old Left had become increasingly moderate: "The Old Left began with a whoop of revolution and sank into a whimper of reconciliation – thanks to Russia; the New Left started in a spirit of moderation and ended calling for nothing less than revolution – thanks to America" (ibid: 219). They shared the fear of human annihilation with the former Trotskyist part of the Old Left. They differed from them in that the New Left stressed America's responsibility for preventing such destruction. In general, they did not know very much of the East Coast old-left traditions and internal conflicts as they often came from other parts of the country and often from middle-class Republican families. In its early stage, the New Left was not

---

25 For detailed histories of the American New Left see Katsiaficas 1987 and Gitlin 1993.

in a narrow sense 'Marxist', but nevertheless remained hostile to U.S. anti-Communism. Activists looked for space to manoeuvre at the margins of capitalism – especially in the Third World and its national liberation movements. Receptive to Freudian psychoanalysis, they also saw the human unconscious as a site for political intervention. Their interests in Marxism extended to the "early Marx", "cultural Marxism" (as developed by the British New Left), and the concept of alienation (as elaborated especially by Existentialism and the Frankfurt School). Their interest in liberation movements temporarily attracted many to Maoism. Their political goal, apart from the concrete demand for an end to the war in Vietnam, focussed on a vague demand for the replacement of "the system" by participatory democracy. The New Left in the United States turned out to be a rather short-lived movement, disintegrating into factional struggles: some embraced militancy while others pursued intellectual careers in the expanding academic sector, tried to liaise with social movements or retreated from activism by the early 1970s. However, some of their achievements were impressive: they managed to halt the draft, contributed to the withdrawal from Vietnam, and developed an understanding of politics that facilitated the emergence of the Women's Movement and other social movements. Although they did not succeed in democratising the universities and could not convince them to cut their ties with the arms and military technology industries, these reformers radically modified the academic disciplines and curricula in higher education. Their influence became most visible in history departments in the 1970s and in English departments in the 1980s. Interestingly, despite the New Left's critique of the Old Left for sticking to anachronistic and economistic problematics or for siding with the United States in the Cold War and Vietnam, in the 1970s a number of the New Leftists became contributors to, and editorial board members of those Old Left Magazines that had not moved towards the emerging New Right. This integration allowed for a combination of old-left concerns about how to achieve socialism with new concerns about gender equality, environmental issues, and grassroots movements and thus initiated a more open debate on possible agencies and strategies for radical social change.

In the 1970s, a new division appeared between different sections of the intellectual left in the United States: while some started drawing heavily on Foucauldian and post-structuralist critical theory imported from Europe (especially from France), others remained in the tradition of socialist or materialist analysis. The first tendency in particular became widespread in the academic world and provoked New Right assaults on "cultural and moral relativism", "epistemological irrationalism" and "political correctness". Leftist thinkers who did not follow this trend found themselves in an odd situation. They agreed with the New Right on some of its criticisms, but were still labelled by the Right as part of the same broad left – especially because they shared a concern about "minority issues" with the postmodern left. Left thinking in the 1970s became very much a university affair; extra-university activity reached its nadir in 1979/80. In the 1980s, a renewed interest in old American radical traditions emerged (cf: Ostendorf & Levine 1992) – a concern supported by several thinkers associated with the journal *Dissent*, such as Richard Rorty, Michael Walzer and Irving Howe, for example (cf. Rorty 1982, Walzer 1983, Howe 1986). The rupture of 1989 thus affected an intellectual left that either claimed to retain the basics of materialist historiography and political economy, or instead claimed to reinvent a new radical perspective from old domestic traditions.

2.4. *Dissent* and *Monthly Review*

Dissent

For Irving Howe, the leading figure behind *Dissent*, the publication of a journal became an escape route out of what he regarded as sectarian politics (cf. Isserman 1993: 88-9). For the New York intellectuals, magazines had always been the most important medium of political debate and disagreement. With *Partisan Review*'s move to the right, a vacuum emerged that was first filled by the journal *Politics* (founded in 1944) whose contributing editors included several future *Dissenters*. The actual founding of *Dissent* in 1954 resulted from a feeling of political helplessness (as Howe later explained, whenever left intellectuals do not know what to do, they set up magazines), but also from dissatisfaction with the shape of the left in the United States and the climate of McCarthyism (cf. Plastrik 1979: 3). *Dissent* developed under the "shadow of the two Josephs" – Stalin and McCarthy (Cohen 2004: 4). This explains its originally planned name "No!". The journal wanted to be a forum for open debate – albeit within certain limits. It called itself "democratic socialist" and stood for a critical support of U.S. foreign policy in the Cold War. It disagreed with those who saw the U.S.S.R.'s nationalisation of the economy as a progressive step and thus took a staunch anti-Deutscherite position. Yet on the other hand, it did not participate in the "Leninophobia" of other (former) Trotskyists (cf. Wald 1987: 324). The peculiar spirit and perspective of this "Quarterly of Socialist Opinion" might best be explained through a few quotations. For Irving Howe, *Dissent*'s theoretical reflections were a process of self-cleaning: "Year by year we shook off remnants of ideology, till we seemed to have nothing, at times, but the motivating ethic of socialism; yet we wanted thereby to hold fast to the socialist vision, to give it new strength and value." (1979: 6). A commitment to democracy remained absolutely central:

We provided a platform for Herbert Marcuse when he engaged in principled debates with Erich Fromm on psychoanalysis and politics; we parted company with him when he suggested that civil liberties should be reserved for the virtuous, with the voice of the sinful to be stilled. We printed some of C. Wright Mills's most significant essays, but we turned against him when he listened with admiration to the appeals of Castro. (Coser 1974: 4)

An external perspective on the magazine's version of socialism was provided by the liberal Joseph Epstein, writing in the twentieth anniversary issue: "*Dissent*'s editors themselves, while insisting on their socialism, have tended to wear it lightly. Their approach to socialism, they have always claimed, is not to a fixed piety and their concentration has been on 'problematics' of the subject" (1974: 161). The journal was, according to an observation by second-generation editor Mitchell Cohen, opposed to determinism but not to utopianism. Over the years, this position has remained remarkably constant, though, in the 1980s, *Dissent* described itself as "democratic left" rather than socialist and in 2004 Cohen offered his readers a wide variety of self-identifications of *Dissenters* – "democratic socialists", "liberal socialists", "social democrats", "social liberals", and "liberal left" (cf. Cohen 2004: 4). Another defining feature, distinguishing *Dissent* from the other journals in this study, is its suspicion against 'grand theory', including supposedly over-abstract versions of historical materialism and political economy.

These misgivings influenced the choice of topics: the journal consistently focussed on actually existing political movements, on social democratic parties in other countries (with particular sympathies at times for the British Labour Party and the various Scandinavian Social Democrats), on the reflections of disillusioned European intellectual leftists – "refugees from the International" (Isserman 1993: 92) – as well as on those of Eastern European dissidents. In the 1950s, *Dissent*'s mood was not so much one of despair as of anger (cf. Walzer 2004: 11). Contributors controversially discussed the 'mass-culture thesis' and celebrated the uprising in Hungary and the emergence of the African American Civil Rights Movement. The latter provided hope for the emergence of further radical movements in the United States, hence *Dissenters*' pessimism about the possibilities of political change mellowed slightly. Its greatest success story was perhaps the extensive coverage of Michael Harrington's work on poverty that culminated in his important study *The Other America* (1963), many of whose findings were published in advance by *Dissent*.

The journal welcomed the emergence of the New Left in the 1960s, having anticipated several themes that became associated with the students' movement: the insistence on human emancipation, democratisation, and decentralisation of power. Nevertheless, their relationship was complicated by a number of differences. They disagreed over Vietnam – whereas Howe and others argued for negotiations (at least before the Tet offensive), the New Left demanded the immediate withdrawal of American troops. *Dissent* remained anti-Communist, whereas the New Left, though not pro-Communist, still rejected anti-Communist sentiments. They also clashed on more theoretical issues; whereas *Dissenters* had mostly abandoned Marxism, the New Left was increasingly attracted to the "early Marx", and whereas *Dissent* abhorred politically motivated violence, the New Left sympathised with Maoism for a time. Finally, there were cultural differences. *Dissent* retained the New York intellectuals' admiration for modernist high culture and was deeply suspicious of popular culture, while the New Left stood for a cultural anti-elitism. Despite the efforts by individuals, such as Michael Walzer, who acted as intellectual interlopers between the New Left and the magazine, "a sense of disappointment, of hurt pride, and toward the end, of ironic resignation flavoured *Dissent*'s attitude toward the New Left" (Isserman 1993: 122). Nevertheless, in the 1970s, a number of important figures from the former New Left began to contribute articles to the magazine. This change brought the generations of the 1930s and the 1950s closer to each other (cf. Cohen 2004: 4) and prompted Howe and other *Dissenters* to revise their view of new social movements, especially feminism (cf. Wald 1987: 333).

During the 1970s, the journal held its political course in general. However, since others raced to the right or turned to postmodernism it created an impression of moving to the left. Despite its mentioned scepticism about 'grand theory', the journal took a hostile position towards poststructuralist anti-foundationalism and political eclecticism. This stance made it ambivalent to the issue of identity politics and deeply suspicious of 'political correctness' and its associated 'cultural relativism' (cf. Cohen 2004: 5). In many of the contributions of the time, one could find "regret for a gone era of reform" (Bromwich 2004: 110). The journal suffered, like the American left as a whole, under the experience of Reaganism, which it regarded as the worst onslaught on liberal-left achievements and thinking since the 1950s. However, it tried to avoid futile laments about being confronted with an over-powerful enemy (cf. Phillips 2004: 170). Additionally, it faced problems with recruiting younger contributors: due to the ever increasing specialisation among university intellectuals, only few were willing and able to submit articles with the generalist perspectives the journal preferred. When the Eastern Bloc collapsed in 1989, *Dissenters* felt more ambivalent about the events than might be expected from an originally anti-Communist collective. While they welcomed the disappearance of dictatorships and state violence, at the end of the neo-liberal 1980s, they were at the same time deeply concerned about future developments within Eastern European societies.

For Alan Wald, *Dissent* suffered for most of its history from an anti-theoretical perspective that prevented it from seeing the structural deficiencies of capitalist societies (cf. 1987: 334). Similarly, Maurice Isserman diagnosed that, for example, U.S. foreign policy was analysed almost exclusively on the basis of case studies rather than systematically or systemically. The journal was not willing or able to realise that the United States' role in the world was not decided by competent or incompetent specialists and politicians, but resulted instead from the context of a geo-political system of power (cf. 1993: 106-107). For the whole Cold War period, *Dissent* was, to a certain degree, a Janus-faced journal: it defended the merits of liberal democracy against radical leftists and criticized its shortcomings in discussions with liberals.

Monthly Review

Like *Dissent*'s, the foundation of *Monthly Review* in 1949 was a reaction to the obvious left retreat in the United States in the late 1940s. For the founders and the early contributors, the New Deal liberal-left coalition had been replaced by a Cold War liberal-conservative coalition (cf. Phelps 1999: 8). The idea was to set up an "independent socialist magazine" (this was its subtitle) in order to sustain and further open debate among the non-orthodox Marxist left in the United States. This group basically consisted of an alliance of people who had united behind the Wallace presidential campaign in 1948 and were no longer willing to accept the leading role of the Communist Party which had reacted to a hostile public climate with increased authoritarianism (cf. Buhle 1991: 197). The founders, Paul Sweezy and Leo Huberman, "believed roughly in [the] extension of the New Deal into state socialism, with heightened democratic participation and international détente" (ibid: 198). Although the New Deal Coalition had already started disintegrating, the journal's founders remained convinced that it was necessary to develop a Marxist theory more closely related to American society and less axiomatically founded on Leninism. However, as Sweezy and Huberman explained in the 1953 article "A Challenge to the Book Burners", they were in no way anti-Communist. Instead, they described their position as "socialist, Marxist, non-Communist, but willing to cooperate with anyone, including Communists, on agreed aims and by agreed methods" (1953: 159).

This claim to cooperate with anyone was taken very seriously and established *Monthly Review* as a journal that tried to reach beyond academic contributors and intellectual readers. In the early years, the theoretical heads behind it were Sweezy and his friend and collaborator Paul Baran. As a former assistant of Joseph Schumpeter at Harvard, Sweezy was sentenced to three years in prison in a McCarthyite trial for his involvement in the Wallace campaign – a verdict that later was overturned by the Supreme Court. At the time, Baran was the only Marxist tenured professor at a U.S. economics department. Both formulated individually and jointly a theory of capitalist development that, by the mid-1950s, had become known as the 'Monthly-Review School'. They worked to support their major premises through numerous articles in the journal, most written from a historically informed materialist perspective (cf. Hopfmann 1999: 398). According to their basic assumption, crises were inherent to capitalist development and thus unavoidable and, therefore, fine-tuning strategies such as Keynesianism were doomed to fail. Furthermore, large and strong national economies were able to externalise these crises, a process that made imperialism a structure of domination intimately linked with capitalism. The task of the left, and particularly of left intellectuals, then was not to devise more sophisticated strategies of social and economic engineering, but to oppose capitalism in all its economic, cultural, political, ideological and social dimensions. *Monthly Review*'s notion of socialism, consequently, was the overthrow of capitalism in all these aspects, but most importantly, the transformation of property relations, the abolition of private profit as guiding principle for economic decision making, and the creation of a society in which the producers would control the conditions and results of economic activity. This position differed radically from a social democratic perspective, though many contributors' personal histories in New Deal agencies resulted in a gradualist approach towards achieving these goals. *Monthly Review*'s particular strength lay in its coverage of the mechanisms and intricacies of 'externalising' capitalist crises. They analysed developments in the Third World in great detail and became early populariser of dependency and world system theory.[26] André Gunder Frank, Immanuel Wallerstein, and especially Samir Amin all became frequent contributors. Later, the editors concerned themselves with another form of externalisation: the problem of environmental devastation. In this context, the magazine searched for alternatives to the growth principle underlying neo-liberal, social democratic, but also many socialist strategies.

Despite viewing capitalism and especially finance capital as a system acting globally, *Monthly Review* insisted on the national arena as being central for anti-capitalist politics. Thus they were interested in, and supportive of, local labour and popular struggles in the United States and everywhere else. Like other leftists in North America, they reflected on working-class conservatism in the climate of the 1950s, but did not show much interest in the mass-culture thesis. While the magazine's particular strength lay in its editors' expertise in political economy, beyond this they published

---

26 According to Ellen Meiksins Wood, also the British journal *New Left Review* was at certain stages in its history very interested in developments in the Third World. Unlike *Monthly Review*, however, they focused more on vanguard movements and parties than on popular struggles (1995: 30).

contributions by numerous innovative left thinkers of the time and, in several cases, articles by the same persons who wrote for *Dissent* – among them C. Wright Mills, William Appleman Williams, Todd Gitlin, and the British New Left authors Raymond Williams and Ralph Miliband. In the words of Christopher Phelps, the journal became an "arc of continuity" between the Old Left and the emerging New Left in the 1960s and profited from the rise of the latter through fresh debates and rising circulation numbers (1999: 18). Despite these cross-generational tendencies, the journal still belonged more to the Old Left than to the New:

[I]t seems fair to say that *Monthly Review* was a journal of the old left that extended its sympathies to the new, that from the beginning it held certain beliefs identical to the new left's central tenets, and that it was further shaped over time by interaction with the movements and events of the 1960s, serving as one place of fusion for overlapping generations of the left. (ibid)

Obviously, the relationship between *Monthly Review* and the New Left was less contentious than between the latter and *Dissent*. This cordiality was facilitated by more common theoretical ground and also by generally similar positions both against the war in Vietnam (*Monthly Review* had criticised American involvement in Indochina as early as 1954) and on U.S. foreign policy (which according to the journal's definition of capitalism was imperialist by necessity). However, the magazine did not accept the early New Left's anti-Marxism; it still insisted on the centrality of class struggle in any strategy for radical change and saw all forms of oppression as linked to the class hierarchy within capitalism. Furthermore, *Monthly Review* shared the New Left's enthusiasm for liberation movements in the Third World and was initially intrigued by Maoism, but moved towards more sober analyses of post-revolutionary societies after the failure of the Cultural Revolution became obvious. Again, the Reagan and Bush years were conceived of as a time of left retreat, though the editors (the economist Harry Magdoff had accompanied Paul Sweezy since Huberman's death in 1969) had expressed less enthusiasm about the 1960s as an era of reform.[27] Like *Dissent*, the journal stuck to its original course and reacted

---

27 Harry Magdoff, 1913-2006, became co-editor of Monthly Review after Leo Huberman's death in 1969. As an auto-didactically trained economist, he had

sceptically towards the academic integration and post-modernisation of the American left, and especially to its substitution of psychoanalysis and discourse theory for historical-materialist political economy as explanatory tools of social phenomena. As a result of the unsupportive political and theoretical climate, its influence on the academic left declined in the 1980s.

Another problem for *Monthly Review* was its relationship with and views of the states of the Eastern Bloc. Contributors criticised the regimes' authoritarianism, but at the same time partly excused it, attributing its cause to the introduction of socialism in such 'backward' countries, the failure of revolutions in Central Europe after the end of the First World War, and U.S. pressure and aggression in the Cold War. On the one hand, they condemned the Soviet army's crushing of revolts in Hungary and Czechoslovakia and the suppression of Solidarnosc in Poland. On the other hand, they accepted the nationalisation strategy in the U.S.S.R. as a horrendous – but nevertheless to a certain degree successful – step towards modernisation. They saw the states of the Eastern Bloc as 'transitional', as no longer capitalist but not yet socialist, and hence always in danger of sliding back into capitalism.[28] For a short time in the mid-1980s, they hoped for a democratised socialism as the successful result of the Gorbachev reforms, but became very critical of their content (and implementation) after the restructuring failed and the feared backslide to capitalism actually occurred.

Monthly Review was, to a certain degree, a pan-American journal. Its eyes were never directed exclusively towards developments in North America and Europe; it also closely followed political struggles in Latin America, as in the 1970s and 1980s, when the journal took an interest in liberation theology. The philosophy tied in nicely with the *Review*'s emphasis on the ethical dimension of Marxism, which had already been responsible for its openness to the New Left, the Women's Movement and environmental concerns. For most of its history, the journal focused on political economy (and in this context was occasionally criticised for its adventurous use of statistical material to prove its central theses [cf. Hopfmann 1999: 398]). Its

---

    held jobs in the New Deal administration and later wrote on the nexus of capitalism and imperialism.

28 For a summary of Paul Sweezy's view on the U.S.S.R., the Eastern Bloc and Yugoslavia as transitional societies which moved back to capitalism see van der Linden 2007: 209-210.

focus broadened with regard to historical, sociological and environmental questions when Ellen Meiksins Wood (for a couple of years) and John Bellamy Foster accompanied and later replaced the old editors. *Monthly Review*'s most distinctive features – its global perspective, its environmentalism and its effort to reach beyond academia – influenced its reactions to the changes of 1989.

2.5. Similarities and Differences among the American and the British Intellectual Lefts

The journals introduced were all set up by leftwing intellectuals at a particular historical conjuncture characterised by the first Cold War, a conservative hegemony – moderate in terms of welfarism but radical in its anti-Communism – in the leading countries of the West and a break (at times hesitant and reluctant) with a dogmatic Marxism which subordinated working-class emancipation beyond the Soviet sphere of influence to the interests of the Moscow leaderships. Against this background and alarmed by the possibility of an East-West confrontation which could lead to a nuclear war and human self-annihilation, the intellectuals surrounding the journals started discussing questions that developed into the agenda of a proto- or pre-1968 New Left. The British thinkers looked to intellectuals in the United States like C. Wright Mills for inspiration, but also to the two American journals which had been founded several years earlier (cf. Chun 1996: 207). The intellectuals' older generation in both countries was heavily influenced by the experiences of the 1930s, whether or not they supported the Popular Front and backed the Allies in the Second World War. The journals can, to a certain extent, be regarded as the brainchildren of single intellectual fathers (Irving Howe, Paul Sweezy, E. P. Thompson, Perry Anderson, and Ralph Miliband) who stood for particular versions of historical materialist analysis and who (apart from Thompson) retained their influence over the respective publication well into the 1990s, or in the case of Anderson until today. Despite important differences listed below, they were united by the act of producing historically informed analyses of political and economic power relations, struggles and developments. Although working on different levels of abstraction, this enabled contributors to submit articles to one of the other journals – which in fact happened frequently. Each journal searched for potential historical agents of change – labour organisations, left-of-centre parties, and social movements. All of them viewed the events of 1968 with a sceptical sympathy for the revolting students, struggled with their new forms and themes of political activism, integrated some of these issues into their own agendas, and provided shelter for several of the former activists once the revolts had died down. All became deeply concerned about the ideological radicalisation and rising self-confidence of the Right from the mid-1970s onwards and perhaps even more by the start of what is called the Second Cold War, at the end of the decade. With feelings of losing out in the 1980s, they placed high hopes in the attempts at reforms in the Soviet Union from 1985 – hopes they had soon to abandon.

The differences between the journals often mirrored specific features of and developments within American and British society. In Britain, the labour movement, the Labour Party, and class conflict played a central role. In the United States, with its more fragmented and ethnically divided society, where, the Civil Rights Movement, one of the strongest ever popular movements, emerged around ethnic identification during the formative years of the two journals. In Britain, the spectrum of the political mainstream extended slightly more to the left than in the United States, where even the revisionist British Labour Party appeared progressive. It also stands that some of *Dissent*'s positions which in Britain could have been found in publications close to the Labour Party were 'far left' in the American context. In the United States, the break with the New Deal and World War II climate was fundamental and gave way to Cold War anti-Communism, whereas in Britain, the war ushered in the era of the welfare state. The two American journals strongly disagreed with each other on many substantial political questions. The two British publications' differences were, first of all, generational and slightly less about questions of politics – although behind their controversies over epistemology lay problems of the possibilities and limits of historical agency and thus also questions of political strategy.

Each of the magazines has always had its own project, identity, and priorities, reflecting their editors' and contributors' political and personal backgrounds and perspectives. *Dissent* put great effort into defining democratic socialism *practically* and for this purpose analysed concrete policies instead of discussing 'grand theory'. Most *Dissenters* did not see themselves as equally distant from the United States and the Soviet Union, but closer to the former. Many of them shared a left Zionism. Their experiences as Jewish Americans or former Jewish Europeans played an important role for their political perspectives. *Monthly Review* focused strongly on political economy due to its conviction that capitalist crises (and their externalisation) explained the dynamics of domestic and international politics. This notion of inevitable crisis explained its concern with international power structures, environmentalism, and its opposition to reformism. *New Left Review* was the most theoretically inclined of the publications. Thus it focused on political philosophy and, additionally, on world history. It was deeply involved in following (and shaping) the vogues of post-1968 left intellectualism. It published a wide variety of critical theory, far transcending the boundaries of Marxism and socialism. Hence it was more open to (although often critical of) poststructuralism, but, at the same time, perhaps the least consistent of the journals in terms of political perspective. Like *Dissent* and unlike the two other publications, *New Left Review* took a consistently supportive position towards European unification since the early 1970s. *Socialist Register* was most thoroughly concerned with structures and mechanisms of power, both internationally and within the (British) state. On questions of international political economy, it was close to *Monthly Review* but more systematic in the analysis of domestic power relations and struggles. More than the others, it stressed the importance of designing democratic institutions suitable for a socialist state, although it had problems with translating this into concrete scenarios.

All journals, with the exception of *Dissent* due to its Trotskyist origin, had problems in defining their relationships towards the Soviet Union and the Eastern Bloc. They oscillated between foregrounding the progressive content of the U.S.S.R.'s and the East European states' nationalisation programmes – which made them post- or non-capitalist – and criticising their violations of their own populations, especially their working classes – which made them authoritarian. This fluctuation put the journals in a vulnerable position once the states of the Eastern Blocs had collapsed. Despite their differences and inconsistencies concerning these questions, all were aware that the discursive nexus between the term socialism and the forms of governance associated with the Eastern Bloc – a nexus whose formulation was, as they all, including *Dissent*, agreed, a central ideological device of the capitalist West in the Cold War – would still cause profound inhibitions to the formulation of socialist or radical projects after state socialism's end.

III. Crisis and Re-orientation: Evidence from the Journals

1. THE MOMENT OF 1989: EMOTIONAL RESPONSES TO THE COLLAPSE OF THE EASTERN BLOC

This chapter sheds light on the mood in which analyses among the intellectual left were formulated in the years after 1989. By focusing on the personal, emotional, immediate aspects of intellectuals' reactions, it sketches out an important part of the framework within which to understand the more academically detached and more sober reflections discussed in later chapters. The emotional link to the Eastern Bloc, whether one of sympathy, anger, discomfort, or protectiveness, overshadowed and influenced what contributors thought and wrote about its disintegration. Obviously unexpected by most of them at the time, the collapse provoked 'spontaneous' reactions in all the four journals. Such statements peaked in the years 1990 and 1991 and became less frequent from 1992 onwards. At their core were questions about what the altered conditions meant for radical intellectuals individually, for their generations of the left as a whole, socialised in times of the Popular Front or the Cold War, and for the chances of left political projects in Britain and North America.

New Left Review

Feelings in *New Left Review* oscillated between relief, mourning, and unease. Relief was founded on the hope that with overdue changes in the societies of the crumbling Eastern Bloc, new socialist beginnings would become possible – not only there but also elsewhere. This view, formulated, for example, by Robin Blackburn in the introduction's first quote, which termed great-power communism an "unhappy spirit begging to be laid to rest" and to be replaced by something new, was obviously strongest in the early months and years after 1989 (1991: 173). However, such sentiments soon disappeared behind more ambivalent feelings. While socialist and radical intellectuals welcomed the revolutionary agency of Eastern European people who had brought down those state socialist regimes which had denied them certain basic rights, the character of these revolutions was not unproblematic. It was defined, as Jürgen Habermas stated, by a "total lack of ideas that [were] either innovative or oriented towards the future" (1990: 5). As a consequence, intellectuals became increasingly uneasy about the directions which political developments took in the former Eastern Bloc. Lucio Magri, a leading member of the Italian *Rifondazione Comunista* described the mood change over the months after the autumn of 1989:

When the Berlin Wall came down the judgement of many people was one of euphoria. They saw the coming of a new historical period marked by world cooperation, disarmament, and democratic advance which would provide a clear opportunity for democratic socialism with a human face. Now we can see that the reality is different and much harsher. (1991: 5)

The reality turned out to be a situation in which capitalism stood triumphant and where people in Eastern Europe embraced it whole-heartedly even if ill-informed. In this context, the hope for a human socialism appeared illusory. Over the following years, it became increasingly clear that the abolition of state socialism meant the introduction of an even more radical, liberated capitalism – especially since it was paralleled by the collapse of the Western labour movements and by the fizzling out of Third World radicalism (cf. Ahmad 1994: 96).

However, grief was not limited to the loss of the revolutionary moment of 1989 which had been appropriated by those interested in the restoration of capitalism. At least some contributors felt obliged – despite all their previous criticism – to express their mourning over the disintegration of the Soviet Union. G. A. Cohen, philosopher and analytical Marxist, made no secret of his deep feelings of regret:

It is true that I was heavily critical of the Soviet Union, but the angry little boy who pummels his father's chest will not be glad if the old man collapses. As long as the Soviet Union seemed safe, it felt safe for me to be anti-Soviet. Now that it begins, disobligingly, to crumble, I feel impotently protective toward it. (1991: 9-10)

While this position appeared paradoxical, Cohen explained why it was not:

[A]lthough I have long since sustained little hope that things in the Soviet Union might get substantially better, in a socialist sense, there is, in certain domains, and people are prone to overlook this, a vast difference between nourishing little hope and giving up all hope. The small hope that I kept was, as it were, an immense thing, since so much was at stake. And now that residual hope has to be forsworn. So a feeling of loss is not surprising. (ibid: 9)

Furthermore, the feeling of loss was likely to have serious psychological consequences. For those who, like Cohen, had been socialised into a socialist culture as children and had continued to understand themselves as part of it as adults, the collapse marked the end of a relationship that was far from harmonious but nonetheless extremely important. The tradition's sudden end transformed it into traumatic experience:

What is more, depression about the failure of the Soviet Union, as it supervenes in those of us who reluctantly rejected its claims decades ago, perforce has a complex structure, one element in which is self-reproach, since what is lost is a long since denied (yet also fiercely clung to) love. (ibid: 13)

Critics of the Soviet Union, feelings disappointed over its inglorious performance, had not necessarily stopped projecting their dreams into it – even if it had not been socialist, it was the part of the world that could and should have.

However, despair among contributors to *New Left Review* was not limited to the collapse of the Eastern Bloc. Rather, it became an additional blow in a long series of political defeats that had to be accepted at least for most of the 1980s. The experience of powerlessness against the Thatcherite dismantling of many progressive gains for which the labour movement and other social movements had struggled turned out to be particularly hard to bear for the generation politically socialised around 1968. They had started out with some optimism that critical intellectuals could make a difference and install elements of a libertarian socialism. This generational project, as Lynne Segal explained, was in shambles:

Today, depression, cynicism or political turnabouts are hard to avoid, even knowing we are not the first – and will not be the last – to face the defeat and disorderly retreat of the ideals, activities and lifestyles that transformed and gave meaning to our lives. Depression hits hardest when the withering of former struggles and aspirations begins to feel like personal defeat; often ending the friendships, the shared activities, and the opening up of public spaces, so necessary for the survival of any sense of optimism in the future. (1991: 81)

The biographical consequences for this generation were grave as she pointed out later: "Ten years of defeat for almost all egalitarian and collectivist endeavours has caused many of us on the Left to fall into chronic mutual abuse, to fall upon our own swords or to fall – some never to raise again – onto the analytic couch" (ibid: 82). She argued that all socialist ideals and aspirations were threatened by illegitimacy in the aftermath of 1989. She deplored the "gloom of witnessing the erasure of the history of such struggles: an erasure which stems not only from the mainstream media, but from sections of the Left as well, busy exchanging new ideas for old, or else recoiling memoryless from the corpse of Soviet socialism" (1991: 82). For others it seemed to constitute a problem which of the socialist ideals of the recent past could be retained and retrieved – even if Western socialists had not hesitated to distance themselves from the Eastern Bloc. Jürgen Habermas questioned the sustainability of socialist commitments in a post-communist world when he discussed what the changes meant for German society: "It [the West-German non-Communist left; SB] does not need to let guilt by association be foisted on it for the bankruptcy of a state socialism that it has always criticized. But it must ask itself how long an idea can hold out against reality" (1990: 10).

Faced with this situation, the majority of authors encouraged each other not to surrender and recommended a certain level of stubborn perseverance.

It remained an important task to stick to the principles of socialist critique in order to avoid both the stagnation of social theory and the spread of political agony – especially since the triumph of capitalism was likely to be less stable than anticipated by many:

As the light of socialist hopes and aspirations fades, and the need for clear vision and historical perspective grows imperative, we might look to the owl of Minerva, trusting she will neither be dazzled by the fires of capitalist celebration (or crisis?) nor succumb to the absolute darkness of despair. (Therborn 1992: 17)

Critical intellectual work on capitalism and the limits of capitalist democracy remained important, as contributors frequently reminded each other, especially if they agreed with Göran Therborn's diagnosis that "as the twenty-first century approaches, no labour movement, no anti-imperialist movement, no surviving socialist regime, is offering a convincing vision of a socialist future" (1992: 21). Since the need for political change was more important than ever, intellectuals should keep up their nerves – as many contributors urged though most of them not as elegantly as Jacques Derrida:

For it must be cried out, at a time when some have the audacity to neo-evangelize in the name of the ideal of a liberal democracy that has finally realized itself as the ideal of human history: never have violence, inequality, exclusion, famine, and thus economic oppression affected as many human beings in the history of the Earth and of humanity. (1994: 53)

According to Immanuel Wallerstein, future developments could be hardly anticipated at the moment. He expected the horizon to stay open for a long time of up to fifty years – this amounted to a "bleak period" during which a new world system would emerge in a slow and complicated process, a system either more or less democratic and egalitarian than the previous one (1994: 4). From left intellectuals, this prospect required open-mindedness but also a certain sense of programmatic direction and, above all, stamina:

You may think that the programme I have outlined for judicious social and political action over the next twenty-five to fifty years is far too vague. But it is as concrete as one can be in the midst of a whirlpool. First, make sure to which shore you wish to swim. And second, make sure that your immediate efforts seem to be moving in that direction. If you want greater precision than that, you will not find it, and you will drown while you are looking for it. (ibid: 17)

Socialist Register

The reactions in *Socialist Register* in many respects resembled those in *New Left Review*. With the collapse of the Eastern Bloc, contributors believed, the chances for the realisation of a socialist society had declined everywhere. Joel Kovel, still shocked by witnessing what for most of his life he had considered as hardly thinkable – the victory of anti-Communism – was convinced that the demise of the state-socialist regimes reinforced a neo-liberal onslaught on Western labour movements and would make the life of what was left of the latter extremely difficult – particularly in the Unitred States (cf. 1992: 254):

The dream of the [U.S.; SB] bourgeoisie had come true: the proletariat had withered away; anti-communism had helped secure class struggle on the most favourable possible terms to business, leaving in its wake a largely oppositionless society characterised by the accommodation of labour to capital, the functional identity of the Democratic and Republican Parties, and the most threadbare left-wing politics of any nation in modern history. (ibid: 263)

The problem remained that however one judged the states of the Eastern Bloc, they had been the only alternative to capitalism ever realised, as the editors Leo Panitch and Ralph Miliband stressed in their editorial to the 1992 *Register*, which focused on the question of a new 'world order' (cf. 1992: 1). Both of them had expressed severe criticisms of the Eastern Bloc's lack of democracy. The disappearance of these negative characteristics was still to be saluted. Nevertheless Panitch and Miliband emphasised:

What is a matter for bitter regret, on the other hand, is something else altogether: the disappearance of the hope that existed at the beginning of *perestroika* in the Soviet Union that this might in due course produce something that would begin to resemble socialist democracy, on the basis of a loosened but predominant public sector. This hope turned out to be an illusion. (ibid: 4)

Richard Levins was convinced that socialists everywhere had to acknowledge a defeat of immense proportions and that this defeat was only the final result of a process of several decades of decline in Eastern Europe and of defeats in the capitalist parts of the world (cf. 1990: 328). Like Cohen in *New Left Review*, he commented on the personal dimension this had: "Half a century ago, my grandmother could assure me that my grandchildren would live in a socialist republic. It now seems unlikely" (ibid). Once more, it is obvious that although contributors held deep reservations about the political realities in the Eastern Bloc, they had regarded it as indispensable for, and as the most likely area of, moves towards socialism. For Levins, the present situation constituted a nadir, but he seemed to remain convinced of a dialectical movement of history: "We are living in a difficult time, a low point between periods of upsurge, when revolutionary optimism looks like a cruel joke." (ibid: 345) Again, this constituted a call on intellectuals to stick to their convictions and not to give up on the principles they believed in. Joel Kovel however feared that this would become increasingly difficult because the commensurability of these principles, of understanding history through the category of class struggle, might be lost. He seemed to be less certain about the reliability of reassuring dialectical moments in the future, or he seemed to suspect that they would be misread. If transformative criticism was regarded as quixotic in the future, any attempts at political change worth its name could be easily suppressed (cf. 1992: 264). These proposed developments were to have most dramatic consequences:

A profound weariness and cynicism occupies the place where critical/dialectical thinking used to occur. Since the underlying structure which makes society intelligible is erased, society becomes a mystery, its various phenomena merely strung together like the words of a game of Scrabble, and as easily forgotten. Thus even factual understanding of the world is lost. (ibid)

Arthur MacEwan expressed a feeling of insecurity – perhaps socialist intellectuals had themselves lost understanding of the world? More wholeheartedly than others he conceded that the collapse of the Eastern Bloc posed serious questions concerning the feasibility of socialism. Even if, as he agreed, a socialist society had never been constructed in the U.S.S.R., at least one difficult question remained: "[W]hy is it that our efforts will lead to something better?" (1990: 312).

Socialists, and the intellectuals among them, were in the defensive. Still, they remained important. For instance, they should support attempts to prevent further damage and protect the bad against the worse – a domesticated capitalism against a liberated one. To this purpose, they should act not as a vanguard anymore but as a rearguard, "defending the gains of 150 years of struggle, acknowledging the reality of the defeat and evaluating the reasons for it, regrouping and preparing for the second wave of revolutionary upsurge. It is an agenda of years and decades" (Levins 1990: 329).

Dissent

Dissent's reaction to the events of autumn 1989 was more positive. Initially, at least, the main thrust of comments emphasized the positive effects, not just for the people in Eastern Europe but also for the Western left – they had been freed of the burden to continuously explain that they did not sympathise with what the Eastern Bloc declared to be socialism: "Intellectually, Stalinism evoked keener discomforts than did Nazism, since here the enemy seemed to have come out of 'our own' milieu, that of the left. Stalinism used words and symbols representing our hopes" (Howe 1991: 63). Given the journal's Trotskyist roots and anti-Soviet perspective, these reactions did not come as a surprise. More amazing, perhaps was how soon the euphoria of 1989 was left behind. Irving Howe stated already in the summer of 1990 that his main feelings were scepticism and uneasiness by now (cf. 1990: 301). The roots of this change of mood lay in the directions developments in Eastern Europe took and perhaps also in Howe's later realisation that the era of revolutions had come to an end (cf. 1992: 144).

Still, also for *Dissenters*, the collapse of the Eastern Bloc and the subsequent rapid introduction of capitalism came as a surprise, even if they had close contacts with opposition circles in Eastern Europe. Norberto Bobbio, for example, the Italian liberal socialist who repeatedly wrote for *Dissent*, described the events breathlessly as "total overturn of a utopia, of the greatest political utopia in history [...], an overturn into its exact opposite" (1990: 340). This seemed to imply an interpretation similar to Habermas's in *New Left Review* – the revolutions of 1989 were characterised predominantly by negative motivations. They had to be understood as protests against the state-socialist regimes rather than as the attempts at creating something new. The revolutions initiated the introduction or restoration not just of capitalism but of a variety which, for *Dissenters*, was the worst option: Anglo-American, neo-liberal capitalism. While already Stalin had turned socialist utopia into dystopia, the abandoning of any idea of socialism could now introduce a free-capitalist dystopia.

For the intellectual left in the United States, the conjuncture of 1989/91 could cause serious biographical problems. Ann Snitow, for example, expected difficulty for the two generations of *Dissenters* to come to terms with the altered global context: "As a cultural group, we U.S. leftists (Old and New now shovelled together by recent events) may not recover spiritually from 1989. Our utopianism took root in other soil. Children of the cold war, we are not likely to be elected to the future." (1994: 14). Dennis Wong agreed and argued that the events of 1989 had to be interpreted as the "death knell of socialism as a credible and attractive political goal" (Rule & Wong 1990: 481) and that, among left traditions, only reformist social democracy could profit from its demise (ibid.). Whether this would allow *socialist* intellectuals to adopt new functions seemed to be not entirely clear. Two Hungarian dissident leftists resident in the United States argued that, if they intended to play a role in the future, democratic socialists had to accept new tasks which they had for a long time avoided:

This perplexity of (noncommunist) socialism is a highly revealing feeling, conveying the message that noncommunist socialism has not faced seriously the complex issue of the historic achievements and internal limitations of its own theory and politics. The critique of communism seemed to have spared socialism this unpleasant task, which can no longer be postponed. (Fehèr & Heller 1991: 105)

As a consequence, writers expressed deep insecurity about how to proceed in this "moment of political and intellectual confusion" (Howe 1992: 143). Obviously, most of them retained a feeling that there still was a difference between 'radicalism' (or democratic socialism) and liberalism (or social democracy), but found it difficult to exactly define distinctive features. The following words stem from the opening paragraph of a *Dissent* symposium in 1994: "Are we now advocates only of an American version of social democratic reformism, reduced to piecemeal opponents of the liberal status quo, urging only that things be made a little more democratic? Can we still project some radical hope?" (Editors of *Dissent* 1994: 7). In their responses, many tried. Yet in this symposium other voices proved more afraid of failing to make a radical break with the past than of giving up on radical change: "[I]f we keep trying to project radical hope by sticking more or less to our main arguments from the past, will our efforts be credible?" (Berman 1994: 9).

In principle, radical intellectuals were still needed: the collapse of Communism had not put an end to the 'social question' within capitalism. In no way had capitalist democracies solved all the problems, which were linked to social inequalities, exploitation and oppression – characteristic features of capitalism. Socialism had tried to address these issues and had not found adequate solutions. However, the need to find solutions remained and intellectuals could play a role in finding them – ideally before a new period of political unrest began. Bobbio, at least, did not doubt that future social struggles lay ahead and, differing from Howe in this respect, he did not even preclude the possibility of revolutionary change:

In a world of frightful injustices to which the poor are condemned, crushed by unreachable and apparently unchangeable great economic powers, including those that are formally democratic – to think at this juncture that the hope for revolution has been extinguished only because the communist utopia has failed is tantamount to closing one's eyes in order not to see. (1990: 341)

Monthly Review

In the pages of *Monthly Review*, writers expressed a feeling absent in the other journals: anger. It was a reaction to, for example, self-congratulatory statements by conservatives, but also by liberals like Robert Heilbroner (who occasionally wrote for *Dissent*), claiming that capitalism had won the contest with socialism. These statements were viewed as pure propaganda. Carl Marzani, who wrote an extended article "On Interring Communism and Exalting Capitalism" which appeared as *Monthly Review*'s first piece in January 1990, asked: "Which contest? If the 70-year-old contest was military, then neither side had won; if it was economic, the conclusion was premature; if cultural, it was debatable" (1990: 2). The author went on to explain that the United States and other Western states had proven impotent in terms of preventing moves towards socialism in many places: "What we are witnessing in our day is the grand failure, not of communism, but of the capitalist attempt to prevent or destroy any socialist state, whether the Soviet Union, Cuba or Nicaragua" (ibid: 3). Nevertheless, for leftists associated with *Monthly Review*, the future of socialism was insecure after 1989 and it depended to a great extent on what would happen to the Soviet Union, a point that the editors emphasised in spring 1990:

> Socialists all over the world have not only an interest but a personal and political stake in what happens in the Soviet Union in this coming and decisive phase of the process that began with Gorbachev's accession to office in 1985. We can only hope that the outcome will be positive and that it will set the stage for a following phase of economic recovery. (*Monthly Review* 1990: 17)

As soon as this hope had to be abandoned, the mood changed: Miliband, who had close ties with the editors of *Monthly Review* made the claim that "[n]o socialist could mourn the passing of oppressive regimes; but the sequel to that passing has, from a socialist perspective, been profoundly disheartening" (1991: 18).

Some authors, however, tried to reassure each other that even if the Soviet Union followed the rest of the Eastern Bloc and disintegrated, this would not disqualify socialism as a political goal. Paul Sweezy provided solace by analogy and with a certain trust in the *longue durée*, when explaining that in the late Middle Ages the first attempts at installing capitalism had also failed but developments had soon made its rise inevitable (cf. 1993: 6). A restoration of capitalism in the Eastern Bloc would also be just a temporary phenomenon. Like Marzani, Michel Löwy argued that the West had not defeated and killed socialism – but he argued his case rather differently: "One cannot die before being born. Communism is not dead, it is not yet born. The same applies to socialism." (1991: 33) Following this line of argument, the journal published optimistic statements from authors such as Howard J. Sherman. He advocated grassroots models of socialism and expressed his hope that the Eastern European revolutions would provide a "wonderful opportunity to begin the construction of a democratic socialist society" (1990: 22). He enthused that "[w]e are thus witnessing an end to statism and the possible – still fragile – beginnings of the worldwide triumph of socialism" (ibid). Again, this symbolised the hope that the disappearance of the state-socialist regimes would free socialists from elaborations that they intended to build socialist societies radically different from those that 'really existed' and that democratic experiments would be granted space and time in Eastern Europe.

Generally, contributors to *Monthly Review* claimed that there was no reason to be perplexed by the events of 1989/91 because they had been predictable – and Samir Amin claimed that in fact he had predicted them for thirty years (cf. 1992: 43). Like the other journals, if writers in *Monthly Review* expected tremendous problems for the Western left and their intellectuals after 1989, they explained these problems as the results not just of the "collapse of neo-Stalinism" but also of the political "bankruptcy" of social democracy and of left defeats in the Western world over the preceding years (Singer 1994: 87). The problem for *Monthly Review* was that developments elsewhere were not encouraging either: in 1993, the left was forced to digest not only the recent end of the Soviet Union but also the defeat of the Nicaraguan Sandinistas, new problems for an isolated Cuba, and the demise of Marxism-Leninism in Africa (cf. Meisenhelder 1993: 40).

Also in *Monthly Review* writers saw important tasks for intellectuals and repeated that they should not submit themselves to the dismal situation at hand because otherwise they would become part of an "unholy alliance, between capitalist triumphalism and socialist pessimism" (Wood 1994: 9). Contributors agreed that a portion of socialist optimism, based on sober and critical analysis continued to be of utmost importance. John Bellamy Foster quoted Cornel West who had emphasised precisely this point. West related his admonition not only to the end of the Eastern Bloc but also to the intellectual and political *zeitgeist* in the West and demanded that "social theory wedded in a nuanced manner to concrete historical analysis must be defended in our present moment of epistemic scepticism, explanatory agnosticism, political impotence (among progressives), and historical cynicism" (1993: 14).

Coming to Terms with the Crash
Between the journals but also between British and American intellectuals the similarities in spontaneous, emotional reactions to the events of 1989/91 outnumbered the differences. All agreed (though *Monthly Review* took longer than the other three journals to come to this conclusion) on the definite demise of the Eastern European variant of state socialism. Common to them also was the emphasis that the regimes they witnessed crumbling did

not represent their models and visions of socialism. Nevertheless, they expected the collapse would have consequences for their reflections in the future. They expressed doubts that the world was on the route to socialism (as Richard Levins's grandmother had been convinced) and some were even unsure that socialism could still serve as a guideline for an emancipatory politics. They were convinced that the Eastern and the Western bloc would be affected by the changes in Eastern Europe, either positively, as a minority of optimists believed (through freeing socialism from the association with the state-socialist regimes), or negatively, as a growing majority of pessimists was convinced (with the freeing of capitalism from the necessity to make concessions to its critics). This 'liberation' of capitalism was the consequence not only of the collapse of its systemic alternative, but also of the weakness of Western labour movements, and the fossilisation of Third World left nationalism.

Interestingly, emotional feelings were more strongly expressed in the pages of *Dissent* and *New Left Review* than in the other two journals. This is surprising, given *Dissent*'s post-Trotskyist origin and *New Left Review*'s broad-church approach. However, the generational difference between the writers in the journals is important here: *Monthly Review* and *Socialist Register* were still more dominated by an older generation of leftists who had had to survive similar ruptures before, for example, in 1956. They seemed to have more trust in the emergence of new movements and struggles. In the other two magazines the '1968' generation had a stronger presence, a generation that had always distanced itself from the Eastern European states and originally shared very optimistic and voluntarist perceptions of social change. This optimism became increasingly qualified by the experiences of the economic and political crises of the 1970s and the beginning of the dismantling of welfare capitalism in the 1980s. Paradoxically, 1989 came as a further blow in a long series of defeats. The pieces by Cohen, Segal, and Snitow – all born in the 1940s – can serve as examples.

The two British journals seemed more inclined to feelings of mourning and regret over the collapse of the Soviet Union or the failure of its attempts at reform than the American ones. In the case of *Dissent*, the early reaction consisted of relief and elation, later more and more replaced by unease. In *Monthly Review*, a mixture of anger and unease seemed to dominate. Most likely, this can be explained geographically – for the British and the West European intellectual left, Europe, including Eastern Europe, served as a frame of reference in a way it did not for American intellectuals who were at the same time more inward looking – focusing on the United States – and more internationalist through taking into account parts of the world beyond Europe. When *Monthly Review* expressed pessimism, it reflected developments in Latin America as much as in Eastern Europe.

Dissenters were the only group of writers who demanded a radical re-direction of intellectual work. The task amounted to defining new versions of democratic socialism which should not shy away from borrowing from and communicating with social democratic varieties. Contributors to the other journals were more concerned with continuity. They should not abandon their former positions and follow their colleagues on the roads to political reformism and – to use Cornel West's formulation – epistemological relativism even if it would take a long time to gain clarity about the exact shape of future struggles for socialism.

2. Assessments of State Socialism

Finding the adequate words for, and the right relationship to, developments, deformations and debates in the Soviet Union and the Eastern Bloc had always been complicated issues for the Western radical left. Evidence in the journals suggests that matters did not become any easier after the end of the Cold War. Even though most socialists and Neo-Marxists had seen the Eastern European countries as spent forces by the 1960s and 1970s and had subsequently turned to seemingly more promising developments elsewhere (for example, to China), interest in the Soviet Union again intensified with the Gorbachev reforms of the 1980s. Unfortunately, hopes were disappointed soon, as these experiments began to crumble. This chapter looks into the analytical attempts at summarising the achievements and failures of the Eastern Bloc in the four journals. Intellectuals wanted to know what went wrong, why it went wrong and what lessons could be learned from the large-scale but eventually failed attempts at implementing socialism in a considerable part of the world. The overall explanations and interpretations that were formulated would influence the directions in which theorists looked in order to design the details of a new socialist project. Contributors generally commented on four different issues: (1) the economic development of the Soviet Union and the Eastern Bloc, (2) their power structures and apparatuses of government and governance, and (3) the consequences of the Cold War for their economic and political realities. From these three dimensions, reasons for the collapse (4) could be deduced. The journals' common aim was to find adequate, differentiated judgments on the achievements and failures of the state socialist experiment that differed from the Western triumphalism that was perceived to be dominant at the time.

New Left Review

On the topics listed above, most serious disagreement existed and controversial debate took place in the journal's pages. The deliberations over the Cold War proved especially heated; though the long-term debate on 'exterminism' still continued, it became marked by an even more fundamental struggle. Positions were divided, ranging between those (the minority) who saw the Soviet experiment as an unmitigated disaster and as those (the majority) who were convinced that this judgement needed qualification. Such differences resulted in normative evaluations not only of the Soviet Union, but also of the United States and its allies and of their treatment of countries which questioned their hegemonic position in global politics – and thus also in different suggestions on future strategic imperatives for socialist politics.

Assessments
Several authors emphasised that economic development in the Eastern Bloc had been a success, if measured against pre-revolutionary levels of wealth. Fred Halliday and Göran Therborn remarked that its people lived relatively well when viewed from a global perspective and thus industrial modernisation could not be interpreted as unconditional failure (cf. Halliday 1990: 15; Therborn 1992: 28). Additionally, Therborn elsewhere hinted at statistical evidence that the Eastern Bloc's economic performance was not seen as an "unmitigated disaster" even by its own population (1993: 187-8). Moreover, contributors remarked that other parts of the world, which had remained under capitalist domination, did far worse:

Indeed there can be no doubt that the loss of human life, and the extent of physical suffering in the capitalist third world in the 1980s greatly exceeded that experienced in the countries ruled by Communist bureaucracies – a dismal comparison which does nothing to justify the stifling tyranny exercised by the latter but does put it in perspective. (Blackburn 1991: 174)

Through achieving industrialisation, whose immense human costs the authors did not ignore, the Eastern Bloc managed to narrow the gap to the advanced capitalist nations of the West. (cf. Therborn 1992: 26-7). Authors reiterated the well-known fact that, during the 1960s and still in the 1970s especially, there was widespread fear in Western countries that they might be overtaken in economic terms by the Eastern Bloc, especially as long as De-Stalinisation seemed to signal the parallel transition to a more humane and possibly also to a more productive social and economic order (cf. Blackburn 1991: 211-2). Though Halliday conceded that this had been an exaggeration of economic advance in the Eastern Bloc, he pointed out that it formed part of the rationale of the Cold War (cf. 1990: 15) and Therborn underlined that "impressive growth" had continued until recently (1992: 20).

These analyses of course generated the question of how economic shortcomings were to be explained. Here one could find statements by sceptical voices such as that of Nicos Mouzelis who criticised Therborn's "overly positive" account of the Soviet economy. He pointed out that industrialisation had already started in tsarist Russia and would have continued without revolution (1993: 182). Hence he contradicted the widespread Marxist narrative of the Herculean task of transforming pre-industrial Russia into the industrialised Soviet Union (cf. ibid). Hence, unlike Therborn, Mouzelis did not trace back the collapse of the Eastern Bloc to a conjunctural crisis of its economy, but to fundamental structural deficiencies (cf. ibid: 183). Other writers were less sure and described the undeniable failure that followed the transformation to an industrial economy, which they still considered as an economic success, as a relative one. In their view, the failure could be traced back to two causes: firstly, the Eastern Bloc never succeeded in delinking from the capitalist world economy but took a subaltern place in it (cf. Halliday 1990: 19). Delinking would have required the modelling and creation of a system alternative to capitalism. Instead, they remained in the state of a "socio-economic hybrid" (Blackburn 1991: 193). In recent times, they had become, partly against their will, increasingly integrated into the global economy, but, as hybrids, were in no way equipped to deal with its uncertainties and rapid changes (cf. Hobsbawm 1992: 60).

As the second mistake, writers diagnosed the particular mode of economic planning, which Blackburn described as the crudity of the link between micro-decisions and macro-decisions in the production process (cf. 1991: 213). This led not only to the dissuasion of innovation and creative development (which would also have needed some form of socialist democracy) but also to an extended system of fixing, the trading of favours and thus the persistence of a complex web of mutual obligations (ibid: 214). This had not only economic consequences, but ideological ones as well – a point Blackburn wanted Marxists to accept:

Socialists are, not without reason, suspicious of the ideological forces generated by the capitalist market […]. But it should also be acknowledged that the pattern of nationalized property in the Communist states also produces unlovely ideologies – notably an intolerant nationalism and an excessively tolerant attitude towards traditional patriarchy. (ibid: 235)

Others added that inhuman aspects were not restricted to the ideological level but manifested themselves in forced labour and super-exploitation – something which Karl Kautsky had already criticised when he observed the agrarian collectivisation process (cf. Wollen 1993: 87). These characteristics could not be explained without the Cold War, as Mary Kaldor pointed out. The Eastern Bloc's economy, especially under Stalin, remained a war economy, organised primarily for the purpose of countering Western threats – from Marshall aid to nuclear weapons. Later, some piecemeal corrections were implemented in order to move towards a more differentiated economic strategy, but these were overshadowed from the 1970s onward by the need for austerity policies, which arose from trade deficits with the West. Their consequences of social displacement, Kaldor argued, eventually destroyed the remaining legitimacy of the Eastern European governments (cf. 1990: 29-30). While Mike Rustin was convinced that the main reason for the collapse of the Eastern Bloc experiments was economic failure rather than a lack of democracy (cf. 1992: 100), there were also other voices: "The defeat of Communism has thus been the defeat of a type of social formation which gave too little scope for popular initiative and pluralism, or self-recognition and self-activity (whether collective or individual), either in economic life, politics, or culture" (Blackburn 1991: 236). It was this critique of over-regulation that led some contributors to agree with Fukuyama's thesis that Communism was not able to satisfy humans' longing for 'thymos', for the chance to develop as individuals and to receive appreciation for their activity, creativity, work, and achievement.[1] Joseph McCarney expressed this dissatisfaction as a trespass against "freedom":

It is surely not at all fanciful to see these people in a Hegelian perspective as having grasped the central truth of the modern world, that freedom belongs to their nature as human beings, and as having grasped also the contradiction between that nature and their actual conditions of life. (1991: 22)

Many contributors qualified their critical perspective by a belief in the Soviet Union's and later the Eastern Bloc's beneficial impact on parts of the world beyond their direct sphere of influence. The following considerations by Blackburn were echoed by several authors:

While the peoples of the Soviet Union have good cause to rue the horrendous cost of Stalinism, the survival of the Soviet Union has had huge, and often positive implications for those outside Soviet borders – most obviously the immense and irreplaceable Soviet contribution to the defeat of Nazism but also the real, though less quantifiable, Soviet contribution to persuading Western ruling classes to cede ground to anti-colonial liberation movements and to make concessions to their own domestic labour movements. [...] The Bolshevik victory of 1917-20 or the Soviet role in the victory of 1945 did not put socialism on the agenda, even in Russia, but, in conjunction with antagonisms internal to the leading capitalist nations and empires, they did

---

1 Francis Fukuyama's well-known book *The End of History and the last Man* (1992) claimed the triumph of 'liberal democracy' and denied the possibility of further systemic changes. Fukuyama based his thesis on the assumption that liberal democracy was best able to satisfy the universal konging for both economic efficiency and individual recognition by society. While writing his book, however, the author seems to have developed his own doubts whether liberal capitalism would really be the 'end of history'. In some passages, he obviously feared deterioration into an authoritarian capitalism.

help to bring about a new global order, both limiting and prevailing forms of capitalist and imperialist power. (1991: 192-193)

Along similar lines, Lucio Magri conceded that it had been fundamentally wrong for socialists not to criticise Stalinism, and the bureaucratic authoritarianism that followed it. Nevertheless, he suggested to not ignore their constructive role in international politics:

But for decades another side also continued to operate: the side of national independence; the spread of literacy, modernization and social protection across whole continents; the resistance to fascism and victory over it as a general tendency of capitalism; support for and actual involvement in the liberation of three-quarters of humanity from colonialism; containment of the power of the mightiest imperial state. (1991: 7)

This anti-imperialist dimension was celebrated as the most unambiguously positive one. Halliday, for example, declared that "[i]t is for Brezhnev, as much as anyone else outside South Africa itself, that credit for cracking the racist bloc should go" (1990: 15). Writers unanimously contended that despite internal political inadequacies, the Eastern Bloc was a force for good in the rest of the world – making not only the defeat of Nazism possible (the reluctance with which Stalin took up this task was not mentioned), but allowing for decolonisation and posing as enough of a threat for capital to make it concede to the institutional arrangements that became associated with the golden age of social democracy. Magri summed up the consequences of the Eastern Bloc's disappearance in the following way:

For the oppressed, it means the passing away not so much of a model [...] as of an ally and support. And with it is going a legacy of cultural autonomy which the common sense of Marxism, in its most diverse forms, deposited in the world much more widely and deeply than in the Communist parties alone. (1991: 7)

Concerning political achievements, not much in the pages of *New Left Review* could be read as a defence of the Eastern Bloc's record. Only Paul Auerbach pointed to the credit that should be given "for advancing broad-based literacy and culture, in spite of the debilitating effects of totalitarianism and isolation from the rest of the world" (1992: 23-24). These concessions, however, were undermined by the political system itself: "The inability to use this human potential in even a moderately effective way is a weighty indication of the failure of the command-administrative system of government" (ibid). Nevertheless, the systems were not totalitarian in the sense that there was no chance of reforming them. Therborn hinted at the examples of Hungary, Slovenia, and the Soviet Union itself to prove that 'change from above' was possible (cf. 1993: 187). And Halliday added bitterly: "The historical irony is that communism has lost its appeal just at the moment when it has demonstrated a new political potential, an ability to change that theorists of totalitarianism and many within the Soviet system had doubted" (1990: 14).[2]

The most problematic issue for socialists was certainly the lack of democracy in the Eastern Bloc. Comments were numerous and dealt with the problem of introducing socialism in one, or as had often been claimed, in a 'backward' country. Giovanni Arrighi explained ways in which Marxist principles were violated in this process. The revolutionaries developed interests different from those of the world proletariat and sought to catch and keep up with the wealth and power of leading capitalist states. According to Arrighi, realities in Russia required to take sides with that section of the proletariat suffering mass misery and thus to develop a coercive form of rule in which the party controlled the state which in turn controlled civil society. Arrighi defined this as a double substitution with the vanguard first standing in for a mass organisation (Leninism) and then also for the ruling functions of the bourgeois state (Stalinism). Since the Russian revolutionaries were successful in this effort, up to the surprising point where the Soviet Union gained super power status, they also successfully transformed Marxism into an ideology of coercion and industrialisation. At the same time, they still claimed to represent the interests of the world proletariat as a whole and accused those sections that formulated interests at variance with their own, especially the increasingly strong social democratic wing of the labour movement, as traitors. By splitting the world labour movement, they "provided the world bourgeoisie with a valuable ideological weapon in the

---

2 Halliday saw this potential however just as a hypothetical one. He argued that 'socialism with a human face', as, for example, behind the Prague spring risings, had never been possible under Cold War conditions because of the Western multi-party alternative (cf. 1990: 20).

struggle to reconstitute its tottering rule" (1990: 59). Arrighi nevertheless claimed that the strategies chosen by the Russian revolutionaries did not constitute a 'betrayal' of Marxism:

Rather, [...] it describes Marxism for what it is, a historical formation that conforms to the actual unfolding of the Marxian legacy under circumstances unforeseen by that legacy. Or to rephrase, Marxism was made by bona fide followers of Marx but under historical circumstances that were neither prefigured for them nor of their own making. (ibid: 57)

Blackburn drew a similar sketch of developments in the Soviet Union. However, he also contended that it was, at least from a traditional Marxist point of view, delusory to try building Marxism in one backward country (cf. 1991: 176). Revolutionaries could not help but fall prey to political voluntarism (ibid: 189). He described and gave reasons for the processes which guided the revolutions of the 20th century into increasingly authoritarian directions:

The would-be socialist revolutions of the twentieth century have all taken place against a background of war-devastation and capitalist failure and each has had to struggle with a heavy weight of economic backwardness as well as military encirclement. In each revolutionary process there have been primitive elements of democracy, as hitherto excluded and suppressed layers of the population asserted their elementary interests, but in each case a centralizing political and military apparatus, while giving stability and direction to the revolution, has also foreclosed democratic development. (ibid: 176-177)

Several other voices came forward with characterisations of state socialism's defects, such as the disastrous skipping of historical stages (cf. Mouzelis 1993: 185), attempts at accelerating history (cf. Wollen 1993: 93), economism, statism, Jacobinism (as another term for vanguardism), Eurocentrism (cf. Magri 1991: 12), or the attempt at achieving radical change through ruthless leadership (cf. Miliband 1994: 12).

These deficiencies resulted in an authoritarian top-down structure which made political democracy as impossible as economic democracy and popular planning. Hence the political and the economic problems were clearly linked. Eric Olin Wright claimed that this was precisely the critique Neo-

Marxists expressed with regard to the Eastern Bloc – without democracy, socialist institutions could not be sustained and would degenerate into intractable power centres and networks, serving their own interests (cf. 1993: 22). All this could be summarised, in Kautsky's words, as a "barbaric road to socialism" (quoted in Wollen 1993: 86). Or perhaps not to socialism but to something else – for example, to "authoritarian collectivism" which was the exact opposite of the "socialized individualism" that Miliband saw as the goal of socialism (cf. 1994: 4). Critique was meticulously historicized and carefully balanced and contributors maintained that the possibility of political change had existed in the Eastern Bloc for most of the time. To this end, Kaldor identified 1968 as the turning point which convinced the population of the futility of further strivings for socialism (cf. 1990: 30). Therborn disagreed and claimed that until 1980 all uprisings in the East had been socialist in character (cf. 1992: 20). Only Mouzelis condemned the entire time span and disagreed with the others, claiming that comments by contributors (in this case, Therborn's) were "based less on sober analysis than on a reluctance to accept that the Soviet experience was from beginning to end an unmitigated disaster" (1993: 182). He countered that once human costs were taken into account, the situation could not be taken as a success story in any way (cf. ibid). The issue, however, was not the degree of success of the endeavour, but rather the problem was whether it was legitimate to use categories of relative or absolute failure when describing the lack of fundamental democratic principles. Another question was whether explanations for the deficiencies were to be found in the Eastern Bloc's internal structures only. The evidence above has shown that for most authors such an explanation was too narrow. Rather, the historical framework of system competition and geo-politics also needed to be taken into account.

The Impact of the Cold War
The Cold War was central to these additional considerations. Debates over how to interpret the Cold War had reached a peak in the early 1980s when Edward P. Thompson popularised his notion of 'exterminism'.[3] This con-

---

3   Thompson interpreted the second Cold War – which had started in the late 1970s – not as an element of the 'competition' between a capitalist West with an expansionist tendency and the state socialist East reacting to this aggression (and

cept was criticised by many intellectuals associated with *New Left Review*. Unlike Thompson, they interpreted the Cold War as one between capitalism and state socialism – and as one in which capitalism acted as the main aggressor. Halliday reiterated this position after 1989. He maintained that the end of the Cold War signalled the end of an era in which the Western states had been predominantly concerned with containment of the Soviet Union – an era stretching back to the Versailles treaty (cf 1990: 10). The "global, ultimately irreconcilable, conflict between two different kinds of society and political system" had come to an end (Halliday 1990a: 149). It had done so not because the capitalist West had lost its opponent – as Thompson seemed to indicate – but because the Western countries had succeeded in subjugating it (cf. ibid: 148; Ahmad 1994: 96). Despite the general disagreement, the journal also provided a forum for dissenting voices which restated the 'exterminist' argument, as was done by Thompson and Mary Kaldor. Though both 'exterminists', their positions differed slightly from one another. For Kaldor, Atlanticism and Post-Stalinism were compatible, part of one system (cf. 1990: 33). It had been one of Western Marxists' major mistakes to ignore this:

Even though the Western Left was, for the most part, sharply critical of Stalinism, it still characterized the Cold War as a conflict between capitalism and socialism. It described the West as 'capitalist' and the East as 'socialist', and explained the conflict in terms of the expansionary nature of capital and the unwillingness of capitalism to tolerate any alternative. (ibid: 25)

Thompson in contrast underlined that he interpreted the Cold War as an inter-systemic conflict which had, however, developed a self-reproducing dynamic and a logic of its own (cf. Thompson 1990: 140). Immanuel Wallerstein argued along similar lines. He identified a Cold-War system that

---

neither the other way round). He regarded the Cold War as following the self-governing logic of 'exterminism' in which both sides amassed ever larger supplies of weapons and became dependent on economic and political agents interested in maintaining them. Both the 'West' and the Eastern Bloc had become tied as symmetrical components to this dynamics. Peace movements in East and West scandalised this situation and tried to make people aware of its immense dangers (cf. New Left Review 1982).

left a part of the world for the Soviet Union where anti-systemic forces that had come to power after 1945, were co-opted to the capitalist world economy, and created their own inequalities and power centres. The same Cold-War system created a hegemonic bloc from North America via Western Europe to Japan, backed 'moderate' decolonisation in the Third World and a certain degree of redistribution in the states of the capitalist core. But the regime contained repressive elements – from the gulags in the East via one-party states in the Third World to McCarthyism and anti-Communism in the West. This system, for Wallerstein, constituted the logic of the Cold War – and the risings of 1968 were directed against the many faces of this system in East and West (cf. 1994: 9-11).

Why was this debate still important after the Cold War had ended? Kaldor was convinced that the Western left had been seriously weakened by lending critical support to the Eastern Bloc or by its anti-anti-Communism – but still, some chances remained for a renewed socialism (cf. 1990: 36). Thompson shared this view, especially since he did not interpret the end of the Cold War as an unconditional victory for the West:

In a logic of reciprocal interaction, if one side withdraws it may have profound effects upon the other, just as the wrestler who suddenly loses an antagonist may fall to the ground. [...] If the Cold War is no longer 'self-reproducing' we can expect other (more traditional, less mystifying and less ideological) pressures to reassert themselves. But let us wait a few months before we can decide that it is 'capitalism' which has triumphed *tout court*. (1990: 141)

In other words, for Kaldor and Thompson, new possibilities emerged with the end of the confrontation between East and West which, to a certain degree, had been achieved by progressive forces on both sides.[4] Most contributors to *New Left Review* seemed less optimistic. If the West had won the Cold War, popular movements had nothing to do with its end and, even

---

4   Jürgen Habermas was more cautious in his judgment. Although he agreed that changes in people's political opinion obviously had consequences, it was hard to determine how important the peace movements had been for the end of the Cold War (cf. 1990: 21). He was also convinced that developments had moved beyond Jürgen Kuczynski's idea of a self-purifying reform process on the road to socialism (ibid: 6).

worse, the victory signalled the disappearance of the only systemic alternative that had existed to capitalism. While for Thompson this view amounted to a perverted version of Western triumphalism, Halliday insisted that the process of disarmament from 1987 onwards was already a sign of the Eastern Bloc's defeat and any attempts of the former state socialist countries to develop a third way were "swept aside by the combined pressures of their own populations and Western state and financial interventions" (1990a: 149-150).[5] Therborn supported this position, linked socialism to the epoch of modernity and questioned whether it still represented a realistic alternative (cf. 1992: 21). At least for the moment, the end of state socialism seemed to suggest the end of the socialist project as a whole.

Reasons for the Collapse

The question remained as to what exactly had caused the collapse. Contributors suggested two reasons: Halliday described the first one as the Eastern Bloc's internal entropy. Even if economic failure was only a relative one, it was decisive. It was the West, the core of the capitalist world, against which the economic performance of the Eastern Bloc was measured (cf. 1990: 17-19). The catching-up or overtaking of the Eastern Bloc, feared by many Western politicians, did not happen. Instead, increasing economic problems, ecological devastation, falling birth rates, declining life expectancy and growing crime caused a diminishing legitimacy of the ruling elites in the eyes of the public of the Eastern Bloc. The governments were neither able to develop a post-industrial strategy (that was needed from the 1970s onwards) nor to muster new sources of political legitimacy:

By the 1980s the industrial and military capacities of Communism were waning assets. The previous achievements of industrialism bequeathed new tasks, beyond the scope of industrial modernity. The Second World War generation was ageing and thinning out biographically, and their expertise of little value to a Cold War stabilisation of the continent, symbolised by the Helsinki agreement. Radical structural changes were needed. We know now that this led to the end of Communist

---

5   Halliday also agreed that the collapse of the Eastern Bloc was the result of public mass action. But he disentangled the events of autumn 1989 from the end of the Cold War (cf. 1990: 5).

socialism, or socialist claims, and to an attempted restoration of capitalism. (Therborn 1993: 186)

However, Therborn again maintained that there were some successful moves towards modernisation, led by Communist leaderships, for example, in Gorbachev's Soviet Union, in Hungary and Slovenia in the 1980s. However, they obviously came too late. In general, the public upheaval seemed to be as much a consequence of entropy as an activity that caused the collapse. Yet it also contributed to it – the state socialist apparatuses became ground between internal forces such as Charter 77 and Solidarnosc and the pressures of capitalism (cf. Blackburn 1991: 236). Secondly, the Eastern Bloc, not least due to economic weakness, lost the Cold War (cf. Ahmad 1994: 96). The confrontation not only prevented a healthier economic development in the Eastern countries, it also made the export of socialism to the West impossible. Hence, socialism as a political system had to be developed in a limited geographic area, in one country or in a small number of countries. Such constraints were likely to cause difficulties (and to vindicate Marx's thesis of the necessity of revolution on the *international* level).

For Therborn however, it was not all elements of socialism that had collapsed, rather, after a peak of socialist influence in about 1980, decline had set in. Nevertheless, socialist measures such as planning and redistribution were still widely used. Hence, "the current crisis of socialism in the west did not follow an accumulative series of failures but, rather, constitutes a changed perception of the prospects for socialism from that of a very recent historical peak of impact and influence" (1992: 26). Others, such as Eric Hobsbawm and Wallerstein, interpreted the collapse of the Eastern Bloc as just one expression of a more general crisis which was not restricted to one particular political, economic or ideological system: "For, at least in the zone of Western civilization and economic development, neither past experience nor the ideologies and theories inherited from the pre-industrial past or developed since the eighteenth century, seem to fit the situation of the last quarter of this century." (Hobsbawm 1992: 58) What the Eastern Bloc proved unable to cope with was not a 'healthy' capitalism but capitalism in crisis. This crisis would continue (cf. ibid: 59). State socialism, however, had died due to its lack of democracy and its defeat in the Cold War.

Socialist Register

Although the issues discussed in *Socialist Register* were mostly the same as those in *New Left Review*, the emphasis was slightly different. Whereas, for example, the debate on the adequate conceptualisation of the Cold War played only a minor role in *Socialist Register*, the authors showed a stronger interest in comparing the failures of state socialism with the deficiencies of capitalism. Different opinions became clearly visible on a number of questions, for instance, on the quality of the Gorbachev reforms or on the degree to which the Eastern Bloc formed part of one world system.

Assessments
Like in *New Left Review*, a number of voices emphasised the economic and social achievements of the Eastern Bloc, also in comparison to the capitalist West. Some authors set out to question both the normative standards and the empirical bases of judgment prevalent in the West. One example was Ellen Meiksins Wood's article on "The Uses and Abuses of Civil Society" from 1990. She took issue with social conditions in the United States and hinted at horrendous infant mortality rates in Washington D.C., extreme discrepancies between wealth and poverty in New York City and Los Angeles as well as a deficient education system and widespread drug abuse throughout the United States (cf. 1990: 80-81). She listed similar problems in Britain and went on to ask:

If these are the successes of capitalism, what standards should we then use in comparing its failures to those of the communist world? Would it be an exaggeration to say that more people live in abject poverty and degradation within the ambit of capitalism than in the Soviet Union and Eastern Europe? (ibid: 81)

Similarly eager to diffuse capitalism's rosy image, Robert W. Cox echoed Therborn's defensive statements in *New Left Review* that socialism's economic planning was not without successes and had created an educated population, health provision, and an equitable distribution of life necessities (cf. 1991: 177). Although he admitted that this had been achieved at great cost such as police terror, war casualties and the victims of collectivisation, he – like Wood – posed the question: "But was the cost more terrible than the suffering caused by the impersonal market forces of capitalist industrialization? There is little basis to conclude that it was, though the socialist experience was compressed into a shorter space of time" (ibid). Miliband also pointed to the high levels of inequality in capitalist countries and criticised that decisions by large and transnational corporations had consequences for ordinary people who could not control these decisions. He concluded that the assumption on which a beneficial capitalism was built, the good invisible hand of the market, was "belied by the whole experience of capitalism" (1991: 379). And also Joel Kovel expressed the problem of how to measure the value of individual freedoms usually associated with capitalism against the safety of a social infrastructure that the state socialist countries had provided:

How to justify the fact that those released from the bondage of Communism would have to give up guaranteed rights to housing, employment and education, and their factories with recreation clubs and day care centres, for structural unemployment, inflation, gross differences in wealth and widespread banditry? (1992: 258)

In short, contributors agreed that the "first attempt to build socialism" (Richard Levins' term) had achieved a great deal in terms of social and cultural improvements (1990: 330) as well as unprecedented levels of equality and security. However, they also accepted that these – according to them impressive – stories of extensive development, based on rapid and reckless industrialisation, had to be qualified by taking note of the horrendous human costs. (cf. Miliband 1991: 377; Panitch & Miliband 1991: 3).

Furthermore, serious economic deficiencies made it difficult or impossible to maintain the flattering social achievements over time. The Eastern Bloc never succeeded in organising a highly centralised and sustainable economy that could do without markets as regulating mechanisms (cf. MacEwan 1990: 312). In the end, with *Perestroika*, they deliberately and officially re-introduced markets (Immanuel Wallerstein described the governing groups of the Eastern Bloc even as the last true believers in market liberalism [cf. 1992: 104]). The question remained as to why did economic and organisational difficulties turn out to be so insurmountable? Just like in *New Left Review*, it was argued that the Eastern Bloc failed to set up an alternative world system. Instead, the Soviet Union (and later the Eastern Bloc) tried to develop 'socialism in one country' and became, as such, integrated into the capitalist world economy (cf. ibid: 102). Under these circumstances, it was impossible to design an economy that was superior to, or at least qualitatively different from, the capitalist one (cf. Lebowitz 1991: 365). Even as early as the 1930s, the Bolsheviks organised production along the lines of capitalist management structures. This affected the re-emergence of quasi-class hierarchies in society with not only a managerial class but also a primary and a secondary labour force (cf. Cox 1991: 174, 180). Thus, planning could not be pursued on the base of economic or social rationality, rather it became a bargaining process between interest groups. This led to power struggles and alienation just like in capitalism (cf. ibid: 180-181).

Some writers listed a number of political achievements and expressed sympathy for, or solidarity with, the political leadership groups. Again, there was a tendency to compare the East and the West – for example, when Arthur MacEwan argued that the states of the former had been created by committed Marxists, whereas the Western leaders with their human rights rhetoric were simply cynics (cf. 1990: 312). Nor were the Eastern Bloc's governments staffed by "mere scoundrels and stooges", as Miliband assured the readers (1991: 377). Rather, they acted under immensely difficult circumstances (cf. Cox 1991: 170). Several contributors hence questioned which was the correct approach towards criticism. Cox, for example, explained that many assessments of the failure of 'real socialism' were inconsistent with a socialist theory of history – a perspective that considered real society to be the product of struggle rather than the ideal result of a project led by intellectuals on the basis of a Marxist blueprint (ibid: 169-170). He was convinced that certain developments towards a higher level of democracy could be detected in the Soviet Union's history. He observed, for instance, the emergence of a rudimentary civil society during the Brezhnev era and explained that the party acted as a link between it and the state institutions (cf. 1991: 178-179). Finally, like in *New Left Review*, contributors emphasised the positive effects the Eastern Bloc had caused beyond its own borders, notably in the Third World – less as a model than as a provider of material support:

This aid was hardly costless in terms of the political, ideological and economic courses into which such regimes and movements were often channelled, but at the same time it was often a critical lifeline. The prospect of not standing alone against the massive military, political, economic and ideological power of a hostile capitalist world was an important condition of struggle against oppressions and exploitation in the 'third world'. (Panitch & Miliband 1991: 5)

Despite all qualifications, writers published detailed criticisms of political failure. Above all, they hinted at the lack of democracy (stemming from either the beginning of the socialist experiment or else resulting from introducing democratic structures but then allowing them to swiftly lose all real content [cf. Levins 1990: 338]) and the inability to create a socialist consciousness among the populations. MacEwan's argument that meaningful and sensible planning was impossible without a democratic social and political environment pointed to the link between economic and political failures. He argued that the abolition of markets and market relations might have been a step towards the creation of democratic political structures, but alone it proved insufficient (cf. 1990: 312). For him one of the most serious weaknesses of Marxism was not having taken the problem of democracy, of establishing democratic structures, seriously enough (ibid: 314). Miliband described the consequences such failings had for revolutionary leaders and those coming after them:

Their tragedy and that of their successors was that the system they built or accepted was based on unchecked power, and demonstrated to perfection how deeply corrupting such power is, and how wasteful and ultimately inefficient is economic management under its auspices. (1991: 377)

This meant, as Panitch and Miliband explained, that centralist economic and political systems and the concept of the vanguard party were, in the end, ultimately discredited (cf. 1991: 18). Moreover, critics could no longer maintain the notion that a state under workers' control was in and of itself a progressive achievement (although there was difference of opinion whether workers control had ever existed in the Soviet Union [cf. MacEwan 1990: 315]). MacEwan raised the topic of pre-revolutionary Russian 'backwardness' and of the alleged imperialist threat – the classical argument for justifying the lack of democracy in the Soviet Union. He contested the argument's validity and, obviously not believing in the chance of world-scale revolution, explained that there would always be a threat of imperialism (ibid: 314-315). Socialism would have to learn to live with this threat or it would not live at all. The problem, furthermore, had not so much been backwardness but the belief in productionism – the plan of accumulating wealth in the present, in order to provide a suitable socio-economic environment for a more democratic socialism in the future (cf. ibid: 316): "Thus the valid idea that the full development of socialist democracy and 'socialist man' requires a material base became the justification for a single-minded pursuit of economic growth and callous disregard for the self-determination of the people in the present" (Levins 1990: 331). This productionism had not only been substituted for human emancipation (and on the way neglected issues such as equality, the liberation of women, humane working conditions), it also had reduced the socialist experiment to an economic competition with the capitalist West. Levins concluded that this meant that socialism had not moved far enough from capitalism (cf. ibid: 340). A similar idea was forwarded by Wallerstein: the one-country version of socialism meant that Leninism developed aspects of a 'liberal Socialism' which made it compatible with the liberal world order and its breakdown a symptom of the liberal order's demise (cf. 1992: 102-104). Authors were convinced that a more radical break would have been necessary to provide space where socialist ideas could develop and take shape. Ideally, economic change and political change should have occurred side by side. Only then would social consumption, the absence of unemployment and economic crises be valued sufficiently by the population (cf. Levins 1990: 330). Michael Lebowitz stated that the economic strategy failed to produce or to educate human beings for whom the requirements of socialist production were self-evident. Nowhere, he claimed, had a civil society with a socialist common sense emerged (cf. 1991: 365-367). Instead, as Panitch and Miliband noted, with their productionist success stories – impressive as long as one focused on economic development only – they had destroyed people's creativity (cf. 1991: 3). The most strongly worded political critique came from Daniel Singer; he accused Stalinism of being a curious mixture of oppression and an almost religious belief in a particular doctrine and, hence, quite the opposite of a self-organised, democratic system, able to energise and use the creativity of the people (cf. 1993: 251). All intellectuals seemed to agree that the Soviet Union's and the Eastern Bloc's reliance on state-centred, top-down mechanisms of decision making had eventually undermined their political and moral authority. Nevertheless, some theorists remained circumspect in their judgment and hinted at the problems always present in attempted reforms: "As Macchiavelli long ago warned, the necessity of reforms can never be acted upon without danger, the danger being that the state may be destroyed before having perfected its constitution." (Cox 1991: 171) This seemed to be even truer when this internal risk was accompanied by an external threat – such as the Cold War.

The Impact of the Cold War
Socialist Register's interpretation of the Cold War differed in some respect from the versions discussed in *New Left Review*. They were less interested in conflicting interpretations like exterminism versus capitalist aggression and socialist self-defence. Their obvious main point was that, during the Cold War, the capitalist threat was experienced as reality in the Eastern Bloc, whether this concern was justified or not:

External opposition to established socialist regimes, whether or not intended, whether or not justified, provoked responses from the socialist leaderships in the realms of foreign policy, production, and the form of state that have nothing intrinsically to do with the socialist idea *per se*. (ibid: 172)

This perception remained important even if revisionist historiography had challenged the view that the alleged threat was as real as the socialist countries' leaders claimed. From war communism and New Economic Policy onwards, it influenced the states' structures and activities (cf. ibid: 172-174). On the Western side, the Cold War had left its marks too – for example, with the central role for the arms industry which was a key element of capitalist growth and depended on the maintenance of arms production (cf. Singer 1993: 255). The discursive and ideological consequences were equally important. Kovel even suggested naming the Cold war the "Forty Years War" after the Thirty Years War – in order to highlight that also the former in his view had quasi-religious, ideological dimensions. In the end, the West had succeeded in tying up terms like 'democracy' and 'freedom' with their own political systems (1992: 254). Kovel additionally hinted at the scars the Cold War left in the West. Speaking in particular about the United States, and describing the reconstitution of the country as a "national security state" that managed its "empire" through terror and cooptation, he claimed that the U.S. population became anti-Communist (ibid). This construction made international solidarity among working-class people impossible, weakened the labour movement at home, and stabilised the political system of the United States: "[A] nation welded together against Communism sees itself as identical with its state and ruling class" (ibid: 256-7). Avishai Ehrlich further added that these ideological struggles had world-systemic effects. The most serious was a domestication or bringing-into-line of all states who tried to break free from the bipolar confrontation and to follow alternative political logics (cf. 1992: passim). The authors were unanimously convinced that the Western powers' goal of containment was reached in so far as the Cold War contributed to the marginalisation of socialist struggle in the West, further complicated democratic-socialist innovation in the East, and effectively blocked 'third ways' in other parts of the world.

Reasons for the Collapse
The overview of economic and political failures listed in the pages of *Socialist Register*, as well as the comments on the Cold War, suggest various reasons for the collapse of the Eastern Bloc. One of the major causes was Stalinism – "in either its bloody form or its more common authoritarian and bureaucratic form" – which was "not the necessary outcome of Marxism" but nonetheless tragic (MacEwan 1990: 317). Perhaps the failures of Stalinism could have been corrected if the socialist states had been granted more time to do so. The problem, at least according to Levins, was that capitalism was still the 'natural' system of the 20th century. He argued that really new societal norms and arrangements needed long periods of time in order to develop, and he compared the formation process of the Soviet Union to the slow rise of democracy in the United States:

Seventy years after the Bolshevik revolution, we see nationalist rioting in the Soviet Union; 70 years after the American Revolution the massacre of Native Americans was still in full swing and opposition to slavery was still a fringe movement. A hundred years after the revolution, Jim Crow laws were being imposed throughout the South. Seventy years after the Bolshevik Revolution, the formal but hollow structures of socialist democracy are just being revitalized; 70 years after the American Revolution we were still only halfway toward women's suffrage and more than a century from Black enfranchisement. 70 years after the Bolshevik Revolution, the labour movement struggles for more direct workers' control and strikes threaten to bring down Communist-led governments; 70 years after the American Revolution union organizing was still the criminal offence of 'conspiracy to increase wages'; and now, two centuries later, unions are in decline. (1990: 333)

Later in the same article, the author referred to an argument that was shared by Wallerstein and Hobsbawm in both *Socialist Register* and *New Left Review*: the terminal crisis of the Eastern Bloc could not – at least not for long – hide the structural problems that had taken hold of the liberal capitalist West (ibid: 345). The collapse was just one consequence of structural problems in the world system as a whole.

It has already been noted that several writers regarded reforms as dangerous as they destabilised the structural and institutional set-up of a society. The risk proved even greater if they came late and were introduced in an inconclusive way. Miliband emphasised the incoherence and inconsistency of Gorbachev's reforms and Levins pointed out that in the second half of the 1980s a rhetorical Marxism had been substituted by a naïve liberalism in the U.S.S.R. (ibid: 341). However, this only explained why the belated attempts at rescuing the state socialist systems did not succeed. More decisive had been the long-term inability to firmly anchor the socialist experiment in the hearts and minds of the population, the only agent who in the long run could defend and sustain it. Lebowitz referred to Brecht's tailor of Ulm (who wanted to fly without proper wings) and related his fate to that of societies supposed to become socialist while being insufficiently equipped with knowledge and experience of the value of the socialist experiment but instead attracted by promises to materially overtake people living under capitalism. Participants in the struggle for socialism thus had been poorly equipped and ill-prepared for their tasks. Lebowitz concluded that "[n]o one should ever try again to fly with those things that only look like wings" (1991: 369).

Dissent

Unsurprisingly, *Dissent* evaluated state socialism more negatively on the whole. This clear position resulted in a briefer treatment of the issue. There were no direct attempts to balance the shortcomings of capitalism with those of state socialism. Furthermore, the journal expressed an alternative opinion on the Cold War, which identified the Soviet Union as the major aggressor, though this view was not shared by all contributors. However, like in the others, in this journal one could find traces of traditional Marxist arguments on the difficulties of developing socialism in a 'backward' country as well as indirect comparisons of state capitalism and socialism which warned against too complacent a view about the current historical situation.

Assessments

Exemplary evidence of the former type of argument could be found in editor Mitchell Cohen's article, "Theories of Stalinism. Revisiting a Historical Problem" (1992).[6] Here Cohen restated the original economic success of the Stalin era's modernisation programme, but contrasted it with a later stage in which economic organisation and state bureaucracy became increasingly anachronistic, a situation that was alleviated for some time through the emergence of a civil society from the ranks of the techno-scientific and intellectual strata of the population (ibid: 189). More importantly, the journal worked to counter the exaggeration of capitalism's successes. Unlike the qualifying remarks found in *Socialist Register*, no one attempted to question the ethical scales of failures (for example, by comparing, state socialism's beneficial impact on Third World countries with capitalism's exploitation of the peripheries). However, *Dissent* did feature warnings against triumphalism that echoed those in the other journals. The Canadian Bob Rae described capitalism as a remarkably tenacious system of power and values, but hinted at its serious limitations and contradictions – to produce opulence and squalor simultaneously; to make technological achievements possible, but at the price of ecological disasters; to allow for individual triumphs for a few and hardship for many (cf. 1991: 42). Further, he explained:

Capitalism's ability to 'deliver the goods' economically has been much exaggerated. As a political system, it fails miserably to address the ordinary needs and demands of its citizens. As a moral system, it utterly fails to enlist people's will to a shared freedom, to justice, to equality, to community, or to love. (ibid: 45)

---

6 Mitchell Cohen, born 1952, served as co-editor of *Dissent* from 1991 to 2008, works as political theorist at Baruch College and City University of New York Graduate Center. His work focuses on social democratic theory, political culture and cosmopolitanism.

Though *Dissenters* saw no need to regret the end of state socialism and did not have much to say about its economic achievements, they nevertheless feared that the domesticating effect it had had on the Western bloc would disappear and make capitalism even less considerate.

That the Soviet Union's and the Eastern Bloc's economic performance constituted a disaster (initial modernisation notwithstanding) – this view was almost universally shared in contributions to *Dissent*. For its explanation, many authors referred to Marxist arguments. Shlomo Avineri, for example, repeated the issue of the problematic skipping of historical stages and hinted at Lenin's *New Economic Policy* as an attempt to bridge the gap from pre-capitalism to socialism that ended in failure and produced an economic system that could by no means be called socialism (cf. 1992: 8). *Dissenters* were not overly concerned with the question of what label the economy deserved instead, though Howe referred to the observations of his once-ally Max Shachtman, who subscribed to the characterisation of the system as one of 'bureaucratic collectivism'.[7] For Howe, this was a label more negative than those of 'state capitalism' or 'degenerated workers states' because it implied the development of a new exploitative social structure where the bureaucracy had become almost a fully-fledged ruling class. Yet this was an isolated statement; instead an altogether telling silence testified to the view that the collapse of the Eastern Bloc did not deserve much attention, except for the question in what directions its countries would move now (cf. 1991: 69).[8]

The journal's initial optimism about the direction which changes could take in Eastern Europe was dependent on the notion that certain social achievements of its former systems could not be abandoned without causing collective outrage. They had provided levels of social security and social consumption that had become important for their populations. For this reason, Dennis Wong argued that people in Eastern Europe did not

---

7 Max Shachtman, 1904-72, was expelled from the CPUSA in 1927 and moved via Trotskyism to social democracy. He became a source of inspiration for U.S. neo-Conservatives

8 The developments in Eastern Europe were observed with an increasing pessimism by *Dissenters* who initially had believed in a spread of European-style social democracy but then had to observe that, to the contrary, a liberated capitalism was gaining strength (see Chapter III 1.3.).

want capitalism *per se,* but the fruits of capitalism (cf. Rule & Wong 1990: 482). It remained to be seen what they would turn to once they realised that the latter depended on the former. In addition, like in the other journals, authors argued that the Eastern Bloc had achieved its most substantial effects elsewhere; as without its domesticating effects, capitalism would have collapsed. Only one author, who did not belong to the inner circle of the journal, Eric Foner, pointed in an exchange with Eugene Genovese (who surprisingly un-self-critical criticised the left's lack of self-criticism) to the 'great achievements' of the Soviet Union as they were mentioned in *Socialist Register* and *New Left Review*:

Genovese generates a great deal of passion, but never gets around to explaining precisely why anyone on the left who supported even part of the USSR's 'political line' (which at various times included anti-Fascism, promotion of colonial independence, and opposition to the war in Vietnam) bears moral responsibility for the crimes of Stalinism. (1994: 379)

Yet on the whole, *Dissent* defended fewer aspects of the Eastern Bloc's political, social and economic realities than the other journals, though this did not signal a wholehearted embracing of capitalism on the part of its writers. As Genovese stressed, "I do believe that socialism is finished but am no more enamored of capitalism than I ever was." (1994: 388)

While the list of achievements was short, that of political failures was long. The most fundamental disappointment was that the overthrow of capitalism did not translate itself into a reign of freedom, a movement which was instead suppressed or postponed after the revolution:

Indisputable, however, even more than the failure of the communist regimes is the failure of the revolution inspired by communist ideology – that is, the ideology of the radical transformation of a society considered oppressive and unjust into a completely different, free, and just society. (Bobbio 1990: 339)

Wong argued that the whole concept of a sudden and comprehensive shift from one stage to another was a mistake, as it was based on a simplistic understanding of political change: "Today the very concept of socialism seems to me too evocative of totalistic solutions, as in the phrase, still widely used by thoroughly principled democrats, 'the transition to socialism', which implies a once-and-for-all passage across a demarcated dividing line" (Rule & Wong 1990: 483). Once this premise was given up, it became indefensible to monopolise power through measures such as the disbanding of the constituent assembly, as in revolutionary Russia, and replace it with centralised planning of all social and economic developments. Mitchell Cohen expressed a very negative view of what happened in the transitional process:

> In short, self-declared Marxists came to power in Russia lacking all preconditions for socialist goals, and had to accomplish what capitalism did in the West – thereby converting Marxism into a program for modernization and industrialization rather than emancipation – while eliminating those segments of the citizenry most 'advanced' in know-how and political culture. (1992: 188)

These shifts had serious repercussions for the post-revolutionary society that developed; the producers did not become the ruling class, but rather a proletariat dominated by strata of bureaucrats. Discussing the study *The Gorbachev Phenomenon* by Moshe Lewin, Cohen described what this meant for the character of the modernisation process the Soviet Union embarked on:

> The social bases for the Stalinist state were, therefore, badly collectivised peasants 'flanked by millions' of poorly urbanized peasants governed by ill-prepared bureaucratic strata of rural and semi-rural origin. In the meantime the party was transformed from supervisor of change into 'an adjunct of the economic bureaucracy'. The party became étatized, lost its political nature, and the Stalinist system became a party-state-economy 'bureaucratic matrix'. (ibid)

This configuration of political power had serious consequences for the social structure of the Soviet Union. Several contributors mentioned the persistence of class relations. In fact, the bureaucracy had become the new ruling class (though some questioned whether it really constituted a class) and ruled over an oppressed and alienated proletariat. Far from being a homogenous post-revolutionary subject, this proletariat was split along ethnic and community lines. Maintaining this hierarchical and conflictual order required authoritarian power. Some authors stressed that the Eastern

Bloc should be regarded as authoritarian rather than totalitarian, but nevertheless conceded that its ruling mechanisms contained a large amount of terror and violence. Cohen depicted the difference between the Leninist and the Stalinist phase of terror: while under Lenin the apparatus of violence was used against imagined or real enemies, under Stalin it was directed against the Communist Party itself – a move which killed what might have been left from a revolutionary socialist ethos. He continues, "[u]nder Lenin, the USSR was a one-party state; under Stalin it was an unparty state, with (surviving) card holders functioning less as members of a political party than as clergy under an infallible pope" (ibid: 184). Despite liberalisations after the Stalin era, the Soviet system was not able to integrate the creative potential that lay in the emergence of an intellectual class and elements of a civil society (ibid: 189). This view seemed consensual, but authors disagreed on the roots of these developments in the U.S.S.R.. Some, such as Howe, accused Soviet leaders of "violating Marxist prescriptions and expectations" (1991: 70). This perception was shared by many who, for example, blamed a blend of different elements of political culture – such as the application of Marxism in the form of a positivist Leninism which owed a lot to nineteenth-century scientific thought in general (more than to Marx's method of critique) and to a traditional Russian positivism (cf. Cohen 1992: 184-186).[9] Others contradicted and claimed violence to be not the consequence of the perversions of Marxist ideology, but instead of the ideology itself. Eugene Genovese even went a step further by not limiting this judgment to Marxism, but extending it to all radical egalitarian movements – whose victories were always followed by despotism and cruelty – though he was convinced that the Soviet Union broke all records for mass slaughter (cf. 1994: 375). Genovese's position, however, did not represent the majority opinion in *Dissent* and his intervention met with a great amount of criticism. In particular, Cohen blamed him for drawing the wrong conclusions from the disastrous Soviet experience:

---

9   Cohen explains that this positivist-scientific approach was widely shared, for example, by Mensheviks like Plekhanov who stated that Marxism should be understood as Darwinism applied to social science (cf. 1992: 186). Beyond Russia, schools of thought such as British Fabianism would qualify for a similar category. For a critical discussion of left perceptions of history, determinism, positivism and agency see Morgan 2003.

If there is something to learn from the willingness to see millions die in the short run for utopia in the long run it is that the form and content of politics shape one another. Many ex-communists – especially those who became neoconservatives – try to expunge the content without questioning the form. (1994: 378)

This idea of a procedural approach to socialism, one which would take the form of politics seriously enough, became the guiding principles of the journal's work in the next few years and explained its high interest in issues such a market socialism, associative democracy and communitarianism.

The Impact of the Cold War
Dissent's peculiar opinion on the Cold War, called the second-and-a-half-camp position by Isserman, has already been mentioned. Nevertheless, comments resembled those in the other periodicals. For Irving Howe, writing under the impression of recent events in 1990, the conflict ended with a "decisive victory for the West (in part for democratic capitalism, in part for social democratic welfare states, with the relative weight of these two still to be determined)" (1990a: 87). In another contribution, the end was interpreted as a compromise: the capitalist states had integrated so many socialist features that it was incorrect to claim that with the collapse of the Eastern Bloc all elements of socialism had been abandoned. Still, Howe repeated that fear of Communism in the 1950s had been justified and restated his conviction that the revisionist historians had been wrong (cf. Howe 1991: 64). Paul Berman supported this view with his argument that large sections of the American left had tainted the United States with many more crimes than the country had actually committed (cf. 1993: 100). This position (though not shared by everyone on the editorial committee) distinguished the journal from other left and post-left positions – from the 'hard left' to the neoconservatives – who were, however, not completely banned from its pages as Genovese's intervention as well as the responses by Eric Foner and others proved.

Reasons for the Collapse
The reasons for the collapse of the Eastern Bloc were seen as closely linked to its internal development. Even if the West won the Cold War, its ability to win had to do with its opponent's internal weakness. Daniel Bell listed three main reasons as the immediate causes of the implosion: the failure of the economic model, the failure of ideology and the crumbling of the 'empire' that the Eastern Bloc constituted (cf. 1990: 172). These were, of course, related to each other and to the authoritarian nature of the state socialist system (cf. Howe 1990: 87). Under particular historical conditions, authoritarianism became vulnerable because, as Howe explained, masses could act on their own, without leadership and without a vanguard (cf. ibid: 89). Elsewhere he sketched out the framework in which this was likely to occur: "The events in the Soviet Union show that, as in Germany and Italy a few decades ago, all the socio-political forces, good and bad, suppressed by the total state have a way of reappearing once a bit of freedom is allowed." (Howe 1991: 71) While authoritarianism led to insurrectionism, economic inefficiency led to the restoration of private property relations. However, if not socialism in all its aspects had been abandoned, and if not a pure capitalism had won, but one that had been forced to make numerous concession to the working classes, then an epoch of supposedly clear alternatives between two systems had come to an end for *all*, rather than only for those living in Eastern Europe.

Monthly Review

There are important differences between *Monthly Review* and the other publications with regard to the discussion of state socialism. On the one hand, in the early 1990s, contributors to *Monthly Review* still retained some hope that the eventual rescue of a renewed Soviet Union was possible. This perspective was shattered beyond repair with the unsuccessful attempt at ousting Gorbachev in the summer of 1991, which led to the final break-up of the U.S.S.R. On the other hand, several important journal contributors expressed their divergent views on the nature of the Soviet state. Despite differences, most seemed to agree that it had been neither socialist nor state-capitalist. Whereas before interest in power relations and mechanisms of decision-making in the Soviet Union had been only limited, this now changed[10]. Writers also discussed the values and weaknesses of the Gorbachev reform project in relation to these considerations. For obvious reasons, the Soviet case was treated as important for socialists all over the world. Its importance, once more, seemed to stem less from its internal political and economic contradictions, problems and weaknesses, than from its role in a global class struggle in which it was just one actor, although a major one, in the anti-capitalist camp. The Cold War, it seemed, had not yet ended – even if the collapse of the Eastern Bloc was an important victory for the forces of capitalism.

Assessments

Carl Marzani remained the only author who argued for labelling the Soviet Union as "socialist". On the surface, he disagreed for pragmatic reasons with those who insisted on finding other ascriptions – he saw no sense in ignoring a term that was so widely used. Yet at the same time he licensed a reading of the U.S.S.R. as, at least in some sense, socialist:

My chief objection [against calling the USSR 'post-revolutionary'; S.B.], however, is one of political tactics: the current appellation is so deeply ingrained that attempts to change it would be sterile. It is simpler and more effective to use Isaac Deutscher's epigram, 'Socialism in a backward country is backward socialism'. (1990: 24)

The other contributors backed Sweezy's interpretation of the Soviet Union as 'post-revolutionary'. Alberto Prago criticized Marzani heavily for paying insufficient attention to the U.S.S.R.'s violent and authoritarian aspects (1990). He suggested that critics speak of the "Soviet system" or follow Paul Sweezy's proposal because socialist or communist societies required political and economic democracy (ibid: 53-54). Sweezy himself explained that the lack of democracy resulted in an authoritarian class society with state ownership and central planning (cf. 1990a: 7). Elsewhere he formulated a similar diagnosis about Cuba, which he described as pursuing a partic-

---

10 Marcel van der Linden speaks of Paul Sweezy's "agnostic theory about classes" in the Soviet Union: Sweezy simply observed the existence of "a ruling class [...] of a new type" without further elaborating on the mechanisms and relations of domination (2007: 210).

ular form of "Caudillismo" – a term that stands for power concentrated in a 'chief' – characterised by a mixture of bureaucratic patronage systems and political repression (1990b: 19). Unsurprisingly, in *Monthly Review* Miliband also emphasised that the U.S.S.R., in general, and Stalinism, in particular, fundamentally contradicted central tenets of socialism (cf. 1991: 18). Perhaps more astonishingly, others questioned whether the Eastern Bloc could really be seen as non-capitalist or even post-capitalist. While Michel Löwy in his "Twelve Theses on 'Really Existing Socialism'" thought it could at best be described as non-capitalist (cf. 1991: 33), Istvan Mészáros was even more careful. He introduced a distinction between capitalist systems and those dominated by capital and categorised the Soviet Union as an example of the latter (cf. Monthly Review 1993: 13). It was easier to destroy capitalism than the power of capital which reproduced particular socio-economic relationships and priorities and thus inhibited the emergence of a radically different form of societal organisation. The Eastern Bloc had developed divisions of labour, a hierarchical structure of economic command and it retained the priority of capital accumulation in economic considerations (ibid).

Listings of the Soviet Union's economic achievements however were few in *Monthly Review* and they included a comparative dimension, contrasting its industrialisation process with that of the United States. Carl Marzani pointed out that the Soviet Union built its industries without using child labour whereas in the United States in the early twentieth century coal mines were still staffed with children not older than eleven years (cf. 1990: 25). Others added that, unlike the United States, it modernised without slavery. Several authors deplored the discrepancy between the system's considerable economic and social achievements and its lack of democracy (cf. Monthly Review 1991: 20). Generally, primitive accumulation worked well in the Soviet Union, economic problems began after this expansive phase (cf. Singer 1990: 76-77). However, even if this early stage was successful in economic terms, it should be considered as state-led growth rather than as a move towards socialism (cf. ibid: 77). Contributors stressed the similarities and the links between the post-revolutionary and the capitalist countries. Samir Amin suggested that common ground lay in the predominant role of economism: technological modernization and industrialisation as priorities and as precondition for social progress (cf. 1992: 46). Amin criticised that the collective identities and political solidarities that had existed had been sacrificed for such purposes – when, for example, collectivisations, carried out in the name of efficiency and technological progress, had destroyed the class alliance between peasants and workers. At the same time, this allowed for the development of a Soviet bourgeoisie (ibid). Because of their shared developmental priorities, the Western and the Eastern Bloc remained parts of the same economic system. Victor Wallis explained the ecological problems of the non-capitalist countries as consequence of the capitalist climate in which they had to survive. When the Soviet state took over and then continued with habits inherited from capitalism (such as the satisfaction of private ambition), the practice proved to have detrimental effects on the internal level and also externally, propagated by the fear of falling behind the West economically (cf. 1992: 2). Forced into competition with the capitalist West, the Eastern Bloc eventually lost.

Yet the Eastern Bloc did not lose without having its own successes, some of which were political. The fact that communism became a movement with considerable backing owed a great deal to the irrationalities of capitalism, under which many people suffered and from which it promised an escape route via rational planning. Like in the other journals, several writers suggested that among the Eastern Bloc's political accomplishments was the domestication of capitalism in many parts of the world. Demonstrating by their sheer existence that alternatives to Western-style capitalism were possible, they destabilised its reign. Tom Mayer, who reviewed the 1991 issue of *Socialist Register* (*Communist Regimes: the Aftermath*), was convinced that this threat would continue to function even if the regimes themselves had – with exceptions such as Cuba – disappeared (cf. 1992: 60). With this positive effect, it becomes understandable that the revolution of 1917, despite its substitutionism and all its problematic outcomes, was not judged as a mistake – even by severe critics of the U.S.S.R. like Amin (cf. 1992: 45). The same author observed occasional attempts at correcting the problems which had resulted from substitutionist revolutions in agrarian countries, for example, in China's cultural revolution, which he described as strategies for strengthening "popular classes" (workers and peasants) against the bureaucracy (ibid: 46-47). The other great historical achievement of the Soviet Union was once again the defeat of Nazism – with this victory, Marzani suggested, the Soviet Union and socialism had proven their raison d'être (cf. 1990: 3). This triumph bestowed both legitimacy and prestige on the regime (cf. Monthly Review 1990: 7). Closer to the present, Marzani hinted at another achievement which backed his Deutscherite interpretation – the Soviet Union was able to produce a Gorbachev, to reform itself 'from above' through its ruling class, and to attract people in many parts of the world to socialism once more. Again in a comparative view, he pointed out: "People may well catch on to history's gargantuan jest: the 'sick' system produced Mikhail Gorbachev, the 'healthy' one Ronald Reagan" (1990: 15). Marzani's article appeared in early 1990. Later, contributors were more likely to mention Gorbachev's initiatives as one of the failed attempts at reforming the Soviet system and perhaps even as the most disastrous one.

As in the other journals, a great deal of attention was reserved for a critique of the Soviet Union's political mistakes and deficiencies. One of the most outspoken critics, Alberto Prago, insisted that the country's success in defeating Nazism did not say anything about its internal qualities. He accused others like Marzani to be apologetic about the countless state-sponsored crimes, the resulting terror, its victims, and the system's bureaucracy. If Gorbachev was seen as one of the system's achievements, these darker aspects needed acknowledgement too (cf. 1990: 54). Although other contributors' assessments were often milder in tone and blamed the hostile climate for driving the Soviet Union into authoritarian postures of self-defence, in principle they also criticised the same crimes and bureaucracy. Sweezy explained that all the numerous socialist revolutions of the 20th century struggled with the form of a post-revolutionary state's institutional set-up and its distribution of power (cf. 1990a: 6):

The new revolutionary regimes were able to overthrow and expropriate the old rulers, and to this extent they succeeded in laying the foundation for a socialist society. But the life-and-death struggle to develop and protect the embryonic new society gave rise – whether inevitably or not remains a matter for debate – to a military-style cleavage between the leaders and the people which in time, and against the will and intentions of the original revolutionaries, hardened into a new self-reproducing system of antagonistic classes. This was obviously not the restoration of capitalism: that would have been the result of a victory of the counter-revolution, not of a development clearly internal to the revolutionary regime itself. (ibid: 7)

Löwy agreed that the leading class in fact excluded the workers and the majority of the population from political power. Ideologically, the upper stratum of post-revolutionary societies discredited individual political and human rights as bourgeois while in reality they were fruits of victorious working-class struggles (cf. 1991: 33). Sweezy and Magdoff emphasised that not only the Soviet Union and the Eastern Bloc suffered from this problem, but also other socialist countries such as China (cf. Monthly Review 1991: 1). And addressing the situation in Cuba Sweezy explained:

From a socialist point of view, there is much to criticize in Cuban society, most importantly that it is not democratic and after 30 years shows no sign of evolving toward democracy – using the term in its authentic Marxist sense of a society in which the associated producers are in charge of their own lives and destiny. (1990b: 19)

Others hinted at the direct contradiction between post-revolutionary practice and the democratic principles Marx had laid down in his essay on the Paris Commune (cf. Wallis 1991: 6-7) and argued that this practice had contributed, just like the counter-revolutionary threat and fascism, to the destruction of the original revolutionary Marxist tradition (cf. Löwy 1991: 39). These discrepancies harmed not only the workers, or to use Amin's terminology, the popular classes, but also the rulers; originally most of them had not been careerists, but in many cases had suffered greatly for their convictions before they came to power. They had to be seen as victims too – who fell prey to power's corrupting tendencies. For Miliband, the only chance to avoid the traps of power lay in the implementation of a system of checks and balances which facilitated critical debate and safeguarded accountability. Socialism, in other words, could only be democratic socialism and needed a formal democratic context (cf. 1991: 20). Without such a framework, the Soviet Union and the states of the Eastern Bloc had developed a class antagonism with the nomenklatura as a quasi-bourgeois class – or a ruling elite (cf. Meisenhelder 1993: 40) – that even tried to behave like the one in the West and was consequently regarded by the working classes as their enemy (cf. Amin 1992: 44).

This was the tenor of *Monthly Review*'s description of the material realities of power. In parallel, there was an ideological dimension with, according to voices in the journal, two main features: voluntarism and superhumanism. Miliband explained that for many revolutionaries and for many leaders in the post-revolutionary societies, a belief in socialism was understood as a quasi-religious commitment. While it could sustain people, it could just as well invite a type of voluntarism that tried to install a completely different order too quickly and with insufficient consideration of those who did not share the religious commitment (cf. 1991: 19-20). This arrogance became even more dangerous since it was accompanied by what Kovel described as a quasi-Nietzschean super-humanism that would without hesitation sacrifice the individual human being for the benefit of the human species – a perspective that most Bolshevists shared and that found its ultimate expression in attempts at 'radicalising' Marx and introducing communism immediately. The author hinted at Pol Pot's Kampuchea as a case in point (cf. 1994: 40-41). These mistaken interpretations of socialism had harmed its chances all over the world: "An exorbitant price is still being paid for this confusion of the Stalinist nightmare with the socialist dream" (Singer 1990: 74). Since the left elsewhere in the world had remained too hesitant in condemning the failures of the post-revolutionary states, it was suffering the consequences too. As Singer concluded in a later article, this timidity explained, at least to a certain extent, why all genuine popular movements had developed outside, or even against, the traditional left over the previous twenty-five years (cf. 1994: 97).

The Impact of the Cold War
Several writers seemed convinced that the political leaderships of the Eastern Bloc were not alone to be blamed for the deformations their experiments in socialism had produced. Defence against Cold War pressures played an important role in justifications of authoritarian measures. Hence, interpretations of the Cold War were given considerable space in the journal's pages. Contributors unanimously argued that the capitalist West ought to be seen as the main aggressor in the confrontation. For the Soviet Union, the problems of rapid industrialisation under conditions first of war and then of the Cold War era became almost insurmountable (cf. Monthly Review 1990). The idea that the West had won was accepted only relatively late. In early 1990, Marzani, commenting on Western triumphalism, still doubted that this was the case (cf. 1990: 2). In terms of economic and military strength, the United States and the U.S.S.R. (as well as their systems of allies) were almost equal. That the United States tried to outperform its

opponents generated negative consequences for both – the United States suffered from a trade deficit, as well as a run-down, under-financed infrastructure and was overtaken economically by Germany and Japan (ibid: 11-12). The author even interpreted Reagan's sudden shift from hostility to cooperation with Gorbachev's U.S.S.R. as a sign that the United States were unable to keep up with the arms race (ibid: 14). For both sides the question of whether they could win the Cold War was one of survival, but, perhaps, for capitalism even more than for socialism. Sweezy explained that the West had to prevent the Eastern Bloc to prove its historical superiority over capitalism:

Centrally crucial was the question of whether the socialist leaders of the revolutions would be able to steer a course toward the creation of new societies increasingly capable of realizing the aspirations and ideals of the socialist faith. If so, it would be only a matter of time for the struggle to be decided in favor of socialism. (1993: 2-3)

For this reason, the Western, and especially the U.S. ruling classes put a great deal of effort in obstructing all moves towards socialism. Internally, the U.S.S.R. mutated from ally to enemy and internationally, its security interests were demonised as imperialist (ibid: 3-4). Since the West had reached a higher level of economic development, it profited more from the arms race and could more easily integrate the weapons industry into its patterns of production (ibid: 5). In the 1970s, at a time of serious crisis when capitalism's future seemed at risk once more, the West intensified its ideological onslaught on the Eastern Bloc and argued that all radical changes would lead to totalitarianism: "In the mid-1970s, when a deep capitalist economic crisis followed student protests, the system felt threatened. The *gulag* campaign – the discovery of latter-day Christopher Columbuses, the *nouveau philosophes*, of Soviet concentration camps – came to the rescue" (Singer 1990: 88-89). The combination of economic, military and ideological pressure finally decided the Cold War – by 1993, *Monthly Review* writers accepted the 'defeat' of the Eastern Bloc and the Soviet Union: "So capitalism won the Cold War and in the process snuffed out whatever chance there may have been that the revolutions of the twentieth century could or would provide successfully working models of socialism" (Sweezy 1993: 3-4). In another piece, Sweezy repeated these arguments and described the Western aggression as a counter-revolutionary attack with an inevitable outcome, given the global distribution of economic power (cf. 1994: 4-5). Nevertheless, he clarified that the collapse of the Soviet system should not be reduced to external factors: "Its defeat in the great showdown of the second half of the twentieth century owed as much to its own internal divisions and weaknesses as to the strength of its opponent" (ibid: 7). The disastrous consequences of the Cold War, however, extended to the Western left as well. It was never able to effectively counter the argument that socialism manifested itself in the realities of the Eastern Bloc, especially since those who made the claim could not agree on a definition of 'true socialism' (cf. Vilas 1990: 93; Bell-Villada 1991: 53). The Western left was also unable to disentangle 'democracy' from its association with the capitalist West and hence it could do nothing against, in E. P. Thompson's words, the substitution of the European class struggle by the bloc struggle (cf. Wood 1994: 13). In the early 1990s, there seemed to be nothing they could do against claims of the 'end of history', against the argument that there were no alternatives and against the hegemonic conflation of the "collapse of Communism", the "failure of socialism", and the "death of Marxism" (Wallis 1991: 7).

Reasons for the Collapse
Several authors discussed the question in how far the Gorbachev reforms had contributed to the final collapse of the Eastern Bloc. In an editorial entitled "Perestroika and the Future of Socialism", the writers criticised the belief that the positive sides of capitalism could be introduced without the negative ones (cf. Monthly Review 1990: 15). This was utopian thinking in the most negative sense and was explained with the observation that intellectuals acted as the moving forces behind the reform programme. Intellectuals, according to the authors, were among those people who profited most from advanced capitalism. Eastern European intellectuals seemed to imagine themselves in the roles their peer groups played in capitalist societies:

Capitalism, whatever its faults and shortcomings, has created in a few of its most advanced units a standard of living and a degree of security for its most fortunate citizens far beyond anything available in any other form of society, whether earlier or contemporary. Among these fortunate citizens are many in the arts, sciences and professions whose status in their respective countries is below that of the ruling establishments but who live well, are influential in their own communities, and enjoy a wide latitude to dissent and criticize. (ibid: 13)

With regard to the reforms' contents, from a human-rights and democratic perspective, there was much to applaud, in terms of its economic programmes, there was a lot that went wrong. For Löwy, the whole package of renewal formed a

mixed blessing, combining a remarkable opening (*glasnost*) with a market-oriented economic restructuring (*perestroika*) which endangers some of the traditional rights of workers, and some very positive initiatives for nuclear disarmament with a substantial reduction of support for third world revolutions (particularly in Central America). (1991: 34-35)

Also Amin took issue with the utopianism of the "school of Novosibirsk" which he identified as the think-tank behind the Gorbachev reforms and explained that their goals were not socialist – at least not in a Marxist sense:

They [the school of Novosibirsk; SB] imagined a pure and perfect self-regulating market which required – Walras had understood this and Barone had expressed it by 1908 – not widely dispersed private property but a totally centralized means of production and the bidding for access to it on the part of all people, who would be free to designate themselves as sellers of labor power or as entrepreneurs. This old Saint Simonian dream of scientifically managed society (Engels was the first to have seen it as nothing but capitalism without capitalists), when pushed to its furthest limits, expressed the economistic alienation of all bourgeois ideology, whose unreal and utopian character was demonstrated by historical materialism. (1992: 48)

For Amin, it seemed clear that the unrealistic idea of capitalism without capitalists would eventually be transformed into a more ordinary capitalism with the emergence of a real bourgeoisie (which would replace the Soviet quasi-bourgeoisie) and a class system. While the Gorbachev reforms were guided by positive intentions, these would be thwarted by their inadequate theoretical foundations and thus contribute to a reintroduction of capitalism.

Of course, these reforms were only the straw that broke the camel's neck. The roots of the Eastern Bloc's problems were inextricably linked to its emergence. In this respect, no fundamental difference existed between the authors of *Monthly Review* and those of the other journals. The most baroque picture of the roots of the 1989 collapse was drawn by Singer:

We were clearly watching the twilight of a reign, the end of an era, the collapse of regimes that were the result of revolutions not only carried out from above but imported from abroad. We were also attending the final funeral of Stalinism as a system. In February 1956, in his famous 'secret' indictment of Stalin, Nikita Khrushchev stunned the faithful by revealing that the corpse of their demigod was stinking. The shock was terrible. Yet it took a third of a century for the system based on this cult to be dismantled throughout the empire. (1990: 74)

But the reasons did not start with Stalin either. Also Singer recurred to the old hope that the Soviet revolution should have spread to, in socio-economic terms, more 'advanced' countries but failed to do so. For the author, the reason did not lie in the treacherous behaviour of the social democrats but at least partly in the "abortive search for a shortcut" (ibid). Thus he suggested to interpret the whole Soviet period as a historical parenthesis rather than a new era. Sweezy added that the lack of popular support necessitated the military presence of the Soviet Union in all Eastern European countries (cf. Sweezy 1990: 20). Under the surface, this could only strengthen the resistance of the population. Amin pointed out that this opposition did not develop into an overtly political revolt but became a process of depoliticisation which alienated the people from the political class (cf. 1992: 45). The author admitted that he had underestimated the extent of depoliticisation and wrongly believed in the chance for the systems to move to the left rather than, as they recently did, to the right (ibid: 47). Also Miliband conceded to have put a "naïve" faith in the transformability of Communist regimes into socialist democracies (1991: 18). With a depoliticised population the setting-up of a coherent socialist system, independent from capitalism, became even harder to realise than it already was. Paul Sweezy tried to formulate a synoptic view on the multiplicity of problems:

The [socialist] breakaways occurred in weak and relatively underdeveloped parts of the global capitalist system and were consequently never able to compete on equal terms with stronger and more developed parts of the system. From the very beginning, therefore, they had to devote all their energies to the most elementary tasks of survival against the determined efforts of the capitalist leaders to bring them back into the fold. Under such circumstances, these societies were unable to construct a coherent socialist system comparable to the global capitalist system from which they had broken away. Their industrial trajectories reflected not only their socialist ambitions but also their varying histories and the special weaknesses with which they were burdened from the outset. (1990: 19)

Like some of the voices in *New Left Review*, several authors claimed that the real turning point had been 1968 rather than 1989. After the Prague spring upheaval, no further attempts were made at reforming the Soviet system into democratic socialism but only to replace it by something else (cf. Singer 1990: 80). Still it was not merely the obvious difficulty of achieving such modifications that produced this change of direction among revolutionary movements. It was also an ideological offensive from the side of the capitalist West:

To understand why a Tadeusz Masowiecki, once a progressive Catholic trying to reconcile Socialism with Christianity, becomes prime minister who presided over Thatcherite privatisation or why a Vaclav Havel, who a few years ago described himself vaguely as a socialist, no longer does so today, one must keep in mind the extraordinary change in the ideological climate. (ibid: 82)

The author pointed to the failed moves to the left among various social democratic parties (and in the case of France, governments) which contributed to this climate of 'there are no alternatives' (ibid). Since these changes coincided with the culmination of economic difficulties in the Eastern Bloc, characterized by Istvan Mészáros as a stagnation in the accumulation process, and with the desperate attempt at keeping pace in the arms race, the collapse was inevitable (cf. Monthly Review 1993: 14; Singer 1994: 88). 1989 had to be explained by a combination of economic weakness, a crumbling political authoritarianism, a global ideological shift to the right, and a merciless arms race given priority by both parties in the Cold War.

The Deficiencies of Really Existing Socialism
It has become obvious in this chapter that in their evaluations of central aspects of the state-socialist systems, contributors reached very similar conclusions in the various journals. The overall critique of the Eastern Bloc's lack of democracy remained the most important of these. All agreed

that the regimes did not do themselves any favours with the suppression of open discussion and democratic debate. Some authors were more willing than others, however, to seek out explanations for these mistakes – and so to a certain extent implicitly justify or excuse them. Despite their differing degrees of tolerance, authors unanimously argued that the absence of democracy had not only seriously harmed the *political* development of the Soviet Union and the Eastern Bloc, in general, but had also greatly impaired their *economic* performance. The restrictive measures not only failed to convince the population to embrace socialist ethics (or as *Socialist Register* would describe it, to cultivate a socialist consciousness); they also stifled people's creativity, which, if instead allowed to flourish, would have helped to put the Eastern Bloc's economy on a far more solid foundation. Still, the Soviet Union could claim a number of economic successes: especially the industrialisation of the pre-industrial society which had been achieved after 1917 – even if only with terrible human sacrifices. For those who had survived and for later generations, economic modernisation had afforded citizens a modest level of wealth, material security and social equality. Finally, in several ways, the state-socialist system had helped capitalism to survive; the Soviet Union had played a central role in rescuing Europe from fascism and the Eastern Bloc had protected the West from a number of market-radical follies and indirectly supported the introduction of a domesticated capitalism that had felt forced to make concessions to its working classes. The countries of the Eastern Bloc had also contributed to the process of decolonisation that would have been even more cumbersome and protracted without their anti-colonial position. Although authors agreed nearly unanimously on these matters and provided similar interpretations of empirical evidence, this concurrence did not mean that specific issues were given the same weight in each of the different journals. Industrialisation provides an excellent example; while some mentioned it only in passing, for others, it constituted a central point.

Overarching agreements aside, focal differences were marked amongst the journals. For example, although the gigantic task of Soviet industrialisation was acknowledged, their economic performance was judged differently. For some authors (most in *Dissent* and a few in *New Left Review*), it amounted to a complete failure, while others held a more sympathetic or stratified view. Contributors also disagreed as to when and why these disastrous tendencies started or when they became irreversible. It is interesting that these questions played an important role in the American journals – *Dissent* concentrated its discussion of authoritarianism and totalitarianism very much on the Stalin era. *Monthly Review*, on the other hand, contributed a counterfactual reflection on the role Trotsky would have played if the struggle between him and Stalin had ended differently. The negative evaluation of Trotsky does not come as a surprise: the split between Trotskyists and Communists had played a prominent role in the American left for a long time. Context can also explain why certain issues were treated more or less prominently in certain journals; for example, the issue of a basic level of social security seemed more worthy of mention in the American journals (as Europeans were less easy to impress in this respect). The British journals, on the other hand, devoted more space to applauding the Soviet Union's role in the Second World War; for the British left, the war still had tremendous importance and the journals represented strands of the left who had supported the popular front strategy. The coverage of the Cold War also differed, though these divisions did not run between the British and the American publications. *New Left Review* and *Dissent* had explicit and strong geo-political orientations, although the former also published opinions at variance with its perspective. *New Left Review* identified the West as the main aggressor, whereas *Dissent* named the Eastern Bloc. For the other two journals, the political-economic perspective seemed more important than the geo-political one; which means they paid less attention to the Cold War. *Monthly Review* took the strongest interest in a detailed analysis of the Gorbachev reforms. This focus followed from their opinion that the Soviet Union had never been *post*-capitalist but rather *non*-capitalist. Hence classes did still exist in Soviet society and the journal interpreted the Gorbachev era as a period of class struggle. The notion of non-capitalism was shared by *Dissent*, albeit in very different ways. In the British publications, the Deutscherite notion of post-capitalism had been more widely embraced – and the shock that the Gorbachev reforms could usher in the restoration of capitalism was consequently more serious. Altogether, while the collapse of the Eastern Bloc did not provide a reason for regret, the global consolidation of capitalism certainly did.

3. THE STATE OF THEORY

The production of politically relevant theory had for long been the main occupation of socialist intellectuals – theory should point the ways towards more equal and just societies. For intellectuals as a group, theory had a double function: it formed a common base internally and served as a marker of distinction – from other groups of intellectuals and political activists – externally. This chapter analyses the discussions on the most important inspiration for socialist intellectuals – the writings of Karl Marx. Additionally it investigates what additions and alternatives to, or corrections of, Marxism writers tried to find in reflections by other theorists from or beyond the Marxist tradition. To call these 'classics' seems justified in so far as the individuals and groups chosen by intellectuals were either from earlier eras of emancipatory struggles, well-known, or presented in a mood of reverence (even if accompanied by critique, as, for example, in the case of Rosa Luxemburg).

3.1. Marxism

The discussion of Marxism, of the texts authored by Marx and of the texts interpreting them and developing them further, always a central part of the discussion of the intellectual left, was transformed in the aftermath of 1989: at least to a certain extent, it developed into a meta-discussion on the question of whether further exchanges on Marxism remained theoretically sound and politically useful. Even before the collapse of the Eastern Bloc, the journals had acted as forums of debate as to whether Marxism as a nineteenth century social theory still bore relevance for the problems of, for example, the stratified welfare societies of the late twentieth century. Writers in the 1980s took issue with interventions from theorists who argued for moving beyond Marx or at least radically modifying his theories and approaches. However in the early 1990s, some critics additionally raised the question of whether there was some element inherent to Marxism that was responsible for Eastern Europe's authoritarian regimes and perhaps also some intrinsic factor that had ushered in their demise. This question of responsibility – or even guilt – was one of the two major problems raised at the time. Dealing with it included asking whether Marxism had been affected *as a theory*, or even scientifically falsified, by the events of 1989 or whether it would play a role in the future.

The second major issue grew out of the first, but was more theoretical: it was about Marxism's fundamental nature and status. Was it a complete system of thinking or just one social theory among many? Was it still a theory of history? Did it (still) have to say something useful about political strategy? Or had it been reduced to an approach to political economy or to a vague spirit of critique? These broad questions led to more concrete ones: should particular and problematic issues of Marxism be corrected by looking to other systems of thought? Or was a thorough reading of Marx, and the many theoreticians in his tradition, (still) the best way to bring Marxism (and socialism) forward? Two issues seemed particularly important – they were, of course, older than Marxism itself: (a) was there a direction in history or was it an open, contingent process? (b) Were events shaped by structural determinants or by human agency? Authors dealt with these questions in numerous statements, critiques, self-critiques and defences.

Attempts at finding answers to these questions went directly to the heart of socialist intellectuals' views of the world. Consequently, none of the periodicals achieved unanimity over the issues discussed. In all, one finds continua of positions ranging from a more radical questioning of Marxism's basic tenets to views maintaining that the whole edifice of Marxist theory was more or less unaffected by recent events. The question to be discussed in this chapter is whether these continua were of equal size in each of the journals and whether clusters of voices could be found around particular positions on them.

New Left Review

Only two contributions explicitly mentioned the question of Marx's 'responsibility' for the negative aspects of the Eastern Bloc's social and political system: one by a central figure of the First New Left, E. P. Thompson, and the other by one of the main representatives of the Second New Left, Robin Blackburn. Interestingly, the former, who would only very hesitantly have called himself a Marxist at the time, defended the Marxist tradition against any such allegations: "[T]he current fashion of attributing a vaguely defined 'generic Stalinism' to the original bad faith of 'Marxism' is as disreputable as was last year's fashionable celebration of the guillotine as the authentic outcome of the enlightenment" (1990: 143). Blackburn, then editor of *New Left Review*, and at least in terms of theory a much more straightforward Marxist, dedicated one chapter of his extended article on "Socialism after the Crash" to "[t]he responsibility of Marxism", and the argument embraces the thesis that what happened in the Soviet Union and Eastern Europe could not be disentangled completely from Marxism (cf. 1991: 177): political leaders in the state socialist countries had appealed to Marx and tried to implement institutions inspired by Marxism – for example, public ownership and popular welfare. According to Blackburn, Marxism's major problem was its partial adherence to the 'simplification assumption' which relied on the belief that with the creation of social justice, antagonisms in society would come to an end. Blackburn suggested that in the Eastern Bloc neither commodity and money relations had been abolished nor had the need for the rule of law and checks and balances in political decision making structures been transcended. Traditional Marxism provided insufficient guidelines for how to deal with such a situation (cf. ibid: 177-180).

Even if they did not reflect on Marxism's responsibility in such a direct way, most contributors were convinced that Marxism was strongly affected by recent changes. They differed in their perspectives about the nature of such transformations. Eric Olin Wright, when discussing the consequences for and the future of Marxist class analysis in consideration of the events in Eastern Europe, spoke of a combined theoretical and political challenge to Marxism (cf. 1993: 23). Having spent most of his intellectual life performing analyses of class, he regarded the former as more serious: "If the collapse of these regimes undermines the theoretical arguments about the feasibility of transcending private property and capitalist class relations, then these elements of Marxism are seriously threatened" (ibid: 21). Though he was not sure about empirical proof to substantiate these arguments, he had no doubt that a previous feeling of certainty had disappeared to a critical degree:

Even if one believes that the empirical evidence remains highly ambiguous on these matters, and that democratic socialism remains a feasible and desirable alternative to capitalism, it is still difficult to sustain the concepts of socialism and communism with the certainty that once characterized Marxism. Without such concepts, however, the whole enterprise of Marxist class analysis falters. (ibid: 22)

Although he maintained that empirical evidence still needed to be analysed, he complained that many intellectuals did not have the nerve to wait until it had: "[T]he events of the late 1980s have nevertheless helped to accelerate a growing sense of self-doubt and confusion on the part of many radical intellectuals about the viability and future utility of Marxism" (ibid: 16). Similarly, Joseph McCarney emphasised the detrimental and disheartening influence of triumphant right-wing discourse (cf. 1991: 29). The decisive point was that Marxism could not be sealed off from such condemnation. The pervasiveness of claims of Marxism's uselessness might transform them into a self-fulfilling prophecy.

However, others argued that this made up only one side of the coin. Jacques Derrida, in his article "Spectres of Marx" which appeared in *New Left Review* prior to his book with the same title in 1994, explained that Marxism was still very present and that all claims of its death just proved the point that it still existed and was still relevant (cf. 1994: 40): "We all live in a world, some would say in a culture, that still bears, at an incalculable depth, the mark of his inheritance, whether in a directly visible fashion or not" (ibid: 33). Derrida intended to offer a 'deconstruction' of the 'end of Marxism' and 'end of history' discourse but proposed, as several writers criticized, a future for Marxism only as a rather vague 'spirit of critique'. Derrida regarded what was left as "a certain emancipatory and *messianic* affirmation, a certain experience of the promise that one can try to liberate from any dogmatics and even from metaphysico-religious determination, from any *messianism*" (ibid: 54; original emphasis). Others seemed to agree with Derrida and saw Marxism's future role as rather modest but nevertheless as existing. Jürgen Habermas, for example, claimed that it was still useful as a critique of capitalism (cf. Habermas & Michnik 1994: 11). An ecumenical point of view was characteristic of those who did not believe (anymore) in the omniscience of Marxism and claimed, with Norman Geras, that as a comprehensive social theory plus leading ideology of popular struggle, it was irreversibly finished (cf. 1994: 106). On the other hand, Geras rhetorically asked whether Marxism was dead (cf. ibid: 105) and responded to his own question: "Judged as an intellectual tradition of the kind of breadth and wealth that this one has encompassed, the very question of its end is comical. No less. Of no other intellectual tradition of comparable achievement would such a question ever be posed." (ibid: 105-106)

What united all authors was that they agreed they had to react to the uncertainties with which they felt confronted after the collapse.

Wright declared: "I continue to believe that Marxism remains a vital tradition within which to produce emancipatory social science, but I also feel that in order for Marxism to be able to play this role it must be reconstructed in various ways." (1993:16) Through such refashioning, Marxism might become less holistic than it was once assumed to be, but remain helpful for understanding and dealing with causes of oppression. Wright identified three levels of Marxism: class analysis, theory of historical trajectory, and emancipatory normative theory (cf. 1993: 17). He explained the strength of this combination: "Marxism attempts to theorize the inherent tendencies of historical change to follow a particular trajectory with a specific kind of directionality" (ibid: 18). Later he pointed to the task of Marxist social science "to focus on the ways in which alternative futures are opened up or closed off by particular historical conditions" (ibid: 24). A more detailed definition, emphasising again the historical-philosophical dimension, was provided by Sayers:

> Marx's critical method is an immanent and historical one. It is based on the premiss that the grounds for a critical perspective are to be found in existing social conditions themselves. [...] Social reality is contradictory. Negative and critical tendencies exist within it, they do not need to be brought from outside in the form of transcendent values: they are immanent within existing conditions themselves. Thus Marx's social theory, so far from undermining his critical perspective, provides the basis on which it is developed and justified. (1994: 68)

All these definitions hinted at Marxism's specificity and strength – its particular combination of ontology, epistemology and strategy – but also at its problems: Marxism was, as Sayers put it, on the one hand 'scientific' and on the other not 'value-free' (ibid: 67). What would happen to the three levels once one of them was called into doubt for normative reasons? Could Marxism's epistemology and strategy survive once its ontology had been proven wrong as it arguably had by recent events? Given its holistic character, what characterised its relation with other social theories – could it learn from them or had innovations to come from a re-reading of Marxist texts?

Among many contributors, one could observe a tendency to look for clues in Marx's writings themselves about how to come to terms with the changes of 1989/91 and the questions which followed from them. McCarney, for example, explained that the collapse of the Eastern European governments did not contradict the Marxist theory of history. Quite to the contrary, he insisted that Marx himself had never believed that communism could exist and survive as a local (rather than global) phenomenon (cf. 1991: 28). In the same article, he pointed to a kind of dialectical humour as an important means for surviving at the historical conjuncture of post-1989:

Yet students of dialectic, with the example of Hegel and Marx in mind, should be able to keep their humour. They will be aware that humour is itself a dialectical weapon, liable to the kind of reversal that strikes back at those who wish to exploit it. Hence, they will be alert to any signs of transforming irony in the present situation. (ibid: 29-30)

Arrighi also emphasised that recent events could be read as a proof of Marxist perspectives: the Polish union *Solidarnosc* closely followed Marxist ideals – they did not rely on vanguardism, did not represent selfish interests, and did not fall prey to separatist tendencies – and its success vindicated the theory's assumptions, prognoses, and recommendations (cf. 1990: 63). In a similar vein, McCarney reiterated the relevance of Marxist historical theory, which he considered proven by recent events in Eastern Europe:

It need not be feared that the tradition of thought Marx founded when he set Hegelian dialectic the right way up has been rendered obsolete or irrelevant by the working out of the historical process which has been its true object from the beginning. On the contrary, there is now everything to fight for so far as that tradition is concerned (1991: 38).

Even those who believed that Marxism had to be criticised and corrected nevertheless felt obliged to excuse the theorist Marx by situating his writings in the context of nineteenth century industrial capitalism (cf. Habermas 1990: 11). They pointed out that Marx and Engels had themselves been conscious of the historicity, the 'ageing' of their standpoint (cf. Derrida 1994: 32). They also stressed that certain omissions in Marx's corpus of work had to be explained via his wish to distance himself from the not only utopian but at the same time doctrinaire socialisms of the nineteenth century which were likely to produce dictatorships in the name of some version of vanguardism (cf. Blackburn 1991: 180). These statements reveal the wish to show solidarity with Marxism as a certain system of thought before criticising it.

The first technique used by authors to display support was to list the many elements of Marxism that were still important. First of all, its political vision was still needed: for Robin Blackburn, at least some elements went beyond mere criticism and still acted as useful guidelines for the construction of a political project:

If some of Marx's rhetoric now seems overly simple, this emphatically does not apply to the previously cited aphorism which sums up his vision of the principle which should govern the future society: that the precondition for the free development of each would be the free development of all. (ibid: 233)

This meant arguing less the scientific but more the political and the moral case for Marxism. Together with socialism, Marxism simply remained indispensable as long as opposition to capitalism was needed. This formed the core of Derrida's definition of Marxism as a 'spirit of critique'. But the moral case was argued also by others such as Aijaz Ahmad, who regarded Derrida's definition as too vague, his position as too performative, and his argument as not sufficiently analytical:

One reason for being a socialist can be far simpler than 'awaiting' the 'event-ness' of the 'messianic promise'. Theoretically, socialism arises from within the contradictions of capitalism. Morally, opposition to capitalism is its own justification since capitalism is poisoning human survival itself, let alone human happiness. In the present circumstances, the resolve to overturn this globally dominant system does indeed involve what Ernst Bloch once called 'utopian surplus'; but the utopian aspect of communist imagination need not translate itself into 'the messianic'. (Ahmad 1994: 94-5)

Secondly, Marxism's theoretical and methodological achievements were also highlighted. Contributors considered a number of ideas in Marx's writings and, more generally, in Marxist theory to be as indispensable as ever. Often these essentials were situated not too far from the respective authors' academic backgrounds and specialisations. Most were still convinced of the theory of labour and of the necessity of a nuanced class analysis. Wright emphasised the specificity of the Marxist class analysis, which interpreted the existence of class antagonisms as the result of property relations and the exploitation of workers (the decisive difference to Weberian class theories), and tied it to the utopian vision of creating a classless society (1993). Additionally, no one would have denied the importance of the sphere of production for the organisation of societies, and no one would have totally abandoned historical materialism as a scientific method. For Sayers, the historical materialist method should be extended to the area of ethics, values and ideas: "For it questions the idea that the history of ideas of justice can be understood in terms of the logic of those ideas themselves; rather we must look to the development of the social forms which give rise to them" (1994: 82). Therborn listed three basic elements of what could be called a Marxist belief system: firstly, inequality and injustice had to be understood as the outcomes of capitalism and imperialism, class rule and exploitation. Secondly, the possibility of radical social change was inherent in the development of capitalism, and finally, the historical agents potentially achieving such change would be the exploited and oppressed people (cf. Therborn 1992: 18). Another important aspect was suggested by G. A. Cohen who pointed to the Marxist theory of reification and used the relationship of money and freedom in capitalism as example – a lack of money meant a lack of freedom (cf. 1994: 15). He explained: "To have money is to have freedom, and the assimilation of money to mental and bodily resources is a piece of unthinking fetishism, in the good old Marxist sense that it represents *social relations of constraint* as *things* that people lack. In a word: money is no object" (ibid: 16; emphasis in original). For McCarney, more abstractly, it was only a question, the question of what was the nature of a human community that realised freedom, which formed the core of a philosophy influenced by Marxism (cf. 1991: 33).

Several authors took up the question as to whether Marxism was teleological and working under the assumption of a clear direction in the movement of history. Sayers suggested distinguishing teleology from directionality. He defended directionality as a necessary part of Marxism as both a comprehensive social science and a political project by arguing for a strong version of a historical materialist theory of change: "Our present condition of disharmony and alienation is not ideal; but there is no question of going back. The true content of the idea of a harmonious life lies in the future; and it can be attained only by going through a necessary stage of division and alienation" (1994: 78). He insisted that this perspective was non-teleological because, unlike some conservatives and liberals in the early 1990s (such as Francis Fukuyama), it did not set a particular turn in history as its end (ibid: 82-3). He also maintained the notion that socialism for Marxists needed to be understood not as a moral ideal, but instead "as a concrete historical stage which will supersede capitalism and which will be the outcome of forces which are at work within present capitalist society" (ibid: 69). As mentioned above, he was concerned in his article not only with the movements of history as such, but also with the genesis of ideas of justice which he saw not as developing in a closed and timeless space of ethics (as, he claimed, *New Left Review* contributors and analytical Marxists like Geras and G. A. Cohen did) but within historical change and social struggles. Since human nature itself was produced and modified in history, and historical developments gradually led to a more rational control over material and social life, ideas of justice would, in this process, become increasingly rational (cf. ibid: 82).

Even if in fact Marxism still had much to offer, this did not mean it was beyond criticism. Authors demanded two types of corrections: On the one hand, they identified areas that, from a nineteenth century perspective, could not have been foreseen or were missing for another reason. Arrighi, for example, argued that classes in the original Marxist sense had ceased to exist under conditions of managed and corporate capitalism which had emerged since the 1940s. In this context, anti-systemic forces were marginalized politically, thus destabilising Marxism theoretically even more intensely in 1989/91 (cf. 1990: 34). On the other hand, *New Left Review* published individual voices, though far from the journal's 'mainstream', which claimed the definite end of the theoretical usefulness of at least a certain version of Marxism; David Marquand explained in short critique of economic determinism that the idea "[t]hat politics can be a sort of cart, dragged along by the horse of economics, has no place outside the fairytale worlds of classical Marxism and classical economic liberalism" (1994: 25). For most writers, problem with the reliance on Marxism was that the philosophy contained internal contradictions. Robin Blackburn hinted at the "simplification assumption", the idea that once capitalism was superseded, all social conflicts would disappear and all required societal structures would automatically emerge; premises which collided with the "developmental assumption", the belief that new structures had to be created actively (1991: 180). According to Blackburn, both positions could be found in Marxism and thus he argued, in his tour-de-force through Marxism and other socialist theories and programmes, for a new open debate on socialist theory and strategy which would start from the developmental assumption which required creative, utopian and strategic thinking.

Contributors went on to identify topics for reflection upon which traditional Marxism did not have much to offer. Among them was the problem of environmental destruction. Influenced by the pioneering spirit of industrialisation and by its promise of material wealth, Marx considered the domination of nature as positive and denounced affection for natural beauty as sentimental. He did not anticipate ecological problems resulting from the human mastery of the natural environment. Both Ted Benton and Jürgen Habermas pointed to this problem and Benton not only stated that Marx's aspiration to control all natural and social processes would result in an ecological disaster but, commenting on Marx's derogatory remarks on people's leisurely Sunday walks, complained that "[c]ontempt for such apparently trivial sources of 'ordinary' pleasure, wonder and engagement with the world has long been an Achilles heel of orthodox Marxism" (Benton 1992: 71, cf. Habermas 1990).[1] While this criticism was widely shared among the contributors, another contradiction figured even more prominently into discusions – the failure to sketch out the institutional arrangements of a socialist democracy and the workings of a socialist economy. Especially Habermas noted Marx's restricted and instrumental view of constitutional democracy, his insistence to limit the possibility of real democracy to communist post-political democracy, and his reluctance to

---

1 Ted Benton was engaged in a long debate with Reiner Grundmann over not only the philosophical and ethical justifications of an anthropocentric versus a biocentric environmentalism but at the same time also about the status of Marxism. To muster authority for his arguments, Grundmann simply referred to Marx, for whom humans lived in and against nature, and hence declared an anthropocentric Marxist environmentalism to be justified (cf. 1991). Interestingly, Marxist concepts and theories were even used when Marxism was criticised. The following quotation from Ted Benton, can serve as an example: "The notion of the ultimate vulnerability of all natural and social processes to the human will is purest *idealism*. For a civilization to live as if it were true would be to court ecological catastrophe" (1992: 63; my emphasis).

provide, beyond the dictatorship of the proletariat, any suggestions for institutions during a transitional period leading towards socialism (cf. 1990: 12). Blackburn shared this view and presented a vast and heterogeneous list of socialists who had discussed democratic decision-making procedures and socialist goals within the sphere of production (1991). Some writers located a third omission in Marx's work (though this remained controversial): his failure to contribute to a theory of justice. This became a particular concern of Geras, who diagnosed this deficiency as a negative side effect of Marxism's restricted focus on identifying material preconditions and social forces of change rather than its ethical principles (1992: 66-67).

A further criticism of Marx's writings took issue with his understanding of society and political agency. Firstly, writers regarded his concept of society as too holistic because he had depicted it as composed exclusively of a number of antagonistic and rather monolithic "macro-subjects" acting in their rational interests which stood in conflict with each other (Habermas 1990: 11). The resulting problem was that

[t]heory in this way blinds itself to the resistance inherent in the system of a differentiated market economy, whose regulative devices cannot be replaced by administrative planning without potentially jeopardizing the level of differentiation achieved in a modern society. (ibid)

This neglect of differentiation went hand in hand with an incomplete understanding of, and exaggerated trust in, the working-class (ibid). Wright (who also called Marx's class concept "too macro" [1993: 29]), Geras and Sayers, in different ways, suggested that the source for potential political change was not in the existence of wage labour, but instead in the experience of inequality from which people suffered (cf. Geras 1992: 68; Sayers 1994: 77). This correction was not only more in line with the character of political struggles in the twentieth century, it also had the strategic advantage that all oppressed groups would, in principle, become potential agents of change. Their intention was not to dismiss class as the main determinant of numerous aspects of social life, but to acknowledge that people might have contradictory class positions and to account for non-exploitative forms of oppression (such as those directed against an underclass excluded from the production process and socially marginalised). Of course, this perception was not new, as Wright himself admitted when he said that for most contemporary Marxists the class conflict was not the only social conflict, and he insisted that all emancipatory strategies would still need to deal with class inequality, namely with the distribution of material resources, the economic surplus, and with time (cf. 1993: 28). The rest of Wright's article attempted to develop a revised form of Marxist class analysis, foregrounding different forms of exploitation as the central issue rather than restricting exploitation to wage labour. In practice, a refined class analysis would be helpful for the forging of class alliances in political conflicts (cf. ibid: 35).

Marx's restrictive and "macro" approach to class was explained as the result of a belief in human rationality that was also traced back to philosophical developments of his time. According to Habermas, Marx had believed not only in the possibility of rationally organising economic life but that its superiority – compared to market economies – would become clearly visible and thus automatically discredit capitalism as a system (cf. 1990: 11). Several writers suggested that such rationality was less straightforward and much more constructed and ambiguous than Marx had thought. In response to this oversight, Blackburn contended that Marx's developmental assumption, that contradictory and conflicting perspectives and priorities would continue, was clearly superior to his simplification assumption (cf. 1991: 180-181). These arguments also served as explanations for the unexpected longevity of capitalism. Two contributors working in regulation theory, Robert Brenner and Mark Glick, formulated this thesis very clearly:[2]

The reason why Marx's outline is problematic lies in the epistemological position that humans could understand the world they created much better than the world that is naturally given [...]. [H]e does not reckon with the possibility that human objecti-

---

[2] Regulation theory analyses the role of the state in societies with capitalist economies. Having abandoned the perception of the state as merely serving capitalist interests, regulation theorists see the state as a coordinator of conflicting interests which contributes to capitalism's stability even if acting against the interests of individual capitalists. Generally, regulation theorists distinguish different forms of capitalism characterised by specific accumulation regimes – maintained with the support of state institutions.

fications, such as modern social relations, may become so complex that they are no longer susceptible to everyone's understanding. (1991: 117)

Such difficulties in understanding the social world became a major obstacle to socialist agency and thus to political change. Without clear evidence that socialism was superior, it became harder to argue for socialist policies. These critical observations on the status of Marx's writing set tasks for the future work of radical intellectuals. Of course, modernising Marxism had preoccupied them for a long time, but the fact that they reiterated this need at the historical moment of 1989/91 meant that they treated it with renewed urgency. Indeed, a great deal of the theoretical reflections in *New Left Review* tried to fill these gaps. What Geras described as the need to combine a "scientific" approach of identifying agents of social change and a utopian approach of inventing futures became the guideline for these intellectual activities (1992: 69). A certain amount of creative imagination, obviously, had to be brought in order to progress beyond the rationalist determinism of what Geras called the "real tendency" theory of Marxism (ibid: 65).

Two objections to these teleological, historically-directional and, to varying degrees, determinist perspectives were put forward in *New Left Review*: allegedly, they were analytically simplistic and politically dangerous. Regulation theorists pleaded for a more complex and historically-specific understanding of capitalist regimes. Thus they stressed agency in the widest sense: it manifested itself in class and other political struggles which created socio-institutionally defined structural forms and hence shaped different phases within, and models of, capitalism. Their modes of production could not be sufficiently explained by Marx's theory of history and development (cf. Brenner & Glick 1991: 46-47). Theorising and political strategy had to be attuned to historically and spatially specific social conditions and power relations. Politically, the strong version of historical materialism could have, in the eyes of its critics, two negative consequences. It could either lead to the self-stylisation of revolutionary vanguards as being exempt from the moral regulations of their time. Habermas suspected teleological perspectives to encourage revolutionary elites' wishes to accelerate history and hence to violate ethical standards (cf. 1990: 12). Or it could simply lead to apathy – the opposite of vanguardism – because socialism would become possible only after the exhaustion of capitalism (cf. Wright 1993: 16). According to Wright, Marxists would be better served by taking a 'weak' historical materialist position, one that would look for historical possibilities instead of trajectories and hence grant a central place to agency, but at the same time, warn against elitist vanguardism (cf. ibid: 24).. Therborn supported these arguments by pointing out that the polarisation between the industrial working class and the capitalist class never took place on the anticipated scale (cf. 1992: 22-23). The possibility of change was inherent in capitalism. It *could* be achieved by the oppressed and exploited, but that was all. In other words: voluntarism, not of a Leninist version but one based on agreed-upon ethical standards, formed a necessary precondition for movements towards socialism. Voluntarism's purpose was not to accelerate the movement of history but to influence the direction of history's movement. Auerbach called in this context for a dialectical, an interrelated and reciprocal understanding of processes at the level of economic base and societal superstructure and demanded that scholars take the institutions of the latter much more seriously as possible levers for political change:

In its twentieth-century development, the dominant tradition emanating from this ideology [Marxism; SB] has concentrated on the importance of changes in the economic base of society as the mechanism through which it would *then* be possible to deal with questions of human development. Superstructural issues such as education have been perceived as secondary. This tradition is dominant despite the fact that it was precisely failures in aspects of the 'superstructure' that motivated many individuals' radical political activity in the first place – individuals for whom superstructural work such as education was often the dominant mode of human and professional activity. (1992: 9-10)

Hence for 'weak materialists', the political and the analytical argument went together – agency was needed because a "real tendency" could not be relied on. Agency had to stick to ethical principles in order to avoid the dangers of vanguardist isolationism. Marxism was not dead, but Leninist vanguardism obviously was. However, on the continuum ranging from Marxism as a privileged system of thought to a much weaker and more open spirit of critique writers in *New Left Review* took extremely different positions and thus testified to the journal's political and theoretical pluralism.

Socialist Register

In *Socialist Register*, statements about the responsibility of Marxism for really existing socialism were rare. The voice coming closest to such a position was that of the editor Miliband who proclaimed that the events of 1989/91 had cut Marxism to size and that socialists should welcome this development (cf. 1990: 360). This formulation can be read as an implicit acceptance of some responsibility of Marxism. No one contradicted Miliband, but other authors put the emphasis differently and expressed deep scepticism about the lessons which several other groups of Marxists seemed to draw at such times when they felt that non-Marxists considered them partially responsible for the atrocities of the Eastern Bloc's regimes.

Contributors to *Socialist Register* remained convinced that Marxism was not discredited by recent developments and they expressed deep unease about the fact that many (former) Marxists acted as if it was. Geras's position is already apparent from what he wrote in *New Left Review*. In *Socialist Register*, he added that Marxists should, of course, be self-critical but not make a "mess" of their Marxist past (1990: 32). Richard Levins insisted that Marxism's tomb was empty, even if some former Marxists gave up Marxism altogether and others cut it down to a programme for a capitalism with a more human face and transformed themselves into post-Marxists or "petty-empiricists" (1990: 333-334). The annual edition printed further harsh criticisms of what its contributors regarded as the 'retreat of the intellectuals'. One of the most outspoken among these critics was Ellen Meiksins Wood who had received the *Isaac Deutscher Memorial Price* a couple of years earlier, awarded for her book *The Retreat from Class* – meaning, the intellectuals' retreat – and thus claimed some authority on the matter:

> We live in curious times. Just when intellectuals of the left in the West have a rare opportunity to do something useful, if not actually world-historic, they – or large sections of them – are in full retreat. Just when reformers in the Soviet Union and Eastern Europe are looking to Western capitalism for paradigms of economic and political success, many of us appear to be abdicating the traditional role of the Western left as critic of capitalism. (1990: 60)

This task of criticising capitalism was of continuing importance, even if Marxism was on the defensive, as MacEwan wrote with regard to the United States (cf. 1990: 311). Nonetheless, this countering force was needed more than ever at a historical conjuncture characterised by triumphant capitalism:

> Just when more than ever we need a Karl Marx to reveal the inner workings of the capitalist system, or a Friedrich Engels to expose its ugly realities 'on the ground', what we are getting is an army of 'post-Marxists', one of whose principal functions is apparently to conceptualize away the problem of capitalism. (Wood 1990: 60)

This reaction was judged to be untenable since Marxism was not only not discredited by the collapse of the Eastern Bloc but also continued to be the only system of thought capable of demystifying the realities of capitalism.

No one in *Socialist Register* defended an absolute and dogmatic reading of Marxism. Nevertheless, it remained more than one theory among many: rather a world view that an identifiable group of people shared and developed collectively in ceaseless debate. This debate needed to become aware of and look to academic and political debates elsewhere for help – it could not survive in isolation. In how far such incorporations would and should transform Marxism itself was not entirely clear. For some, it seemed enough to fill Marxism's gaps. Others, however, demanded a more open approach: Levins, for example, saw a need for inspiration – not just from sources from which Marxism had always learnt (English political economy, French socialism, German philosophy) but also from contemporary movements such as feminism and environmentalism (cf. 1990: 342).

Geras discussed Marxism's scientific and epistemological status in detail. He conceded that its central theoretical claims could not be proven (cf. 1990: 5). This lack of veracity had repercussions for its reputation and relevance: in the eyes of many, even if they regarded socialism as an attractive model of social organisation, they had developed doubts about its plausibility after 1989, and asked questions about its practicability and, coming back to the old question of revolutionary agency, who could put it into practice and with what strategies (cf. ibid). On the theoretical level, Geras raised the question of whether retaining central tenets of Marxism despite their unproven status would amount to an epistemological absolutism – especially since as a system of thought it employed a notion of truth. He denied the charge with the argument that a third position existed between the extremes of cognitive absolutism and cognitive relativism – and that a third position of probabilistic knowledge should be occupied by Marxists. In other words, Marxism interpreted history along probable lines but was open to criticisms of these interpretations as suggested by others in rational discourse – among them Marxists themselves (cf. ibid: 18-19).

Geras received support through similar reflections by MacEwan. The latter further elaborated on the notion of probabilistic knowledge through defining Marxism as a holistic and thus as different from a totalistic system. MacEwan repeated that Marxism did not provide explanations for all problems – nor every strategy for their solution – even if it was both a social theory and a political world view which aimed at 'getting the whole picture'. In addition, he insisted that any such world view was heterogeneous, containing a plurality of views and controversial debates (cf. 1990: 317) or – as Amy Bartholomew put it – formed an "internally diverse and contested terrain" (1990: 244). The source from which to draw probabilistic knowledge, according to MacEwan, was history. History was theory and hence a guide to current issues (cf. 1990: 324). *Socialist Register* offered some reflection on what a theory of history could mean. Contributors to the journal generally agreed that a structurally determined directionality of history was an overly simplistic perspective. Marxism could not, as Geras repeated, explain all historical developments and social relations. However, he maintained that a 'third way' existed between determinism and pluralism: some factors might be more decisive and influential than others. In terms of history, the alternative to teleology was not necessarily circularity, and in terms of politics, the alternative to a hermetic functionalism was not necessarily contingency (cf. 1990: 5-9).

Such a perception of Marxism could still be extremely valuable for social theory and political strategy. Paul Cammack, for example, discussed what Marxism could contribute to political scientists' renewed interest in state theory and to the 'new institutionalism' and showed the limitations of those two approaches in terms of explaining the widespread long-term persistence and occasional rapid change of institutions. These phenomena, as Cammack argued, could only be accounted for by the central role of class conflicts within the formation processes of society. Marxism, as a theory of history, was needed in order to transcend what he called statism's "theoretical emptiness" (1990: 156). He suggested that its "concern with the institutional requirements for state capacity supplements rather than replaces a broader theoretical analysis" (ibid: 159). He claimed that statists and institutionalists failed to integrate the historical dimension into their reflections – to their own disadvantage. Concretely, he saw two errors:

> The first is the polarization of theory on the one hand and history on the other, as in the rejection of grand theory in favour of historically situated case studies, and the treatment of Marxism as functionalist and teleological, which rules out the possibility of a dialectical *theory* of *history*, and recognition of Marxism as one such theory. The second is a failure to approach Marxist commentaries on the state in the context of the wider corpus of Marxist theory, from which they cannot be detached. (ibid: 168; original emphasis)

Equally important as the intricacies of state theories, Cammack communicated his perspective in an interesting way. Illustrating the merits of Marxism as measured against the approaches of 'conventional' political scientists[3], he claimed the authority of non-orthodox sympathisers of Marx:

> We shall find [in statists' and institutionalists' writings; SB] strong confirmation of Sartre's observation, recently recalled by Michael Löwy, 'that Marxism is the ultimate possible horizon of our age and that attempts to go beyond Marx frequently end up *falling short* of him'. (ibid: 152; original emphasis).

It seemed to contributors to *Socialist Register* that Marxism's most important achievement lay in its provision of a theory of history. Some of them criticised not only non-Marxist social scientists but also other Marxists for not handling this merit carefully enough. In an article that analysed the situation of the left in France, George Ross accused Louis Althusser of having led Marxists into an intellectual cul-de-sac through replacing historical causality with a more abstract "deep structure" (1990: 203):

> [The] Althusserian turn undercut perhaps Marxism's greatest political appeal, its purported capacity to lay bare the various motors of historical development and make them accessible to rational, progressive human action. The connection between the Althusserian reformulation of Marxism and real politics became ever more tenuous, leading eventually to a political and intellectual impasse. (ibid)

---

3 His list included theorists such as Stepan, Krasner, Skocpol, and Nordlinger (cf. Cammack 1990: 147-152).

With this statement, Ross revealed his conviction that Marxism ought to play a political role as well. It entailed more than an analytical approach to social developments: it served as guide to political action.

The view of Marxism as more than just one among several theories was supported by a reiteration of its main contributions to the explanation of social relations, conflict, and change. Miliband pointed out that its central tenets, especially the class division of society which resulted in struggles, were still intact (cf. 1990: 361). Authors named essentials such as the idea of class contradictions as the primary divisions of society, the problematic of money and the out-of-fashion notion of 'false consciousness' as elements of such a theory – elements they considered to be as valid as ever (cf. ibid; Harvey 1993: 10; Norris 1993: 58-59). MacEwan listed three basics which he regarded as particularly important parts of Marxism: the labour theory of value, the theory of accumulation, and the theory of crisis (cf. 1990: 319). These essentials could not only explain why conflict between employers and workers was inevitable, why choices of technology in the production process were a product of struggle and thus had to be understood as social rather than as technical decisions, why the inclusion and exclusion of groups of the population comprised a tool for avoiding a falling rate of profit, or why economic crises were intrinsic to capitalism rather than accidental (ibid: 319-323), it could also provide a source of energy for political activism:

Socialists of all types have emphasized the way that workers are victims of capitalism, but Marxism stands out because it also emphasizes that workers are actors in creating their own history. This way of looking at things can provide an injection of power to workers struggles. (ibid: 321)

The belief that workers were actors became even more important with the notion of "relative autonomy". Geras accepted that the economy was not all-explanatory but nonetheless omni-present in political structures and pointed out that the debate of reductionism, though once important, was now a tired theme (cf. 1990: 10-11). While he admitted that economic determinism was reductionist indeed, he insisted that an anti-positivist explanation of one phenomenon through features of another, for example, through economic requirements, was not (ibid: 11). Wood added that, as a consequence, it was above all in this respect that Marxists differed from other theorists. Commenting on the debate about civil society, she explained that Marxists interpreted states and civil societies as also dependent on the context of political economy and the power structures it produced. Others conceded, however, that certain traditional understandings such as the primacy of productive forces in social relations and conflicts had always been a deterministic distortion of Marxism (cf. Lebowitz 1991: 358). Michael A. Lebowitz discussed in this context one of *Socialist Register*'s most central beliefs that the possibility of working-class political agency should be taken seriously:

Those who fall prey to its [Marxism's] determinist message can never explain why Marx believed that the political economy of the working class he elaborated in *Capital* was so important that it was worth sacrificing his 'health, happiness and family' or why he never ceased to stress that workers make themselves fit to found society anew only through the process of struggle. Rather than reflecting Marx's position, the thesis in question is characteristic of a one-sided Marxism that has lost sight of the subjects of history. (ibid: 359)

He added that a determinist understanding would mean that history was now on the side of capital – if relations of productions were changed once they had become fetters of the productive forces, then recent developments would mean that the re-introduction of capitalism was in the interest of the productive forces (ibid: 348-349). The alternative, Lebowitz emphasised, was to see capitalism's triumph not as historical necessity but as consequence of workers' belief in its necessity (ibid: 358). Thus, conceptions of 'false consciousness' and of the contentious relationship between interpretation and reality could shed light on the questions of directionality, determination and agency.

The notion of "false consciousness" proved more relevant than ever in a time of 'there-is-no-alternative' and 'end-of-history' discourse (Norris 1993: 58-59). Closely related to the topic of consciousness was the insistence on the continuing importance of critical theory – its analysis of instrumental reason and its claim "that social transformation can only come about through the intentional, self-conscious actions of human agents" (ibid: 86). Theorists had important insights for the post-communist world: changes in the social realm would lead to changes in human beings and an intensified capitalism would, therefore, leave its scars within people themselves:

> At the same time, critical theory saw that the hope for 'true individuality', with its capacity for critique and resistance, was fast disappearing with the intensified encroachment of capitalism into all areas of human existence, or what Habermas would call 'lifeworlds'. (ibid: 86)

George Ross explained that even if one agreed that the collapse of the Eastern Bloc had revealed certain deficiencies in Marxism, an alternative existed to abandoning it. He recommended a look into French intellectual history and sketched out how Sartre and others in the post-1956 situation formulated a revisionist defence of Marxism which developed into existential Marxism. It took issue with the Algerian War and, under its impression, formulated refined theories of state-society relationships (cf. 1990: 195-204). Similar revisions would be possible now. More concretely, Geras accepted that Marxism had serious gaps and deficits and he named several of them. Its worst political deficiency was class reductionism. Marx himself, Geras claimed, had not suggested that a classless society would end individual antagonisms (cf. 1990: 13). A few pages later, he referred to Isaac Deutscher who also had pointed out that even socialism would not solve all predicaments of the human race (cf. ibid: 16). However, these statements reflect a certain ambivalence: it seems as though Geras, by using the term 'individual antagonisms' for non-class based conflicts, saw a difference between these and structural antagonisms (which seemed to be identical with class antagonisms). This differentiation implicitly comes close to a repetition of the primacy of class oppression – a position frequently criticised by feminist and anti-racist theorists. For Geras, these gaps in Marxism posed no problem – they should be used as opportunities for thought. In his metaphorical language, occasionally difficult to decipher, he seemed to propose using Marxism as an overall framework and adding certain elements that had been dealt with inadequately or not at all by Marxists. Filling gaps meant adding new aspects to Marxism which was different from correcting its potential mistakes. Apart from a new understanding of class, such additions concerned, for example, the future role of politics. Whereas for a long time traditional Marxism had emphasised the 'withering away' of politics and the state, Geras now insisted that politics would only disappear as organised power of one class over another but not as a set of institutions regulating the public sphere of a society. However, this assertion entailed a different form of state and politics – one subordinate to rather than superimposed upon society (cf. ibid: 27).

Nevertheless, a number of modifications were needed. Geras dedicated a long section of his 1990 article to Marx's failure to sketch out a classless society and – since the state would not wither away – its political institutions and he encouraged Marxists to learn from other traditions in this respect, notably from liberalism which had invested much more effort in theorising institutional frameworks that offered protection by and against the state (cf. ibid: 26). Geras received support from Immanuel Wallerstein who stated that for too long the reflections on the shape of classless and socialist societies – something he called "utopistics" – were frowned upon as diversions from struggling for state power and national development (1992: 110). Another correction which had to be made was to engage in debates over welfare and social needs. As Linda Gordon suggested, like conservatives, Marxists had been sceptical about needs discourses because they regarded them as essentialised constructions which disguised the interests of hegemonic cultural and economic actors (cf. 1990: 191). Another reason for their lack of engagement was the assumption that under socialism needs would be satisfied automatically and welfare programmes would thus become superfluous – a perception which Gordon criticised as gender-blind (ibid: 171).

An example of a complete article dealing with corrections of Marxism – though one taking up discussions that had started already before 1989 – was Amy Bartholomew's "Should a Marxist believe in Marx on Rights?", published in 1990. This article is interesting not just in the positions it took but also in the ways in which it referred to Marx in support of its arguments. Rather than offering an outright criticism, Bartholomew started with suggesting the use of Marx's own understanding of a "rich personality" as the basis for a Marxist discussion of rights (1990: 246). She admitted that Marx himself had treated rights ambiguously (cf. ibid: 247) because he saw them as results of particular configurations of social power and believed that workers' interests should not masquerade as universal interests. Instead, Bartholomew argued that in twentieth century capitalism any attempt to take Marx's position seriously would require supporting the notion of rights:

We can take support for the position that if Marx believed communism was a place lacking class conflict and lacking a state in the coercive sense of the word at least, then either he did or should have supported the rights in capitalism which protect people against the existing state and capital (e.g. the right to strike). (ibid: 250)

Thus taking Marx seriously could also mean drawing conclusions from his work which he himself did not. In order to do so, one could turn to other topics in his work, for example, as Bartholomew suggested, to the issue of liberty. The author explained that Marx had a much more comprehensive idea of liberty than liberals because he complemented their negative definition of the concept with attributes like individuality, community, freedom, and choice. Hence negative liberty was a necessary but insufficient precondition for the Marxist concept of liberation. This meant that rights – the right to assemble, to vote, or to strike – could facilitate the process through which the proletariat developed class consciousness and political awareness and, as a consequence, would start the proletariat fighting for the Marxist, comprehensive concept of liberty (cf. ibid: 252). On a more concrete level, on the question of the right to privacy, the author disagreed with Marx more fundamentally: she maintained that while Marx had wished to abolish the differentiation between the public and the private spheres, contemporary Marxists should argue for retaining this difference and call for 'equal opportunities' to choose their privacies:

A socialist conception would not be the anxious privatism that dominates the current conception of privacy. Rather, a socialist privacy right would require a reconceptualization of, and material commitment to, among other things, *freely chosen private spaces*; not only the ones where I just happen to be stuck by virtue of my class, gender and race or other source of a relative lack of power. (ibid: 256; original emphasis)

Bartholomew's contribution argued on two different levels. On the one hand it reflected on the importance of 'bourgeois' concepts (such as civil and political rights) for socialist struggles. Yet on the other it also proposed how to deal with Marxism as a historically specific body of social and political theory rather than as a trans-historical system of thought – the writing of 'Marxism' as 'marxism' attained symbolic importance here. The theory should be used as a point of intellectual departure rather than taken for a holy script:

> I do not accept that even if Marx and the 'marxist' tradition had rejected rights, a contemporary marxist could not believe in rights. Clearly, we should care what Marx said, just as we care what any other major social theorist said. And as 'marxists' there must obviously be some degree of agreement – what that degree is, of course, is properly a matter of lively debate. But it is necessary to distinguish between textual fundamentalism, which is to be rejected, and serious study and evaluation. (ibid: 246)

Finally, Bartholomew pointed out that she regarded one central problem of Marxism and socialism as not adequately solved at the time of writing: socialist strategy's tensions over means and ends (cf. ibid: 256). In her view, the discussion of rights was a valuable way for sensitising oneself vis-à-vis this tension.

In a similar vein, Arthur MacEwan warned against taking Marx's productivist bias, his ideas of economic development, too seriously. He argued that productivism had for a long time hampered Marxist economic strategy and distorted it into support for Keynesianism. In more theoretical terms, this development had obliged the association of productive advances with human progress. Marxists, he was convinced, should stop defining welfare (and progress) as ever more people obtaining and consuming ever more products. Instead, more efforts should be made to achieve non-material goals such as equality, a humane work environment or the liberation of women (cf. 1990: 316). Some authors were convinced that Marxists were well-equipped to theorise on and to find solutions also to environmental problems even though these topics had not been an issue in traditional Marxism. Levins thought about a new and more holistic understanding of historical materialism which perceived human history as the continuation of natural history. Historical change, thus, had consequences for the relationship of (human) organisms and the natural environment. Along the lines of feminist demands for integrating reproduction into analyses of production, Levins saw a need to consider renewal, consumption and waste within analyses of production and reproduction. On the one hand, this led to an enlightened productionism which reflected the consequences of production on the environment. On the other, it constituted a critique of an ecologism that was in the past based on the mythical idea of a balance between nature and human beings (cf. 1990: 343-344).[4]

Eleanor Macdonald suggested a further correction concerning Marxism's conception of itself as a system of thought, a modification which she distilled out of a critical discussion of the work of Jacques Derrida: instead of clinging to the idea of non-ideological knowledge (scientific knowledge in the terminology of structural Marxism, or empirical knowledge, as analytical Marxists would say), Marxists should concede that there were no areas of knowledge untouched by ideology (cf. 1990: 232-233). They should put more effort into discovering the relationship between interpretation and reality – "different forms of ideological mystification" (ibid: 241). A scepticism of grand theory should not stop short of Marxism itself: "What this means for Marxists is that the foundational character of the 'economic' realism, and the corollary privileging of the category of 'class' in political analyses, must be continually drawn into question as a sufficient programme for useful political interpretation" (ibid). Nevertheless, for contributors to *Socialist Register*, Marxism retained a very privileged role in their theoretical reflections. Especially its theory of history – understood flexibly – was of central importance. Most writers saw Marxism more as a system of thought than as a spirit of critique.

Dissent

Contributors to *Dissent* had long awarded Marxism a lower status than had their British colleagues and their (former) opponents working in conjunction with *Monthly Review*. Their move away from Marxism was less the consequence of theoretical considerations than of political ones. For the older generation, estrangement began with a Trotsky-inspired opposition to the Soviet Union and the popular front and later led to an Atlanticist opposition to the allegedly expansionist authoritarianism or, as some said, totalitarianism of the Eastern Bloc. For the younger generation in *Dissent*, politicised around 1968, Marx had always been just one inspiration among many. Looking for alternatives to Marxist orthodoxy, the journal not only published materials from Eastern European dissidents but also retrieved

---

4 Levins quoted Ernesto Galeano who underlined the active nature of human ecology: "We are what we do, but above all what we do to change what we are." (Quoted in Levins 1990: 343)

writers such as Carlo Rosselli, a member of the Italian partisans and a theorist of liberal socialism. Hence for most contributors Marxism constituted just one possible point of theoretical departure and certainly not a holistic system of thought. Furthermore, *Dissent* had started questioning the usefulness of Marxism for the politics of the Western left long before 1989. Many of its contributors considered Marxism responsible for the changes of 1989/91 which they – at least in the early days – unambiguously applauded as the liberation of the people of Eastern Europe. For many *Dissenters*, Marxism as it had been translated into practice in really existing socialism had revealed the shortcomings of Marxism as theory.

Marxism's central problem in *Dissenters*' eyes was the 'simplification assumption' which caused not only a neglect of politics but even made them illegitimate. If 'right' and 'wrong' were given and obvious, institutions of political debate and for procedures regulating political struggle would become obsolete (cf. Ryan 1990: 437). The post-Marxist Cornelius Castoriadis made exactly this observation and added that Marxism formed a special case within a more extended school of thought with an uncritical belief in rationalistic scientism which had all too often produced ideas of orthodoxy – once a position was legitimised by 'science', opposition to it became heterodoxy (cf. 1992: 221). Contributors to *Dissent* thus discussed the question of whether there was any relevance at all for Marxism in the future more extensively than the other journals.

Most authors started out from the observation that Marxism was in decline – but it was pointed out that this phenomenon did not start in the late 1980s. Tying theoretical decline to the political realities in the Eastern European countries, most agreed with Castoriadis's claim that Marxism's collapse had been obvious for thirty years (cf. ibid: 221). The question remained, however, whether this collapse was total – also for Marxism as theory – or whether any aspects of Marxism should be salvaged. Occasionally writers claimed its continuing relevance. Robert Dahl, for example, suggested that, all mistakes notwithstanding, "[m]any of the criticisms of capitalism advanced by socialists were essentially correct" (1990: 226). What remained, however, was a relatively vague idea of critique. Gus Tyler, for instance, wanted to abandon the scientific approach: "Is Marx valid today? Yes, if we allow for the factor of uncertainty and if we admit that there are, in the real world, no pure forms" (1991: 109). He hinted at the demands formulated in the *Communist Manifesto* which called for an end to the proletariat's immiseration and, in Trotskyist terminology, constituted 'immediate demands' which, by and large, had been fulfilled in the twentieth century (at least – though Tyler did not make this specification – in the metropolitan regions of capitalism). Thus his argument might be understood as suggesting that Marxism had succeeded in so far as its 'sensible' demands were concerned. Shlomo Avineri claimed that exactly this had happened over the last decades – both the demands of Marxism and the threat of a possible overthrow of capitalism had allowed social democracy to win concessions:

It is likely that one day, when someone tries to immortalize the person who inspired the complex developments that led to the rise of this system, Karl Marx will, ironically, be seen as the harbinger of this developed neocapitalist world, in which moral suasion, economic interest, and fear of revolution combined in a potent mixture to yield a more humane transformation of a system whose predatory beginnings threatened to destroy it from the outset. (1992: 11)

This made, as he pointed out, the industrialised countries of the West the 'most socialist' ones. This observation could be interpreted in a positive light – but Gitlin, for example, warned that serious problems continued to exist which Marxism was as unable to solve as liberalism. He considered not only recent global threats such as environmental destruction, but also worried about the aspirations which gave rise to identity politics. What they articulated, he suggested, was a demand for commonality politics, for a recognition of the value of community and of the interests of groups, opposed to the universalism (and its companion, individualism) of both traditions of thought, Marxism and liberalism. The ideas of 1968, obviously, had been attempts at bridging the gap between universalist and commonality politics (cf. 1993: 74-75). In short, *Dissenters* understood the events of 1989 primarily as a further and maybe final blow to a Marxism in decline as a political theory. They varied in their opinions about what it had – unintentionally – achieved and what should replace it – either a democratic socialism or a left communitarianism.

However for some contributors, Marxism remained important enough to be worth the attempt of a radical overhaul – which would have far-reaching consequences for socialist theory and strategy. As in the other journals, corrections were understood to have both a theoretical and a political dimension. First of all, the central perception remained the abandoning of an uncritical belief in a rationalism that could replace politics:

What socialism involves, if not a measure of collective social control over decisions that under pure capitalism are left to actors in the market place, I do not know. But what has to be abandoned is any thought that we shall achieve Marx's vision of a world in which 'society' rationally chooses what to consume, how to produce, and how to distribute it, as if 'society' was a single individual writ large. (Ryan 1990: 437)

Castoriadis pointed out that to make such alterations would amount to a liberation of Marxism (or socialism) from the capitalist imaginary that hampered it: from the centrality of production and economic growth, the mythology of progress, the mastery of humans over nature and themselves, the acceptance of work as a specific sphere of social organisation, and the existence of a bureaucracy (cf. 1992: 221). Gus Tyler summed up these suggestions by claiming that it was "timely to make two small adjustments in Marx: first, instead of economic determinism, substitute societal indeterminism; second, instead of 'forms' substitute norms to guide human behavior – individually and collectively" (cf. 1991: 110). The over-reliance on economic and scientific rationalism reflected an insufficient consideration of the discursive, ideological and organisational dimensions of societal life. As again Castoriadis explained, Marx had failed to see that humans produced not only tools and history but also significations and institutions. This realization had repercussions for political struggle. Others added further miscalculations: Daniel Bell, for example, portrayed classical Marxists as believing that socialism would overcome scarcity and thus it would only have to find ways of distributing products rather than organising production (cf. 1991: 50). Its idea of economic planning was closely linked to its trust in unlimited growth. Another mistake, according to Shlomo Avineri, was Marxism's neglect, its negative or instrumental view of nationalism – he called nationalism Marxism's "black hole" (1990: 447). This reduction of nationalism to a pre-modern phenomenon or, in Hobsbawm's words, to a "building block of capitalism", had resulted in a lack of support for "national liberation" as such (ibid: 448-449). Nationalism, however, was one of the issues on which *Dissent* differentiated between classical and neo-Marxism. Avineri conceded that some theorists of the latter variety had come to terms with the autonomous, emancipatory power of nationalism (ibid: 452). Finally, the French writer Michel Wieviorka suggested a shift of emphasis concerning the role of work in socialist theory. The concept of work should not be interpreted a euphemism for wage slavery and in the twentieth century oppression was at least as likely to stem from exclusion as from exploitation:

What counts now is not social relationships, but the lack of them; not the relationship of domination to exploitation, but the growing separation between the excluded and those who 'belong' – who continue to work, to earn a salary and to consume. [...] Today no one would seriously claim that by casting off its chains, the proletariat will liberate all humanity. The worst crises are no longer those of exploited workers, who now seem to occupy a privileged position – one they want to protect – but rather those of men and women deprived of work. (1994: 249)

Castoriadis took up the issue of agency and determinism. He identified two dangers in traditional Marxism's teleological-determinist approach: on the one hand, it simply ignored the possibility of agency and thus of choice and the existence of alternatives, on the other, it de-legitimised opposition and popular struggle because history was on the side of those who claimed to represent it. He insisted that the idea of a future better than the past would make politics meaningless, that historical change would be regarded as automatically positive and that altogether this amounted to a religious rather than a self-critical approach (cf. 1992: 223). He pleaded instead for the importance of politics: "The choice when brought to bear on the form of institutions, is politics properly understood. And for reasons mentioned above, it is this possibility of choice – thus, of politics – that Marx's conception makes impossible" (ibid).

Nevertheless, he remained convinced that useful elements in Marxist theory could be picked for a project of social and individual autonomy and its "kernel", free thinking, created through human actions:

[W]hat remains is what I have called 'the other element' in Marx: the element that stresses human activity, affirms that humans make their own history under determinate conditions generally without knowing it, and asserts that we have to find in actual historical reality the factors tending to transform this same reality. (ibid: 222)

For most *Dissenters*, Marxism had been reduced to *one* inspiration for reflections on socialism. They privileged Marxism's humanist elements over its scientific claims. For them, the writings of Marx could only make limited contributions to a critical perspective of the left.

Monthly Review

Monthly Review was the journal which came closest to 'traditional' Marxist positions – though the spectrum of opinions it published was wider. Thus it was not surprising that it commented only rarely on the responsibilities of Marxism for the deficiencies and the eventual breakdown of the Eastern Bloc – which it acknowledged as final and irreversible later than the others. The only voice which drew a direct line between Marxism and the lack of democracy in the socialist states, once more, was Ralph Miliband – Miliband was held in high esteem by the editors of the journal. He hinted, in an article called "Socialism in Question", at Marx's and Lenin's beliefs in forms of semi-direct democracy and explained: "I do not believe that this is a good recipe for the socialist exercise of power, not at any rate for a very long time to come, when a new breed of people will have been produced by a prolonged experience of socialist relations of life" (1991: 21). Others, among them Michael Löwy in his article "Twelve Theses on the Crisis of 'Really Existing Socialism'" (he chose this title as late as 1991), denied that such a direct link to Marx could be drawn and blamed anti-Marxist rhetoric for doing so:[5]

> Nobody would make Descartes responsible for the French colonial wars, nor Jesus for the Inquisition, even less Thomas Jefferson for the U.S. invasion of Vietnam. But it has been made to seem that Karl Marx built the Berlin Wall and nominated Ceaucescu the leader of the Romanian Communist Party. (1991: 36)

This view was balanced by several contributors' observation that most Marxists had long been too apologetic about the countries of the Eastern Bloc – countries that they had, as Alan Wald admitted, despite all scepticism felt close to (cf. 1991: 61). Wald's remark was meant as a warning against moving on too easily to a barely altered version of Marxism without

---

5   This line of argument was very similar to Thompson's critique in *New Left Review* on blaming the French Revolution for the guillotine.

taking notice of what had happened. It was directed against Manning Marable, author of an article on "Remaking American Marxism" (1991), which Wald criticised for its strategic proposals. In Wald's eyes, Marable propagated a continuation of vanguardist and democratic-centralist decision-making structures though now in alliance with social democrats from the left wing of the Democratic Party (cf. Wald 1991: 61-62). Similarly, Alberto Prago took issue with Carl Marzani's view that the defeat of the Eastern Bloc was declared prematurely and that its societies had achieved much more than was commonly admitted (cf. Marzani 1990). Prago conceded that Marxists (like Marzani and himself) should have begun much earlier to critically examine the Soviet Union and the states of the Eastern Bloc: "He [Marzani; SB] – and I and other Marxists – should have employed it [Marxism; SB] in examining the nature of Soviet society, *before* the Khrushchev revelations" (1990: 54; original emphasis). The exiled Hungarian Marxist István Mészáros took up the topic of critique and pointed out that 20th century Marxists had either failed to address moral and political questions or were prevented from doing so by Stalin's ban on political theory and philosophy. Under these circumstances, Lukács's and Kautsky's reflections remained isolated (cf. 1993). Western Marxists avoided the issue and preferred to move into new theoretical terrain:

In this context, even Marx's own position could be, and has been, grossly misrepresented. The peculiar notion which labelled Marx 'a theoretical anti-humanist' – a notion born partly out of ignorance and partly out of a quite undeserved respect for Stalin's position which condemned preoccupation with these matters as inadmissible 'moralizing' – is a well-known example of such misrepresentation. (ibid: 33-34)

Hence, contributors to *Monthly Review* seemed to be generally convinced that although Marxism was not responsible for the deficiencies of the socialism of the Eastern Bloc and of the changes of 1989, Marxists to a certain extent were. Their abstention from critique and independent thought had diminished chances for a future radical political model because they had failed to rescue Marxism from being associated with Stalinist bureaucratic systems (cf. Löwy 1991: 35). This failure would have repercussions for the importance and status of Marxism after 1989: while Marxists believed that its strength was as important as ever in a historical situation dominated by a triumphant capitalism, this opinion was shared by few contemporaries. Löwy contended that Marxists should blame themselves for this situation because many had exempted really existing socialism from Marxist critique. Nevertheless, he declared majority opinion to be wrong:

What is being thrown away with the (extremely dirty) bathwater – the anti-democratic, bureaucratic, often totalitarian nature of the non-capitalist societies and of their system of centralized planning is the baby – the idea of moving beyond capitalism toward a democratically planned economy. (ibid: 37-38)

Löwy suggested an ensemble of features which Marxism still had to offer – a philosophy of praxis, the dialectical materialist method, the analysis of commodity fetishism, workers' self-emancipation, the utopia of a classless and stateless society (ibid: 39). He quoted Marx in order to propose that after 1989 Marxism had to be more than ever a "ruthless criticism of all that is" (ibid). He also referred to other Marxists when pointing out that the 'principle of hope' also belonged to its central tenets (ibid: 39-40). This hope, called by others the visionary or the utopian element, was central for many contributors (cf. Wallis 1991: 9; Kovel 1994)

Since authors were aware that as a system of thought and as a political programme Marxism was seriously affected by recent events, they discussed how to handle this situation. The most promising way out of this impasse for *Monthly Review* was to return to Marxist basics – as evidenced by their extended debate on Cornel West's book *The Ethical Dimension of Marxist Thought* which attempted an innovative reading of Marx, one based more on its moral than on its scientific claims. Although written in the 1970s, in 1993 West's study was debated in the journal with the intent of introducing a discussion on an 'ethical Marxism'. One of the journal's contributors to the discussion defined the relationship between the events of 1989/91 and the relevance of Marxism as dialectical rather than unidirectional: Guillermo Bowie explained that "[i]t now seems that socialist thought has entered a new phase that forsakes Marxist thought and praxis. The loss of faith has both contributed to and resulted from the collapse of European socialist states." (1993: 38) Confusion over the state of affairs was not limited to the fate of the Eastern Bloc, but characterised Marxist philosophy in the West too (cf. Monthly Review 1993: 22). Feasible or possible alternatives seemed few at the time; socialist thought had not entered a new phase but stopped at a dead end (cf. Kovel 1994a: 54). Cornel

West himself described the Marxist left as facing a threefold challenge in this situation – one organisational, one intellectual, and one existential (cf. 1993: 57). This echoed the position of Paul Buhle who saw Marxist theory in an odd predicament after its geographical dislocation from its base in the Eastern Bloc, faced with the shrinkage of its assumed political agents – the working classes – in the West and confronted with the epistemological pessimism cultivated in postmodern social theories (cf. 1990: 43).

Contributors united around a shared belief in the theoretical superiority of Marxism even if some of them enhanced the philosophy with elements of postmodernism and new historicism – this was how Allison Jaggar characterised West's work mentioned above. Jaggar pointed to the holistic nature of Marxism that set it apart from "bourgeois social science" with its focus on ossified and isolated facts (1993: 20). She then defined Marxism as simultaneously descriptive, explanatory, critical, and prescriptive and as necessarily calling for changing the world (ibid: 21). In other words, a thorough Marxist analysis would still have the capacity to generate an adequate political strategy. Such a perspective implies that even after 1989, Marxism remained a comprehensive system of thought and as such more than one mere social theory among many. Revealing statements include those by Kovel, written in an obituary for Miliband, which listed Marxism's many different dimensions:

There are of course many facets to Marxism, from deep philosophical presuppositions such as materialism or dialectics to a particular/economic analysis of current events. But class struggle is the conceptual linchpin inasmuch as it is here that Marxists have to *fight* for the truth they believe in. (1994: 52; original emphasis)

Important as the different dimensions are, the most central issue came towards the end of his passage: Marxism is something to *believe in*. The problem of belief – often more closely related with religion and politics than with theory and analysis – provokes the question of the base on which it is built. Is belief – and are the ethical guidelines following from it – completely arbitrary? Contributors hinted at the possibility of avoiding ethical foundationalism and absolutism as well as relativism. This became the central topic within the discussion on Cornel West's work when he argued that Marx had developed a concept of justice that based social criticism on discursive rather than trans-historical values. Such a position allowed for the combination of Christian values such as service, love, and humility with socialist ones like freedom, justice, and equality (cf. Jaggar 1993: 20). Jaggar, in her critical evaluation of West's arguments, remained sceptical about his discursive approach to justification – which put West on a line with Kant, the pragmatists, Rawls and Habermas – and proposed instead a dialectical and procedural – in other words, a more traditionally Marxist – approach:

> If contemporary leftists were explicit in expressing an epistemic as well as political and moral commitment to creating the social conditions that would facilitate more open discussion and critical dialogue, this would dispel the spectres of relativism and even conservatism that otherwise haunt West's conventionalist conception of justification, despite his declared aim of exorcising them. (ibid: 27)

Foster pointed out that these debates revived an old tradition of reflections on how to find 'moral objectivity' and to convince critics, which included Marxists such as Norman Geras who according to Foster had accused Marxism of using moral judgment but rejecting morality, that a difference existed between 'soft' – historically specific, discursively constructed – objectivity and relativism (cf. 1993: 10-12).[6]

With the discussion of Cornel West's work, *Monthly Review* made clear that it considered the development of a socialist ethics to be important and that Marxism was indispensable for such an undertaking. West described Marx's move from a search for philosophical certainty to a focus on social criticism and change, accompanied by a move from philosophical to theoretical language.[7] While West accepted that there was no human essence

---

6 Foster distinguished three quests for moral objectivity: Engels's teleological quest (which regarded proletarian morality as the root of a socialist morality to become fully developed through the transcendence of class divisions), Kautsky's naturalistic quest (which located the base of morality in human needs and human nature), and Lukacs's ontological quest (which combined historicism with a belief in an essence of human beings and came closest to West's considerations)(cf. Foster 1993: 11-12)..

7 Others disagreed with West's description of this move as a smooth and straightforward operation. Jaggar, for example, suggested that there were continuing tensions in Marx's work between 'philosophy' and 'theory' (cf. 1993: 23)

and that human identities were the products of the ensemble of social relations they experienced, he believed in their capability of developing improved forms of humane moralities in *collective* processes – through community-wide agreements which created more just and more equal societies (cf. Foster 1993: 12-15). Foster illustrated this point with an example: "It is not to nineteenth century moral philosophers, after all, that the world owes the conviction that slavery is evil; rather the world was forced to acknowledge the reality of this evil as the result of an historical struggle for human freedom" (ibid: 15). If this experience was generalised, Foster believed that one could argue in the following way: "In short morality was not a form of philosophical truth that could be abstractly advanced or defended, but something real, in the sense that it was the object of struggle for communities of individuals actively engaged in the changing of the conditions of human community" (ibid: 13). It was this tying of morality to collective struggle and discursive action that distinguished moral historicism from both, moral relativism and moral essentialism. In this sense, Marxism provided a very useful toolkit for the development of a socialist ethics.

Authors in *Monthly Review* argued for a weak form of historical directionality but did not explicitly defend economic determination. In an anonymous "Review of the Month" with the title "Where are we going?" published in 1991, the editors explained how they tried to draw lessons from history. They contended that the past had opened up certain routes and closed others: "If there is a science of history, it has to do not with predictions but with identifying and studying these determinations of the past with a view to making meaningful choices for the future" (Monthly Review 1991: 3). If there was any foundation for determinist ideas, these seemed to lie in the interrelationship of human beings and social conditions rather than in the social conditions themselves. This premise constituted the spiritual element in *Monthly Review's* outlook which set it apart from the other journals. Amin explained that human beings were metaphysical beings because they questioned the meaning of their lives (cf. Amin 1993: 49). As a consequence, they possessed a desire for transcendence which manifested itself in revolutions (cf. Buhle 1990: 50). To combine such a desire with knowledge gained from analyses of the past remained, according to the journal, the task of Marxists – especially in a time when others declared the end of history. For West, Marxism combined a moderate historicism with the search for a new foundationalist approach to ethics – for the purpose of finding philosophical justifications for moral choices.

Monthly Review remained convinced that, objectively, Marxism remained as relevant for the future as it had always been – as long as, to use Wood's phrase, social relations were embedded in economic relations (cf. 1994a: 20). As Victor Wallis explained in one of the articles which tried to reformulate tasks for the American left: "In short, capitalism is as damaging as ever, and the longer it hangs on, the more dangerous it gets. The objective basis for Marxism – the systematic search for an alternative to capitalism – has therefore never been stronger" (cf. 1991: 6). Capitalism inevitably produced its 'other' and Marxism still provided the most appropriate theoretical model for this other. Hence its relevance rested on political conditions and on its theoretical achievements. The fact that capitalism had developed in unforeseen directions in the 20th century did not make Marx's work less valuable because this process had not challenged, as Harry Magdoff pointed out, the essentials of Marx's laws of motion (cf. 1991: 1). Others argued that the importance of Marxism had been vindicated through recent changes in the U.S. class structure, as Richard A. Cloward and Frances Fox Piven made clear. The preceding two decades had seen a "new class war" that had produced, in Marxist terminology, a "reserve army of labor" and thus weakened the workers' bargaining power (1991: 26-27). Nevertheless, capitalism had produced additional problems, environmental destruction perhaps being the gravest. *Monthly Review* took ecological problems even more seriously than the others. It argued for a politicisation of ecology (cf. Weston 1990) and listed Marxism as one among the radical ecological perspectives alongside deep ecology, social ecology, bioregionalism, and eco-feminism (cf. Yih 1990: 16). All of these positions shared a fundamental critique of the prevailing social, economic and political order (ibid). Yet contributors were convinced that Marxism was better equipped for the pursuit of a radical environmentalism than the other approaches because it entailed possibilities for combining issues of justice and equality with environmental concerns and could thus avoid the traps of quasi-Malthusian misanthropy. The central contribution that Marxism could make to environmentalism consisted of the understanding of the politics of ecology as the politics of production and exchange (ibid: 24). Using the tools of dialectical materialism and theories of accumulation, Marxism could also provide a theoretical framework for environmental political action that was superior to approaches such as ecological anarchism or deep ecology (ibid: 19).[8]

Victor Wallis in pointing out that Marxism was "bigger than Marx", argued that the label should be attached to all people who worked in analysing and for overcoming the systematic dimension of oppression (cf. 1991: 10): "Marxism is important because instead of just dealing with oppression on a case-by-case basis, or even with all the forms of all the oppressions at once, it deals with the *totality* of oppression in all of its interrelationships" (ibid: 8). This notion of totality made Marxism indispensable. Even if groups suffering from particular types of oppression were not aware of this totality, the oppressive structure used it to their advantage. This structure consisted of the capitalist class and "the entire complex of economic, military, and cultural instruments over which this class presides" (ibid). Only Marxism, Wallis believed, could prevent oppressed people from engaging in futile struggles against single oppressions and isolated phenomena, which would mean "to settle for a merely spasmodic response-mechanism to the framework imposed by capital" (ibid: 9).

Another important insight of Marxism which, according to Wood, was in danger of getting lost in the aftermath of 1989 was the pervasiveness of compulsion as an organising principle of market relations. In an article which commemorated E. P. Thompson and his work, she argued against a reading of Marx that interpreted the change from feudalism to capitalism as progress and liberation, and instead explained it like Thompson had as a process in which social relations became embedded in market relations (1994: 15-20). The contemporary relevance of this interpretation lay in the tendency among Marxists to regard markets as parts of emancipatory projects rather than as instruments of class power which, in the late twentieth century, were used to control labour and to discipline Third World countries and the 'new democracies' of the former Eastern Bloc (cf. ibid: 39).

---

8   At the same time, the journal was very critical of Marixsm's deficiencies in this field. They clustered around a quasi-liberal understanding of productionism and progress, based on scientific rationality. Yih criticized Marx's theory of value in particular because it was restricted to labour time and ignored the 'consumption' of nature involved in the production process. Accordingly, the value of nature remained unclear and, consequently, easy to 'externalise' (cf. 1990: 21-23).

Finally, Marxism was able to explain the unavoidable link of capitalist success and failure. Such a perspective, based on Paul Sweezy's theory of accumulation and overproduction, interpreted the expansion of the forces of production and the simultaneous growth of misery as mutually dependent (cf. Magdoff 1991: 1). This insurmountable problem of capitalism was ignored by those organising political change in Eastern Europe. Contributors to the journal claimed that in the early 1990s the collapse of the Eastern Bloc was interpreted as a quasi-natural incident which proved the inescapability of capitalism's economic laws. Marxism was as needed as ever for a deconstruction of this myth. Amin emphasised in this context that Marx's most important contribution to political economy consisted of the distinction between the laws of nature and the laws of economics. Only an understanding of the 'laws' of the economy as being internal to society – and imposed on parts of it – would open up space for political change (cf. 1991: 48).

Although *Monthly Review* awarded Marxism an important status, it recognised areas where Marxism needed modification. Three broad – and in many ways interrelated – weaknesses were identified. The first concerned the importance of human identity and subjectivity. As Jack Weston argued in his article "For an Ecological Politics of Hope", Marxists should learn to accept that religion and spirituality could play a positive role in social change, a perception that was to go hand-in-hand with transcending the traditional ignorance about 'primitive' societies and their forms of knowledge (1990: 11). Joel Kovel, who in his work tried to synthesise Marxism and psychoanalysis and who reflected on the conditions of human subjectivity, reiterated the point when he explained, with a bow towards Marx, that the latter indeed had accepted a positive function of spirituality (cf. 1994: 33). Kovel suggested that it was "exactly what Marxism needs to reclaim itself in its present dark hour" (ibid: 34). Though he admitted that spirituality constituted an ambiguous concept that had also played its part in Nazism and Soviet gigantism, he maintained that it could have human and social significance and provide the base from which to develop ethical guidelines: "The issue is not to turn Marxists into meditators. It is rather to cultivate a certain needed humility and openness to the wonders of the world" (ibid: 40). According to Buhle, Kovel's work was extremely important because it drew parallels between Marxist concepts of 'consciousness' and religious concepts of 'faith'.[9] Further, Kovel sketched out a Marxist understanding of personality formation that relied not only on Freud but also on Bachtin. Hence it succeeded in transcending the boundary between self and society. The integration of psychological theories was necessary, Buhle suggested, in order to come to terms with 'irrational' developments such as, for example, the recapturing of revolutionary societies through neo-colonialism (1990: 47).[10]

The second important set of corrections concerned Marxism's roots in nineteenth century reality and science. Of course no one doubted that important changes in capitalism had occurred since the early stage of industrialism which Marx and his contemporaries had witnessed. Nevertheless, a number of features were regarded as important enough to be mentioned in the pages of *Monthly Review*. Editor Sweezy excused Marx's exaggerated optimism with regard to the capacity of the working class's ability to act collectively as stemming from the comparatively low level of social stratification and differentiation in the 19th century (cf. Watanabe & Wakima 1990: 1-2). The pervasiveness of class antagonisms at the time could also explain why other differentiations were neglected. Weston mentioned the importance of patriarchy, racism, and condescension in respect to 'primitive' societies as expressions of such anachronistic views (cf. 1990: 11). Löwy traced such deficiencies back to a positivist scientific model which Marxism shared with the mainstream sciences of its time:

As a social scientist Marx did not always transcend the bourgeois/positivist model, based on the arbitrary extension to the historical sphere of the epistemological paradigm of the natural sciences, with its laws, its determinism, its purely objective predictions, and linear development – a tendency pushed to its logical conclusions by a certain kind of Marxism, from Plekhanov to Louis Althusser. (1991: 38-9)

---

9 Kovel interpreted 'revolution' as a desire for transcendence manifested in history (cf. Buhle 1990: 50).
10 Buhle did not make it clear as to which societies he was referring – he did not mention the Eastern Bloc (which to describe as neo-colonised would be questionable). In the America of the early 1990s, Nicaragua might have come to mind as a typical example.

Amin claimed that Marx managed at least to move beyond traditional economics which he described in the following way: "Bourgeois thought is founded on the totalitarianism of the economic, expressed every day in naïve terms by those who say that 'the economy *forces* us to do this'" (1993: 51). Still, Marxism was less successful in overcoming other deficiencies of enlightenment thought which had revolted against religion but "did not, however, substitute for religion anything very convincing, only an insipid behavioralism based on existing social practice" (ibid: 46). As a consequence, bourgeois social science and Marxism shared a mechanistic view of society. Dialectical materialism, according to Amin a centrepiece of what he called "vulgar Marxism", was a reiteration of bourgeois differentiation of nature, society, and the individual. Hence all societies had functioned with some form of alienation –religious, market-oriented, or economic. This disaffection had harmed both human emancipation and theoretical reflection: "The theories of power and ideology were blocked [by 'vulgar Marxism'; SB] in their development and reduced to the pseudotheory of 'reflection'" (ibid: 52). Under this assumption, human emancipation became identical with an increase in production and wealth.

Thirdly, several contributors demanded a number of concrete changes, for example, a transcending of Marxism's latent Eurocentrism (cf. Boggs 1990: 14). Guillermo Bowie welcomed West's intervention as an "indigenization of Marxist thought, i.e. as an attempt at applying Marxism to North American culture and society where issues of racism, sexism and religious faith figure prominently" (1993: 37; see also Vilas 1990: 102; Cushman-Wood 1993: 27-30). As early as 1990, Prabhat Patnaik called for the revival of one particular strand of Marxist theory and analysis that while though earlier had constituted a central element, was at the time was almost forgotten: the issue of imperialism. For the author, its disappearance from debate was surprising because its importance had never been doubted (cf. 1990: 1-2). Patnaik was convinced that a modernised theory of imperialism could provide insights not only into U.S. interventions in Central America, but also into recent changes in Eastern Europe (ibid). He suggested that the concept of imperialism could explain why socialism did not develop more successfully in the 'peripheral states' of capitalism and why Herbert Marcuse and numerous U.S. Marxists had erred when they had put their hopes in peripheral challenges to the metropolises (ibid: 1-5). Patnaik was convinced, and quoted Althusser to support his argument, that theoretical concepts could not be discarded "like old shoes" – they came back and haunted you (ibid: 6).[11] To expect moves towards socialism from the peripheries rather than from the centres, posed, of course, a challenge per se to classical Marxism. Nevertheless, the analysis of the possibilities of such activities became a requirement according to Kovel. He explained once more that whereas Marx had anticipated the capitalist economy's coming to power, thinkers now had to deal with the maturation of capitalist society – the penetration of capitalist principles and relations into all parts of the globe and all areas of life (cf. 1994: 53). To focus on such changes in detail, as Jaggar suggested, should become the core task of Marxism in the years to come and this embracing of a modest analytical Marxism did not make its work less important. It still could fulfil the

> urgent political task of developing historically specific accounts of structures such as modes of production, state apparatuses and bureaucracies, and socially detailed analyses of how such structures shape and are shaped by cultural agents. These theoretic analyses will make no pretensions to philosophic necessity; instead, their adequacy will be determined experimentally and empirically. They will be fallible but still rationally and empirically warranted. (1993: 23)

However, Marxists had to move beyond their traditional concern with analytical work, as Miliband explained: "But the strength of Marxism has never been that it offers ready-made solutions to contradictions which are an intrinsic part of real life: it is rather that it highlights these contradictions and challenges us to find ways of resolving them, or at least of attenuating them" (1991: 25). In this sense, moving beyond analytical work meant moving beyond Marxism: although writers did not use the terms of utopia and utopistics, their emphasis on values and ethics pointed into exactly this direction. Many contributions must be read as appeals to bridge the gap between analysis and belief; as claims that linking politics to morality was inescapable and that all major works on political theory were at the same time works on ethics at the same time (cf. Mészáros 1993: 34). Generally, contributors to *Monthly Review* considered Marxism to be an important

---

[11] Looking back from the early 21st century, this indeed was a prescient statement although the debate on 'new imperialism' focused more on the post-Cold War era.

social and political-economic theory – but as one that needed complementation, especially by timely reflections on ethics.

3.2. The Retrieval of Classics from the Radical and Socialist Traditions

Although Marxism was not abandoned in the journals, it was widely accepted that it needed new inspiration to find meaningful responses to the questions posed by the changes of 1989/91. Therefore, many intellectuals began to reconsider the contributions of thinkers from a more broadly defined socialist or radical tradition. Among those retrieved were some, such as Rosa Luxemburg, who had always been held in high esteem. Yet the list also included others who had been harshly criticised in the past, for example, Karl Kautsky. One finds interesting differences between the journals in terms of the space devoted to these re-readings and in how far they transcended their theoretical core positions. These differences are telling with regard to how seriously contributors felt challenged by recent changes but also concerning the question as to what they considered to be the most urgent renovation work.

New Left Review

A serious discussion of 'classics' took place in the pages of *New Left Review*. The journal published two complete articles, one by Norman Geras and one by Peter Wollen, devoted to re-evaluating the works of Rosa Luxemburg and Karl Kautsky. A considerable number of additional names were listed and their ideas were more briefly discussed in two other articles.[12] Luxemburg had long been treated with great sympathy, because, having been one of the most strongly committed Marxists, she had been heavily critical about vanguardism and the lack of democracy in the revolutionary Soviet Union. Her perspective, however, included tensions and

---

12 *New Left Review* had always been more interested in discussing left social theory than *Socialist Register*. This might explain its more comprehensive coverage in the early 1990s. This contradicted Anderson's earlier thesis in his *Considerations on Western Marxism*, that the Western Marxism of the interwar years had been formulated in a period of defeat and pessimism and was thus only of limited value for a renewal of socialist thought (Anderson 1976).

ambiguities that were well-known to left intellectuals. Norman Geras, probably the British political theorist most familiar with Luxemburg's work, emphasised, just as Daniel Singer, several of these points including her conviction that change had to come from below (cf. 1994: 95), her "instrumentalist" view of parties, leaders, and parliaments (ibid); and her belief that since the shape of socialism was not pre-defined but an "open horizon" (ibid: 97) the revolution always had to stop and criticise itself (ibid: 96). In terms of the latter, she claimed that in order to do so, a strict adherence to formal democratic principles had to be guaranteed: "As in the manner so in the product of it, much remains to be determined through the experience of the process itself. And this requires that what would today generally be called liberal norms of political life must govern that process" (ibid). According to Luxemburg's thinking, emancipation through oppression of liberties seemed to be a contradiction in terms: "[J]ust because what is envisaged is an emancipation, those carrying it through have to be free in their constructive enterprise." (ibid: 100) She spoke of "sacred personal opinions", freedom of the press, the right of assembly and the importance of public life – but as Geras pointed out, this was not a "revisionist" position. Rather the goal of socialism and communism in the Marxist sense remained a "regulative idea", committing the open and democratic process to concrete values and goals (ibid: 98-100). As the most important goals in Luxemburg's work Geras listed working-class liberation, social equality, an end to exploitation, communal property, a planned economy and socialist democracy (ibid: 100). These were, according to him, "a set of very general principles, to be realized in institutional forms that have yet to be worked out." (ibid)

The most interesting part of Geras's article on Luxemburg concerned the ambivalences in the latter's work. He conceded that with her famous formulation of "socialism or barbarism", Luxemburg broke with Marxist historical and economic determinism. However, Geras criticised the fact that she remained entrapped in what could be called a 'moral determinism'. She left no doubt that there was but one outcome of democratic agency – socialism – and that Marxism was *the* system of thought to be employed in the emancipatory struggle of the proletariat (ibid: 105). This parochialism had consequences for those studying Luxemburg's work: "While it may not strictly gainsay the freedom of the one who thinks differently, it does suggest there is not much point in thinking too differently" (ibid). Geras instead proposed a more open struggle for emancipation:

> How can any outcome be that certain, so much of whose exact shape and content, empirical working out, practical trial, variation and negotiation, is still so open? Socialists have every reason to hope and strive for the kind of world they do. But to count on the certainty of its democratic achievement when there is so much to be settled in both the 'what' and the 'how' of it, this has been a mistake, not only of Marxist thought. Socialism may be a possibility, and that is all. (ibid: 102)

He gave two reasons why he regarded the critical re-reading of Luxemburg to be important: firstly, the analysis of the ambivalences in her work suggested that deficiencies existed in Marx's writings themselves. They could not be explained away as distortions for which others, for example Lenin and Stalin, had to take responsibility (ibid: 94). Secondly, for reconciling socialism's struggles with democratic procedures, the retrieval of socialist classics could provide help, but only up to a certain extent: "This may perhaps contribute something to a wider process of democratising socialist thought: in the sense here, be it noted, not of rendering democratic what was not; but of seeking to make more democratic what has always aspired to be so" (ibid: 94-95). For Geras, the lesson to be drawn seemed to be the prioritising of democratic principles over the achievement of socialism. While socialism was a possibility, democracy was a necessity. However, he did not make this point explicitly, perhaps because doing so would have made him, according to his own argument, a 'revisionist'.

More surprising than expressions of sympathy for Luxemburg was the rehabilitation of Kautsky, whom twentieth century leftists – including those from the 1968 generation, at least according to Peter Wollen – generally had little time for (cf. 1993: 92). Wollen argued that a return to Kautsky could be helpful in the climate of 'post-communism' since the latter was a thinker who had been not only criticised but treated as a traitor by all – Eastern Bloc Communists, Trotskyists and Western Marxists (ibid: 86-87). He explained that the importance of Kautsky lay in three aspects of his work: Kautsky had been convinced of the need to accept formal democratic principles, he had developed a theory of ultra-imperialism and he was opposed, at least in most of his statements, to any attempts at accelerating history. These assumptions amounted to a critique of vanguardism which led Kautsky to condemn what he called the "barbaric road to socialism" in the Soviet Union, based on forced labour and super exploitation (ibid): According to Wollen, "for Kautsky, this policy flew in the face of reason, democratic values, and, most important of all, Marxism. [...] This was indeed, in Gramsci's words, the 'revolution against *Das Kapital*'" (ibid: 87). In the early 1990s, the criticising of the undemocratic turn at the end of the Russian revolution was, of course, a position often taken. Interestingly however, Wollen linked this critique with a new emphasis on a differently understood scientific, deterministic approach:

Now that the collapse of Soviet Communism has changed the situation once again, perhaps it is time to reconsider Kautsky and the 'classical Marxist' tradition he represented. Indeed, perhaps it is time for a more general reappraisal of scientism, historicism and economism, the principal evils his work was said to represent. (ibid: 92)

This scientific approach should not be revived in order to develop a new version of a hermetic, determinist teleology, but to identify features that were indispensable for a situation in which a transformation towards a socialist society would become possible and might actually start. Wollen pleaded that academics should take seriously the historical materialist insight that socialism could only be attained once capitalism provided certain economic preconditions such as a sufficiently advanced development of productive forces, which would allow for the achievement of "full democracy" and the political hegemony of the working class (ibid). With regard to internationalism, the author drew parallels between Kautsky's "ultra-imperialism" and Wallerstein's world-systems theory. Both described a "long-range system alternation between rivalry and hegemony within capitalist world-systems" (ibid: 93). Ultra-imperialism could eventually create a situation in which change on a global scale emerged as a realistic option – then, and only then, would socialism become possible (ibid). Wollen argued with Kautsky that Lenin's strategy had been wrong and that it had started a process which reduced Marxism to a self-serving orthodoxy. He observed a more recent tendency, represented by Ernest Mandel and Fredric Jameson, which again was too 'optimistic' in its observations of capitalist crisis and retreat (ibid). However, as in the case of Luxemburg, Wollen admitted that Kautsky's approach was also not free of ambivalences and that the clarification of such was an important task for left intellectuals in times of post-communism:

> At the same time we should also note how Luxemburg, Lenin and Kautsky all fell prey, in different ways, to the wish to accelerate history. Socialists should accept that it may be better to have a realistic hope, however historically distant, than a false hope based on a deformed foreshortening, however immediate and close at hand it may seem to be. We should once again give priority to the goal rather than to the movement. We must reverse the terms set so disastrously in the Soviet Union, where indeed the Communist movement became everything and the goal of socialism nothing. (ibid)

Obviously Geras and Wollen (and Luxemburg and Kautsky) agreed on some points and disagreed on others. Whereas Geras emphasised agency (proceeding towards socialism on a democratic road), Wollen stressed structure (the preconditions for a transition to socialism must exist). Both of them, however, saw formal democracy as central and, moreover, both refrained from giving detailed accounts of the institutional set-up of a socialist society which other authors in *New Left Review* prioritised as the major task of the time.

Additionally, Robin Blackburn who traced back the deficiencies of the Soviet Union to certain shades of Marxist theory presented a list of famous names and discussed their potential for offering corrections and alternatives to Marxism. The core of his article's critique was directed against the Soviet Union's interpretation of the dictatorship of the proletariat as a bureaucratic party dictatorship. Blackburn emphasised that this substitution was criticised by Kautsky (who as Lenin's teacher felt personal responsibility) as well as by numerous other individuals and groups from the Mensheviks to the Eurocommunists (cf. 1991: 179) as it gave rise to the two main pathologies of the Soviet system: the neglect of political liberties (ibid: 191) and the inability to organise a differentiated economy (cf. ibid: 200). Blackburn explained that Kautsky had diagnosed the intricate linkage between these two defects and that the latter had hinted at the incompatibility of military-like command structures with a creative workforce (cf. ibid: 198). Blackburn called for a reconsideration of all those writers and activists who saw themselves in the Marxist tradition, but who in turn had contradicted the Soviet Union's claim to represent the only valid version of the

Marxist programme, opposed press censorship and arbitrary state power, and gave priority to democratic practices – from Kautsky and Trotsky via the Austro-Marxists to C.L.R. James. However, Blackburn also went one step further. He pointed to alternative sources of socialism from nineteenth century utopian novels to anarchists like Bakunin (cf. ibid: 183; 187). Although Blackburn suggested listening to such individuals, in many cases he remained unconvinced of the alternatives they suggested. For example, though he entertained Bakunin's criticisms that the Bolshevists had too narrow a definition of the working class and that the 'revolutionary state' was in danger of being ruled by a 'scientific intelligence', Blackburn remained sceptical both of the anarchist's alternatives and, furthermore, of all suggestions which laboured under the simplification assumption and expected the withering away of the state and institutional politics (cf. ibid). He preferred those approaches which combined decentralised forms of democracy with versions of market socialism – a list ranging from Proudhon via Bernstein to political economists like Oskar Lange and Karl Polanyi (cf. ibid: 183; 185; 204-208).

Giovanni Arrighi also featured Eduard Bernstein when he reflected on the making and remaking of the world labour movement since the nineteenth century. Arrighi's article was not primarily concerned with the retrieval of certain intellectual traditions, but rather with establishing which theories of socialism were most adequate for fundamentally different phases of capitalism. Arrighi suggested understanding Marx and early Marxism as children of their time, as belonging to a first phase of industrial capitalism, witnessing the apogee of market relations and the bourgeois society. In its second phase, beginning in the last decade of the nineteenth century, this form of capitalism ran into crisis and was transformed in ways unforeseen by Marx and the early Marxists. This stage and the accompanying attempts to come to grips with the difficulties of overproduction and social unrest changed the role of the state and of formal political democracy. Bernstein, according to Arrighi, was one of the first critics to recognise this altered structural context. Analysing developments in Britain in the 1890s, Bernstein wrote that political democracy had changed from a tool of subordination of, to a tool of emancipation for, the working class and had increased the British working class's standard of living (cf. 1990: 40). Moving on to a third stage of managerial and corporate capitalism, Arrighi maintained that Bernstein's belief in the possibility of a peaceful move towards a more humane capitalism was validated through the examples of Britain, the United States, Scandinavia and Australia (cf. ibid: 42). Arrighi identified a certain strategy of reformist labour struggles that on the one hand became possible in this stage and on the other contributed to its dynamic. According to the author, Bernstein was, in other words, among the first to identify

> the path [...] of energetic and well-organized movements capable of exploiting whatever opportunity arose to transform the increasing social power of labour into greater economic welfare and better political representation. In this context, the goal of socialist revolution never became an issue, and revolutionary vanguards of the proletariat found few followers. (ibid)

Arrighi thus underlined the importance of Bernstein's approach for the second and third stages of capitalism and its superiority in comparison to those revolutionary Marxist strategies that would have been relevant for the first. However, the third stage of capitalism had, since the late 1970s, come under threat from the increasing importance of the global market and foreign direct investment. Arrighi pointed out that with these changes, and with a fourth stage of capitalism which in many respects resembled the first, the political strategies suggested by the early Marxists might gain a new relevance. The *Communist Manifesto*'s predictions about the emergence of a world labour movement might become more realistic in the early twenty-first century than they had been in the twentieth. Though first and foremost an attempt to sketch out likely future developments in class relations and struggles, at the same time, Arrighi's article appeared to be a warning that late Marxists should neither mistakenly abandon Marxist theory at a time when it was likely to become increasingly relevant, nor move on to thinkers who were as likely to look as outdated in the fourth stage of capitalism as Marx had done in the third. In other words: although Bernstein's observations had been farsighted and remained relevant and although Marx's theories had not anticipated the development of capitalism in the twentieth century, this did not make Bernstein necessarily more important. Arrighi argued for a synthesising rather than for a polarising interpretation of socialist 'classics'.

Socialist Register

Socialist Register contributed only a few thoughts to the discussions about socialist 'classics'. However, they published two articles from American writers, Daniel Singer and Manfred Bienefeld, who did mention Luxemburg and Trotsky, albeit only in passing. Singer repeated what he considered to be Rosa Luxemburg's most important message: socialism could not be implemented from above. This position had consequences not only for socialist strategy but also for the contours and details of a future socialist society:

Socialism, to echo Rosa Luxemburg, cannot be a Christmas present for those who voted well; it is by definition a conquest from below. Hence, it cannot be built thanks to a blueprint drawn at the top and imposed from above. The vision of a different society must be elaborated collectively and in the open. It must take into account the spectacular changes in the capitalist world and answer all the awkward questions (e.g. whether the greatly altered working class is still the main agency of historical change). (1993: 253)

Singer's passage must be read as a suggestion to look carefully at what political struggles were going on at grassroots level and to collectively design the institutional set-up of socialism in the process of building it. Singer thus compliments Luxemburg's sentiments as an important procedural approach to the development of socialism.

Unlike Luxemburg, Trotsky was criticised in the pages of *Socialist Register*. Bienefeld argued that Trotsky's ideas of a global political strategy and the attempt of setting up a global socialist state were correct analytically and in principle. In practice, however, they were useless (1994: 122). This statement carries three messages: firstly, to return to Luxemburg, the struggle from below had to be fought on a lower and more accessible level than the global. Secondly, the national state still constituted a major political frame of reference.[13] Thirdly the Trotskyists in Britain and North America, who saw their analyses vindicated by recent events in the Eastern Bloc, could not suggest a realistic way forward.

---

13 This became one of *Socialist Register*'s central positions when it involved itself in the globalisation debate from 1992 onwards.

These two references were all that *Socialist Register* contributed to debates on classics beyond Marx. This paucity remains surprising, given the fact that editor Miliband was one of the most creative thinkers on democratic socialism.

Dissent

In *Dissent*, most articles mentioning classics from the socialist tradition focused on issues such as market socialism or associative democracy rather than on detailed reconsiderations of individual contributions to socialist theory. The one exception, where a complete article honoured a particular thinker, was not a comment on, but a reprint of, a reflection written by the Italian activist Carlo Rosselli on "Liberal Socialism" in the 1930s. As Nadia Urbinati explained in her introduction, Rosselli regarded socialism as a moral ideal and free of (Marxist) orthodoxy. He wanted to develop an alternative to determinism and open up space for human agency. He regarded liberalism and socialism as having the same roots in the old traditions of European political thought and even as being dependent on each other: "[A]s Rosselli stressed, socialism needs political and civil liberties; in turn, these liberties need a politics of social justice to remain alive" (1994: 115). Rosselli formulated a version of liberalism that required socialism for its completion:

Liberalism in its most straightforward sense can be defined as the political theory that takes the inner freedom of the human spirit as a given and adopts liberty as the ultimate goal, but also the ultimate means, the ultimate rule of shared human life. The goal is to arrive at a condition of social life in which each individual is certain of being able to develop his own personality fully. (1994: 117)

Rosselli considered a liberal socialist to be a believer in the possibility of such a society who was nevertheless opposed to dogmatism, and involved in grass-roots work rather than in a revolutionary struggle aiming at occupying the commanding heights of the economy. This strategy bore the chance of gradually democratising the organisational structure of the state and the economy (ibid: 120-123). His reflections paralleled Luxemburg's view that the exact content of socialism would become clear in the process of its creation and that therefore self-reflexive moments, and a spirit of self-critique rather than of dogmatism were essential:

In this doubt, in this virile relativism that gives a powerful impulse to action and wishes to leave plenty of room for human will in history; in its critical demon that obliges one continually to review one's position in the light of fresh experience; in this faith in the supreme values of the spirit and the marvellous animating force of liberty, end and means, climate and lever, lies the state of mind of a socialist who has sailed away from Marxist seas and touched land on the shores of liberalism. (ibid: 123)

Whereas in *New Left Review* the bureaucratic command structure of the Soviet system was criticised for both its violation of human liberties and its economic inefficiency, in *Dissent* the issue of civil liberties was given priority. This was because the journal focused more closely on the 'totalitarian' regimes of the twentieth century. The sympathy for representatives of Italian socialism like Rosselli lay in the fact that they had developed distinctive features reacting to both Stalinist orthodoxy and fascist dictatorship. Or, as Nadia Urbinati put it, some of the Italian thinkers had understood that the defeat of liberalism was also a defeat for socialism (ibid: 115). As leftwing intellectuals frequently of Jewish backgrounds, contributors to *Dissent* took all totalitarian tendencies very seriously and usually situated their origin in an uncritical faith in human power. Consequently, as Jeffrey C. Isaac explained in his article on "Civil Society and the Spirit of Revolt", *Dissenters* held those intellectuals who had become careful about change induced by human will in high esteem – he listed artists and intellectuals such as Iganzio Silone, Victor Serge, Dwight Macdonald, Simone Weil, Albert Camus, George Orwell, and Nicola Chiaromonte (cf. 1993: 357-359). The message of Isaac's article echoed Rosselli in stating that socialists' priority should be to involve themselves in grassroots associations and loose alliances rather than to fight for state power. This negative understanding of the state and the belief in the permanent danger of state tyranny led to brief statements of sympathy for anarchists and syndicalists (cf. ibid: 360), but also for American radicals, such as Tom Paine, Elizabeth Cady Stanton, Eugene V. Debs, and Norman Thomas (cf. Wilentz 1994: 384-385).[14] Other writers pleaded for a more positive understanding of the

---

14 Editor Irving Howe nevertheless explained that he did not see himself as an uncritical follower of theories of totalitarianism. He insisted, following David Riesman's critique of Hannah Arendt, that 'totalitarian' regimes had very differ-

state and quoted John Dewey, who in the 1930s had argued similarly to Bernstein in the late 19th century, that civil liberties should be appreciated as protection *by* the state rather than *against* it (Brody 1994: 62). Without such a changed perception of the state, David Brody suggested, the civil rights revolution of the 1960s would have been impossible (ibid).

The critique of vanguardism played a central role in *Dissent*, as did the perception – an orthodox historical-materialist one – that the preconditions for a transition to socialism had not been present in Russia. However, this absence did not mean that the country had never had a chance to develop into the direction of a socialist society. Although Howe agreed with Isaac Deutscher that Soviet totalitarianism could and would change (cf. 1991: 69-70), this concurrence did not qualify Deutscher, in Howe's eyes, as one of the classics to whom one should now return. Howe contended that Deutscher had been morally wrong in stating that Stalin fulfilled a cruel but necessary task and that he was analytically wrong when assuming that a well-functioning planned economy would lead to a self-organised liberalisation. In fact, Howe found evidence of the contrary: "It now seems quite the other way round: that it is the crisis of the economy and the failure to provide material well-being that have provoked *glasnost* and *perestroika*" (ibid: 69). The choice of classics that were worthy of reconsideration was similar to the selection in *New Left Review*. It included Luxemburg and Martov (1990a: 184-186) and still paid attention to the ideas of the Trotskyists. Mitchell Cohen wrote an article, "Theories of Stalinism. Revisiting a Historical Problem", where he sketched out how criticism of the Stalinist system had developed from Trotsky himself to Milovan Djilas and Max Shachtman in the 1950s and how different conceptions emerged as to how to best understand the Soviet Union (as a degenerated workers state, as neither capitalist nor socialist state, as a state ruled by a new class, as a bureaucratic collectivist state, as a state with or without a rationale to its policies for the improvement of the living conditions of the proletariat). Cohen's relationship to these thinkers remained ambivalent. Like Howe, he seemed convinced of their reflections' superiority compared to the historically unspecific accounts of Arendt and, more so, "cold warriors" like J. L. Talmon and F. Hayek. He drew no direct line from Lenin to Stalin (1992:

---

ent roots, structures and functions. The analytical use of the concept of totalitarianism was thus very limited (cf. 1991: 70).

183, 190). However, he complained that even such Trotskyist and post-Trotskyist thinkers had not been serious enough in considering the particularities of Russian political culture (ibid: 190).

If classics could to a certain extent be helpful in analysing the failures of the Soviet Union, they were less useful in developing ideas for alternatives (beyond liberal socialists' and existentialists' commitment to democracy). However, Shlomo Avineri named a number of theorists who had developed ideas of a leftwing nationalism – an issue he granted similar importance to as had Manfred Bienefeld in *Socialist Register*. Whereas Marxists like Luxemburg and Lenin had an instrumentalist perspective towards nationalism, others came forward with more positive views (cf. 1990: 450). Avineri mentioned Moses Hess, who had described a national community as a Hegelian element of mediation and was convinced that while a revolution would abolish classes and national conflicts, it would not annihilate nations and their identity as the "individuality of a people" (ibid: 454). The Austro-Marxists provided a further important example with their emphasis on the importance of cultural empowerment in a polyglot society with a large non-German proletariat (ibid: 455). They imagined internationalism not as the opposite of nationalism, but as peaceful coexistence of nations in a pluralist structure. Finally, Avineri hinted at a Zionist socialist, Chaim Arlosoroff, who had blamed the abstract internationalism of socialists as the root of the destructive working-class nationalism that exploded in the First World War (ibid: 456). Altogether, *Dissent* presented a large number of classical figures from the socialist tradition, with those proposing ideas for a liberal socialism seemingly deemed most important.

Monthly Review

Monthly Review invested more effort in finding alternative sources of socialist imagination than any of the other journals. The value of such sources was measured less by the details of the models some of them had developed than in the spiritual guidance they could provide. The conviction that the spiritual dimension of socialism needed more consideration proved central to the journal's reading of classical thinkers. Contributors looked into three different bodies of political thought: into the "left wing" of the English revolution of the seventeenth century, represented by Gerrard Winstanley and the Diggers and its repercussions in early America (Sweezy 1993: 1), into religious thought and into theories developed in the context of the anti-colonial struggle. Apart from these strands, contributors also mentioned (but more in passing) several of those classics from the Marxist tradition that were discussed in the other journals as well – above all, Rosa Luxemburg. Löwy echoed the democratic dimension of Luxemburg's thought when explaining that the latter had criticised the abolition of free elections in the Soviet Union as early as 1918 (cf. 1991: 33). Singer emphasised another element in Luxemburg's thought: she believed that the socialist revolution – better understood as a transformation – would be a protracted global process with periods of advance but also of retreat during which sticking to socialist principles and setting personal examples was all the more important (cf. 1990: 73). As in the other journals, a list of further illustrious names of early critics of the Soviet union was presented to the readers. It included Leon Trotsky, Christian Rakovsky, Isaac Deutscher, Abraham Leon, Heinrich Brandler, Willi Münzenberg, Victor Serge, and André Breton (cf. Löwy 1991: 34). Trotsky, unsurprisingly, played a rather ambivalent role and was severely criticised in the journal's pages. Kovel explained that Trotsky shared with other Bolsheviks a Nietzschean superhumanism which travestied Marxist humanism and overestimated humans' capacity to change the shape of the world and of their own nature and character: "For Trotsky's spiritual grandiosity contains within itself the failure of Bolshevism to achieve socialism. Its impulse towards gigantism and hardness is paired with an indifference to the individual." (1994: 37) Hence Kovel expressed scepticism that those horrors associated with Stalin would have been avoided had Trotsky come to power in the U.S.S.R. Amin also included Trotsky in a genealogy of "vulgar Marxism" which, he insisted, had not begun with Stalinism but in late-19th century Germany. Amin referred to a Marxism that had substituted historical necessities for ethical imperatives – a tendency he also diagnosed in Leninism and (though to a lesser degree) Maoism (cf. 1993: 52).

More interesting than these considerations, which evidently mirrored *Monthly Review*'s customary anti-Trotskyite perspective, were those that moved farther beyond the Marxist tradition. Suggestions peddled in the journal ranged from the communality and spirituality located in the traditional life of Native Americans to the moral foundations of existentialism. In an interview, the British musician and protest singer Billy Bragg went furthest in depicting socialism as a collective moral spirit whose embodiment could be found in the past rather than in the future. Though he did certainly not represent *Monthly Review*'s mainstream opinion, his reflections were nevertheless published in its pages:

[T]he ideals of what socialism is about, the call of socialist feelings and humanitarian hopes which existed long before Marx, as far as I am concerned, are still valid. We need to trace back before Prague '68, before Hungary '56, before Stalin, before the Russian Revolution, before Marx, before the whole industrial revolution, to look at the collective societies which existed then. Take the Native Americans. They know how to deal with the environment and the relationship of the individual to one's surroundings. We've lost that because capitalism demands individualistic materialism. (Batstone 1991: 23-24)

Whereas this statement stresses communality and collectiveness as central elements of socialism, Istvan Mészáros, quite to the contrary, emphasised its often neglected individual dimension. For him, socialism became possible only after a conscious personal decision against capitalism. Jean-Paul Sartre was the thinker who pointed this out most markedly:

Sartre was a man who always preached the diametrical opposite [of the idea that "there is no alternative"; SB]: there is an alternative, there must be an alternative; you as an individual have to rebel against this power, this monstrous power of capital. Marxists on the whole failed to voice that side. (Monthly Review 1993: 10)

These two poles became equally important for *Monthly Review* contributors' quest for ideas – they tried to link personal responsibility for pursuing socialism with a common spirit in which to do so. The effort to establish such a link explains the selection of the further sources discussed in the journal's pages. Early Anglo-American radicalism provided inspiration. Notably the Levellers and Diggers were applauded for their "advanced ideas of egalitarianism" but they were complemented by specifically American fighters, for example, the "Regulators", who were recruited from the 'lower orders' and struggled against the landed aristocracy in North Carolina (cf. Magdoff 1991: 3). Even the 'Great Awakening' of the 1760s was interpreted as a radical political movement and the authors explained that the American revolution was not only an anti-colonial uprising, but also a struggle over more radical or more restricted versions of democracy. Unfortunately, those forces who argued in the *Federalist Papers* against 'excessive' democracy and for a retreat from the egalitarianism that had characterised some of the states in the years directly before the foundation of the United States proved stronger than the anti-property wing (ibid: 3-4). The U.S. constitution, thus, was a document of defeat as much as an achievement. Bragg also mentioned the Diggers of the seventeenth century and characterised them as the first liberation theologians. Further, he pointed out that the antagonism of religion and social liberation was a feature specific to European history. Religion itself, however, did clearly have socialist implications (cf. Batstone 1991: 26). This argument built a bridge towards the second and the third strand of political thought – religion and national liberation.

The treatment of religion was surprisingly prominent in the journal's pages: it went back to the classical figures of Buddha and Jesus but also took notice of the social gospel theologian Rauschenbusch and his impact on Martin Luther King. In the case of Buddha, Kovel explained the human and social significance of mysticism: "Recall that Buddha's meditative insights into the illusory nature of the self led him to call for the care of all suffering creatures" (Kovel 1994: 39). John Brentlinger constructed a surprising alliance of Jesus and Che Guevara, interpreting them both as examples of revolutionary Christianity, which consisted of the feeling of love and responsibility for other people and nature, and presented the Nicaraguan case as an example where spirituality had been integrated into the revolutionary struggle (cf. 1992: 28-34):

The revolutionary Christian speaks of following Jesus, of putting love into practice by building community. It is because of the commitment to practice that the revolutionary Christian is revolutionary, and confronts the necessity for ridding the world of capitalism and building socialism. (ibid: 35)

Guillermo Bowie also mentioned the religious aspect of Guevara's struggle and drew parallels to Martin Luther King: both men were concerned with the possibilities of making ethical decisions in the face of, and perhaps against, European modes of cultural and economic domination (cf. 1993: 41): "This moral imperative, rather than the cold, detached, manipulative ethic of the European capitalist, was the guiding principle of Guevara's praxis. In this respect he was at one with Martin Luther King" (ibid: 39). However, this spiritual commitment was not all; at least some writers warned against blurring all boundaries between different anti-oppressive projects. Interestingly, it was a theologian, Darren Cushman-Wood, who insisted on bearing in mind these differences. In an article on the economic thinking of King and Malcolm X, he clearly hinted at points where they parted company with Marxist approaches. Although Malcolm X adopted some Marxist ideas, for example, when he regarded black people as the reserve army of labour needed in capitalist relations of production, he still considered the class conflict as subordinated to the "race" conflict (1993: 30). And Martin Luther King remained within a reformist Keynesian framework in his suggestions on the redistribution of wealth (ibid: 33).

It is a bit surprising that a journal as strongly committed to internationalism as *Monthly Review* did not come forward with more classical figures from the anti-colonial movements. Comments remained largely limited to the frequently mentioned examples of revolutionary Nicaragua and Cuba and to Che Guevara. Yet one article introduced another thinker – Amilcar Cabral. Cabral insisted on the importance, under conditions of imperialism, of national liberation struggles and emphasised the need to form an alliance between workers and peasants on the one hand and petty bourgeoisie and intellectuals on the other. Only the awareness of a national interest would allow the "class suicide" of the more privileged sections – the subordination of their selfish material interests to the interests of the whole society and the integration in a "nation class" (Meisenhelder 1993: 41-46). Finally, Cabral, like many others, emphasised that after successful liberation an institutional set-up was needed that prevented people from achieving permanent positions of power (ibid: 47).

3.3. Marxism and Radicalism

The reflections on Marxism and on classics from the socialist and radical traditions show that Marxism was far from dead for most socialist intellectuals. Most agreed, however, that it was seriously harmed even if only a small number of them were convinced that Marxism had to accept responsibility for the realities as they had existed in the Eastern Bloc. Some authors even suggested that the recent changes in the (former) state socialist countries vindicated core elements of Marxist theory, though they had their doubts that even these affirmations would help Marxism in the future. While all intellectuals accepted that Marxism had been 'cut to size', they disagreed as to 'what size' this was. *Dissenters*, looking back over a long history of criticising at least certain strands of and elements in Marxism, wanted to retain only the 'other Marx': particularly the 'early Marx' who stressed human agency and fit into a category usually described as 'socialist humanism'. In *New Left Review*, for many writers the main function of Marxism was reduced to its critical and analytical dimension – either as a 'spirit of critique', resembling a vague and general perspective, or a system of critique, posing questions about the bases of a critical social theory and methodology. *Socialist Register* and *Monthly Review* as well as some contributions to *New Left Review* pushed for a more prominent role for Marxism. For them it came far closer to a holistic edifice of thought, even if one with overt gaps and covert mistakes.

All journals agreed on a number of achievements which they considered to be Marxism's most important: The concept of class, the historical-materialist method (understood flexibly as an illuminator of influences and tendencies rather than as a tool to dogmatically identify historical laws) and the notion of reification (which linked the material with the psychological world) were highly esteemed. On the other hand, most writers were willing to at least partially excuse Marxism's deficiencies on the basis of Marx's and Engels's historicity as nineteenth-century thinkers: historical context, authors conceded, explained the failings of Marxism's utopian vision (with regard to the details of a socialist society), its 'simplification assumption', determinism and its neglect of questions of ethics and justice. Nevertheless, these were serious defects which had to be corrected. Further issues, such as ecological considerations, constituted gaps which could be filled by applying elements of the Marxist methodology itself. At the bottom line, what remained of Marxism as political project was the central role of class struggle, albeit in a radically re-conceptualised form.

In their attempts to re-conceptualise problematic elements of Marxist and other theories, contributors looked to various 'classics' from the left tradition. It is here, in each group's canonical preferences, that one first finds differences between the British and the American journals. Although all of the journals investigated the writings of several 'classical' figures in order to find inspiration for the conduct of grassroots bottom-up struggles, the Americans' choices were dramatically more eclectic. Presenting figures ranging from Italian liberal socialists to Jewish socialist Zionists and from the Diggers to Jesus, the American writers claimed adherence to a *radical* rather than a Marxist-socialist tradition. The British lists were much shorter, although they also included surprises such as writers of nineteenth-century utopian socialist novels or Kautsky. One could conclude here that these differences testify to Therborn's thesis: the two groups could be characterised by their differing political routes in the twentieth century, where European movements were more ideologically-driven while those in North American were more socially motivated.[15] In *Monthly Review* one finds another element often identified as central to American political culture: a commitment to 'community' which formed a constant compliment to the journal's insistence on the necessity of fighting the class struggle. For *Dissenters* the question of whether Marxism and classics of socialism provided openings for totalitarianism played a prominent role, pointing to the importance of the twentieth-century European Jewish experience for the New York intellectual scene in which the journal had its roots. Surprisingly little attention was paid to the experience of third-world classical theorists. While a few names were mentioned in passing – such as C. L. R. James and Ernesto Che Guevara – only Amilcar Cabral was addressed in a complete article. Neither the struggle against British imperialism nor the opposition to U.S. dominance in Latin America seems to have provided inspiration for intellectuals in Britain or the United States. Regardless of their judgement on the future status of Marxism, their search for alternative approaches remained predominantly restricted to heterodox European and North American political traditions.

---

15 For Therborn's argument, see p. 32, footnote 9.

4. Out of the Impasse: the Search for Models

With universal agreement that socialism would not fall into place overnight but had to be developed through well-designed institutions, radical intellectuals saw a need to move beyond a mere critique of capitalism. They had to answer the question of how a socialist society and a socialist world would like. On the one hand, this task required an engagement with 'utopistics'. On the other, it could analyse existing models and institutional arrangements. All the journals took both of these routes.

4.1. Dimensions of Democratic Socialism

The previous chapter has shown that radical intellectuals criticised Marxism for its lack of imagination of the shape of a socialist society and for its disregard of democratic procedures. Thus it became an important task to think about the structures of a socialist society and the institutions of a democratic socialist political system. This involved the discussion of four questions: (a.) what would be the most important principles on which to build the edifice of democratic socialism? (b.) What institutional forms were required to make it work – did models of such institutions exist? In how far would they differ from the institutions of liberal or – as most authors would say – capitalist democracy? (c.) Which preconditions had to be met in order to make democratic socialism a realistic option – for example, with regard to the distribution of power in society? Would international power constellations allow societies to move towards democratic socialism? What were, overall, the chances for realising such a project? (d.) Finally, what dilemmas would people committed to the building of democratic socialism face? How, for example, should they deal with likely opposition to their project?

New Left Review

New Left Review dedicated a great deal of space and energy to new reflections on the basics and chances of democratic socialism. A number of well-known writers as diverse as André Gorz, Jürgen Habermas, Ralph Miliband, and Kate Soper contributed to this discussion – which they obviously considered crucial at this historical moment. However, from the members of the journal's editorial board there were, apart from Robin

Blackburn's far-reaching article "Socialism after the Crash" (1991), only contributions by Fred Halliday (rather in passing) and Norman Geras. Most of these thoughts, formulated as either complete articles on the issue or as fragmentary sections and reflections within essays on other topics, were concerned with defining the basic values, principles, goals and priorities of democratic socialism or with institutional structures required to organise and sustain it.

Principles and Core Elements of Democratic Socialism
Authors introduced a number of definitions of socialism and democratic socialism. According to Therborn, the most important core values of a socialist culture were universal equality and solidarity (cf. 1992: 32): "In a nutshell, socialism is about the availability and the distribution of material resources; about understanding, explaining and changing them by way of a new mode of production and/or of distribution" (ibid: 25). This was a very general definition which left open whether this egalitarianism moderately meant a *more* egalitarian society or more radically one in which *all* inequalities had been dissolved (ibid: 63). Some authors, such as G. A. Cohen, strongly argued for a radical egalitarianism where "the amount of amenity and burden in one person's life should be roughly comparable to that in any other's" (1994: 11). He made this point with reference to a non-Marxist authority:

And whereas rewarding productivity which is due to greater inherent talent is indeed morally intelligible, from certain ethical standpoints, it is nevertheless a profoundly anti-socialist idea, correctly stigmatized by J. S. Mill as an instance of 'giving to those who have', since greater talent is itself a piece of fortune that calls for no further reward. (ibid: 13)

Eric Olin Wright, disagreed and explained through the example of class differences, that classlessness served as a utopian vision but in practice the reduction of "classness" functioned as the "operative norm" (1993: 25). Democratic socialism would become a rolling process, a move towards a utopian, egalitarian vision. While no unanimity existed about the extent of material equality, it remained similarly open as to within which framework it should be achieved. For Wallerstein, there was no doubt that relative equality had to be achieved on a global level because "[w]e can contribute nothing to a desirable resolution of this terminal crisis of our world-system unless we make it very clear that only a relatively egalitarian, fully democratic system is desirable" (1994: 16). This perspective, of course, called for reflections on the problem of a standard of living that could be reproduced on a global scale. Kate Soper tried to find solutions to this issue. She argued that if one took Wallerstein's goal of relative global equality seriously, one had to distinguish between basic human needs (she listed nutritional food, clean water, protective housing, non-hazardous work and physical environments, appropriate health care, security in childhood, significant primary relationships, physical security, economic security, appropriate education, safe birth-control and child-bearing) which had to be made available for everyone and human wants which must be questioned (cf. 1993: 121). Hence, she called for a new "erotics of consumption" and explained: "In this sense, being realist about needs may require us to be utopian about wants, and the political force of any theory of basic needs prove dependant on the imagining of a new hedonist vision" (ibid: 127-8). She based a socialist environmentalism on these theses, which differed from some strands of deep ecology in so far as it did not demand a radical reduction of consumption from everyone but tried to strike a balance between satisfying the basic needs of the poorest, worst-off sections of global society and a less destructive relationship to nature.

Miliband agreed that material equality constituted a necessary precondition for democratic socialism. Nevertheless, he pointed out that liberation had to go beyond the redistribution of material resources (cf. 1994: 13). Like him, writers unanimously subscribed to the claim that socialism depended on democracy. However, at the same time it stood that democracy needed a redistribution of power and at least relative equality in order to attain real meaning – if it was understood as "egalitarian" rather than as "hierarchical" democracy (Honderich 1994: 62). While some contributors were convinced that democracy understood along democratic socialist lines had been a central element in all 'schools' of socialism and that all attempts at accelerating movements towards socialism had constituted perversions of its theory (cf. Miliband 1992: 112), others urged socialists to become more precise in their own understanding of democracy – for example, on "relations between state and nation, man and citizen, the private and the public, and so forth" (cf. Derrida 1994: 50). Habermas, on the other hand, argued that a radical conception of democracy was all that was left of socialism (cf.

Habermas & Michnik 1994: 11). For most authors, the concept of democracy was not restricted to the political sphere but extended to democratic decision making in other parts of societal life, especially in the economy. Authors disagreed on the more concrete forms that this extension could take; Honderich, for example, remained sceptical of Miliband's and Robert Dahl's propagation of workers control. In any case, Miliband argued, socialism gave fullest meaning to democracy (cf. 1994: 3), while socialists' relationships with existing forms of capitalist democracy remained complex and instrumental. Finally, the environmental dimension was especially mentioned in numerous contributions. Some authors seemed to feel (but only rarely addressed) a possible tension between socialist and environmentalist goals. However, André Gorz explicitly dealt with this problem when demanding the redistribution of labour not only to save time for socially purposeful activity beyond work but also to reduce the economic activity's destructive consequences for the natural world. He described "eco-compatible industrial civilization" as a social project that had to be achieved democratically through self-limitation (1993: 64).

The commitment to public ownership remained, perhaps most strongly, from classical socialist thinking within a democratic-socialist perspective. This did not require the socialisation of every business and all economic activity (and not necessarily the complete abolition of market mechanisms), but certainly of a part large enough to become the *dominant* form of ownership – a project that went beyond the mixed economies during the golden age of social democracy and models such as Sweden. Yet differences were not just about the degree of public ownership; the authors were at pains to point out that public ownership was about *collective* social ownership rather than about the *state* as the institution to monopolise economic decision making. They agreed that public ownership was no panacea but was, nevertheless, to be preferred over a private system and above all to be controlled by democratic decision making. Miliband pointed to its superiority: "[E]xploitation under public ownership is a *deformation*, for a system based on public ownership does not rest on and require exploitation; under conditions of democratic control, it provides the basis for the free and cooperative association of the producers" (1992: 110). For him, public ownership was an indispensable part of socialism because:

[C]apitalist democracy [...] may not seriously challenge the power, property, privileges and position of the people at the top of the social pyramid – more specifically, the holders of corporate power on the one hand and of state power on the other, linked as they are in a difficult but very real partnership. (ibid)

In short, without the abandonment of privilege linked with large-scale private ownership, there was no chance of creating a democratic-socialist society.

Since the writers in *New Left Review* expected a long and complicated process of transformation towards a socialist society, its exact shape and its most important values could not be determined in detail, but only generally from the present. Socialism, according to Habermas, was only available in the form of an "abstract idea" – but in connection with radical democracy it would be approximated in a rational, non-exclusive discourse which could find solutions to global problems in everyone's interest (cf. 1990: 15-6). There was a parallel in the writings of Miliband who believed in the possibility of a

civic virtue, according to which men and women would freely accept the obligations of citizenship as well as claiming its rights; and they would find no great difficulty in the cultivation of a *socialized individualism* in which the expression of their individuality would be combined with a due regard for the constraints imposed upon it by life in a society. (1994: 4)

Socialism remained as something like an 'open horizon' – a guiding moral principle acting as a compass in order to solve the problems of the present. The route taken (to follow the direction defined by the compass), however, had to be strictly governed by "liberal norms of political life" (Geras 1994: 98).

Reflections on Institutional Arrangements
The institutional set-up of a democratic-socialist society was also a widely-discussed topic. There seemed to be two basic assumptions: one rather in line with traditional Marxist thinking, the other at variance with it. As already mentioned, contributors were still convinced that planning was necessary within a socialist economy. New, however, was their belief that some kind of state would remain indispensable for the foreseeable future

because the introduction of socialism was now defined as a never-ending process rather than a sudden qualitative leap to a new stage (cf. Miliband 1992: 113). Rather than holding on to the 'simplification assumption', writers started thinking about the constitutional and institutional set-up of a democratic socialist state, or for a democratic state that would move towards socialism – a state characterised by great complexity:

Simple-minded socialism, or a socialism adapted to simple conditions, has imagined that the logic of social choice can be just as intelligible and definite as an individual's decision to slake their thirst by drinking a glass of water. But without at all abandoning socialism it is quite possible to recognize that social need and public good have to be arrived at by complex, tentative and negotiated ways – indeed this could be seen as the very essence of genuine socialism. (Blackburn 1991: 208)

Without planning of economic activity, the principal goals of socialist change – reduced inequality and an environmentally less-damaging mode of production – had no chance of being achieved. This planning, however, should not take the form of centralised, bureaucratic state guidance but of democratic, grassroots, rational decision making. Blackburn described the task in the following words:

The harsh contrast of wealth and poverty in the modern world – and the spectre of ecological catastrophe – demand global and regional planning but they also require a framework of economic cooperation which encourages responsible initiative and innovation in a myriad of citizens. (ibid: 233)

His solution required the ability of people to communicate "rationally and effectively" and thus reasserted Habermas's ideas of the ethics of communication (1990: 15). Whereas Habermas, in keeping with his model of communicative action, believed in the theoretical possibility of arriving at solutions in everyone's interest (though he did not dare to predict whether economic and state apparatuses could be transformed to work on the base of rational discourse [ibid: 16]), Miliband was less optimistic and assumed that conflicts and tensions would persist (cf. 1992: 113; 1994: 12). With several authors, Wright suggested that the implementation of a basic income would at least partly weaken the "coercive character of capitalism", "deproletarianize" working-class people, (1993: 26). This would enable them to take decisions on ethical rather than material considerations. Most forcefully, the link of social income, social citizenship and communication-based democratic socialism was argued by David Purdy in his article, "Citizenship, Basic Income and the State":

> More generally, if the ethos of social citizenship takes hold, people may be less inclined to take a narrow, sectional view of their interests and more receptive to the claims of wider moral communities, including those of their fellow citizens, humanity as a whole or, for that matter, of other sentient species and our common planetary home. (1994: 42)

André Gorz also considered basic income as a chance to combine less work and consumption with more autonomy and existential security and thus as a chance to transcend the profit-based economic rationality of capitalism (cf. 1993: 65). Ideas on the exact shape of decision-making institutions remained limited to hints at workplace and community democracy. Writers obviously agreed with Habermas that the concrete set-up had to be established in practice on a trial-and-error basis (cf. 1990: 16).

Regardless of its final shape, none of the suggested measures would make the state in a democratic socialist society obsolete: "The power of the state in such a society would be variously constrained; but [...] the notion that state power, and therefore state coercion, would no longer have a substantial place in the conduct of affairs belongs to the realm of fantasy, at least for the relevant future" (Miliband 1994: 7-8). Miliband envisaged a structure in which a strong state, a vivid civil society, and democratic practices controlled and checked each other. Thus the rule of law, the separation of powers, civil liberties, and political pluralism would stay in place, but a democratic socialist civil society "would give them much more effective meaning" (1992: 113). Blackburn also pointed out that formal structures were needed since it was unrealistic to expect the emergence of a transpersonal socialist mind. Socialist change would develop as result of meetings of minds – and these had to be organised and formalised (cf. 1991: 208). Just one of the writers thought – given that there was no automatic historical move towards socialism – about how to deal with potential decisions to instead turn round and move away from the socialist course: Ted Honderich explained that a normative commitment to socialism (or to increasing equality and environmental sustainability) had to be constitutionally codified in a manner similar to civil rights in what he called "hierarchic democracies" (1994: 63). In this sense, socialist democracy meant both the institutional extension and transcendence of capitalist democracy (cf. Miliband 1994: 13).

Apart from these widely-shared beliefs, one could find reflections on particular institutional tasks. Prominent among these was Immanuel Wallerstein's insistence on devising mechanisms to organise the redistribution of wealth on a global scale. He suggested a process of "rational reconstruction" that reversed the global North's appropriation of the surplus produced in the South. Rather than being regarded as "remedial charity", such a mechanism was central to the whole project of global democratic socialism (1994: 17). Another author highlighted the educational aspect of democratic socialism. Hinting at the observation that the societies coming closest to its principles were the best educated ones, Paul Auerbach called for a radical reconstruction of elitist and class-selective education systems where the reproduction of hierarchies should be replaced by genuine equality and by spending more resources on poorer and weaker pupils (cf. 1992: 31). Finally, one contribution argued for considerably less radical measures with regard to economic and social policy than suggested by other authors. Mouzelis, in strongly criticising Therborn's reflections on "The Life and Times of Socialism" (1992), pleaded with intellectuals to refrain from anything more than an indirect control of the economy and targeted social benefits. Accompanied by the suggestion to expand democracy downward and gradually to the workplace, neighbourhood and local community, this view seemed to take on board some communitarian themes of the time (cf. Mouzelis 1993: 184).

Auerbach's reflections on education point to Scandinavia as an entity from which democratic socialists could draw lessons. However, whereas it could probably serve as a model for relative educational and material equality, it could hardly demonstrate democratically organised economic planning or a state checked by a strong civil society. For these elements, authors had to look elsewhere and did not find very much. Blackburn suggested reconsidering the merits and historical experiences of syndicalism as models for planning (cf. 1991: 207). Auerbach hinted not only to Scandinavia's but also to Japan's capitalism because he saw also the latter as based on cooperation and group-loyalty (cf. 1992: 13). David Marquand, in writing in his capacity as a specialist on the EC/EU, suggested that the left should develop a new version of the early post-war European federalism based on the idea of subsidiarity (cf. 1994: 25). Generally, he seemed convinced that lessons could be drawn from stabilising economies and societies in difficult situations. Hence he also hinted at the example of the early developing United States and its forms of democratic decision-making (ibid: 26).

Requirements
With the abandoning of teleological determinism, the question of preconditions for, and chances of, moves towards democratic socialism became urgent. The probably most fundamental precondition was expressed by Miliband: socialists needed to believe in the capacity of humans to act in unselfish ways (cf. 1994: 5-6). Without this belief, all ideas about the most important principles and the most suitable institutional set-up were moot. However, it was exactly this perception of humans' sense of collective responsibility that seemed questionable – more than ever in the face of the capitalist restoration in the Eastern European states. Cohen thus pointed to studies which emphasised that even among the managerial classes in capitalism, there were many people who aimed at the maximisation of cash results, but who did so out of a desire to make positive contributions to the society to which they belonged, rather than for selfish reasons (cf. 1991: 19). Auerbach took insights from management studies a step further: "The question naturally arises in the minds of socialists: if group loyalty and cooperation are important components of economic efficaciousness at the level of production, will this not be true a fortiori for society at large?" (1992: 13). Democratic socialism required attempts at changing society's superstructure, for example, its political culture and political ideas, its rationalities. While Gorz argued that only a new rationality (able to recognise alienation and what was called 'externalities') could establish a new economic order, Wallerstein urged a rationality that was capable of overcoming the Eurocentrism on which it was based for the last 200 years (cf. Wallerstein 1994: 16-17). Paul Auerbach added that only a highly educated population would be able to survive: "We also need an educated population because the world that population inherits will be an extremely dangerous one. The only hope for survival is that some sober, rational thinking will keep the race afloat a little while longer. It won't happen by luck" (1992: 33).

Apart from these reflections on general preconditions, there were other deliberations that were more concrete: Halliday pointed out that the chances of socialism in the West depended to a high degree on the willingness of the parties of the Western left (in fact, he meant the former Communist Parties) to criticise capitalism again (cf. 1990: 20). This leads on to the question whether there was a realistic chance for a democratic socialism to be implemented. Two positions existed in the pages of *New Left Review*, which were not necessarily mutually exclusive. The first was expressed by Geras when he explained the openness of future developments in the following way:

But socialism now, it must clearly also be acknowledged, is *utopian* socialism – in the way Marxists used to mean that. It is a moral ideal; a protest; the refusal to take for acceptable, much less for the best, what is today triumphantly commended as being that. And no one presently knows how, or even if, socialism will be achieved. (Geras 1992: 69)

The second opinion was, for example, put forward by Hobsbawm who formulated, also in the footsteps of Rosa Luxemburg and implicitly echoing her socialism-or-barbarism dictum, that there was no alternative:

[S]ocialists do not, and cannot, accept Adam Smith's view that the pursuit of self-interest by every person will produce socially optimal results, even when they accept that it may maximize the material wealth of nations – which it only does in specific circumstances. They cannot believe that social justice can be achieved simply by the operations of capital accumulation and the market, and they agree with Vilfredo Pareto that a society which had no specific place for social justice and morality cannot survive. (1992: 62)

This reversal of the Thatcherite slogan 'there is no alternative' (because without moves towards socialism, destruction on a global scale would become inevitable) was often reiterated in the magazine's pages and it was explained above all via the dire conditions in the global South and ever-increasing environmental problems everywhere. The chances for survival depended to a high degree on the flexibility and creativity of people who in changing alliances worked for progressive change (cf. Wallerstein 1994: 17).

Questions and Dilemmas
In the end, a number of questions remained open in the pages of *New Left Review*. These were posed by single contributors, but most of the time not taken up by the others. Consequently, a real debate on these issues did not develop. However, they are still worth considering because they reveal dilemmas and a sense of helplessness. The first of these problems was formulated by Honderich. Agreeing with other contributors that vanguardist and dictatorial routes to democratic socialism were undesirable, he remained at the same time convinced that a peaceful transformation from "hierarchic democracy" to "egalitarian democracy" was impossible (1994: 65). Socialists faced a dilemma because such change would inevitably lead to civil war and thus worsen the life situation of those at the lower end of the social hierarchy, thereby harming the very people whose situation's improvement was the socialists' original political goal (cf. ibid: 66). Yet even if such a society could, in fact, be established, problems would continue:

It remains a fact that for a society to persist in Egalitarian democracy is for it to be in a way of existing that requires defence against determined adversaries within and without. There is the possibility, then, that the Principle of Equality will not justify the continued defence of an Existing Egalitarian Democracy. (ibid)

Perhaps this problem seemed less insurmountable for all those who believed in the possibility of human beings to decide rationally and beyond their narrow self-interests. However, not even Miliband, who certainly was convinced that they could, would completely rule out the necessity of violent and authoritarian self-defence (cf. 1994: 10-11). Finally, some contributors raised the question as to whether progressive and emancipatory struggles should still be fought in the name of socialism. Blackburn, for instance, seemed to have doubts: "The future belongs to a diversified socialism, a 'socialism without guarantees', or even to some new concept more adequately embodying the goals of the left and the creative impulses of anti-capitalist movements" (1991: 239). Blackburn was seconded by Cohen: "The socialist aspiration was to extend community to the whole of our economic life. We now know that we do not know how to do that, and many think that we now know that it is impossible to do that" (1994: 11). Obviously, contributors to *New Left Review* still had to come to terms with the question whether the future belonged to a struggle for democratic socialism or to what Jürgen Habermas called a struggle for radical democracy.

Socialist Register

New considerations of the meaning and the shape of democratic socialism played an important role during the early 1990s in Socialist Register as well. According to the editors, the rethinking of these topics was made necessary by not so much the collapse of the Eastern European regimes, as by the perception, shared also among intellectuals, that Western socialists had backed and defended their practices. As Miliband and Panitch explained in their introductory article ("The New World Order and the Socialist Agenda") to the 1992 Register, many on the left shied away from using concepts like "socialism" any more – they followed the "prophets of postmodernism" (like Jean-Francois Lyotard) into a retreat from 'mega-sagas' (1992: 20). The editors were very critical of this defensive movement and regarded it as operating under false assumptions:

It is impossible to say how long the ranks of the left will be plagued by this fashion, but it is clear that it is an intellectual mood that was very much based on a caricature of contemporary socialist aspirations as inherently totalitarian. This ignores the extent to which the aspirations of socialists in every era, and not least of the new left of the 1960s (taken together as encompassing a new generation of radicals and an older generation of socialists and communists), entailed not a future constructed on a model of disciplined proletarian homogeneity but rather of genuine pluralist democracy in which the state would be subject to a freely associated society. (ibid)

Generally, the mood in the publication oscillated between a confidence that spoke of the supposed end of socialism – as what Richard Levins called a "eulogy behind an empty grave" – and a sober admission that to claim that Western socialists were not affected at all would not lead very far (1990). Practically, this meant to restate what had been stated (but not necessarily heard) before – most importantly, thoughts on democratic socialism. Many of the reflections on democratic socialism in the annual of course came from its editor, Miliband, who had throughout his career worked on this question but intensified his efforts after his hopes that a reformed Soviet Union might provide a suitable model had been destroyed. Because

Miliband was so central to the *Register* and because also several other contributors simultaneously wrote for *New Left Review* (like Wallerstein and Geras), a number of similar ideas and proposals figured in both publications. Yet there were interesting differences too. Above all, the narrowing down of democratic socialism to only radical democracy (on the basis of Habermasian rational decision-making) was nowhere suggested in *Socialist Register*. This abstinence was linked to a second difference: the scope of each journal's work. Discussions of the means and relations of production and especially the question of how to democratise their organisation had always found a more central place in *Socialist Register*. Finally, the second editor, Leo Panitch, also contributed a special angle based on his conviction of the central roles national states still played in a perceived era of globalisation. Indeed, for many writers in the *Register* the national state remained the most important arena of struggle for a democratic-socialist society.

Principles and Core Elements of Democratic Socialism
Socialist Register provided three basic definitions of socialism. Miliband emphasised its democratic dimension in his article "Counter-Hegemonic Struggles" and described it as the extension of democracy to all spheres of societal life (1990: 356). Democratic decision making would create a society (this was his second definition) that consisted of what he called genuine communities (cf. ibid: 363). These definitions were accompanied by a more orthodox Marxist comment from Lebowitz who maintained – within the context of a contribution which warned of giving too much away of Marxist approaches – that socialism should still be seen as a transitional phase, a stage on the move from capitalism to communism (cf. 1991: 361). Obviously, several intellectuals regarded these definitions as important tools to make their idea of socialism distinguishable from the authoritarian, repressive perversions (as Arthur MacEwan put it) with which the term was associated (cf. 1990: 324). Additionally, like in *New Left Review*, the holistic claim of socialism was seriously contested, or at least seen as in need of specifications. This was, for example, Geras's argument, who intended to save Marxism from simplistic critiques through stressing its self-conscious modesty. Thus he explained that (socialist) feminism and (socialist) anti-racism had their own specific objectives (cf. 1990: 30):

Beyond continuing to register how different forms of domination can often feed off and mutually reinforce one another, socialists have to recognize that socialism, ambitious and difficult of attainment as it has proved to be, is one goal, relatively distinct from other emancipatory goals; which are of their own pressing urgency, the obstacles and resistances to them being the source of plenty human misery and stifled potentialities. [...] Any battle against one grave systemic injustice diminishes itself by ignoring other such equally grave injustices, or by making light of them. (ibid)

Specific objectives could, of course, be conflicting or contradictory. Thus democratic decision-making had an important role to play. However, although a great deal of thought was spent on explaining democratic socialism, such clarifications focused more on the differences between socialist and capitalist democracy than on terms of structural details. Levins, for example, stated that

[t]he difference between socialist and bourgeois ideas of democracy remains valid: while the one aims at the mobilization of the creative and critical intelligence and knowledge of the whole people on behalf of a common enterprise, the other is organized around the management of dissent within a safe domain and the competition for office. (1990: 339)

He explicitly welcomed the achievements of bourgeois democracy which succeeded in terminating particular abuses and thus helped the liberation struggles of the oppressed classes. Hence, it should not be dismissed but incorporated and invigorated (ibid). The core idea for Levins consisted of an activist democracy, in the attempt at using the intelligence of all people for problem solving and the corrections of errors in the organisation of economics, politics and social life (ibid: 345). Cox added that there were three meanings of democracy: a bourgeois version of liberal pluralism, a socialist meaning of producer self-management (under conditions of central planning), and a third meaning, also socialist – but unlike the second without historical precedence and yet to be realised – of popular participation in central planning (1991: 184). This final version constituted the most attractive way forward for a new socialism (ibid).

Such a project could only work under conditions of equality. The goal of equality appeared of course quite often in the pages of *Socialist Register*, but again it was Wallerstein who gave it the most radical meaning by insisting that it had to be understood globally (cf. 1992: 108). He reiterated a perspective formulated one year earlier by Miliband who claimed that "'[a] radical alternative', as I understand it, simply means the creation of a comparative, egalitarian, democratic, and ultimately classless society, to be replicated in due course throughout the world" (1991: 349). Interesting in Wallerstein's contribution was the suggestion to develop a collective, group-related understanding of equality which he saw, liberalism's official high esteem for individualism notwithstanding, at work also in capitalism. He wanted to replace the group ideology of "survival of the fittest" with another: the recognition of equal rights of all groups in a reconstructed world system – while acknowledging that individuals should never be reduced to being nothing but members of groups, collectives or 'masses' (1992: 107-8). Apart from this perspective, which integrated associationalist and communitarianist elements, also more traditional interpretations of equality were published, which understood it as a matter of redistribution of resources, income, and working time. Redistribution was required to limit economic growth, and such reallocation should be accompanied by an economic strategy that prioritised national and local needs, along the lines of the programme of the Bennite left in the British Labour Party of the late 1970s and early 1980s (cf. Panitch 1994: 89-91). Such a programme – this lesson could also be drawn from the Benn experience – would be impossible to realise without restricting the power of capital (cf. Albo 1994: 163). Finally, and the ultimate goals should not be neglected as Singer wrote in his "In Defence of Utopia", for Marxists, the pursuit of equality entailed the replacement of exchange value by use value (1993: 255). This move would also contribute to a more cautious treatment of the natural environment (cf. Albo 1994: 166). At the same time, this strategy aimed at changing the dominant view of labour as a private commodity (cf. Lebowitz 1991: 363).

Equality, democracy and environmental sustainability served as general points of orientation. More concretely, authors were convinced of the superiority of, and, for both moral and strategic reasons, the necessity of public ownership. On the one hand, private ownership was declared to be morally inferior: Miliband admonished that private armies were universally seen as abominable, but other private enterprises not (cf. 1991: 387). On the other hand, only democratically controlled public ownership could muster the material preconditions for initiating and maintaining the move towards a socialist society by ending the power imbalances inherently linked with systems of private ownership:

> There are, however, reasons other than 'efficiency' for wanting a mixed economy with a predominant public sector. One crucial such reason is that public ownership removes from private hands the control of assets and resources which [...] are of essential importance to society. (ibid)

The pragmatic way forward thus required an alternative economic strategy and a change in the ownership of the means of production in order to move towards social justice and the extension of democracy (cf. Albo 1994:166-7).

Like the contributors to *New Left Review*, the authors in *Socialist Register* could envisage the achievement of socialism only as a long-term process (cf. Wallerstein 1992: 108). The goals and principles to be popularised in order to convince people were not new – but the central place for democracy could not be mentioned often enough at the historical conjuncture of the early 1990s. The task of working for a socialist future was more than merely a political decision. It was based on a particular understanding of human beings and the human condition which distinguished socialists from conservatives and liberals. This understanding, at least according to John Griffith in his discussion on the status of rights maintained that:

> Socialists are different again [from conservatives and liberals; S.B.]. They believe humanity to be composed of social animals, a collection of individuals who are inseparable from the society in which they live. From conception until death they are integral part of society. Their problems arise from this. This is the human situation, perhaps the human tragedy. In this society there are no natural rights, only those which society has conferred. (1993: 123)

Reflections on Institutional Arrangements
Since the sphere of work played a central role for socialist principles, the shape of the production process and its control were at the core of the *Register's* reflections on the organisational features of a democratic socialist society. A great deal of thought was spent on issues such as more democratic workplace structures, the redistribution of work, democratic planning of employment as the major tasks a democratic socialist state had to organise

(cf. Albo 1994: 164-166). The authors understood a socialist democracy as an institutional arrangement that followed established democratic procedures while at the same time actively pursuing the empowerment of working people (cf. MacEwan 1990: 324-5). Moves towards socialism required, as institutional foundation, the socialisation of the most important means of production and the creation of democratic, decentralised decision-making structures (cf. Lebowitz 1991: 367). The latter aspect, that of decentralisation, was crucial for autonomous work control (cf. MacEwan 1990: 325). It seems that the authors did not want to introduce this model too abruptly; instead they envisaged a gradual process, where the production process was carefully planned (in order to serve a number of functions defined on the basis of democratic socialist values) and this planning became more and more decentralised over time (cf. Levins 1990: 338). Their model constituted a mixture of subsidiarity, grassroots democracy, and workers control. Levins, for instance, suggested measures such as the participation of volunteers in working committees of legislative bodies, the extensive nation-wide discussion of suggested legislation, the compulsory reporting-back of elected representatives, and collective leadership (ibid). Albo intended to set up national and sectional planning structures (cf. 1994: 164). Bienefeld demanded a version of subsidiarity that would leave decision making decentralised and as much as possible in the realm of the market (and to a certain extent allow private ownership) – as long as the framework of social and environmental sustainability was not violated (cf. 1994: 125).

Institutional arrangements such as these relied – as already stated – on a number of preconditions: the private sector should be subordinate to the public sector (cf. Miliband 1991: 386). This suggestion not only echoed the critique of the British left that the private had always dominated the public sector in the UK, but it was also founded on the idea that the public sector was the 'base' from which to build new, non-competitive social relations (ibid: 388). Secondly, as Panitch expressed it, it was necessary to restructure the hierarchy of state apparatuses. Thirdly, since contributors to *Socialist Register* assumed these developments would take place on the nation-state level, protectionist strategies were essential: these would include capital controls and some trade controls to allow inward industrialisation instead of export-oriented growth (cf. Panitch 1994: 90; Albo 1994: 163). Finally, such arrangements would require a world system that did not privilege one mode of growth and sanction all others, but instead allowed for different paths of economic development (cf. Albo 1994: 163) and additionally penalised the causing and export of environmental "externalities" (ibid).

The last point was important: the institutional set-up needed not only to empower the weaker parts of society, it also had to fulfil a number of normative considerations, nationally and internationally, derived from the debate on democratic-socialist goals and priorities. For example, it had to serve environmental purposes, such as, through the acceptance of tariffs that allowed countries to implement or maintain high social and environmental standards. It had to support the expansion of a democratically controlled third sector of social and cultural services. Finally, it had to work towards overcoming the sexual division of labour and the creation of a non-racist, non-militaristic, and generally non-competitive society which rewarded caring as a socially helpful activity and transformed the welfare system from a stigmatising into an empowering institution.

Obviously all this could not be achieved by a free association of individuals. Hence, a strong state was needed, at least for a "young" socialist society, as Miliband explained. However, this state had to be constitutionally controlled as well as checked and complemented by popular power (cf. 1990: 357). Miliband and Panitch insisted that "[t]he socialist project is not about more or less state but about a different kind of state" (1992: 23). Concretely, the constitutional arrangements would have to be radically revised. One important question, however, remained: how to deal with the resistance to such alterations? Again, the authors seemed to understand opposition primarily in terms of class antagonism. Thus Bienefeld suggested addressing the problem in the following way:

It [the group of those who profit from the institutional arrangements in capitalist states; SB] must be persuaded by argument and by the threat of political opposition to accept a political compromise through which it can regain its social and political legitimacy, in return for agreeing to recreate sovereign political spaces within which capital, labour, and other constituencies can bargain and in which the resulting agreements can be forced, in which the process can establish social, political, ethical and environmental priorities and trade them off against efficiency; and in which full employment can be pursued as an overriding priority. (1994: 112)

When looking for models that could provide direction or inspiration, the contributors listed three very different types of experiments. Firstly, Foster hinted at the U.S. New Deal and especially its *Works Progress Authority*. The project's importance lay in the fact that it did not follow a capitalist logic but instead, in its job creation programmes, considered where people lived, what their capabilities were and acted on these premises. Foster agreed with *Monthly Review*'s Paul Sweezy and Harry Magdoff who were involved in setting up New Deal policies, that lessons could be drawn from the programme: it showed the way for a concrete anti-capitalist strategy as the beginning of a long revolution (cf. Foster 1990: 278). Secondly, Levins detected forms of grassroots democracy in the states of the Eastern Bloc. He pointed, for instance, to neighbourhood courts which "demystified" the legal process and to the historical example of Makarenko's pedagogical work with communities of orphans (1990: 338).[1] According to Levins, the problem was that grassroots activities had lost most of their real content in socialist countries. Yet he saw parallels with grassroots experiments in other parts of the world – in both, advanced capitalist as well as in developing countries: feminist consciousness-raising groups, liberation theology's base communities, participatory action research, and the educational theories of Paulo Freire (cf. ibid).[2] Finally, there were lessons to be learned from France and Britain in the late 1970s and early 1980s; Albo claimed that France was, in the early years of the Mitterand presidency, more successful in its economic strategy than was normally admitted and had avoided the sharp downturn experienced by most other OECD countries (cf. 1994: 160). Panitch highlighted the eventually abortive attempts by sections of the British Labour Party to implement democratic-socialist decision making both within the party and also in local politics (cf. 1994: 91). All these reflections suggested a combination of grassroots and state-led initiatives for a move towards a democratic socialist society.

---

1 Demystification in this context meant to free the judicial system of the perception that it followed universal or foundational values and needed sophisticated procedures and to anchor judicial decisions within the population and trust their sense of justice and fairness.

2 He added the theories of Gramsci and the work of Che Guevara to his list of precedents and starting points of socialist democracy (cf. Levins 1990: 338).

Requirements
Reflections on preconditions and chances of success for socialist democratic structures were seldom and short. For most writers it seemed clear that the adequate strategy for a democratic-socialist left was to transform the state rather than either to over-ambitiously transcend it (an allegation directed against "ultra leftist" groups) or to be content with shaping it as a 'progressive' competitive state in an era of global capitalism (as social democrats were accused of doing) (cf. Panitch 1994: 87). This transformation required, as already mentioned, a combination of parliamentary and extra-parliamentary activity – especially for bold programmes of economic recovery which could receive their dynamics from building improved public infrastructure. For Miliband and Panitch in particular, it seemed crucial to find a strategy for initiating change which would then, almost automatically, continue to gather momentum (cf. 1992: 23). They described democratic socialists' task as "giving people a sense that something can be done about the crisis, which is the key to further popular mobilization in even more radical directions" (ibid). This was as true for Western societies as it was for the transformed countries in Eastern Europe, where the removal of dictatorships had generated formally democratic regimes with highly inegalitarian social orders (ibid: 16-7). Linda Gordon raised another issue in emphasising the centrality of utopian thinking (in her case, especially, inventing concrete utopian models of welfare provision) for new dreams and ideas of democratic socialism and liberated societies (cf. 1990: 172). In terms of political geography, it seemed unclear where moves towards democratic socialism were most likely to be started. Generally, writers seemed to expect them from the industrial North rather than from the South and Miliband invested his trust in the few "third way" activists who were still struggling in Eastern Europe; he felt they constituted the best "slender hope" for an emerging socialist society, they should be supported by Western socialists (1991: 388-389).

Questions and Dilemmas
Socialist Register dealt in a more conclusive way with difficult questions than its British sister publication. The problems identified were similar; here contributors also asked themselves what to do in order to secure the gains achieved on the route to a democratic socialist society. In an article on the question whether Marxists should follow Marx' legal relativism,

Amy Bartholomew hinted at possible dilemmas: how to deal with what she still called counter-revolutionaries and how to come to terms with people who demanded "too much" in a period of economic transition from capitalism to socialism? Her conclusion was different from that expressed by Honderich in the *Review*. She claimed that individual rights could be infringed but "as little as possible congruent with the importance of realizing the objective to be secured by that encroachment" (Bartholomew 1990: 259). Hence, she did not completely rule out such infringement – despite all the dangers connected with such restrictions, of which she claimed to be very aware:

> Thus, the commitment [to individual rights; SB] does not entail the conclusion that we never limit or even deny rights. Rather, it indicates that each limitation and denial must be justified and if not abhorred at least undertaken with the recognition that an accumulation of limits and denials chips slowly away at the culture which sustains respect for the protections and entitlements we call rights. (ibid)

No explicit contradictions to this opinion can be found in the pages of *Socialist Register* – one could argue, however, that Miliband's and Panitch's insistence on the transformation of the state accompanied by an incremental radicalisation of the population was at variance with it (as were Bienefeld's suggestions to "convince" the dominant strata of society by argument and the "threat of political opposition" (1994: 12).[3]

As stated above, the transformation of socialism into radical democracy and the abolition and replacement of the term were not backed in the *Register*'s pages. However, it did discuss whether the whole range of emancipatory struggles could be subsumed under the heading of socialism. When Geras pointed out that Marxists had exaggerated the link between achieving socialism and, almost automatically, overcoming all kinds of oppression, he also raised the question whether a society organised on socialist principles was a "good society" or only part of a "good society" (1990: 29-30). He

---

3   Due to its character as an annual publication, there were hardly any debates within *Socialist Register*, unlike in the other journals discussed. Although the editors claimed each year that the *Register* did not have a general line, there were limitations of what counted as acceptable for publication and what not. Bartholomew's article apparently was not beyond this line.

self-critically conceded that the traditional tendency to take the part for the whole had contributed to an over-reliance on the working class as historical agent (cf. ibid). This certainly was not meant as a farewell to the working class. However, the statement underlined a clear commitment to accept the multiplicity and many faces of oppression and the possible contradictions involved in tackling them. This stance made it perhaps easier to be more conclusive about another important issue – that of living standards. Gregory Albo left no doubt that with a reduction of working time – which he regarded as necessary for political, social and environmental reasons – certain cuts in living standards were unavoidable (cf. 1994: 165). It seemed that writers in *Socialist Register* were convinced that there was no use in evading difficult questions and no alternative to coming to terms with the problems of the realisation of a 'good life' everywhere rather than just in the rich global North.

Dissent

More than any other publication, Dissent clearly and emphatically dealt with the questions of values, goals and principles in its reflections on the future shape of democratic socialism. Two problems seemed to be of crucial importance: the relationships of democratic socialists with social (or liberal) democracy and of individualism and collectivism. Obviously, these issues were important enough to be covered not only in numerous articles by regular contributors to the magazine but also by a wide variety of 'externals', ranging from proponents of associationalism via leading post-Marxists, such as Chantal Mouffe, and representatives of the left wing of liberalism in the American sense of the term, to dissident socialists from an earlier era like the Italian liberal socialist and anti-fascist Carlo Rosselli whose work was discussed in the previous chapter. Additionally, the editors found it helpful to look to the other side of the Atlantic: not only to Italian socialism, but also to British political theorists, and to the role model of Swedish social democracy and its welfare state. That Dissent's approach appeared to be even more concerned with ethical questions than that of the other journals could be partly explained with the strong current of political theorists among the magazine's contributors but partly also because of its basic assumption that the problem of what had become of the Eastern European states could not be explained without discussing the ethics and values of socialism. Based on their anti-Communist history, it seemed insufficient for these intellectuals to restrict explanations to Cold War confrontations and the state socialism's internal degenerations. With few exceptions (such as the contribution by H. Brand [1991]), questions of the global political economy (and thus global living standards) and of the concrete institutional set-up of a socialist society played a minor role. As a consequence, the related questions of necessary preconditions of and possible obstacles hindering the move towards socialist societies were dealt with less extensively. However, despite the narrower focus, the normative and ethical questions featured in the journal bore more than sufficient material for disagreement. It is quite obvious, however, that such disagreements were rarely expressed in the open. Contradictory statements appeared side by side in the pages of the journal and this coexistence could be read on the one hand as a commitment to the type of democratic pluralism Dissenters viewed as indispensable for any future moves towards socialism, but on the other as a symptom of what Michael Walzer called the "period of uncertainty and confusion" (1992: 466).

Principles and Core Elements of Democratic Socialism
Dissent came forward with a number of new attempts at grasping the meaning of democratic socialism by means of definition-like statements. These were more diverse than in the other journals and, arguably, often even contradictory. Firstly, authors suggested definitions foregrounding the economic dimension. Robert Dahl characterised democratic socialism as a third way between a planned economy and a free market (cf. 1990: 225). Others put forward a political-economic definition, regarding the essence of socialism as being the primacy of politics over the economy (Ryan 1990: 442). Additionally, there was a class-based, social definition stating that democratic socialism stood for the "effective extension of the liberties of the bourgeoisie to all" (Rosselli 1993: 118). For Dennis Wong, the opposite of socialism was not capitalism but individualism and egoism, thus he transferred, more consequently than most others, the question of socialism from property relations and the organisation of the economy to ethics. Furthermore, there was a 'reformist' definition by Howe, claiming that democratic socialists – despite the necessity of values and utopias – should not try to create a "new man" (1992: 144-145). He was seconded by Michel Rocard, former French prime minister and thus a practitioner of reformism in a moderate, gradualist declaration: "I call socialism the collective wish

for social justice, for less arbitrariness, for a reduction of inequality to a level that corresponds to the distribution of talents, risks, and responsibilities" (Rocard & Ricoeur 1991: 506). Finally, one could also find more traditional historical-teleological definitions like that by Branko Horvat: "Socialism is a phase in the process of the individuation of men and women, of their emancipation from various collectivities (tribe, estate, class, nation), of their progress in the direction of individual self-determination" (1991: 107). Perceptions of socialism thus ranged from innovative ideas of what constituted an individual's 'good life' to a different organisation of the processes and relations of production. Yet no one defended the idea of revolutionary overthrow of the existing order. Socialism did not mean a comprehensive break with exiting forms of social organisation. This position was representative of *Dissent*'s early break with vanguardism. Consequently, the central concept for *Dissenters* was democracy. Its dominant status was repeated in numerous articles which left no doubt that there was no falling-back behind the standards set by capitalist (or liberal) democracy. Not all contributors went as far as Dennis Wong, who suggested substituting "democratic socialism" with other terms such as "social democratic liberalism" or "liberal social democracy" to underline democracy's superior status (Rule & Wong 1990: 485). Others looked at the ways in which the two could be linked.

All *Dissenters* would agree, however, that the form of democratic societal organisation they envisaged was different from the democracy that existed in the United States and in other Western countries – even if several of them regarded the Scandinavian countries as coming rather close to their ideals. The responsibility of the left was to initiate an extension of democracy – some would call it its radicalisation or expansion while others preferred to describe it as a move towards socialism. Among the first group was the post-Marxist theorist Chantal Mouffe: "There are still numerous social arenas and relationships where democratisation is critically needed. The task for the left today is to describe how this can be achieved in a way that is compatible with the existence of a liberal democratic regime" (1993: 81). The centrality of democracy for the authors was related to the centrality of individual freedom, which, as Dennis Wong argued, needed to have precedence over all other values (cf. Rule & Wong 1990: 485). These shifts in focus implied that democratic socialists had to accept the fact that ultimately not everyone would be converted to socialism (cf. Ryan 1990: 437-438).

Judging solely from these reflections one might wonder whether any distinction remained between democratic socialism and social (or liberal) democracy or whether Dennis Wong's recommendation to abandon the term was consistently accepted by the majority of contributors. However, not all writers agreed with him. Two differences were retained in several contributions: the first consisted of the presumed necessity to do more than to just correct the failures and excesses of capitalism. The Canadian Bob Rae expressed this position quite powerfully: "If the best democratic socialism can offer is 'a little more of this and a little more of that', we might as well pack our bags and call it a day" (1991: 45). The second, and related, difference lay in a long-term project which had to be borne in mind and required utopian thinking (cf. Denitch 1991: 103; Howe 1993: 145). The dream of eventually achieving a society that looked radically different from the present and had abolished, for example, wage labour was not ruled out entirely. The only aspect to be abandoned was the infringement of individual liberties in order to arrive there. This hope for change was based on the assumption that socialism did not constitute so much a break with the past as its logical continuation. Horvat, for example, argued that socialism contributed to fulfilling three principles underlying bourgeois revolutions and societies: liberty, equality, and solidarity (cf. 1991: 107). This old triad also became the means by which *Dissenters* believed the contentious relationship of individualism and equality could be overcome. When discussing post-Marxist Paul Hirst's reflections on associationalism, Mouffe conceded that certain types of individualism might prove conflictual, but that such strife could be avoided by recourse to an idea of a republican common good (cf. 1993: 85). Insisting that universalism and individualism had to be seen as related, she explained:

The problem is to understand the individual, not as a monad, an 'unencumbered' self existing previous to and independent of society, but as constituted by an ensemble of 'subject positions', participating in a multiplicity of social relationships, member of many communities and participant in a plurality of collective identifications. (ibid)

These ideas built a bridge on which *Dissenters* could discuss ideas not just of republicanism and republican virtues, but also communitarianism (as suggested, in a left version, by Michael Walzer) and associationalism. They remained sceptical of libertarian versions of these theories and maintained that political institutions were necessary, even if certain critics, such as Horvat, hoped to replace party politics – he saw parties as agglomerations of power – with "citizens' politics" (1991: 107).

As in the other journals, the question of power relations was regarded as very important. For socialists, as Alan Ryan insisted, community could only mean a "community of equals" (1990: 440). This equality did not necessarily mean the levelling of all wealth differentials, but instead its precondition was a redistribution of economic and political power (cf. Horvat 1991: 108). Such reallocations could only be achieved through changes in the organisation of the economy. This view that successful political change required economic change was, of course, not new; it had been essential to many orthodox old-leftists, a line of reasoning which *Dissenters* now partially shared. However, *Dissenter's* arguments for some form of a socialised economy and for the crucial role of economic planning were not restricted to this traditional materialist view; like contributors to *Socialist Register*, they questioned the environmental sustainability of an unregulated capitalism and even its macro-economic sense. For Ryan, an unregulated private economy had intrinsic self-destructive tendencies which had to be controlled (cf. 1990: 439). He saw it as an essential task of socialism to overcome these deficiencies in the economic system (ibid: 440). He denied that the collapse of the state socialist societies had proven that there was no sensible way in which economic planning could reduce the waste of human resources and talents and the irrationalities of unorganised production and distribution (ibid: 442). Neither, he went on, did Hitler or Mussolini discredit corporatist critiques of an unorganised capitalism (cf. ibid). As a result of his article, he pointed out that "[s]ocialism as such must [...] center on the public control of the consequences of an economic system based on private property" (ibid). Others, like Rae, were more straightforward: he declared that in order to make the difference between a productive economy and a casino, democratic socialism had to do more than just control the excesses of the capitalist system (cf. 1991: 43-45). Denitch again went a step further when suggesting to expand workers control over their workplace and to abolish the present concentration of private ownership (cf. 1991: 105). The problem remained how to organise this kind of economic decision making and interventionism, given the fact that, as

Edward Broadbent stated and the experience of the Eastern European states had made clear, state and private ownership were both alienating (cf. 1991: 83). The suggestions published in the pages of *Dissent* included (apart from market socialism) a combination of Swedish corporatism, a socialised sector, and diverse forms of grassroots economic planning. These propositions came from what could be regarded as the left wing of *Dissent*. Joanne Barkan, for example, pleaded for extending the small sector of cooperatives that already existed. These could become a vanguard of self-reliant and responsible economic decision making (cf. 1991: 97-98). Brand wanted to put the lever elsewhere and turned to corporate structures: he saw them as necessary for reducing the influence of shareholders, and for creaming-off and reinvesting dividends (cf. 1991: 99). The structures he proposed were different from those found in ordinary corporatist capitalism: he fancied a tripartite structure of representatives of the public, of the labour force, and of consumer groups (cf. ibid). Only by reorganising the conditions of economic production in such ways could economic liberty become a reality – in a specific sense as it was understood by Carol Rosselli in the first half of the twentieth century: not as a liberated economy but as people liberated from economic coercion and hardship (cf. 1993: 119).

Such liberation would mean the – at least partial – decommodification of labour, of the allocation process of goods and services and, thus, of social life as a whole. Ernest Erber expressed his opinion that it was only once the polity as a whole decided over the allocation of resources, that there could be a chance at satisfying a society's collective needs (and to tackle social and environmental problems)(cf. 1990: 360). Brand further explained that the decommodification of labour in practice meant the massive expansion of a social wage, which should be material as well as security-providing; hinting at the writings of Gösta Esping-Anderson, he envisaged collective social services, unemployment and sickness compensation, employment security, and general income maintenance (cf. Brand 1991: 99). Cohen emphasised that such measures indeed worked towards moves towards a democratic socialist society and put them into the same context as Branko Horvat – using a term from the U.S. Declaration of Independence, Cohen made them a completion of the promises of eighteenth-century bourgeois revolutions: "To go beyond the welfare state is to make its gains irreversible and to democratise the conditions of production. It is to make employment, health care, housing – the basics of human welfare – together with democratic control of the workplace 'inalienable rights'" (1991: 101).

The emphasis on decommodification could be interpreted as an echo of the 'post-materialist' political visions of the new social movements. However, recourse to the agenda of the new social movements occurred only infrequently. Occasionally, environmental issues were mentioned, mostly as an argument supporting the necessity of economic planning (cf. Erber 1990: 360). Rae hinted at the important task of combating the disadvantages of women, disabled people, and visible minorities (cf. 1991: 45) and Ryan, finally, insisted that struggles against disadvantages could not be successful as long as they were not accompanied by the struggle for socialism. He claimed this to be the lesson to be drawn from the experience of the 1960s (cf. 1990: 442). Another parallel to feminist thinking could be found in Mouffe's discussion of Norberto Bobbio which emphasised the need to democratise institutions in all areas of social life: "To democratise society requires, for Bobbio, tackling all the institutions – from family to school, from big business to public administration – that are not run democratically" (1993: 83). Despite the rare exceptions, generally the agendas and the political ideas of the new social movements did not qualify as very important sources of inspirations for *Dissent*'s contributors.

Instead, more than in other journals, writers for *Dissent* stressed the indispensability of a commitment to the primacy of the individual. Most of the time, they did not see this as a problem for moves towards democratic socialism. When they did, the primacy was not questioned – rather it was suggested to abandon the goal of democratic socialism instead. *Dissent*'s principles could be interpreted as being more self-confidently moderate than the other journals': they seemed to be more at ease with reformist and gradualist approaches and did not even necessarily justify these principles as immediate steps towards a far more ambitious distant goal. However, differences of opinion existed between social democratic contributors and the more left wing faction. This pluralism of positions remained responsible for most of the contradictory statements on ideas and goals.

Reflections on Institutional Arrangements
Among *Dissent*'s institutional concepts, market socialism and the state played central roles. For most contributors, market socialism, in which neither private economic privilege nor an over-powerful state could gain a

dominant position in the decision-making process, formed a core element of a democratic socialism. These reflections on market socialism were part of a more general idea of economic democracy. Nevertheless, the state was indispensable – as H. Brand made clear:

> Furthermore, I believe that the state must ultimately guide all *major* investment in productive equipment and structures, human resources, and social infrastructure. This role for the state remains, notwithstanding all that has happened in Eastern Europe, a central problem, perhaps the central problem for social democracy and democratic socialism. (1991: 99)

As already mentioned, such state guidance did not necessarily mean public ownership in all cases, but entailed instead a mixed economy of state and private ownership in combination with cooperative enterprises. Authors admitted that state (or public) ownership might be advantageous in some instances, but they did not see it as the dominant form of ownership in a socialist economy (cf. Rae: 44, Cohen 1991: 101, Urbinati 1993: 116). *Dissenters* obviously subscribed to two broad ideas on the institutional organisation of a democratic-socialist society: The first wanted to democratise decision making in the *economy*, the second in all other aspects of *social life*. Concerning the economy, writers envisaged a corporatist set-up where workers should be members of the boards of directors of either publicly or privately owned enterprises. Above all, they should be involved in deciding the future direction of production – this was seen as a massive extension of liberal democracy (cf. Broadbent 1991: 82). Bob Rae's idea on this issue resembled the abortive Swedish attempts at implementing wage-earners funds which would incrementally de-privatise ownership. He suggested pension funds as a strategy for exerting control (cf. 1991: 44). It was also necessary, according to the writers, to control the banks and thus not only productive but even more financial capital. For democratising society comprehensively (or at least its public sphere – in how far writers agreed with Bobbio's suggestion to democratise all institutions, including for instance families, that were not yet 'run' democratically, was not clear), a legal framework had to be designed that allowed for a democratically controlled interventionist welfare state. Additionally, regulations were needed in such areas as protection of the environment, affirmative action, mandatory paid vacation, universal health, education, and childcare (cf. Broadbent

1991: 82). In order to avoid the development of a concentration of power to such a degree that it might become dangerous for democracy, Horvat suggested extending one of its core ideas: the separation of powers. In addition to the classical division of legislative, executive and judicative he added an administrative, a recruiting and a controlling power (cf. 1991: 108). For Urbinati, such a horizontal separation should be combined with vertical and professional ones; parliamentary democracy should be accompanied by regional autonomy and workshop democracy (cf. 1993: 116). Civil society would thus, as a federation of federations, control the state and reproduce principles of resistance organisation in fascist Italy (ibid). Finally, writers in the magazine came forward with ideas for arrangements of political interest articulation and accountability. Horvat, in accordance with his ambition to replace party democracy by popular democracy, wished to see representatives held responsible to their electors and the people they represented rather than to their parties (cf. 1991: 107). Cohen anticipated a democratic socialist culture built, like the United States, on a two-party system, but unlike the United States, consisting of two socialist rather than two capitalist parties, one of which would be a bit more radical than the other (cf. 1991: 101).

Dissenters' attempts at identifying existing models were mainly historical, as has already become clear; besides resistance Italy and welfare-state Sweden during the golden age of social democracy, they also pointed to developments in the Anglo-American world. Dahl, for instance, repeated Karl Polanyi's argument that British economic, social and political theory with thinkers such as Bentham, Ricardo, Burke, Malthus, Marx, Mill, Darwin, and Spencer had come forward from early on with institutional suggestions for replacing the unregulated economic life of the late eigtheenth and early nineteenth century. As a consequence, Britain's social relations had already in the later part of the nineteenth century been regulated by the state (cf. 1990: 225-226). The necessity of controlling banks had gained respect in the United States during the New Deal era (cf. Ryan 1990: 441). Finally, the United States's experience was important in a further respect – it was based not on the idea of a social contract, but on the republican tradition. It was this perception of collective life not as an infringement to liberty but as an enrichment of the self that, according Mouffe's reflections, would allow the democratic creation of a society that had a common socialist purpose to which the people would subscribe (cf. 1993: 84).

Requirements
Dissenters remained mostly silent on the preconditions and chances of a development towards democratic socialism. Most of them shied away from any teleological perceptions of history and thus from reflections on conditions and factors influencing it. However, they remained confident that social change for the better was possible. Social change seemed linked to the belief in human perfectibility. Though *Dissent* did in fact reprint Rosselli's conviction that the latter was unlimited (cf. 1993: 117), various authorial disagreements as to how far this gradual social improvement would proceed seem to suggest that not all contributors subscribed to Rosselli's position. Indeed, statements of modesty, such as Howe's call for utopias for a *better* rather than a perfect society, or Ryan's doubts that everyone would accept the merits of socialism, do not support a claim of unanimity among contributors. As they did not necessarily ascribe to an unqualified faith in humankind, many authors concentrated instead on the values and institutions that might improve the living conditions of the less privileged and might reduce the destructiveness of capitalism. Improving society obviously had a great deal to do with creative political activity, or as Denitch put it: "I believe that only in societies with a high degree of autonomous self-organisation and a thick set of overlapping movements and institutions, does it become possible to think of moving beyond the limits that capitalist civilization sets" (1991: 104). Despite Brand's opinion that the realisation of certain ideas of socialism depended on the "historical setting of a given society", statements such as Denitch's must be read as a prioritisation of ethics and practical democratic experimentation over materialist analyses of the development of capitalism and the political economy, as well as the power structures of the contemporary world (1991: 99).

Questions and Dilemmas
The main difficulty for *Dissenters* was formulated by its editor, Mitchell Cohen: for them, socialism appeared to be more of a problem than a panacea (cf. 1994: 377). Socialism seemed unduly problematic not only because of the realities of the Eastern Bloc, but also because, as a utopian idea, it expressed how society should look like without explaining how to arrive there, now that the most successful model had failed. The crucial question for socialists thus was how to translate socialist concepts into practice or at least how to move towards doing so and it was this limitation which trig-

gered many of *Dissent*'s circumspect positions. Concrete issues were nevertheless raised and difficult questions asked. However, the answers were not often discussed and the problems hardly ever solved.

The existence of a global economy constituted one of these problems. Brand explained that de-linking from global infrastructures would not be beneficial and had ended in disaster for the Eastern Bloc. He argued that one should instead support global struggles for economic regulation (cf. 1991: 100). The question was not discussed any further and to support which struggles in what ways did not become clear.[4] Ricoeur agreed to the idea of a mixed economy but missed any reflections on the question which parts of economic activity were best left in private hands and in the markets, and where public planning for production and distribution would make sense (cf. Rocard & Ricoeur 1991: 505). The final question concerned the role of the state. While there was widespread agreement of its necessity (even among communitarianists such as Walzer), no one contradicted Paul Hirst when he suggested that both democratic socialists and environmentalists should no longer rely on the state (and should instead work through associations) (cf. 1994: 243). Apart from this fundamental problem, the question remained what to do concretely to limit the power of the state (which was just as likely to be destructive as it was to be beneficial) and how to liberate it from its close ties to economic power – a particularly important task in the U.S. context. Although writers were obviously aware of these problems, they were discussed nowhere in the pages of *Dissent*. Just like in *New Left Review*, this seemed to testify to certain helplessness among thinkers confronted with these problems.

Monthly Review

It was already mentioned that *Monthly Review* maintained its faith in the chance of reforming the U.S.S.R. well into the early 1990s, that they saw the Eastern Bloc's disintegration as anything but the proof of the superiority of Western-style democracy, and that they focussed less exclusively on the not so hopeful situations in Europe and North America than the other three magazines. With such a background, re-thinking democratic socialism

---

4   It was only several years later that *Dissent* started regular coverage of "globalisation", and analysed its consequences for the international economy and for the United States.

was perhaps less pressing a task than for the other journals and their contributors. Nevertheless, *Monthly Review* also published articles dealing with questions of democratic socialism and the organisation of a future economic system which would be both just and sustainable. The specificity of their point of view came from close contact with, and frequent contributions by, dependency theorist Samir Amin as well as activists in Latin America. Obviously, it was the specific ethical socialism of the Latin American left which explained *Monthly Review*'s interest in the moral and spiritual dimension of progressive and socialist thought. Against these backgrounds, the journal's mood seemed to be less subdued than the others' though the questions they discussed were often identical ones. Given this focus, the Review may have felt less threatened by recent developments, which might also explain why the journal paid less attention to institutional questions than, for example, *Socialist Register* – the publication closest to it in terms of political outlook. The definition and explanation of socialist principles and goals, however, received considerable emphasis in *Monthly Review*'s pages.

Principles and Core Elements of Democratic Socialism
Like the other journals, *Monthly Review* offered several definitions of socialism, which were, however, less contradictory than the ones in *Dissent*. Amin succinctly summarised socialism as the replacement of competition by cooperation (cf. 1990: 13). Thus, socialism became capitalism's "significant other" on the world-historical stage, as Sweezy pointed out in 1993 (1993: 1). In an interview with the British singer Billy Bragg, socialism was defined as being "about loving and caring for other people" (Batstone 1991: 25). This definition is one example among several which used humanist rather than political or Marxist language and hinted at the spiritual dimension which a number of writers considered important. The following two definitions differed from those in the other journals in so far as they gave socialism a much broader meaning: for Magdoff, socialist struggle denoted the sum of all struggles for human emancipation whose purpose was to combat racism, nationalist and ethnic rivalries, and patriarchal hierarchies (cf. 1991: 5). Löwy defined a socialist society as "a form of society where the associated producers are the masters of the process of production, a society based on the largest economic, social and political democracy, a commonwealth liberated from all class, ethnic, and gender exploitation and

oppression" (1991: 33). These adaptations combined the classical Marxist version of socialism with the agendas of feminism and the new social movements.

Contributors did not shy away from tall orders: Amin demanded an awareness of the cultural universalism of humanity's project and thus hinted at the global dimension which democratic socialism had to consider (cf. 1990: 28). This was in line with his critique of the privileging of Western traditions and problems. The synthesis of human desires for unbroken community as well as a fully developed individuality (cf. Kovel 1994: 41), and a solidarity that was strong enough to transcend group interests, and sufficiently circumspect to combine environmental sustainability with preferential treatment for the poorest parts of the world's population (cf. Hinkelammert 1993: 110). In the context of a sympathetic evaluation of Cuba, Alice Walker declared: "This empowerment of the poor: literacy, good health, adequate housing, freedom from ignorance, is the work of everyone of conscience in the coming century" (1994: 42).

As in the other publications, *Monthly Review* featured perspectives which claimed that while socialism remained an ideal, a goal unlikely to be fully obtained, it was nevertheless needed as a reference point, or a horizon. Bearing this in mind, Amin stressed that reflections on socialism should only focus on systems of values and not on fully-fledged models of social organisation (cf. 1991: 10). This ethical anchoring was needed because, as Miliband repeated in his argument in the pages of *Monthly Review*, otherwise one was in danger of getting lost in the social and political struggles of the day (cf. 1991: 23-24). Again, he declared the struggle for socialism to be a long-term project. This required the refutation of the assumption that a "true realm of freedom" would replace capitalism overnight. Instead, socialism needed well thought through values and institutional structures and to leave the realm of freedom to future generations (ibid: 20).

Within *Monthly Review*'s discussions of socialism, democracy also became a central theme. Without democracy, there would be no chance to achieve a society that was free not only from economic exploitation but also from class antagonisms and alienation. The democracy envisaged was, however, different from the "formal" one familiar in capitalist states which was as far removed from socialism as was authoritarianism. The search for alternatives to both remained an important issue. Oliver S. Land explained in an article reflecting on the tasks and prospects of socialism in the 1990s:

[O]ne way to account for the parallel failures of the capitalist and self-styled socialist systems is to point out what has never yet been achieved anywhere: the integration of political with economic democracy, of centralized with de-centralized socialeconomic planning, of representative with participatory democratic structures and processes. (1991: 47-48)

Here also, the main strategy was to build on the foundations of liberal or formal democracy and to reform and radicalise it. No one believed in the viability of shortcuts to socialism via the infringement of democratic life, and concurrently, the reflexive, critical and creative potential of a society. Walker addressed this argument, quite poetically, as a friendly warning to the Cuban government:

To Cuba I would say your poets are the heartbeat of the revolution: Because that is what, by definition, poets are. If you force them to eat their words it is the revolution that will suffer indigestion and massive heart attack. Bread is not everything, after all, as women have always stressed: there must be roses too. And the roses of any revolution are the uncertainties one dares to share. (1994: 43)

Space for critical creativity was one thing; but there was also a need to dissolve the present structure of economic and political power. Democracy had to be made sufficiently powerful to prioritise social considerations over those of profit. For the veteran community activist Grace Lee Boggs, this meant "replacing it [the culture of capitalism; SB] with a culture in which the political superstructure, based on popular organisations, controls through conscious choices the development of the economy and of the productive forces. I believe that this is the global project of our time" (1990: 13). In addition, authors often mentioned that the democratic control of economic development was simply necessary for ending environmental destruction. Environmental concern had to become a priority for socialists as both Marzani and Sweezy emphasised (cf. Marzani 1990: 29). To this end, Magdoff more specifically demanded that socialists needed to define economic priorities which considered the limits of what the natural environment could shoulder – unlimited growth and development were no longer regarded as realistic options (cf. 1991: 11). Amin took a similar position and described the concrete consequences which would follow from such a required reorientation: democratic socialists should consciously develop new policies instead of trying to catch-up with capitalism. On the national level, this would mean delinking from the world economic system. On the planetary level, it would require the reconstruction of a polycentric world order (cf. 1992: 50). All this was impossible without some form of public ownership – one in which, unlike in social democratic states, the public sector would be dominant and the private controlled by democratic planning (cf. Miliband 1991: 22).

The question of equality, so prominent in the other journals, was only rarely raised in the pages of *Monthly Review*. It appeared that contributors did not contest the idea that the highest possible level of equality should be strived for and instead only discussed the problem of whether hierarchies and classes, formed on the basis of particular expertise and responsibilities, would continue to exist or could be avoided in a socialist society (cf. Magdoff 1991). In contrast to the relatively light treatment of equality, *Review* seriously debated another aspect which hardly played a role in the other journals: the question of spirituality.[5] In a long and tentative article, John Brentlinger based his call for a more positive evaluation of the sacred on his personal observations in post-revolutionary Nicaragua:

> I am a Marxist and an atheist. Yet seeing has become believing – I agree that Nicaragua is a more sacred land through the sacrifices of its revolutionary martyrs. But what can that mean? Is it possible? I ask this question seriously: can a revolutionary society that is refounding itself and its values re-create the sacred? (1992: 29)

Brentlinger wanted to free socialism from a fallacy which he believed was a vestige of capitalism: the perception of religion and the sacred as outmoded and unscientific ways of thought (cf. ibid: 30). Instead he argued for recognising feelings of love and responsibility for other people and for nature as a form of worldly spirituality – a spirituality that recognised human beings as creators of their own lives and societies and enabled them to notice and correct mistakes. Such a spirituality would transform the self-conception and the strategies of socialism: "It becomes modest and world-wise and speaks of infinite progress and alternative paradigms instead of a single

---

5   Norman Geras's considerations on the ethical and moral implications of Marxist theory, which he published in *New Left Review* and *Socialist Register,* came closest to the question of spirituality and 'the sacred'.

method and a final goal, but it need not abdicate its struggle for progress and faith in a higher society" (ibid: 40). With terms such as 'community' and 'new society', he saw conceptual links between socialist and religious goals and utopias. An appreciation of spirituality was just the logical consequence of coming to terms with religion's positive elements:

> I think we must respect and encourage the positive core that exists in religious spirituality for its concrete valuing of human community and humanity's relationship with nature (on a level that transcends the limits of class, race, and gender conflicts, without underestimating their importance). (ibid: 30)

This "positive core", according to Brentlinger, was deserving of scientific acceptance as it functioned to produce the sacred – which he defined as a valid expression of human life and as "necessary element of any community worth dying for" (ibid: 40). For socialists, relying on such insights and feelings was necessary, in order to find what Raymond Williams had called "resources for a journey of hope" (qtd. in Foster 1993: 8). Finally, Paul Sweezy emphasised that the key ideas of socialism – equality and cooperation – predated its emergence as a set of political ideas and were part of all great religious traditions (cf. 1993: 1).

Another core principle turned up in the pages of *Monthly Review* on many occasions: a commitment to internationalism. This position proved much closer to orthodox socialism, but was nevertheless also shared with religious persuasions. Contributors envisaged not only a polycentric world order in which economic power had been dissolved, but also a termination of the arms race which was unjustifiable by all standards and had served to prevent the development of such a polycentric system through its commandeering of political power (cf. Amin 1990: 27-28; Amin 1992: 50).

Reflections on Institutional Arrangements
Compared to the other journals, Monthly Review's deliberations on institutional questions remained short. Some contributors subscribed to a traditional view on the stages of the revolutionary process and assumed post-revolutionary societies would develop institutional arrangements fitting to their concrete conditions. Accordingly, the development of too detailed a general model would be a futile effort since people at different places had different problems, which in turn required specific solutions and hence also

particular institutional frameworks (cf. Amin 1990: 27). Nevertheless Howard J. Sherman provided a summary of institutional principles which again served to define democratic socialism: "economic democracy, the extension of political democracy to the economy. Socialism is public or collective ownership and control, where the public institutions (the government) and the collectives (or cooperatives) are democratically governed" (1990: 14). Sherman's statement points again to the essential factors of democratic planning, public ownership, and the maintenance of certain market mechanisms. Particularly important was democratic control of new investment in order to avoid its orientation on the principle of profit maximisation (ibid: 21). Mechanisms of subsidiarity were needed to make these decision making structures sensitive to people's local needs but it was also necessary to strike a balance with overall demands such as a global redistribution of wealth or environmental protection (ibid). Thus Miliband emphasised that such grassroots elements were indeed important, but still formed "no substitute for democratic mechanisms in the internal organization of state power" (1991: 21). Magdoff explained which institutional changes would mark the difference between a capitalist democratic and a really democratic state. In his view, the most important institutional alteration to be achieved was the more even distribution of power in society:

Clear-cut policies would be needed to underpin the move to a democracy that is really democratic: affirmative action to bring the people into the corridors of power; leaders who trust and listen to the people; and ways to make leaders accountable, which includes the right of the people to recall political leaders and administrators. (1991: 10)

Such reforms, of course, would have to be applied right to the top level of government (cf. ibid: 6). To maintain such democratic structures, a form of 'permanent revolution' was needed, otherwise functionaries and bureaucracies would become too remote from public control: "To be sure, this dilemma can only be resolved by ongoing, uninterrupted revolutionary practice – a practice that opens the way for the empowerment of the unempowered" (ibid: 10). Most of these suggestions focused on the level of the existing national states. Amin, in contrast, emphasised the importance of global governance. He intended to renew and extend the UN and demanded that socialists should work for the empowerment of the existing embryonic structures of world government. He also called for a global tax that could be used for financing environmental policies (cf. 1990: 28). A certain tension arose with the general thrust of articles which recommended an inward-focussed orientation in terms of community-based economic and social structures (the self-organisation of societal entities that were more or less identical with national states) as the only alternative to the rise of an imperial power – the United States.

Apart from the controversial discussion of the Swedish welfare state in the pages of *Monthly Review*, the journal offered a number of further candidates as possible models. Marzani suggested combining the best of the United States and the U.S.S.R., of capitalism and socialism (supposedly he referred to democratic institutions and economic planning) and saw it as the only way forward (cf. 1990: 30). Additionally, he pointed to the possibility of a red-green project in Germany (based on the SPD's comparatively radical 1980s' programme) as a likely candidate for a future model (cf. ibid: 29). The third example mentioned was Cuba. When analysing the latter, Alice Walker noted a number of achievements that were admirable for poor and, perhaps in particular, African-American people:

Having been born among the poorest, least powerful, most despised population of the United States, spoken to as if I were a dog for asking to use a library or eat in a restaurant, the revelation [during a visit to Cuba in 1979; SB] that black people, who make up between 40 and 60 percent of Cuba's population, and women, who make up half, can share in all the fruits of their labours, was a major gift Cuba gave to me, a major encouragement to struggle for equality and justice, and one I shall never forget. (1994: 41)

Cuba, was one of the last remaining non-capitalist systems and one for which contributors to the journal had much more sympathy than former Eastern European state socialist regimes. Given the United States' longstanding conflict with the island, for a left U.S. journal its survival constituted a particularly serious challenge.

Requirements
There were only scattered and rather eclectic remarks on the preconditions and chances of moves towards democratic socialism. Strongest was the feeling that it required a change in public consciousness:

When more than a majority [*sic*] of the total population realizes its oppression, in both direct and indirect manifestations, and joins together to 'fight the power', the inherently unequal social structure will have to buckle, and a new, yet to be envisioned egalitarian society will rise to take its place. (Kim 1993: 57)

In such conceptions, educational work was obviously more important than the task of creating blueprints for the institutions of a democratic socialist society; without socialist education, there were few chances for the population to come to terms with their oppression. Two strategies were essential for reaching people: old ideas had to be communicated in new ways or in new channels (cf. Marzani 1990: 29), and utopianism needed again to play a more important role in socialism (cf. Wallis 1992: 9). There were also scattered hints at replacing economic rationality and the concept of labour with less-alienating alternatives. Again in line with *Monthly Review*'s positive evaluation of spirituality as constituting an important dimension of consciousness which had been ignored by socialists, Peter Meiksins suggested looking at the traditional mythologisation of craftwork for identifying such alternatives – in which values such as freedom, community, variety, challenge and commitment replaced the fixation on wages (cf. 1994: 53). Clearly, the issue of raising people's consciousness, of sensitising them, played the most important role in preparations for democratic socialism.

Questions and Dilemmas
In *Monthly Review* a number of problems became visible that, like those encountered by *Dissent*, went directly to the heart of the democratic socialist project. Among these was the question of the maintenance of the term 'socialism'. Again, if one believed that giving up certain terms meant abandoning ideas and thus narrowed the number of alternatives available for political change, much more than just a name was at stake. However, when Bragg in his interview in *Monthly Review* claimed that the name 'socialism' was not important, nobody contradicted him (cf. Batstone 1991: 25). Most authors, however, continued to use the term self-confidently. The second problem that *Monthly Review* had to deal with was the question of the degree of equality in socialism. This had two dimensions: firstly, critics asked how to avoid the development of a class of specialists in a democratic socialist society, as similar structures had proved historically disastrous for

state socialist countries. Magdoff discussed this issue extensively and believed that a top layer of specialists remained necessary in a society highly differentiated in terms of economic life. In a similar vain, the question arose as to how to limit specialist influence to its immediate economic tasks without allowing it to become a source of privilege in the wider distribution of power. Sensing how critical the class issue was, Magdoff recommended tackling this problem as soon as possible during a process of transformation towards socialism: "The test of the inevitability of class structure will depend on future attempts to create a socialist *transition* which consciously works not only to do away with the old class system but also to frustrate the formation of new classes and social strata" (1991: 8). The author, though, did not explain how this could be achieved. The second dimension concerned the global applicability of the concept of equality. It would be difficult, and deserved further thought, as again Magdoff argued, to overcome differentials of wealth and power above all between third and first world, but also between peripheries and centres within the first (cf. ibid). Most contributors assumed that the strategy towards such equality lay in delinking from the existing structures of the world economy. Delinking would work as a levelling force, which would strengthen domestic investment and thus in the long run reduce such differentials (cf. Amin 1992: 50). The imperfect and eventually failed attempts at delinking by the countries of the Eastern Bloc were not discussed in this context.

A further problem for writers in *Monthly Review* was how to deal with anti-socialist forces. It was again Miliband who tried to deal with this difficulty. In particular, he expressed unease about two questions: he saw an unavoidable tension between a strong state within a socialist democracy and one that was simultaneously controlled by and accountable to its citizens. This tension, his argument went, could be reduced, but not completely eliminated by representative democracy. It became acute, above all, in the case of violent opposition from the political right. Under these circumstances he considered it to be justifiable to infringe civil liberties. However, it was absolutely essential not to forget that such a strategy was detrimental to socialist society itself and hollowed out its values – and thus had to be restricted to the absolute minimum and abandoned as soon as possible (cf. 1991: 21-22). The only alternative to restrictive measures like these consisted, as Tim Meisenhelder suggested, of the formation of class coalitions – to be achieved by political struggles based on concrete issues rather than theoretical ideals. He pointed to Third World national liberation struggles and although he discussed Cabral's theories on the conditions under which sections of the middle classes might "commit class suicide" and take sides with the working class, he still was not convinced that this could prevent all forms of authoritarian structures. He recommended confining such authoritarian measures to a period of transition: "Militarist organization and 'democratic centralism' may well be necessary for armed struggle and other periods prior to the taking of power but they must be rejected by the very design of 'post revolutionary' political institutions" (Meisenhelder 1993: 47). Clearly, the contributors were not happy with their own answers to these problems and Magdoff asked himself (in words that could be understood in many different ways): "Can socialism be built without major changes in the consciousness and standards of morality?" (1991: 5). It seemed that none of these problems could be solved as long as one had not decided whether socialist equality or democratic processes constituted the more important components of democratic socialism.

4.2. Market Socialism – a Promising Project?

In the United States and Britain, leftwing intellectuals and workers had for a long time thought about alternatives to Soviet-style state ownership of the means of production and its bureaucratic planning system. Figuring prominently among the alternatives – especially in the 1970s – were syndicalism and workers control. In the early 1990s, after the debate had gained renewed urgency with the privatisation and deregulation experience of the Thatcher and Reagan years as well as the rapid disappearance of state ownership in Eastern Europe, thinkers began to intensively discuss the merits and problems of 'market socialism'. The term, originally used for the Yugoslav form of economic organisation and going back to the writings of the Polish economist Oskar Lange, stood for a loose concept, developed into different directions by British and American theorists such as Alec Nove and John Roemer respectively.[6] Among the journals, especially *New Left Review* and, to an even greater extent, *Dissent* took some effort in familiar-

---

6   With Nove's The Economics of Feasible Socialism (1983) and Roemer's A Future for Socialism (1994), both have contributed studies which have become 'classics' of market socialism.

ising their readers with the ideas of market socialism, evaluating their chances, and asking in how far they differed from welfare-state capitalism.

A minority of intellectuals who took sides on these issues criticised it from a Marxist point of view, whereas the majority emphasised the advantages of the market-socialist concept, though to varying degrees. Contributions by the latter analysed the merits of markets, the need to guide or control them, the ways in which markets and socialism could be linked (and why such an undertaking was worth the effort), market socialism's organisational and institutional requirements, and what the preconditions of implementation and how its chances for working smoothly were. Like the opponents of the concept, its proponents took recourse to Marx, discussed the characteristics of the market and reflected on motivations guiding human behaviour.

Dissent[7]

In Dissent, market socialism served the purpose of making the democratic socialism analysed in the last chapter more concrete. Roemer, one of its leading proponents, characterised it as "a politico-economic system in which firms are publicly owned, the state has considerable control of the 'commanding heights' of the economy, and there is democratic control over society's use of its economic surplus" (1991: 562). Thomas E. Weisskopf discussed those elements which distinguished market socialism from state socialism and to a certain degree situated it closer to capitalism:

Market socialism seeks to promote the traditional socialist goals of equity, democracy, and solidarity while maintaining economic efficiency; it proposes to do so by retaining one major feature of capitalism – the market – while replacing another major feature of capitalism – private ownership of the means of production. (1992: 250)

---

7   This chapter changes the order in which the findings from the journals are presented because *Dissent* published the mist details reflections on the issue of market socialism. To analyse them first makes it easier for the readers to get familiar with the concepts of market socialism.

Roemer accordingly declared that while markets were indispensible for an efficient economy, private ownership was not indispensible for well-working markets (cf. 1991: 562).

The market, according to the theories of market socialism, stood for a functional price mechanism which was lacking in centrally planned state economies. This price system was needed in order to guarantee efficiency and avoid bureaucracy and waste of resources. It functioned, however, in an economic system where public or state planning directed investment to purposes that were seen as socially useful. Proponents' opinions differed as to the form and the extent of public ownership and on the question whether collective decisions should be taken at plant level or by society as a whole. Nevertheless, all agreed on the basic principles of economic democracy, on the need to redistribute profits as social dividends, and on the advantages of decommodifying public services. There were different suggestions as to the directive role of banks and managers, the availability of loans, or a basic income for all labourers, but all *Dissenters* maintained that a supervisory state would need to play a central role. In the words of Bob Rae, market socialism should be seen as an attempt to come to terms with the tension of "three realities": planning, democracy, and markets (1991: 43).

Rae went into greater detail when stressing the virtues of markets not just in terms of efficiency but also accountability. He listed realistic pricing, respect for the relationship of supply and demand, the positive effects of competition, the need to serve a public of consumers, an openness for change, dynamism, entrepreneurship and efficient management as the main advantages (cf. ibid: 45). States and governments were usually judged by their populations, as James Rule argued, in terms of their ability to organise economic growth – and an economic system based on markets could produce such growth (cf. 1990: 478-9). These successes were most convincing however, as several writers claimed, where states exercised a certain amount of control rather than followed the Anglo-American model of a laissez-faire economy (cf. Erber 1990: 353). Thus throughout the twentieth century one could observe a tendency towards state-guided and increasingly state-managed capitalism – in other words: state-supervised markets (cf. ibid: 357). If Anglo-American capitalism was one unconvincing alternative, the other, as Daniel Bell emphasised in *Dissent*, could only consist of central planning where people at the levers of economic power would inevitably develop and pursue their own interests (cf. 1991: 52-3). This experience stemmed not only from observing economic life in the Eastern Bloc but also in Western countries.

Contributors believed in the possibility as well as in the necessity of controlling markets. David Miller, who wrote a piece on the detailed workings of market socialism, countered criticism that its proponents were no proper socialists by arguing that the problem for socialism was not markets *per se*, but their effective control (cf. 1991: 413). These positions differed not only from the opinion of New Right economists such as Hayek and von Mises, but also from those of former Eastern European scholars, who had once tried to sketch out ways towards a more efficient and more democratic socialist economy but were now convinced of the futility of any such attempts. Thus the proponents of market socialism heavily criticized, for example, James Kornai's book *The Road to a Free Economy* (1990) with its thesis that there was no 'third way' due to the incompatibility of socialist ethics and market efficiency, which they described as an expression of East European intellectuals' flight from their former 'naïve' belief in the possibility of transforming Soviet-style socialism (cf. Nove 1990: 443). The contributors' optimistic view that it was possible to create controlled but still efficient market relations originated from the perception that, in the West, the public sector with its alleged inefficiency was very often blamed for private sector failure and for budget constraints imposed by the state (cf. ibid: 445). Controlled markets worked better than neo-liberals wanted to admit.

Market socialism was necessary for two reasons: Erber was convinced that the introduction of "market relations without capitalist relations" would be the existential question of ecological improvement and hence of human survival in the twenty-first century (1990: 356). Secondly, the perceived need for social curbing of market relations furthered the left's fundamental goal of equality. Crucial goods and services should be unconditionally available to all regardless of their market position and purchasing power (cf. Broadbent 1991: 83). Authors argued that deregulation was no panacea. Even if it was true that planned economies had not worked it was obvious that neo-liberal models did not either. Nove pointed out, and urged Eastern European economists to consider, that Thatcherite laissez-faire policies had had no beneficial effect on the real-wealth creating parts of the British economy (cf. 1990: 446). Erber observed the same for the United States:

If global market share is the goal, the nation's consumers had better not been permitted to decide on the allocation of resources. Laissez-faire America illustrates why not. The consumers opt for second homes, third cars, snowmobiles, Jacuzzis, and Torneau watches, thereby shortchanging education at all levels, skill retraining of the labour force, housing, and health care – all essential ingredients in mobilizing resources to fight for market share. (1990: 359)

The intellectuals agreed on the need for markets, but they explicitly contradicted the neo-liberal idea that markets constituted a form of, or a model for, societal organisation in general. Quite to the contrary, without control, markets posed a danger for societies. In the words of Paul Hirst,

[t]here is no such thing as a 'market society', for the simple reason that the market is *not* a society. It is a mechanism of exchange that is embedded in other social relationships. In 'freeing' the market, economic liberalism actually weakens those relationships. Societies will be unable to survive, and even to compete economically, if they just accept whatever results uncontrolled market and international competitive pressures produce. (1994: 243)

As a consequence, markets had to be accompanied by civil societies:

So if we are to have a market economy, we also need a definition of citizenship (what I have called 'the public household') that permits individuals to participate fully, in the market as well as the polity, as members of a civil society. A market economy without a civil society is an individualistic monstrosity. (Bell 1991: 50)

Writers disagreed on the 'socialist' content of market socialism. On the one hand, the question of the ownership of the means of production and the distribution of wealth had been thoroughly debated by the left and had acted as markers of difference between liberals (or, in the European version, social democrats) and socialists (cf. ibid). On the other hand, proponents of market socialism argued that state ownership meant neither automatically higher wages nor better working conditions (cf. ibid. 480), nor were private and public ownership synonymous with private and public decision making respectively (cf. Erber 1990: 357). In other words, a fair distribution of wealth and public decision making had replaced public ownership as the guideline for socialist politics. Consequently, the privatisation spree in Eastern Europe did not necessarily mean the abolition of a socialist politics. At least for some writers, market socialism could unproblematically exist on the base of predominantly private ownership – a position that certainly transcended the definitions by Roemer and Weisskopf quoted at the beginning of this chapter:

> I suggest that this may not be the most significant or fruitful point to focus on. Perhaps the government-versus-private dichotomy should give way to a broad spectrum of different auspices for capital. Maybe we should be talking about how 'ownership' might take on meanings and new social content in an egalitarian market economy. (Rule 1990: 479)

Rule argued that the worst form of inequality consisted of people who were better-off dominating public and political decision making (cf. 1990: 479-80). He went on: "It seems to me that government ownership of productive wealth neither guarantees an attack on such inequalities nor is necessary for success in such an attack" (ibid: 480). Finally he insisted that rather than anxiously discussing whether the means used in such an attack could be defined as 'socialist' or not, leftwing intellectuals and activists should redraw the "map of political possibilities" (ibid). Yet, while the writers accepted markets, they did not love them. Apart from the already mentioned strengthening of civil society, this scepticism made them argue for an extension of the public sector, especially of the welfare systems (cf. Erber 1990: 357). In this combination, socialism became, according to Alec Nove, almost identical with "welfare-capitalism-with-a-human-face" (1990: 446). Weisskopf contradicted this perception. He saw a difference in the stronger inclusion of communities and a more fundamental power shift:

> Where market socialism seeks to promote the public interest, greater equity, democracy, and solidarity primarily by transferring capitalist ownership rights to communities of citizens or workers, social democracy seeks to do so by government policy measures designed to constrain the behavior of capitalist owners and to empower other market participants. (Weisskopf 1992: 258)

Dissent published three articles which dealt with the technical intricacies of market socialism (cf. Miller 1991; Roemer 1991; Weisskopf 1992). All of the contributions suggested some mixture of public ownership and management, workers cooperatives with self-management and, finally, limited private ownership. Economic decision making would be supervised in three different ways: by the public as a whole, by a firm's employees, and by the state. The role of the state was particularly complicated. Its task was seen as guiding economic development through an arms-length approach – without directing and thus disturbing its internal dynamics. The major instrument for such an involvement was the planning of investment rather than of the composition and prices of goods to be produced (cf. Roemer 1991: 564). Entrepreneurship would still have a function, as David Miller explained, because its essence, the capability of perceiving the difference between a product's future selling price and the cost of the resources needed to produce it, would remain (cf. 1991: 411).

Critics of market socialism often pointed to the case of Yugoslavia. Did it not prove that market socialism did not work? In the Yugoslavian case, the Soviet Union's influence could not be blamed for the failure. However, according to Tadeusz Kowalik, the Yugoslav model had a number of deficiencies: decentralization and the abolition of macro-economic planning went too far and made the national economy more free-market than in most Western European states. This absence of planning produced collisions between workers' self-management, market mechanisms, and the Communist Party's role in un-systematically determining prices and investment priorities. Hence, Yugoslavia could not be used as an example that market socialism was bound to fail (cf. 1991: 94, see also Weiskopf 1992: 252).

The question remained as to how such non-capitalist markets could be implemented. The authors agreed that the present political climate was not particularly promising. In the Western countries, such a transformation would be obviously difficult to achieve. Several authors hinted towards the Swedish wage earners' funds as bold attempt at a change of power relations. However, this example had simply failed as had all other attempts to implement a radical programme on the nation-state level (as in France around 1980) or even to install grassroots democracy within organisations working in the nation-state political arena (as in Britain's Labour Party a bit later). In Eastern Europe, much more than in the West, the objective conditions were given because, after the crash of state socialism, the question in what direction a future economy would develop was open. Unfortunately, market socialism was not what most people in Eastern Europe wanted (cf. Kowalik 1991: 94). There was, however, a chance for the situation to change once unemployment and economic problems began to affect them more seriously (cf. ibid. 95).

Several open questions remained. It was still unclear whether the move to market socialism needed to be started by governments, labour movements, a broad popular alliance, or at the 'point of production'. Additionally, the question of 'market socialism in one country' constituted an obvious problem that was only occasionally raised and in just one case answered with vague hopes on the European social chapter (cf. Miller 1991: 414). At least some proponents of market socialism seemed convinced that once a transformation process had been set in motion, it would become self-sustaining and would gain intensity since it would, through political measures furthering equality and the decommodification of many areas of public life, move public opinion slowly but dynamically to the left (cf. Roemer 1991: 568).

New Left Review

New Left Review published both positive evaluations and also severe critiques of market socialism. Interestingly, it was G. A. Cohen (who had collaborated with Roemer among others in developing what became known as 'analytical Marxism') who criticised the concept for a variety of reasons but especially because it would not break with the bourgeois profit-centred elements of the market logic. He referred to Marx's critiques of revisionism when elaborating his argument:

But he [Marx; S.B.] did not doubt that reward for contribution *is* a bourgeois principle, one which treats a person's talent 'as a natural privilege'. Reward for contribution implies recognition of what I have elsewhere called the principle of self-ownership. Nothing is more bourgeois than that, and the Gotha critique lesson for market socialism is that, while market socialism may remove the income injustice caused by differential ownership of capital, it preserves the income injustice caused by differential ownership of endowments of personal capacity. (1991: 16)

For Cohen, market socialism was not only deficient because it best rewarded people who were talented but also because it identified and reproduced "mean motivations" as the basis for human economic activity: "The immediate motive to productive activity in a market society is usually some mixture of greed and fear, in proportions that vary with the details of a person's market position. In greed, other people are seen as possible sources of enrichment, and in fear they are seen as threats" (ibid: 18). Cohen conceded, however, that market socialism could be embraced as an immediate political demand and play a part in what Marx called the first phase of communism (cf. ibid: 16). Yet he urged the left not to define market socialism, in a voguish move, as the solution to all problems just because the chance to go beyond it seemed at the moment quite slim: "If you cannot bear to remember the goodness of the goal that you sought and which is not now attainable, you may fail to pursue it should it come within reach, and you will not try to bring it into reach" (ibid: 14). David Purdy also explained that even if market socialism was adopted as a progressive politics, the tension between the egalitarian logic of citizenship and the market tendency to (re-) produce disparate social conditions remained and, as a socialist task, had to be tackled head-on (cf. 1994: 43).

For Jürgen Habermas, the separating out of certain spheres of social life was a necessary feature of complex societies. These areas then had developed their own modes and laws of working, be it in the sphere of political-administrative life or in the economy, which was regulated by the market logic (cf. 1990: 17). Yet such an economy was not necessarily capitalist and thus there was no need for Eastern European societies to return to a fully-fledged capitalist system (ibid). An important question for the left was whether efficiency – which markets supposedly furthered – was at all a socialist goal. This question was discussed by Robin Blackburn:

Some may contest the notion that a socialist economics should seek to emulate the sort of efficiency that is promoted by market competition. In a socialist pattern of economy the overall distribution of demand would be very different from that in a capitalist society and so would be the context and capacity of public regulation. The automatism of the accumulation process – growth for growth's sake – would not be there, nor would the encouragement to a greedy consumerism. Social costs and 'externalities' would be rendered more visible. But both productive and transactional efficiency would still be vital. (1991: 217)

The more efficient an enterprise was, he added, the more it could contribute to social and egalitarian goals (ibid.). Hence efficiency constituted an important element of a socialist economy.

However, authors were convinced that market control was a matter of necessity. They formulated the same arguments as *Dissenters*: As Jürgen Habermas and Robin Blackburn explained in different ways, market economies were indifferent to their 'external' costs – thus sensitising them to social and especially ecological requirements would become a matter of survival (cf. Habermas 1990: 17, Blackburn 1991: 232). Additionally, labour itself would not be treated as a commodity and as a consequence many of the conflicts over the distribution of profits and wage levels, and the threat of wage squeezes would vanish (cf. Blackburn 1991: 217).

In practice, state involvement should be indirect, and limited to the setting up of frameworks for industrial relations, procedures of decision making within a socialist economy in general and firms in particular, and institutions of 'social auditing' (cf. Blackburn 1991: 223). It was not entirely clear whether the resulting form of organisation of the economy as a whole could be best described as syndicalism, corporatism, or economic democracy. What was clear, however, was that a shift of power was needed because managers should no longer be responsible to shareholders but instead to the public and to the employees, that profits would be redistributed and hence an egalitarian drive would gather momentum, and that politics in a market socialist society would be at least as complicated and prone to social conflict as in a capitalist one.

Looking for historical precedents, a number of authors seemed convinced that without Soviet interferences, traditions of reform communism in Hungary and Czechoslovakia would have produced moves towards market socialism and in so doing might have been able to produce systems similar or superior to Western welfare-state societies (cf. Habermas 1990: 6-7).

Monthly Review

Monthly Review also published different positions on market socialism though the space dedicated to the issue was considerably smaller. István Mészáros expressed his view that market socialism would suffer from an insurmountable paradox: the combination of the market's economic extraction of surplus labour with its political extraction in socialism (cf. Monthly Review 1993: 14). Ellen Meiksins Wood diagnosed a fundamental error in the market socialists' perception of the market – she declared that the market was not a sphere of opportunity and choice but rather an instrument of class power to control the working classes and Third World as well as Eastern European countries. Although she conceded, like Cohen in New Left Review, that 'socialist' markets might be less harmful than 'free markets' and some institutions and practices associated with markets might be used in a socialist economy, she saw no reason why left intellectuals – following people in Eastern Europe, whose 'illusions' she understood – should embrace the idea of beneficial market systems because

> it's no good refusing to confront the implications of the one irreducible condition without which the market cannot act as an economic discipline: the commodification of labor power – a condition which places the strictest limits on the 'socialization' of the market and its capacity to assume a human face. (1994a: 39)

A different position was taken by Harold J. Sherman who stated that in a highly complex economy, decentralisation of decision-making was necessary and without markets impossible (cf. 1990: 20). Similarly, even the veteran socialists Harry Magdoff and Ralph Miliband conceded in the pages of *Monthly Review* that the question was not whether markets should exist at all but rather what kind of markets (Magdoff 1991: 15) and what would be their adequate role (Miliband 1991: 23). At the same time, authors warned against claiming a causal link between markets and democracy. Clearly, in the case of Eastern Europe, marketisation was not enough to produce democratic societies (cf. Löwy 1991: 36). To avoid short-term consumerism and to allow for a production for the whole of society's needs, markets, according to Harry Magdoff, definitely had to be subordinated to central planning (cf. 1991: 16-7).

Finally, Harry Magdoff presented a successful case – the United States. His experience as member of the New Deal administration more than fifty years ago made him strongly convinced that, in principle, a combination of planning, markets, a high level of state activism, and a variety of ownership types was possible and could have beneficial effects (ibid).

Socialist Register
Socialist Register obviously saw no sense in getting involved in the debates on market socialism. They contended that with the changes of 1989, discussions about ownership had eventually lost their doctrinal significance – although this shift in political attitude had started long before. Contributors

presented a list of illustrious names to claim authority for their thesis that the 'form of ownership' debate had been abandoned: Gyorgy Lukács, James Kornai, Rudolf Bahro and Oskar Lange were put forward as examples of intellectuals who had in their different ways moved beyond the issue (cf. Cox 1991: 184-5; Lebowitz 1991: 349-50). Cox additionally formulated a position that could be read as an implicit acceptance of the relevance of market socialism for transformative politics. He claimed that models of socialism should no longer focus on producers' self-management, but instead on popular participation in central planning (cf. Cox 1991: 184). On the one hand this could be understood as an approach that privileged planning over market mechanisms, but the acceptance of different forms of ownership would also leave space for markets below the level of overall planning. For *Socialist Register*, market socialism had to be integrated into debates over the extension of democracy to the economic sphere.

4.3. Sweden and other Dreamlands

The hesitance and distance with which Western leftist and Marxist intellectuals viewed the political practice of the countries of the former Eastern Bloc begs the question: which countries, societies, or polities in existence actually resembled the intellectuals' respective ideals of 'socialism'? For most thinkers, the Swedish system came closest to fulfilling such criteria.[8] Sweden, thus, became an often mentioned case study and a widely debated topic in the magazines – the coverage ranged from frequent passing remarks to a number of complete articles.[9] Reflections generally addressed

---

8   The breakdown of the state socialist regimes reinvigorated the interest of left-leaning social scientists in 'models of capitalism'. In the first half of the 1990s, it became common to regard the Rhineland, the Nordic and the Japanese models as superior to the Anglo-American one, with their higher degrees of state intervention and their institutionalised corporatism. This view became increasingly contentious as the 1990s progressed and Anglo-American economic liberalism and Ireland-style neo-corporatism seemed to overtake the others in term of economic growth and the creation of new jobs.

9   Interest was even stronger because in the early 1990s the 'Swedish model' seemed to crumble. In 1991, for just the second time (the first lasted from 1976 to 1982) in almost 60 years, a non-social democratic government had come to

three questions: firstly, could the Swedish system legitimately be labelled as 'socialist'? Secondly, why had it run into difficulties in the 1980s? And finally, what lessons could theorists draw from the Swedish model and from the difficulties which it had to deal with after the end of the golden age of social democracy? It becomes obvious that much more space was devoted to dealing with Swedish society than with any other – none was able to act as a serious rival in attracting the socialist imagination. However, though inordinately popular, Sweden was not the only candidate for intellectual interest. Therefore, this chapter also serves the purpose of further examining those countries which were viewed as having possible socialist elements in their fabric.

New Left Review

New Left Review was the only of the four magazines which did not devote whole articles to the 'Swedish question'. Nevertheless, positive evaluations can be found. For example, Kate Soper attested to Sweden's great success when reflecting on the question how the satisfaction of basic human needs could be achieved on a global scale (cf. 1993: 115). With regard to the level of social security the Swedish state provided to its citizens, it clearly stood out as a role model. For Ted Honderich, the issue of social and material equality in Swedish society was the most central. He applauded the country's comparatively successful move from a hierarchical to a more egalitarian democracy – a move, however, that had stopped or even been reversed by the early 1990s (cf. 1994: 65). Honderich interpreted this setback as a consequence of the problem that any more-radical changes in the distribution of power – which were a necessary precondition for leaving the capitalist logic permanently behind – would always lead to civil war. He left the question open, however, as to whether such a war was desirable and could be won (cf. 1994: 66).

New Left Review did not see the Swedish case as an example of a truly socialist society. Nevertheless, it highlighted its importance for socialists as an example of what Robin Blackburn called "impure capitalism" – a form of capitalism with massive state involvement which was superior to Anglo-American 'pure capitalism' and worth more serious attention by left intel-

---

power and started preparing Sweden for a membership in the European Community.

lectuals – now that capitalism had 'won' (cf. 1991: 228-9). Similarly, Paul Auerbach, in his article on the importance of education for socialist advance, listed Sweden, like the Netherlands, among a group of countries whose populations' above-average levels of education coincided with the widest expansion and most powerful forms of industrial democracy (cf. 1992: 10). For the author, a causal link existed between these two features. Several authors in *New Left Review,* however, hinted at the problem that the Swedish model relied on an exceptionally high level of material wealth. It allowed for a living standard which, for ecological reasons, was far too high to be replicated on a global scale. This anomaly, according to a number of sceptics, limited Sweden's value as a globally applicable guide for thought on a more egalitarian society (cf. Soper 1993: 26; Mouzelis 1993: 184).

For *New Left Review* with its global perspective, Sweden was the most interesting of a number of national economies which did not follow the doctrine of 'pure capitalism'. This heterogeneous group also included countries such as Taiwan, Korea, Japan and Germany (cf. Blackburn 1991: 228-9). Though writers suggested that intellectuals should draw lessons from these systems' corporate structures, their highly regulated industrial relations or their state-led investment strategies, they did not discuss these cases in detail.

Socialist Register

Socialist Register nearly unanimously agreed that the Swedish 'people's home' was very likely the most advanced example of social democratic achievement, but that it, nevertheless, fell short of socialism. Miliband defined the Swedish system as a form of tamed capitalism (cf. 1991: 380). The most important lesson to be learned from the country was that the high degree of domestication became possible through the influence of the particularly strong Swedish labour movement. Even though Sweden did not introduce socialism, *Socialist Register* regarded the standards set in its social-democratic experiments as obviously important enough to invite Rudolf Meidner, one of the Swedish welfare state's main architects, to reflect on the model's difficult state in the early 1990s. In his article, Meidner conceded that Sweden's 'people's home' definitely did not constitute a Marxist project, but nonetheless remained one of "functional socialism", in which capital had been driven from its monopoly position in economic decision making. However, it had not been expropriated:

The Swedish model [...] is reformist in the sense that private ownership and free markets are accepted to a large extent, but it is socialist in so far as fundamental values of the labour movement are built into it. The model is based on a firm socialist ideology but recommends at the same time practical methods to attain the goals. (1993: 219)

In short, this quote could be read as the thesis that the Swedish model conformed to a transformative approach to democratic socialism.

With regard to the question of why the Swedish model had run into difficulties or, as some argued, had to be considered a failure, the differences were more about nuance and emphasis than about fundamental points. Comments clarified, however, that the model failed to develop a transformative strategy and instead remained within the limits of social democracy. Meidner himself was obviously ambivalent. Despite his remark quoted above, he saw the model's shortcomings which, according to him, lay in the non-Marxist approach to socialism during the golden years or else in the Swedish labour movement's "inability to encroach upon private ownership, the very core of the capitalist system" (ibid: 225). Gregory Albo also agreed that the Swedish model did not leave the capitalist logic behind; although he added that this had been tried when Meidner and others had – against massive opposition by the owners of large firms, by politicians even from the social democrats' own ranks and by parts of the public – unsuccessfully tried to introduce wage earners funds in the late 1970s (cf. 1994: 161-2). Lessons should be learned from this abortive attempt: John Bellamy Foster criticised liberal left thinkers' calls for "new social contracts" whose demands (which taken together often resembled the Swedish model) would require a class revolt in order to gain a chance of being implemented (cf. 1990: 277-8). If even Sweden's strong labour movement had proved unable to achieve this, the chances elsewhere were minimal. For Panitch, the crisis of the Swedish model had to be understood as the global crisis of Keynesianism which had also harmed other welfare states (cf. 1994: 82). The fact that this crisis affected Sweden later and less seriously, testified to the greater strength of the labour movement, but not to a fundamentally different economic organisation and political power structure (cf. ibid.). Meidner obviously agreed when he declared the model to have run its cause: "Social democracy has fulfilled its purpose well in a singular phase of Swedish history but must step down as a driving force as Sweden becomes just a small part of a large block of capitalist states. There is no room in this scenario for a specific Swedish profile" (1993: 227).

Though Sweden did not implement a socialist system and although it remained to be seen whether or not its model's crisis would be terminal, the question arose as to whether or not it had created institutional arrangements socialists could learn from. For *Socialist Register*, this seemed to be the case. Again, it was Rudolf Meidner himself who argued that although Sweden had never developed fully-fledged socialism, it had at least in some respects progressed beyond capitalism: "The model combines visions and pragmatism of the traditional Swedish brand. It comes close to what Ernst Wigforss, a leading ideologist of the Swedish labour movement, called 'provisional utopias'" (1993: 219). Despite his remarkable level of self-criticism, Meidner remained convinced of the model's significance: "A de-radicalized labour movement took the lead in developing into a welfare society which aroused admiration and envy all over the world" (ibid: 213). The demise of the Swedish model therefore posed a problem not only for Sweden, but for the left everywhere – how could welfare systems be defended in periods of economic crises (cf. ibid: 220)?

Although Sweden fell short of *Socialist Register*'s expectations in several respects, this is certainly not to say that it was not significant. Sweden proved an incomparable object of study; not only did contributors produce multiple articles investigating the country's social and economic organisation, but more than any other, Sweden proved unique in its ability to foster a tone of sympathetic critique among authors.

Dissent

In many respects, comments in *Dissent* resembled those in the *Socialist Register*. Bogdan Denitch, for example, wrote that the central feature setting Sweden apart from other societies was the power and the self-confidence of its labour movement rather than the extent of the country's welfare provision (cf. 1991: 104). James Rule again stressed the society's egalitarianism, the achievement of which, as he was convinced, the Swedish Workers Party had pursued more wholeheartedly than any other social democratic party, making Sweden a more equal society than the U.S.S.R. (cf. 1990: 479). *Dissent* evaluated the Swedish case highly positively, sentiments which became obvious in a series of replies submitted in response to a question formulated by Robert Heilbroner: how far beyond a "real but slightly imaginary Sweden" would democratic socialists have to move in order to create a socialist society (1991: 96)? One respondent stated that Sweden might already be socialist – though still highly vulnerable and increasingly dependent on a "very imaginary Europe" (Barkan 1991: 98). Others agreed with this perception of vulnerability and shied away from calling a country socialist before the moves towards egalitarianism had become constitutionally codified and irreversible. For Mitchell Cohen, for example, it was a condition of socialism that the population's social rights become "inalienable rights" on a par with the civil rights of the U.S. constitution (1991: 101). Denitch remained convinced that Swedish economic organisation could still be transformed into a more socialist model by introducing workplace democracy and what he called the abolition of the concentration of private property (cf. 1991: 105). Finally, Gus Tyler regarded the question of the model's socialist content as difficult to answer because the constellation of power in Sweden was one which was unimaginable within at least a Marxist perspective on socialism: the proletariat acted as the executive committee of a capitalist state and used it for its own ends (cf. 1991: 110). While this configuration was incomprehensible on the base of Marxist theory, it could certainly qualify as a version of market socialism.

Although *Dissenters* saw the Swedish model as seriously threatened, in their eyes its achievements had not disappeared yet. They critically observed that Meidner's plans for wage earners funds had not only been rejected by Swedish capitalists, but also by the voters. Thus it was argued that one of the reasons for recent problems consisted of the model's internal shortcomings, for example, its paternalism which had increasingly antagonised the Swedish people (cf. Horvat 1991: 108). One of *Dissent*'s contributors, furthermore, hinted, just like Soper and Mouzelis in *New Left Review*, at the problem that the Swedish model relied on a living standard which was too high to be reproduced all over the world. Hence, the Swedish case offered important insights, but could not be used a blueprint for a socialist strategy (cf. Brand 1991: 100).

Ernest Erber listed not only Sweden but also Japan as societies where social considerations rather than market forces guided the organisation of social relations. This linked the two welfare systems otherwise known for their differences: one had been achieved by a strong labour movement while the other had been created by paternalist but caring employers who cultivated a corporatist work ethics on firm level (cf. 1990: 359). Similarly,

Paul Berman claimed that not only Scandinavia but even the Canadian social system – which was quite modest for European standards – could serve as important sources of inspiration for the American left (cf. 1993: 191). Like in *Socialist Register*, however, Sweden received more sympathetic attention in *Dissent* than any other country did.

Monthly Review

In *Monthly Review*, contradictory opinions existed on the Swedish case. One of the authors noted that during the golden age of social democracy in the mid-1960s, Sweden had proved, at least impressive and 'socialist' enough to convince a famous American visitor, Martin Luther King, of the merits of 'democratic socialism' when he visited Scandinavia to receive the Nobel Prize (cf. Cushman-Wood 1993: 24). Other writers in *Monthly Review* were less enthusiastic and debated whether there was any qualitative difference between the Swedish model and other countries' social democratic policies. For Kenneth Hermele, its advantages were mostly restricted to the employees of large firms (cf. 1993: 16). He argued that Swedish capitalism did not differ from capitalism elsewhere (cf. 1993, 1993a), a view that was shared by Peter Cohen (1994: 41). Both of them accused the Social Democratic Workers Party of colluding with large Swedish (and increasingly also with international) corporations. If, however, Martin J. Morand declared that, like elsewhere, also in Sweden 'socialism in one country' had failed, this implied that at least clear efforts had been taken to move into socialist direction (cf. 1991: 26).

One also finds two contradictory opinions on the meaning of Sweden's example for socialists elsewhere. David Vail emphasised its importance for the American left (1993: 24):

I confess a Jekyll and Hyde reaction to the recent policies and tactics of Sweden's Social Democratic Party. When in Sweden, I tend to view the social democrats critically, from a socialist-environmentalist perspective. But on this side of the Atlantic, where even Bill Clinton seems fairly progressive, I find myself much more strongly aware of the social democrat's [sic] past accomplishments and present virtues. (ibid: 30-1; Footnote 1)

Peter Cohen, on the other hand, did not see any sense in speaking of a Swedish model because it did not differ from other social democratic and welfarist institutional arrangements. Furthermore, in international politics it behaved as badly and contradicted any notion of global working-class solidarity – just like any other capitalist country (1994: 43-4).

Although all journals questioned the Swedish model's global replicability (and that of other welfare systems in the highly-industrialised countries), only *Monthly Review* looked for models beyond social democratic Western Europe, corporatist East Asia and liberal Canada (whose attractiveness seemed to depend to a large extent on its difference from the United States). Despite explicit critique, several writers in *Monthly Review* regarded Cuba as such a model. For Paul Sweezy, Cuba set standards in terms of its population's social equality, level of education, state of health, and the quality of the nutrition available to its population – if measured against other 'developing' countries (cf. 1990: 18). For Sweezy, the foundation of its success lay in the popular roots of the Cubans' "own" revolution – distinguishing the island from the collapsed state-socialist societies in Eastern Europe where 'socialism' had been introduced by the Soviet Union (cf. ibid: 17). For the novelist Alice Walker, the model character stemmed from the level of equality Cuba had achieved among the different ethnic groups and from the confident politics of empowerment of the poor (cf. 1994: 41-2). Harry Magdoff pointed elsewhere – towards the Indian province of Kerala where a Communist-led regional government had managed to provide a level of social security for the most marginalised people unknown in other far better-off parts of India (cf. 1991: 12). Magdoff conceded, however, that further progress depended on a deliberate moving away from a capitalist framework of economic organisation (cf. ibid). Without such a shift, Kerala might share the fate of a dramatically richer society analysed by Jim Delahunty (1993) in an article for *Monthly Review*: while New Zealand had been regarded as a "Sweden of the South" until the 1970s, it had become the victim of a free-market renaissance and a signpost of an aggressive neoliberalism in the 1980s. As the only among the four journals, *Monthly Review* identified models which had been developed by Communist governments.

4.4. Europe: Capitalist Club or Site of Struggle and Project for the Left?

One of the major changes occurring simultaneously with the transformations in Eastern Europe was the start of a new stage in the 'European unification' process. On the one hand, the signing of the Maastricht treaty in 1992 signalled an intensification of economic and potentially political integration. On the other hand, the border between Western and Eastern Europe had disappeared. Hence the single market, ratified with the treaty, was likely to have consequences for Europe as a whole. The issue of European unification was deeply controversial for the British and the American intellectual left – representing hope for some and a serious danger for others. The main questions raised in a number of articles, either focusing entirely on these developments or discussing them within the context of analysing changes in global capitalism or the international political order, were whether the setting up of the *European Union* was a progressive step in the sense that it transcended exclusionist nation-state structures and constituted a political block powerful enough to prevent excesses by both a capitalism in the process of globalisation, and the only remaining super power. While few were without doubts about the European project, questions remained as to whether Europe could at least be transformed into a progressive force (and if it could, by what means) or whether it was, quite to the contrary, an administrative structure serving European capitalism and collaborating with the United States. Arguments concentrated on this question of the 'nature' of the *European Union*, but also on the meaning of its recent changes: would the single national states, as a consequence, become less powerful? Its present democratic deficit was only rarely ignored – was it possible to transform the EU into a more democratic entity? What would happen to the welfare systems of the individual national states? And finally, how should the left deal with the unification process? Should they welcome it and try to redirect it towards a more socialist project? Or should they keep their distance, criticise it and look for alternative resources, strategies and models for progressive social change? With the partial exception of the predominantly supportive *Dissent*, where only the European and British former structural Marxist and later theorist of 'associative democracy', Paul Hirst, expressed an ambivalent view on Europe, the journals were split on these questions. The Americans, however, seemed slightly more optimistic than their British colleagues on this issue.

New Left Review

In the pages of *New Left Review*, one finds contradictory opinions concerning the question of Europe.[10] Interestingly, it was David Marquand, non-Marxist and left-of-centre political scientist, who made the clearest case against the possibility of a social democratic Europe. Criticising suggestions by Wolfgang Streeck and Paul Rogers for such a project, published in David Miliband's 1994 compilation *Reinventing the Left*, Marquand expressed his opinion that it was highly utopian and that the *European Union* would remain in the grips of centrist and right-wing political forces even if social democrats were nominally in power (cf. 1994: 19). The problem, according to Marquand, lay in the economic orientation of the *European Union*. The original idea that political would follow economic integration had been unrealistic and only led to an erosion of nation-state power without replacing it with appropriate supranational structures (cf. ibid: 24). The result was a lack of equality between different parts of the EU, an absence of what he called "territorial justice". This was likely to have consequences in the future:

So long as there is no authority to ensure territorial justice, to overcome the centripetal tendencies inherent in a capitalist free-market economy, the periphery will not be able to sustain monetary union; and so long as the periphery cannot sustain monetary union, monetary union will be incomplete. (ibid: 25)

Despite his pessimism, Marquand saw no solution but to reverse emphasis: instead of economic unification, political unification should become a priority and economic variation should not be used as an excuse for delaying political integration, but as a reason for its urgency (ibid: 26). A second

---

10 *New Left Review* had taken a pro-European Community position during the heated debate over British membership in the mid-1970s. For the British left of the time this was an usual step which was widely criticised. See especially Tom Nairn's article "The European Problem" (1972) which constituted the centre piece of *New Left Review* 75, a special issue number with the title *The Left Against Europe?*

voice was that of Aijaz Ahmad, who pragmatically argued the case for EU integration in *New Left Review*. In a side remark within a critical appraisal of Jacques Derrida's "Spectres of Marx", the Indian Marxist agreed with the French poststructuralist that there was the danger of a fundamentalist Christian EU (cf. 1994: 99). Unlike Derrida, however, he regarded the coming of the EU as unavoidable against the background of the ensemble of class forces and power distribution in Europe, and, for him, it was in several respects a progressive move (cf. ibid: 100).

Only a few authors explicitly dealt with the question of whether dwindling nation-state power had to be accepted as an unavoidable phenomenon. David Marquand seemed convinced that the states themselves had initiated the transfer of power from the national to the supranational level. His main critique focused on the poor planning and execution of the transition, which made political interventions for a more egalitarian project extremely difficult or even utopian: "It will be utopian because the national states of the Union have already surrendered too much power to supranational institutions to implement it on the national level, while the institutions of the Union will continue to be too weak to implement it on the supranational level" (1994: 19). If it was true that the political room of manoeuvre of individual national states declined, one of the most important issues for socialist intellectuals was the question of what would happen to the best-developed welfare states in a unifying Europe. The overwhelming majority of contributors were sceptical about the chances of their survival. Marquand expressed his fear of "competitive social dumping", explicitly demanded and pursued by countries like Britain (ibid: 18). This was even more likely, as he pointed out, because political-institutional mechanisms for an adequate large-scale regional redistribution in the form of a transnational electoral, welfare and tax system simply did not exist (ibid: 22).

After these analyses, the question remained for the intellectual left how to relate to this process of European integration along capitalist lines. Both Marquand and Ahmad declared that, despite all scepticism, the left had to join the struggle over the *European Union* in order to make it an open, egalitarian, and internationalist rather than a closed, hierarchical, and fundamentalist polity (cf. Marquand 1994: 26; Ahmad 1994: 100).

Socialist Register

John Palmer, European correspondent of the left-of-centre British newspaper *Guardian* emphasised in *Socialist Register* the progressive aspect of the European project and warned against the simplistic notion that the unification would only serve capitalist interests. In his view, the major protagonists of capitalism were also divided over the question of free trade or protectionism (cf. 1992: 149). According to his perspective, the European right feared the entry of social democratic countries such as Sweden, Austria and possibly Norway which might move the whole EU project to the left – thus changing its current direction (cf. ibid: 152-5). Palmer was convinced that a socialist or at least progressive EU could contribute important stimuli to human emancipation on a global scale (cf. ibid). Stephen Gill, in the same issue of the *Register*, drew a bleaker picture. He strongly doubted that a unified Europe could challenge American and Japanese power in the global economy (cf. 1992: 157). He dismissed the idea that the twenty-first century would be European rather than Pacific as a myth, though he conceded that European monetary union could to a certain degree act as a countervailing force to U.S. power. The U.S. reaction, however, was likely to consist of a move from a Gramscian to a realist form of hegemony – replacing cultural-ideological leadership by military-political dominance. This could not be challenged by the EU, but only by transnational alliances of progressive popular forces. These should work, according to Gill, for a differentiated world order on the base of a global civil society and an international political authority (cf. ibid: 193). Consequently, he criticised the "new constitutionalism" embraced by large sections of the intellectual and political left as an *ersatz* strategy after the end of the Eastern Bloc and as a way of avoiding the problems with organising working-class and grassroots agency for progressive international action. For him, new constitutionalism was just a

> political project of attempting to make liberal democratic capitalism the sole model for future development, with the military forces of the major, 'core' countries reconfigured in ways which, in conjunction with the deepening and spread of commoditization and market forces, add a further disciplinary aspect to the emerging order. (ibid: 159)

This could only lead to a marginalisation of large parts of the population within the core countries and, as a likely consequence, to the formation of a mythical, racist Europeanness, or in other words, to the opposite of the internationalism he envisaged (ibid. 175-6). A similarly negative picture was drawn by Panitch. He described the EU project as one that freed capital from the constraints of nation-state control – a liberation organised by these states themselves who acted as "political authors of the Europe of traders and capitalists" (Panitch 1994: 86). For Panitch, the EU had no chance of becoming a counterforce to the U.S. because, as Nicos Poulantzas had already observed, American capital formed a strong presence within Europe and had fought bitterly, for example, against the European Social Chapter since the early 1980s (ibid). Hence the unification process could be nothing more than a mechanism organising the downward competition between states synonymous with a hollowing out of what had remained of the welfare states (ibid: 85).

The idea of decreasing state power seemed undisputed, although its extent was not precisely analysed and some, like John Palmer, emphasized that states had retained many functions and were likely to do so in the future (cf. 1992: 156). The normative question of whether a transfer of power to supranational institutions was to be welcomed or criticised by the left remained a matter of dispute. Whereas Palmer warned against a quasi-jingoistic defence of national parliamentary sovereignty, most others seemed to fear that sovereignty would be replaced by unaccountable institutions colluding with transnational corporations rather than by a progressive internationalism.

Such a view was directly linked to the problem of the EU's democratic legitimacy. Almost all of those who discussed the issue agreed that a serious democratic deficit existed. Again John Palmer disagreed to a certain extent. He claimed that the intensified integration process in the 1990s would lead to an extended role for the European Parliament and a parallel downgrading of the Council of Ministers (cf. ibid: 150-151). Stephen Gill contradicted this prognosis and suspected that with the 'new constitutionalism', institutions all over the new EU framework would become even more removed from public control (cf. 1992: 165-166)

What would happen to what was left of welfare capitalism? Gill, quoting Ralph Dahrendorf, argued in that German unification would put an end to the German welfare state which in turn would jeopardize welfare in other parts of Europe (cf. 1992: 182). The most likely scenario was, according to Panitch, a Europe-wide move towards the Anglo-American model of capitalism (cf. 1994: 86) and the setting-up of a programme to increase EU competitiveness (cf. Gill 1992: 164). In this context, Gill hinted at the example of "liberalisation", in other words, the privatisation of key industries, which traditionally had been under state control in Western Europe (ibid: 176). For the future, Gill expected a phase of Schumpeterian 'creative destruction' not only for the former state-socialist countries of the East, but also for the West-European welfare states (ibid: 177-8). More optimistically, Palmer argued extensively that the left's new political project should aid the fight for a social or even a socialist Europe. He encouraged the left to use the current opening of a public backlash against the neo-liberal policies of the 1980s in order to develop a supranational economic strategy "which [could; SB] both inform specific transitional demands on social democratic and reformist governments and provide the foundations for a European socialist economic alternative" (1992: 155). He claimed the necessity of a common programme reaching far beyond the economic focus of the *European Union* of the present. He saw a

need to develop prefigurative policies covering such questions as environmentally and socially sustainable forms of economic growth, transnational democratic planning, new forms of European public ownership, conversion from arms production, the encouragement of worker cooperatives, the development of the economy of social caring and innovative applications of human centred technologies. (ibid: 154-5)

With Aijaz Ahmad in *New Left Review*, Singer emphasised that the left had to resist an EU project that was "protectionist, white, ethnocentric and objectively intolerant, racist and repressive" (1992: 156). This entailed the defence of the right of the Eastern European states to join the union (cf. ibid: 152). The left should not restrict itself to demanding the democratisation of EU institutions, but should contribute to the Europeanisation of the labour movement and of other social movements (cf. ibid: 153). For the left, according to Palmer, it was a matter of course that a single market needed transnational trade unions and frameworks for industrial relations on the European level. Singer also argued that opposition to a neo-liberal EU, if it wanted to avoid falling into the trap of jingoism, could only take the form of fighting for a socialist United States of Europe capable of standing up to the United States of America (cf. 1993: 252-3). Other contributors to the *Register* disagreed. Panitch, comparing the debate on Europe to the Quebec question in Canada, claimed that one Canada was not necessarily more democratic than two states and that hence one integrated Europe was not automatically to be preferred over several European states (cf. 1994: 89). Similarly, Meidner saw a potential for reinvigorating public pressure for welfare state projects and their individual commitments and priorities on the national level in opposition to a supranational centralised Europe (cf. 1993: 227).

Dissent

Dissenters reflected on the global consequences of recent developments in Europe. Daniel Bell argued that the EU integration process received further impetus with the unification of Germany, the inclusion of Eastern Europe in a European trade block, and the altered relationship between Europe and the U.S.S.R.. Optimistically, he assumed that close cooperation would bring not only economic advantages, but also the abolition of the Warsaw Pact and NATO (cf. 1990: 174). In a manner similar to Robin Blackburn's arguments about the superiority of 'impure capitalism', Ernest Erber was convinced that, as a consequence of further steps of European unification,

the twenty-first century is not likely to be an American Century. Clinging to the market, the negation of social guidance, we might not even come in second. More likely we will be third, after a united Europe and an Asian-rim dominant Japan operating with strategic planning. (Erber 1990: 360)

Similarly, Donald Sassoon argued in *Dissent* that democratic deficiencies could best be cured by more rather than less integration (cf. 1994: 99). However, the British author Paul Hirst emphasised in the pages of the generally Europhile journal *Dissent,* that on the one hand only international organisations could cope with global problems but that on the other most of them – and he explicitly mentions the EU here – lacked democratic control (cf. 1994: 245).

Despite such sentiments to the contrary, those who expected positive dynamics from the unification process were in the majority; they did not doubt that the age of nation-state social democracy had come to an end (cf.

Sassoon 1994: 94) and so regarded the set-up of the EU as a resource of hope. For David Miller, the Social Chapter constituted even a "distinct harbinger" of a market-socialist Europe (1991: 414). Other writers such as Bogdan Denitch and Donald Sassoon argued that further integration would put the welfare provisions on a new stable foundation and allow for a Swedish model on a European scale (cf. Denitch 1991: 103-105; Sassoon 1994: 97) The advantages of such a development would not remain limited to the members of the EU but would affect Europe as a whole:

It would offer to Eastern and Central Europe and, indeed, to the rest of the world, the model of an advanced society radically different from the neoliberalism peddled by the IMF (International Monetary Fund). It would offer a society in which the values of solidarity prevail over the cacophony of cash registers. (Sassoon 1994: 97)

Such a project needed the support of the left. The vision of *Dissent*'s contributors during the early 1990s centred around what Joan Barkan called a "Very Imaginary Europe", which was needed in order to maintain the "Slightly Imaginary Sweden" regarded by many *Dissenters* as the basis of a project for incrementally introducing democratic socialism (cf. 1991 98). According to Barkan, it was the duty of socialists to join the movement for building this imaginary Europe (cf. ibid). Her view was echoed in the article by Sassoon. Speaking neither of 'socialism' nor of the 'left' but of 'social democracy', Sassoon agreed that social democrats should try to influence the process of European integration as much as possible (cf. 1994: 100). In particular, they should insist that the monetary convergence criteria should be accompanied by social ones (ibid: 99). These social measures were needed in order to also grant the underprivileged a stake in the emerging system of governance. Sassoon had no illusions that the realisation of such a project would need support from political agents far beyond social democracy:

Of course such consensus politics entails acceptance by all parties [...] of the basic features of a civilized society – yes, a society in which inflation is less than x percent, but also one that eliminates the fear of ill health, poverty and want, the indignities of sexual and racial discrimination, and the dangers of environmental damage. (ibid: 100)

With regard to the 'new constitutionalism' criticised by other left intellectuals, he insisted that a European constitution was needed, but that democratic institutions and pan-European labour organisations in both party and trade union form, were of equal importance. Finally, he suggested that a European social democratic programme would contribute to a strengthening of democratic structures in Eastern Europe and criticised social democratic parties for employing a Europhile rhetoric that was not matched by a comprehensive European strategy (ibid: 94-5). Altogether, for *Dissent* the *European Union* had the potential to be transformed into a social democratic or democratic socialist transnational community.

Monthly Review

In *Monthly Review*, world system theorist Samir Amin declared his conviction that Europe was at a crossroads in the early 1990s. It could become either a common capitalist market or, as Amin said in Mikhail Gorbachev's words, 'a common European home' based on socialist principles. Which of the two scenarios would become reality depended on the future of intra-European relations, both on the level of political movements and official policy (cf. 1990: 25). In a later contribution discussing the impact of the 1991 Gulf War, Amin suggested that the war had demonstrated the weakness of the 'alternative European perspective' on the world order and had intensified U.S. influence on Europe via the increased control of oil (cf. 1991: 21). Other writers such as Daniel Singer and Peter Cohen were even more sceptical about the European project. Singer diagnosed the capitalist bias of the Maastricht regulations:

The [Maastricht; S.B.] treaty itself was the logical completion of the whole process of integration, with the common currency and an independent central bank asserting the direct rule of money, while the meagre social chapter confirmed that the rules would not be equal for capital and labor. (1994: 93)

Peter Cohen expressed a similar opinion in much stronger words: "The EU is the first step in the final rationalization of the European capitalist production system, and represents the last act in the tragicomedy of European bourgeois political democracy" (1994: 58). Kenneth Hermele and Daniel Singer agreed that monetary union would only codify the EU's monetarist, high-unemployment, anti-workers and anti-welfare biases (cf. Hermele

1993a: 36). In order to change course and to act as an effective counterforce to the United States, Europe would first have to develop different kinds of societies (cf. Singer 1994: 93). This, however, was unlikely to occur given that NATO and *Western European Union* (WEU), the European Community's 'military wing', would always suppress serious class unrest in Western Europe and prevent Communist Parties from regaining power in the eastern part of the continent (cf. Cohen 1994: 57).

Like Marquand in *New Left Review*, Daniel Singer stressed the diminishing power of national state governments in *Monthly Review*, but he saw the reduction more as a consequence of economic developments than of political decisions. His conclusions, however, were similar to those of Marquand: "With the European Community moving towards a single market, this trend was reinforced by the drastic reduction of the powers of the individual national states without a corresponding increase in the powers of a European state, as if capital decided to run without proxy" (1994: 92). The situation was worsened by the fact that the EU, in general, and the Council of Ministers, in particular, were only accountable to the highest levels of "corporate Europe" (Cohen 1994: 58; cf. also Hermele 1993a: 36). Others urged the readers not to give up hope for a more leftwing Europe – especially, as Robert Vail added in *Monthly Review*, if further progressive countries like Finland, Austria, Norway and Switzerland would join (cf. 1993: 30).

What position should the left take towards Europe? The critics of the Swedish model, Peter Cohen and Kenneth Hermele, argued that Scandinavian leftists, including sections of the Swedish social democrats, were correct to oppose EU membership (cf. Cohen 1994; Hermele 1993: 23-24). They remained unconvinced that visions for a socialist Europe could be provided by Scandinavian welfare state models, and did not believe that EU institutions could transform into agents of radical political change. The opposite position was taken by Daniel Singer, who held the left responsible for asking questions about what kind of economic growth the EU needed, about the purpose of such developments, about the nature of the society which would be built, and about the environmental consequences. If they failed to discuss and answer these questions, the left would disappear and Europe would become like the United States (cf. 1994: 98). He received support from Amin, who despite all his critiques of Europe's role in a postcolonial hierarchical world order, had already some years earlier maintained that a unifying Europe should receive the support of progressive and democratic forces (cf. 1990: 21). Like *Socialist Register* and *New Left Review*, *Monthly Review* argued for supporting European unification – but without illusions.

4.5. Locating Socialism

The number of articles dealing with possibilities and forms of a new radical or socialist project was impressive. These reflections thematically centred on the discussion of democratic socialism. As their writings clearly indicate, equality constituted the most important characteristic of democratic socialism for the authors in all four journals. This awarding of the central position to equality – instead of the abolition of private property or the free association of individuals, for example – testified to a certain modesty and allowed for a variety of conceptualisations of the socialist project. Generally, democratic socialism was not interpreted as following a radical break with liberal democracy but as its completion. Authors held that democracy should become more ambitious and be extended to the economic and the social sphere. In this context, the level of the national state with its institutions and its separation of powers retained its privileged position, even if further levels – and further checks and balances on all levels – should be added. The overall vision was one in which the institutions of government, workplace decision-making and grassroots popular democracy would control each other. As a long-term perspective, many writers expected the role of government institutions to become more restricted and the structures at other levels more powerful. The whole process had to be understood as a large-scale learning-by-doing exercise. The rationale was the necessity of striking a balance of socialism and democracy in order to avoid a turn towards authoritarianism. However, these considerations remained altogether vague. Several authors defended the abstract nature of their deliberations with the anticipation that more concrete models for institutional arrangements could only be developed during the process of moving towards democratic socialism. Similarly, despite the centrality of equality, the issue of the extent of such equality – should a society's individuals become equal or only more equal – was only seldom convincingly addressed. The problem how to create equality on a global level was also raised but nowhere thoroughly discussed.

An alternative to designing democratic socialism from scratch would be to look into existing theoretical models or actual existing cases. Hence intellectuals investigated versions of market socialism. Overall, its evaluation was positive. This model could be supported at least as an immediate demand within the framework of a transformative strategy, but others conceived of it as a comprehensive variety of democratic socialism. Most authors accepted that market socialism retained positive aspects of markets, such as the price mechanism, but left behind negative ones, like the nexus of the amount of private property and the level of political influence. Market socialism constituted a strategy to diversify forms of ownership and thus to further economic democracy.

Among real-world cases, Sweden possessed a privileged position. Although most authors agreed that the country could not be considered socialist, its 'impure capitalism', or 'functional socialism' had reached the highest level of equality imaginable within a capitalist framework. Contributors repeatedly pointed out that the Swedish model had not been granted to the Swedish population, but had been successfully fought for and achieved by an unusually strong and well-organised labour movement. This last point bore relevance for intellectuals' evaluation of the European unification project. While a democratic-socialist Europe would not become a realistic option, opinion was split over the question of whether a social-democratic Europe was imaginable. Even if they had reservations, most authors recommended the left's involvement in the debates over the unification process in order to argue the case of working-class interests and strengthen European labour movements, to fight its drive towards a neo-liberal accumulation regime, to correct the European Community's democratic deficit and to prevent an uncritical alliance with the United States.

While all these issues were broadly shared by the journals and constituted majority opinion within them, a number of important differences found expression too. Such variations concerned, for example, the question of whether a clear line of separation could be drawn between capitalist and socialist societies. While most authors agreed that the constellation of political, social and economic arrangements made a given society either capitalist *or* socialist, some, especially among those writing for *Dissent*, argued societies should instead be placed on a continuum: more versus less socialist. These differing views were related to some extent to the question of how one chose to characterise socialism – by absolute equality or by a comparatively high level of it. Implicitly, this problem provoked the question of whether a country such as Sweden could be close to socialism although its population would count as extremely wealthy and privileged on a global scale and it clearly profited from an unequal global division of labour. As most *Dissenters* shared the more-versus-less-socialism perspective, they additionally raised the question as to 'how much' socialism was advisable. Once more they argued on the basis of their reflections on authoritarianism and recommended balancing projects for socialism with realistic assessments of human behaviour. This question led to fundamental disagreements among the journals. While *Dissenters* privileged individual rights over collective interests, authors in the other journals occasionally and very hesitantly conceded that the infringement of human rights could be justifiable under certain conditions. More exactly, the latter position was only taken by contributors to the European journals. Whereas it could be argued that individual rights have an exceptionally high status in the American political tradition and the contributors to the U.S. journals responded to this history, this interpretation must be qualified: more than any other journal, *Monthly Review* defended the Cuban variety of socialism whose record on the protection of individual rights, to say the least, was mixed.

Furthermore, the treatment of market socialism does not lead to a clear distinction between American and British perspectives. Among the journals most concerned with this topic, market socialism received the most comprehensive treatment in the American *Dissent*. Whereas *New Left Review* conceived of market socialism only as a step towards or a part of democratic socialism, *Dissent* even suggested interpreting the European Social Chapter as a document of market socialism. While the other two journals were less enthusiastic due to market relations' supposed coercive character and consequently argued for a complete break with market principles, their position remained slightly at odds with their evaluations of Sweden, which were at least partly positive and called it an example of functional socialism. It was only in *Monthly Review* that Sweden found any competition: while Sweden was 'functionally socialist' internally, it collaborated with a capitalist and imperialist world system. Cuba was socialist not only in terms of its property relations, but also in terms of the positions it took in international politics. However, it lacked democracy. Clearly, *Monthly Review* viewed Cuba through a critical U.S. lens – many of its deficiencies were explained through the hostile postures to the island undertaken by the American government.

The overall critical support of the European unification process came as a bit of a surprise. In the case of *New Left Review*, given its pro-European position, it appeared almost ironic that they solicited a commentator like Marquand, a member of the Liberal Democrats at the time, to present a negative evaluation of European future and then to advise the left to try and influence the workings of the European system of institutions as strongly as possible. It was only in *Socialist Register* that a number of authors argued explicitly for alternative left engagement – rather than immersing themselves in European constitutionalism, activists should join attempts at building European-wide and global labour organisations. Obviously, the European Community and European welfare states were interpreted more positively from across the Atlantic than from within. The provision of welfare in Europe seemed several steps closer towards 'functional socialism' and writers hoped that a critical mass of countries with 'impure capitalisms' – for example, Sweden and Austria – would initiate a drive towards 'functional socialism' on a European scale.

Altogether, differences between the U.S. and the British journals were not very marked. However, another delineation became more evident: the positions taken by *New Left Review* and *Dissent* seemed more congruent than those of the other two journals. Their moderate positions on democratic and market socialism dovetailed with their evaluations of Sweden and Europe. In *Monthly Review*, and even more in *Socialist Register*, a discrepancy existed between their more radical approaches to democratic socialism and their comments on Sweden and Europe which were quite similar to those expressed in the pages of their sister publications.

5. RE-STARTING HISTORY: AGENCY AND STRATEGY

The end of the Eastern bloc had put into question two basic principles frequently reiterated in orthodox Marxism and theories of Bolshevik-type state socialism: the directionality of history and the power of vanguardist voluntarism as a strategy for 'helping' history's movement. History could no longer be simply considered as the comrade and natural ally of socialists. As post-Marxists would have it: contingency had won over determinism.

Hence, possible agents of social change needed to be found and strategic options analysed. These were important tasks for radical intellectuals. Hence the debate on possible ways forward and the question of who would have to pursue them became an issue intensely discussed in the journals. For all it seemed clear that traditional notions of the working class as the revolutionary agent had been too simplistic. Thus academics invested a great deal of time and energy in working to identify either alternative fighters for change or else find new ways of defining a revolutionary or transformative working class, especially in a global perspective. Related to this search was the question of strategy. Though overlapping with the interpretation of Marxism and the problem of democratic socialism, the focus here was put differently: did revolutions still count as a possibility – and a necessity – for achieving radical social change? If yes – were they part of a transformation process or did they constitute the whole? How to consolidate them? If they were not necessary – or not possible at the moment – what was to be done instead? If a reformist route was pursued, was there still anything that distinguished a socialist from a social-democratic strategy? Did the concept of class struggle still have any political relevance? What was the task of those radical intellectuals who wrote for the journals and who, at least in most cases, wanted to act as organic intellectuals serving the oppressed of the world?

New Left Review

Agency

The question of working-class agency was central for the journal. Writers agreed that on the one hand they could not rely on the traditional understanding of the industrial working class as the agent of revolutionary or any other kind of political change. On the other, the meaning of the term 'revolutionary struggle' should be broadened. Giovanni Arrighi, like many others, argued for a less economistic understanding of revolutionary political struggle and pointed to the examples of South Africa and Poland to show that issues such as religion and 'race', as well as age, sex, and nationality, were important sources of political resistance which were not considered in rigidly class-focused Marxist schemes (cf. 1990: 63). Arrighi went on to explain that in late twentieth century capitalism there was a growing group of marginalized and super-exploited people who were most likely to cause the necessary political unrest once they had, through economic restructuring, assembled enough political power in their hands:

The social power which the cost-cutting race is putting in the hands of traditionally weak segments of the world proletariat is but a prelude to these struggles. To the extent that these struggles succeed, the stage will be set for the socialist transformation of the world. (ibid)

In addition, Norman Geras argued that this change of emphasis in the understanding of the working class had to be accompanied by a modified perception of working-class ethics. Whereas the traditional 'historical necessity' argument had restricted agency to those sections of the working class which had a *material* interest to end exploitation, agency should be seen as belonging to those who formulated an *ethical* interest because they regarded distributive injustice as a moral scandal. As a consequence, the demand for distributive justice was extended beyond those who produced surplus value, namely the industrial workers. Geras was convinced that this broadening was extremely important because "[t]he least that can be said is that this [the emphasis on the proletariat as only historical agent; SB] was a particularism which did not always strengthen, in theory or in practice, the democratic and the humanist sensibilities of Marxists" (1994: 102-103). Elsewhere he further elaborated on this argument and explained that workers had an interest in socialism not as producers, but as those suffering from inequality due to their position at the wrong end of economic relations. Hence they shared their plight with domestic labourers, the homeless, the ill or infirm, the long-term unemployed and all marginalized sections of society (cf. Geras 1992: 68). A coalition of these groups of people should form the core of a new socialist project. Geras emphasised that he did not propose a voluntaristic association of divergent interests, but argued on the base of materialism:

Note that this point is not urged in light of some counter-materialist logic, proposing the more or less free construction or alignment of identities. It remains on the ground of rooted social interests. By a development of the logic immanent to the Marxist case itself, the core constituency of socialism is seen to extend beyond the sites of production as such to all of the dispossessed. (ibid: 69)

Considering all the dispossessed members of society as potential agents of change necessitated changing the socialist agenda in two respects: it had to become global in perspective and it had to incorporate the demands of groups fighting oppressions beyond the economic sphere, especially those of the new social movements. André Gorz developed this argument further – perhaps to an even greater degree than Geras would have wanted. He suggested abandoning the idea that any particular class was the carrier of the socialist project, which in practice meant to leave behind the idea that particular economic situations served as its precondition (cf. 1993: 66).

Apart from hints at the importance of super-exploited people for achieving political change, writers pointed to concrete examples that existed even in this non-revolutionary time. Mary Kaldor saw the revolutionary potential of Eastern European people as recently proven and was convinced that their commitment to political freedom was accompanied – through the experience of relatively egalitarian social systems – by distaste for social inequality. She saw reason to hope that both aspects together would generate stronger demands for social justice on a global scale (cf. 1990: 36). However, hope lay also elsewhere: Robin Blackburn pointed to new proletarian movements in the South – especially in Brazil and Mexico, in South Korea and, like Arrighi, in South Africa – and to a new type of socialist parties in several European countries: he listed Finland, Norway, Denmark, Spain, Turkey and the Netherlands (cf. 1990: 238). It seemed consensual that a revived left in Europe would take a different shape than what it had been before – but was at the same likely to be more similar to the left in the rest of the world. Göran Therborn explained that this European left would become more like the North American – more heterogeneous in its concerns and identities, more sensitive towards cultural issues, more pragmatic and democratic, and looser in terms of organisation (cf. 1992: 32). The global dimension – the concerted agency of the oppressed of the world was repeatedly emphasised. Only one writer, Joseph McCarney, disagreed and suggested leaving the question of political agents to the future – he claimed that Western Marxists' debates about supporters or replacements of the proletariat had been futile (cf. 1991: 31-32).

Strategy
Agency was one thing, strategy another. Most contributors accepted that revolution, however defined, was not on the immediate agenda and many

expressed doubts that a nineteenth century type of revolution was the adequate strategy for political change in the future. Auerbach, for example, suggested that it had been a mistake to concentrate too exclusively on attempts to take over the "commanding heights" of the economy (cf. 1992: 34-5). The crucial issue was to find ways of combining the many different struggles that took place on a global, continental and regional level – fights of environmentalists, migrant workers, anti-racists, anti-militarists, as well as of those sceptical of privatisation in Eastern Europe (cf. Blackburn 1990: 238). This strategy of following multiple progressive causes, the opposite of democratic centralism, certainly contained numerous problems. Among them was the danger of open-mindedness becoming unprincipled pluralism or even cowardice, something Auerbach diagnosed in leftwing reactions to the Rushdie affair (cf. 1992: 22):

It is not given to us now to possess the belief of early twentieth-century radical Marxists in the power of historical materialism as a solution to all problems. But does this mean a surrender to fanatics and True Believers of various kinds? [...] [T]he self-confidence of the fanatic can easily overwhelm the Hamlet-like diffidence of the rational person, unless the latter makes an aggressive defence of at least the *method* of rational thinking as the only relevant device for decision-making on public issues. (ibid)

In practice, this position would require squaring the circle of reconciling pluralism with a clear political position and a plurality of voices with organisational cohesion. Another problem was the assembling of a critical mass of supporters in order to make political demands heard. Thus Lynne Segal, discussing what could be learned from the New Left's identity politics in Britain during the 1970s and 1980s, saw no alternative but to collaborate with the reformist labour movements:

Without access to the resources of strengthened social-democratic reformist structures, as decentralized and accountable as possible, and without strong trade unions, the social movements (particularly as conceived by the theorists of difference) can offer little more than the enjoyment of an endless game of self-exploration played out on the great board of identity. (1991: 91)

Lucio Magri was also convinced that new social movements and Marxists would have to move towards each other. He claimed that the former were not able "to produce a new culture and organisation that will unite with broad masses of workers and marginal layers" (1991: 8). On the other hand, the latter had to embrace new concepts of struggle which lay beyond their traditional ideas of social and political change. He was sure that "cultures and experiences outside Marxism and the workers' movement will make an indispensable contribution. There is certainly nothing fortuitous in the role of advanced Catholic currents in Latin America, or of ecologism, feminism and the peace movement in Europe" (ibid: 12). Magri imagined a combination of forces uniting those still fighting the class struggle and the new movements, which required an agreed-upon political theory and practice in order to be sustainable and successful. The only alternative to unity would be defeat, which would only serve to strengthen the objectionable system that one wanted to transform (cf. ibid: 13). In his view, it was wrong to interpret the collapse of Eastern Europe as a proof that formal organisation was no longer needed: "Precisely because socialism can no longer be separated from democracy, it has all the more need of awareness, programmes, organization and education" (ibid).

Magri suggested developing strategies that were compatible with the present situation in which the left was on the defensive. In this context, struggles had to protect democracy not only against explicit authoritarianism but also – and this view distinguished the left from the triumphant right – against the ever-increasing influence of unaccountable power centres such as international institutions, company regimes, and information and education apparatuses (ibid: 16). Some contributors thought that links with social movements and labour organisations were insufficient as a coalition-building strategy. Allies had to be found beyond the constituency of the left. David Purdy called for an alliance of socialism and liberalism. It could be forged around concrete political demands – he proposed citizen's income because liberals and socialists shared the idea of a justice-seeking state:

Socialists who are critical of classical liberalism but care about personal liberty, have begun to overlap with liberals who are critical of classical socialism, but care about social justice. From this standpoint, it can be argued that universal grants offer the best way to renovate the social rights of citizenship and bring consideration of social justice and questions of economic policy into a common frame of reference. (1994: 37)

Further practical proposals concerned the issue of education. Auerbach urged a comprehensive paradigm shift in Marxist political strategy. Instead of focusing on the economic base, radical change should be achieved through altering the superstructure – he demanded a socialist education programme as important contribution to such a shift. In general, people felt very much affected by 'superstructural' arrangements, and the malfunctioning of institutions at the superstructure level had drawn many into political activism. More concretely, a better-educated public would have more chances of changing the existing system – one of the reasons being that an informed society would prove less easily manipulated by mass-cultural products. Education, hence, could become a lever of emancipation and feared as such by those interested in keeping the status quo:

Right-wing philistinism has roots in seventeenth-century non-conformist religion (the superiority of faith over good works and of feeling over thought goes back to St Paul), but a capitalist utilitarianism ('what is education good for?') is reinforced by the long-term suspicion of conservatives (at least since the time of Plato) that teaching the masses to think has its dangers. A persistent nightmare of the conservative is that an informed and literate population will wrest power from the natural rulers of society and deal directly with the issues that affect their lives. (Auerbach 1992: 18)

Auerbach linked this educational programme to the issue of global survival. Pointing out that the system of the United States, as the embodiment of pure liberal capitalism, was likely to be incompatible with environmental concerns, there were just two alternatives – either democratic socialism or an authoritarian system. A well-educated and well-informed population was more likely to embrace the former (cf. ibid: 20).

But how did writers deal with the question of a violent rupture? Was it stricken from the agenda just for the moment or should it be abandoned as strategy of change altogether? It seemed that most writers shied away from facing this problem. Ted Hondrich's position has already been mentioned: he formulated doubts that a peaceful transformation from 'hierarchical democracy' to an 'egalitarian democracy' was possible. The attempt at changing power structures would be violently resisted and lead to a civil war (cf. 1994: 65-66). He pointed out that a democratic socialist morality might then reject the introduction of egalitarian democracy since this would require actions contradicting its very ethos. In other words, he identified a moral dilemma. Unfortunately, this issue was not replied to by any other writer. Miliband expressed his conviction that revolutions in the sense of a violent overthrow of an existing system were necessary where people had to free themselves from dictatorships, but their consequences were highly ambivalent:

As Lenin once said, 'revolution is the festival of the oppressed'. But festivals do not last very long, and revolution is often accompanied by bitter resistance. The dislocation and suffering this causes greatly affects revolution's redemptive quality, and has a profoundly adverse effect on it. (1994: 11)

Miliband disagreed with Marx and Engels, whom he claimed had regarded revolutions as the mechanism for freeing the working classes from the muck of ages. Revolutions would liberate people from dictators, but muck in the form of entrenched social structures and internalised patterns of behaviour would remain. Hence, the introduction of socialism was an extended process, whether it started with a revolution, as with authoritarianism, or with gradual transformation, as with capitalist democracies (cf. ibid: 10-11).

Generally, contributors saw the need to wait for 'better' times. Many of them clung to a paradoxical hope: things had to get worse in order to get better. Immanuel Wallerstein, for example, explained that capitalism would produce contradictions on a global scale which would threaten the legitimacy of state structures and, as a consequence, produce a situation similar to a civil war (cf. 1994: 15-16). It was likely to be a time of reinvigorated demands of equality – but viewed from a global scale, these would be contradictory: "In short, everyone will be acting somewhat blindly even if they will not think they are so acting:" (ibid: 16). In this situation the left would be needed as a force able to formulate long-term goals and to build an alternative social order. In other words, socialists should prepare for times to come. That they would come was a sentiment shared by many in the pages of *New Left Review* (cf. Kaldor 1990: 36; Auerbach 1992: 34). Gorz expressed this hope most clearly when he wrote about the necessary turn towards a more environmentalist regime: "A few limited disasters, portending the approach of major catastrophes, may be sufficient to speed up the socio-cultural mutation now taking place and make societies lean in the direction of political ecology" (1993: 67). Miliband perhaps best summed up the general feeling when he claimed that socialists had to find a path between reckless voluntarism, which had proved to be terribly disastrous in the early Soviet Union, and an exaggerated caution (cf. 1994: 13). The waiting, thus, was an active waiting, accompanied by the participation in small-scale struggles and by the continuous formulation of critique.

Intellectuals
What were the responsibilities of intellectuals with regard to the agents suggested and the strategies outlined? Writers identified three broad categories of intellectual activity: critique, utopian thinking, and activism. Numerous appeals not to abandon the basics of socialist critique littered the pages of *New Left Review*. G. A. Cohen, taking issue with a document published by the centre-left *Institute of Public Policy Research* (IPPR) which argued for leaving behind central tenets of classical socialist thinking and terminology, pointed out that without well-founded socialist principles, leftwing policy would be impossible: "Fundamental socialist values which point to a form of society a hundred miles from the horizon of present possibility are needed to defend every half-mile of territory gained and to mount an attempt to regain each bit that has been lost" (1994: 5). Hence critique and utopianism played as important a role as ever and were understood as the opposite of accommodation. Halliday even seemed to feel a degree of relief that in the new situation a return to critique was possible: "The critique of capitalism was the starting point of Marxism and socialism and is the point to which, quite properly, that tradition can now return" (1990: 21). Nevertheless, this was not a return to a status quo ante, but required "a reassessment and a realignment not only of Marxism and the socialist movements but of the radical and revolutionary traditions of Western society as a whole" (ibid: 23). This was a task of self-criticism, but also an intellectual challenge to analyse the potential for radical social change, in short, to combine criticism with utopianism and activism in order to prepare moves towards democratic socialism. Halliday, in his exchange with Thompson, urged intellectuals to be realistic about the openings that could be found. Observing that during the Cold War no 'third way' had been possible for non-aligned countries, he did not believe that alternatives

to capitalism had become easier to pursue after its victory. Intellectuals should make sober judgments in order to avoid voluntarism and unrealistic options (cf. 1990a: 150).

What remained to be done then? Several authors suggested continuing work on the analytical tasks that they had pursued throughout their intellectual and often also professional careers. Eric Olin Wright reiterated the importance of class analysis even if he saw it in crisis: the link that originally existed between the nodes of class analysis, class emancipation and historical trajectory had become looser not so much because of historical events, but because empirical knowledge of each of the nodes had increased (cf. 1993: 20-21). The solution could only consist of constructing a new but more flexible model of reconciling these aspects (cf. ibid). Whether this proved possible or not did not seem entirely clear. Whereas the author was convinced that class analysis remained an important investigative tool, he was less sure about "the extent to which such class analysis will be embedded in a broader theoretical configuration that contains the normative commitments of class emancipation and the explanatory aspirations of a theory of historical possibilities" (ibid: 35). Derrida described another task of political-economic analysis when he claimed that critique should be directed towards the link between state and international law on the one side and the market on the other (cf. 1994: 58). By analysing this link, intellectuals could contribute towards a new loose and informal international (ibid: 53). For this purpose, intellectuals would have to work in a non-dogmatic, 'hyper-critical' fashion which, for Derrida, was a deconstructive fashion. In this way, intellectuals could renew and radicalise the Marxist spirit of critique "in the name of a new Enlightenment for the century to come" (ibid: 55). McCarney developed a similar idea about the potential achievements of theoretical work. Rather than seeing it as an internal corrective to the existing economic and social order, he wanted it to clarify the fundamental contradictions within this order:

What is needed above all is an inquiry that will achieve for contemporary capitalism what Marx achieved for that of the nineteenth century. [...] The indispensable contribution is the general conception of capitalism as a system structured by contradictions which are insoluble in its own terms. (1991: 30)

Less ambitiously, Jürgen Habermas saw the relevance of socialist critique not in a transformative capacity, but in its function as important point of orientation within his model of communicative politics. Understood in this way, socialism became a "radically reformist self-criticism of a capitalist society, which, in the form of constitutional democracy with universal suffrage and a welfare state, has developed not only weaknesses but also strengths" (1990: 21). Structurally disadvantaged people no longer had the power to change politics through their industrial muscle, and marginal political causes (environmental concerns, the interests of developing states and refugees) never had. Their only chance lay in convincing society as a whole, in processes which Habermas called discursive problematisation (ibid: 20). This was a process in which intellectuals were needed both as spokespersons and as researchers. The latter role was related to "an attempt to find out *how much strain* the economic system [could] be made to take in directions that might benefit social needs, to which the logic of corporate investment decisions is indifferent" (ibid: 18). He further explained that the former role of spokesperson was indispensable for his concept of public sovereignty, "made fluid by being made communicative, that makes itself heard in the topics, arguments and proposed solutions of free-floating, public communication" (ibid). In this guise, the socialist project was no longer about a break with existing power relations but instead about making people aware of the numerous ways in which one's own interests were bound up with the interests of others.

One of the main differences from nineteenth century capitalism lay in its global expansion in the twentieth. Theorists should analyse what the relationship of first and Third World meant for moves towards an alternative social and economic order on a global scale, now that the second world had disappeared. Blackburn, however, added that such critiques of contemporary capitalism were not enough; a critical balance sheet of the socialism of the Eastern Bloc was needed too. This was simply a question of credibility (cf. 1990: 174).

Utopian thinking did not have to start from nowhere. Halliday, and others, such as Magri, proposed looking at the most likely sources for inspiration: pre-Marxist and non-Marxist anti-capitalism, as well as social democracy, feminism, ecology, and anti-racism (cf. Halliday 1990: 23; Magri 1991: 12). The utopianism some writers envisaged was a utopianism of details, one that acknowledged the need to design complex societies and elaborated decision-making structures. The question in how far one could go when describing details of societal organisation was answered differently by different contributors. Some remained sceptical; G. A. Cohen, for example, was convinced of the futility of describing intricacies of political institutions and practice. He saw utopianism more as an embrace of certain moral principles, such as community and equality, since these remained central even if they had fallen out of fashion. Hence he argued: "A different response to the present predicament is to think the values afresh in a spirit of loyalty to them in an inhospitable time, and what new modes of advocacy of them are possible" (1994: 8). It was not socialist rhetoric which was important according to Cohen, but instead the maintenance of socialist principles (ibid: 4).

Obviously, contributors remained convinced of the centrality of theoretical practice – this was perhaps the only form of political activism that made sense in times of uncertainty. Such a view seemed to engender the following comment by Geras:

More than a century of history gives grounds for caution as to where, if anywhere, the capacity to bring about socialism might be located. All we can do, then, those of us unwilling to embrace the present economic order as the best historical terminus imaginable, is to continue to explore where an interest in socialism might be located and why. (1992: 68)

The only project of 'practical practice' beyond work of research, analysis, and interpretation was suggested by E. P. Thompson; he called for a critical dialogue with former dissidents in the countries of the collapsed Eastern Bloc. They often had become neo-liberals and hence there was not much left of an intellectual left and of socialist imagination in these societies. Finding a common language would be difficult. Thompson nevertheless hoped that such a debate would become a first step towards the global revival of the socialist project (cf. 1990: 145). For him, this dialogue was a matter of necessity. Without it, not even the status quo would last because he interpreted the present conditions in Eastern Europe as a vacuum that, in the absence of a credible left, would be filled by anti-Semitism, nationalism and fundamentalism. Even if one was convinced that things had to get worse before they could get better, the danger was real that they would get too bad. Intellectuals should play their role in preventing this to happen.

Socialist Register

Agency

Not surprisingly, *Socialist Register* also asked about the role of the working class – and much more unanimously and unambiguously than contributors to *New Left Review*, it maintained that there was no alternative to working-class agency. Nevertheless, like *New Left Review*, the journal argued for a broader understanding of the concept and against restricting it to the industrial working class. The frequent hints towards the necessity of building rainbow coalitions and to come to agreements with the new social movements or what some called the new middle class, did not mean, however, bidding farewell to the centrality of class struggle. Rainbow coalitions did not have the purpose of aggregating a plurality of struggles, but of relating them to the centrality of class contradictions. Ellen Meiksins Wood explained this perspective in the following way:

There is another possibility: to differentiate not less but much more radically than even the new pluralism allows. We can acknowledge that, while all oppressions may have equal *moral* claims, class exploitation has a different *historical* status, a more strategic location at the heart of capitalism; and class struggle may have a more universal reach, a greater potential for not only class emancipation but other emancipatory struggles too. (1990: 78)

Yet even if the class contradiction was primary, formations of rainbow coalitions or collaboration of labour organisations and new social movements should be welcomed. For some of the contributors, they embodied a combination of working class solidarity and the specific new middle-class moralistic individualism (cf. Ross 1990: 214). For the American John Bellamy Foster, the formation of the U.S. rainbow coalition in the late 1980s constituted the first sign of a mass political movement for half a century (cf. 1990: 267). In his words what was needed was a "rainbow coalition of the working class" (ibid: 285). He believed that the emergence of such movements constituted an encouraging sign that mass agency was still possible – despite apathy and conformism in formal political procedures:

Beneath the calm surface suggested by these recent voting patterns, however, is a society torn by contradictions born of class struggle, in which there exists a potential for mass political rebellion that would threaten conservative political elites and tear the mask off the US ideological system for all to see. (ibid)

Foster hoped, obviously, that a movement like this could be transformed into something more solid: he suggested that a social democratic party might develop out of it and would have the potential to attract the votes of those fifty-one percent of the American electorate who did not bother to vote in the 1988 presidential elections (cf. ibid). He concluded on an optimistic note, assuming that the end of the Cold War might even have beneficial effects. For him the Jackson campaign had signalled "the beginnings of a crucial unravelling of the internal Cold War political order; an order that requires for its coherence the imposition of an ideological straightjacket that leaves a majority of the population not only invisible but effectively voiceless and optionless as well" (ibid: 286). Such a dynamic could only be strengthened by the disappearance of the Eastern Bloc. Examples like this seemed to serve the purpose of reassuring intellectuals that the 'common people' could still become agents of change – this point was reiterated several times in the pages of *Socialist Register*.

John Saville, retaining the spirit of the first British New Left, urged readers not to forget the role of human agency in developing political ideas different from those of the dominant classes, and not to ignore the fact that slightly improved living standards could just as well lead to radicalisation as to depoliticisation – hence it would be wrong to write off the metropolitan working classes as potential political actors (cf. 1990: 50-56). Contributors wondered if this conception could also be applied to the working classes of the Eastern Bloc. Some suggested that working-class people could – under certain circumstances – become reactionaries (cf. Levins 1990: 341). The danger that this happened at the time in Eastern Europe could not be neglected. However, it might still be the case that these workers carried some remnants of a 'socialist consciousness' with them and reacted negatively only to socialist sloganeering, but not to socialist values (cf. ibid; Lebowitz1991: 368).

Despite such uncertainties, *Socialist Register* stood for a tradition of socialist humanism which was strongly convinced that the 'common people' were able to govern themselves in principle. Miliband personified this premise perhaps more clearly than anyone else. He stated that while many lessons should be drawn from the experiment of state socialism, it was not the case that socialism was impossible and had to end in disaster (1990: 350). Miliband freely admitted that human beings were not intrinsically good, but neither were they necessarily bad. Neither Auschwitz nor the system of Gulags were, according to him, instigated by the 'masses' but by their rulers. Miliband conceded that while Marxists had often overestimated the commitment to radical change of the industrial working class, they were now rather in danger of underestimating it (cf. ibid: 362-363).

What did writers think about agency at the international level? Its importance did not lie in the chance to create a global revolutionary movement, but in the possibility of building parallel movements – under similar conditions in comparable conjunctures – in a number of national states. This position constituted an early contribution to the globalisation debate that began at the time. Panitch in this context expressed his scepticism concerning the emergence of a global democracy or a global civil society (1994: 91). He claimed that globalisation was organised by national states and therefore had to be dealt with at the level of the national state (ibid: 63). Another article thematised the contribution to radical change that could be expected from 'maverick states'. They might become reservoirs of resistance because, after the end of the cold war, they might come under increased pressure to conform. Avishai Ehrlich urged critics to look beyond the main protagonists of the Cold War and believed that these pressures "will be viewed by many states as the further concentration of force, along with wealth, in the hands of a few rich states, increasing inequality and diminishing the chances of others to improve their standing in this hierarchy of states" (1992: 238). Inherent in these statements was the assumption that agents within future struggles for radical political change might threaten the leading capitalist states (and thereby the system as a whole) from two sides – from within through the emergence and consolidation of radicalised rainbow movements with a working-class core, and from outside through the resistance of non-cooperative states within the capitalist world system.

Strategy

To move on to the question of strategy, Socialist Register's socialist humanism was anti-vanguardist. Instead, contributors suggested a transformative approach that transcended the old demarcation line of reform vs. revolution. This approach was not only needed because the times seemed unpromising for revolutions, but also because such revolts were no longer regarded as panaceas. Richard Levins explained in this context that revolutions so far had combined both a conservative and a radical dimension: people wanted to consume in the same way as capitalists and at the same time to destroy capitalism and consumerism (cf. 1990: 336). Hence revolutionary strategy had to take into consideration both of these aspects. Furthermore, progressive policies could become regressive (as they did in the state-socialist countries) and continuous reforms were needed even in a post-revolutionary situation. The transformative approach required the combination of parliamentary and extra-parliamentary activity. With the conviction that the victims of certain oppressions were the main actors in their liquidation, Geras reiterated the strategy of self-emancipation (made more complicated by the rainbow alliances that had replaced the mass-based socialist movements of earlier periods) (1990: 31-32). The tall order of self-emancipation had to be understood as a long-term perspective and should be brought about via two routes: on the one hand through the calling for and support of reformist measures within the existing state structures, on the other through the building of a socialist civil society capable of demanding radical change from the existing state system. In the current climate, this strategy could even turn defensive and entail the protection of the patchy welfare-state reforms undertaken during the 'golden age' of domesticated capitalism from neo-liberal attacks and attempts at dismantling them. For Werner Bienefeld, what was left of the secular welfare state was worthy of safeguarding not because it was perfect, but because presently it was in danger of being succeeded by something worse: "And our struggle must begin by rescuing the secular, territorial national state from those who would abandon it, and from those who would replace it with the disastrous notion of ethnic or religious states" (1994: 97). Linda Gordon, who agreed with this argument and underlined the importance of welfare capitalism's programmes especially for women, explained that a transformative approach should nevertheless go beyond such defence and design new forms of welfare that avoided the stigmatisations and oppressions that usually accompanied welfare provision (cf. 1990: 171). She characterised the welfare states as entities of relative autonomy. Accordingly, a socialist ethics of welfare was needed, since discriminations and disadvantages suffered by women, minority ethnic people, and especially minority ethnic women would not disappear automatically in a socialist society (and welfare programmes would still be needed to organise reproductive responsibilities). Gordon called for an ethics that considered these discriminations and tried to position those suffering from them as those who replaced these structures by something new of their own creation (cf. ibid. 192). It would be wrong, as historical examples showed, to write off welfare programmes as palliatives; they could just as well strengthen militant activism (cf. ibid. 193). Arthur MacEwan explained the transformative approach in more general terms, explicitly claiming in doing so that "[r]evolution is not on the immediate agenda" (1990: 318). He suggested distinguishing between reformist measures that simply worked and thus stabilised the status quo and revolutionary reforms which challenged the existing order and were likely to initiate further reforms. He proposed that, for instance, the necessity of environmental protection measures could be addressed through the demand for public control of companies. This would call into question the traditional prerogatives of capital and hence the core of the capitalist system (cf. ibid.). MacEwan admitted that an explicit commitment to this transformative strategy might alienate Marxists from oppositional popular forces, especially in the former state socialist countries – for him a risk to be borne in mind but nevertheless to be taken (cf. ibid. 319). He shared this position with Foster who was deeply critical of a social critique whose logic was anti-corporate but fell short of anti-capitalism. To attack corporations and to avoid 'naming the system', according to him, damaged the argument since it blamed individuals for systemic failures (cf. 1990: 279-80). Like MacEwan, he proposed the combination of concrete reforms with a long-term perspective:

What is at issue here is a strategy that points beyond simple reform or accomodation [sic], and toward the concrete formulation of a radical reform strategy with a potential mass base in the here and now consistent with the goal of long-term societal transformation, or what Raymond Williams and others have called the 'long revolution'. (ibid: 278)

Gregory Albo explained that the transformative approach was necessarily anti-capitalist: "There is no intellectually honest response from the left to the economic crisis, particularly with respect to unemployment, that does not involve political restraint on the power of capital and a redistribution of work and resources" (1994: 163).

Still, even if one embraced this idea of a long transformation, it could appear contradictory to support reforms within capitalism when one conceived of its inherent failures and contradictions as insurmountable and believed in the inevitability of anti-capitalist struggle. Yet rather than merely pointing to its shortcomings in a cynical manner, Marxists should support also piecemeal reforms (cf. Miliband 1990: 349). However, this strategy bore its dangers: it could generate an over-reliance on state-centred reforms and the neglect of what was going on at the level of (civil) society: "The self-help of popular forces should be seen as quite distinct from negotiating reforms in the structure. This has been precisely the trap into which all anti-systemic forces, even the most militant ones, were led during the liberal ideological era." (Wallerstein 1992: 109). However, as long as socialists remained sensitive to the difference between working *in* the system of the existing state and working *for* it, they could avoid this trap. In order to remain clear about this distinction, "utopistics", to use Wallerstein's term, were required: the imagination of new institutional structures – especially in civil society – to replace older ones situated at the state level (ibid. 109-110).

Panitch emphasised the need to analyse the actual existing power structures with which transformers had to cope. He insisted that the national states still played a central role within 'transnational' political processes (like organising EU integration) and it was these national states that helped organise 'transnational' economic processes (such as globalisation). Applying this to strategy, Panitch referred to the work of Sol Picciotto who called for an analysis of the internal contradictions of the state, exploitation of which would give social movements the chance to intervene. At the same time, states were just a part of the structure of the global capitalist system.

Any optimism that could be detected in the pages of *Socialist Register* had to do with the belief that once detrimental effects of the capitalist order became more visible, they would lead to a gradual radicalisation of the population. Again, this perspective was a variation of the argument that things had to get worse in order to get better. In this context, Bienefeld referred to the historical example of the New Deal which would have been regarded as completely unrealistic as late as early 1929 (cf. 1994: 100). The sketching out of detailed programmes was not so much what was needed in crisis situations of this kind, but rather the support of and solidarity with the movements that already existed. The existence of such movements and the threats they posed was proven by "national fractions of a global elite seek[ing] multilateral protection from domestic political forces, be they Chiapas Indians, Moscow conservatives or persistent social democrats." (ibid: 104)

Intellectuals
The task of intellectuals included steering these domestic political forces into the right direction. Consequently, like in *New Left Review*, *Socialist Register*'s writers also identified the three tasks of intellectuals as the formulation of criticism, utopianism, and activism. Criticism was understood not just as *interpretation* of the world as it was, but as critical *intervention* in discursive struggles. Eleanor MacDonald, elaborating on the work of Jacques Derrida, argued that it was Marxists' and feminists' task to demonstrate that a relationship existed between power and what counted as truths and ethical guidelines. Intellectuals, nevertheless, remained capable of speaking the truth about power. Such a frank interpretation of reality was both epistemologically possible and part of an empowering politics (cf. 1990: 241). It required a concept that was could not be fully grasped with academic or analytical methods – hope: "The challenge to rearticulate an optimism for politics and a trust in interpretation is an immense one, and must start with the ability to interpret in the hope of changing the very experiences that Derrida and the other postmodernists describe." (ibid: 231) Criticism in the spirit of hope – for political change – allowed intellectuals to tell materialist 'truths' about capitalism as a system of power instead of echoing postmodernist and liberal perspectives on the exclusively discursive or rational structures of society. In this context, Wood also criticised associational and communitarian perspectives: "It is perhaps time for us in the West to tell a few home truths about capitalism, instead of hiding them discreetly behind the screen of 'civil society'". (1990: 82) However, demanding the truth was one thing, how exactly to go about speaking it was another. Some contributors went a step backwards and suggested that intellectuals had to look at the concepts they used:

The prospects of a 'brave new world' (some would call it a dystopia) of global capitalism and the imperatives of a range of other global forces require a re-examination of theory and a search for either a reformulation or generation of new concepts and approaches which can begin to capture, at least theoretically, the changes which are actually taking place and the logic of their future trajectory. (Gill 1990: 307-308)

The changing prospects of global capitalism followed from the collapse of the state-socialist regimes. The analysis of which factors caused this collapse also constituted an important aspect of critical activity and a precondition for developing adequate concepts and approaches. Generally, writers demanded a re-politicisation of critical theory. They hoped that such a reorientation would spark off critique in the political sphere and deconstruct the myths which disguised and legitimised politics in capitalist democracies. In the words of Foster, the task was

to advance a politics of truth; to avoid easy compromises; to address the immediate and the long-term needs of the masses of the population and of those who suffer the most severe forms of oppression; to search for the common ground of that oppression; to resist ideological claims that 'we are all in the same boat' in this society; to reject what Mills called the 'crackpot realism' that makes the status quo into a kind of inescapable second nature and closes off the future; to fight market fetishism. In short, to avoid what Raymond Williams called 'long-term adjustments to short-term problems'. (1990: 286)

Foster's article was a plea not to fall prey to but to rather resist what he called "liberal practicality" – a first step towards advancing "socialist practicality" (ibid). Further work on Marxism was essential in order to make sense of the world as a "complex, contradictory and evolving whole" (Levins 1990: 335). Yet, this analytical effort was not enough. One of the most interesting and most difficult tasks for Marxists was educational: to work towards the creation of what traditionally was called a 'revolutionary consciousness'. Such a consciousness could no longer be trusted to develop automatically in times of crisis and change; rather, specialists needed to investigate how it could be tended, while remaining wary lest they themselves succumb to over-ambitious vanguardist aspirations: "The recognition that social changes do not drag consciousness along passively has made the analysis of consciousness formation both under capitalism and in revolutionary societies a major priority for all movements concerned with fundamental change" (ibid: 342).

While criticism had traditionally been one strategy for active 'consciousness formation', utopian thinking now became another. In the post-1989 climate, utopianism had to start with absolute basics in order to suggest, to use a slogan which became popular only later, that another world was possible. Even MacDonald's arguments about hope in the possibility of truthful interpretations of reality could be seen as epistemological utopianism in an intellectual era in which even academic thinking was in danger of sliding into complete relativism. More concretely, writers called for reflections on a socialist ethics, including an ethics of rights. Again, they took the recognition seriously that socialism would never automatically solve all problems and conceded that boundaries needed definition which people should not cross when dealing with each other. Socialist rights were utopian in so far as their base did not lie in capitalist rationality, but instead in the ideal of equality. Utopianism of course also included designing new models of socialism (cf. Panitch & Miliband 1994: 4). The final aspect of utopianism again addresses the question of agency. Gill suggested analysing the possibility of an international and internationalist counter-hegemonic project around which all national and transnational progressive forces could unite (cf. 1990: 308).

Contributors to *Socialist Register* claimed to believe in the unity of theoretical work and participation in political struggles. Leftwing intellectuals should not only *think* about, but also *live* for political change:

[U]nderstanding the world, breaking out of the Great Brainwash, is an exhilarating first step in reaching toward our own liberation. Immersing ourselves as a whole way of life in the struggle for *what might be* against *what is* provides the greatest degree of freedom possible for us in today's world. (Levins 1990: 345; original emphasis)

Concretely, intellectuals should try to help in setting up a renewed progressive movement in the shape of a socialist rainbow coalition as it was described by Foster above (cf. ibid; Foster 1990: 267). Such an endeavour required a clear personal decision not to seek refuge and solace in liberalism and work only for the amelioration of capitalism, but to act as a link between smaller, more radical movements and the centre-left – in the hope of radicalising the latter. Only such a position would allow intellectuals to do that task for which they were needed – to open up new political spaces for thinking and activity.

Dissent

Agency

The reflections among *Dissent* contributors on the question of agency were similar to those in *New Left Review* and *Socialist Register*. The working class was important, but it was neither sufficient as an actor for achieving radical change nor was it necessarily progressive. Alan Ryan encouraged the readers of *Dissent* to say farewell to a number of leftist myths, among them not only the beneficial potential of a vanguard party but also, with regard to the working class, to the solidarity of the proletarians (cf. 1990: 437). Several authors called for a 'realistic' picture of the working class and regarded such a portrayal as a precondition for designing a progressive politics. What did realistic mean in this context? Edward Broadbent made the following proposition: "It seems to me time for socialist intellectuals finally to accept the desire for personal economic benefit as a given element in all human nature but dominant in some only. Linked economically with profit, it can be harnessed to achieve socialist goals" (1991: 84). On the other hand, the ruptures of 1989 proved that people were acting according to their political convictions and not only to pursue their economic interests. As Irving Howe explained: "The events in the Soviet Union show that, as in Germany and Italy a few decades ago, all the socio-political forces, good and bad, suppressed by the total state have a way of reappearing once a bit of freedom is allowed." (1991: 73) Not all of these forces were what *Dissenters* would regard as progressive, but still they felt that it should be possible to intensify cooperation among progressives in Europe – between social democrats, greens and those Eastern-European reform groups which had not embraced neo-liberalism (cf. Joseph 1990: 146). Hence, *Dissent* also conceived of broad alliances and rainbow-like coalitions, and like the other journals, it emphasized that the labour movement still had a role to play in such alliances. Paul Berman reminded readers that Mike Harrington had stressed the importance of the labour movement for the New Deal and the Civil Rights Movement. According to Berman, an alliance between labour movement and new social movements implied the attempt to unite two basic political principles – solidarity and the idea of rights. This combination was essential for achieving further political change (cf. 1993: 98).

Related to the importance of the labour movement was the responsibility of a certain type of intellectual, identified by Richard Rorty in a controversy with Andrew Ross as the archetypical old-left intellectual. According to Rorty, old-left intellectuals had been much more politically useful than new-left ones. He explained: "The utility of the [old] left is illustrated by its role in drafting and passing Lyndon Johnson's Great Society bills. The inutility of Ross's left is suggested by its disdainful refusal to think in terms of drafting and passing bills" (Rorty 1992: 265). The core of Rorty's critique, however, was that the new left *did* have an overly simplistic view of mainstream American political culture. For Rorty, this culture should not be reduced to a tool of American capitalism, but used as a vehicle for circulating radical ideas (cf. ibid: 266). Altogether, he argued that an alliance of intellectuals, politicians and progressives was possible and needed in order to achieve political change.

Although many lessons could be learnt from the old left, political agency could not take the shape it had taken in the 1930s and 1940s. In the late twentieth century, the international dimension had become more important. In an article called "The Future of the Labor Movement in Historical Perspective", David Brody argued that a new labour movement needed not only strong national structures (he formulated his disagreement here with Staughton Lynd, a new left labour historian, calling for a grassroots unionism) but, in addition, also transnational cooperation. In particular, the setting up of NAFTA in 1992 required a response from the labour organisations – in this respect the existence of integrated Canadian-U.S.-American unions should be seen as an encouraging example (cf. Brody 1994: 60-61).

The mental connection with the American labour movement was very strong among the contributors to *Dissent*. However, they also reflected on new avenues for political change beyond labour politics, though, as already mentioned, in close contact with it. Parallel to labour struggles on a national and international level, authors suggested relying on civil societal organisations as agents for political change. Some of the more detailed thoughts came from Jeffrey Isaac, who believed in the importance of a "rebellious" civil society which he explained in the following way: "A rebellious politics is a politics of voluntary associations, independent of the state, that seeks to create spaces of opposition to remote, disempowering bureaucratic and corporate structures." (1993: 357) They experimented with a new type of political organisation characterised by self-constitution and spontaneity, focused on present problems, which did not follow a grand master plan, and made a virtue of self-limitation, awareness of one's own partiality, and self-reflexivity (ibid: 359-60). Isaac pointed to the weaknesses of this type of political organisations too – they tended to underestimate the role of the state and of established organisations and institutions, and their membership was often elitist (cf. ibid: 360). Nevertheless, he hoped that such groups would make an important contribution to the development of a democracy, one which offered more than just political engineering by state institutions. The idea of democracy as self-empowerment relied, to a large degree, on civil societal associations (ibid: 361). However, as Paul Wapner added, the politics of civil society had also to move beyond the framework of the national state. He called for what he called a "world civic politics" in which organisations like *Greenpeace*, *Friends of the Earth* and others worked with traditional pressure and lobby techniques to influence governments but also contributed to global political life (cf. 1994: 389). His article clearly indicated how change could be induced through the work of such groups – even if they were elitist:

Greenpeace's direct actions are based on the notion of 'bearing witness'. This type of political action, originating with the Quakers, links moral sensitivities with political responsibility. Having observed a morally objectionable act, one cannot turn away in avoidance. One must either take action to prevent further injustice or stand by and attest its occurrence. [...] The idea is to invite the public to bear witness as well, to enable people throughout the world to become informed about ecological dangers, pique their sense of outrage, and spur them to action. (ibid: 391)

Strategy
The last quotation leads to the question of strategy. Having abandoned vanguardism a long time ago, for Dissenters there was a choice between reformism from above and self-emancipation. Some voices in the journal stated their optimism that such self-emancipation was possible. Cornelius Castoriadis, for example, despite his complaints about an apathetic and saturated population in the rich countries, remained convinced of the possibility of what he called the project of social and individual autonomy. For him, the core of socialism was likely to be backed by ninety per cent of the people. He seemed to believe that "islands of resistance", another term for Isaac's organisations of rebellious civil society, could be found everywhere

and could become larger (cf. 1992: 224-5). The answer to the question of whether the rebellion envisaged was to be violent or peaceful remained vague. However, Carlo Rosselli, who strongly believed in the possibility of peaceful, gradual and self-organised transformation towards "liberty" – obviously the same as Castoriadis's "autonomy". In his words, "Liberty can never be won through tyranny or dictatorship, or even through being granted from above. Liberty is a conquest, a self-conquest, which is preserved only through the continual exercise of one's faculties and individual autonomies" (Rosselli 1994: 120-1). In the same article, Rosselli suggested that violence might be legitimate as a defence – but only when a proletarian election victory was jeopardized by reactionaries (ibid: 121). That political opposition was necessary and that power had to be won in elections – about these facts there was no doubt in the mind of a liberal socialist. Once the strategy of violent change was ruled out, the question had to be answered as to how to create a block powerful enough to initiate a peaceful transition to a more socialist or more democratic system. Here, Rorty suggested forging an alliance between the poor and the middle classes which, especially in the United States, tended at the time to side with the rich (cf. 1991: 484). Michael Walzer supported this line of argument and, like Rorty, hinted at the relevance of appeals to traditional American values and to the common good for creating such an alliance. Such a coalition would not come about by itself, but required political leadership. Many contributors to the journal shared the conviction that principled leadership was capable of modifying human behaviour, though they shared the belief to differing degrees. Broadbent was quite optimistic:

I remain convinced that sustained social democratic leadership can persuade majorities to modify their behavior. Majoritarian support for tough measures to protect the environment, redress the concerns of indigenous people, yes, even favor trains over cars – all in degrees of emphasis, not as an absolute, is evidence of this. The majoritarian 'followers' often run ahead of their government in demonstrating the continuing relevance of non-consumption-oriented values even in market-driven societies. (1991: 85)

However, political leaders and intellectuals would have to change their attitudes towards the people with whom they wanted to liaise – they should take their personal interests seriously instead of trying to educate them away:

> Although it is true that in the nineteenth century most intellectuals ranging from socialists to liberals like John Stuart Mill condemned the consuming culture of capitalism [...], this has not been true of the working class, including those who constitute the main body of the socialist movement, either in the past or today. Workers, historic and modern, have welcomed the opportunity for access to goods that once were not available or were available only to those with much greater wealth. (ibid: 84)

This needed acceptance and could be integrated into political strategy. Nevertheless, Walzer argued that the 'engaged citizen' had to be supported in order to balance the 'economic man'. It seemed clear that such reinforcement was necessary in order to come closer to achieving Walzer's idea of a powerful civil society – but it seemed also clear that "economic man" would not – and probably should not – go away (cf. 1992: 469).

For *Dissenters*, the emergence of a civil society consisting of associations, movements and organisations of 'engaged citizens' was the most important precondition for political change. Nevertheless, even if such a civil arrangement existed and was in a healthy state, it should not overstretch itself by trying to replace institutional politics, but instead work to influence them from the margins (cf. Isaac 1993: 360; Hirst 1994: 246). On the other hand, it could also take over some of the administrative tasks so far reserved for the state and try to design institutions with the basis of democratic self-government in mind – authors like Paul Hirst thought of tasks such as health provision and education which nevertheless should be financed by the state (cf. 1994: 243). Some contributors more specifically demanded democratic control of economic life along similar lines (cf. Walzer 1992: 469). Others saw a need for further reflection on the regulation of conflicts and struggles between governments and civil societal associations – for example, those surrounding the question of military expenditure (cf. Joseph 1990: 147). All in all, *Dissenters* imagined a political situation where an alliance of different classes, of old and new left, of egalitarians and civil rights proponents could develop sufficient political muscle to change the mould of politics – in the United States but also elsewhere, perhaps even in those Eastern European countries that at the moment seemed to embrace capitalism wholeheartedly.

Intellectuals
It has already become obvious that intellectuals played a decisive role in setting up these democratic structures. Whereas in the previous two journals intellectuals were primarily seen as critics of politicians and institutional politics, in *Dissent* they had to fulfil a double function of criticism and support (as with Rorty's insistence that they had to involve themselves in the intricacies of drafting plans and bills), or of a criticism from within. In line with this, the critique of capitalism also seemed to be slightly different in character: at least for some contributors it was more about improving than about transcending capitalism – reformist rather than transformative: "It seems obvious, then, that the search for solutions to the problems generated by a predominantly privately owned, market-oriented society has been and will continue to be a major element in the political agenda of every democratic society" (Dahl 1990: 227). As the discussion clearly shows, intellectuals should not try to make decisions on behalf of those groups of the population whom they sympathised with. Admitting that they had done so too often, their approach to critique contained a large measure of self-critique. Howe suggested that socialist intellectuals had to accept Eastern Europe's choice to return to capitalism, but nevertheless they should try to engage with them in discussions (cf. 1990: 89). A critical investigation of what went so disastrously wrong in Eastern Europe was of equal importance. It was necessary not only because without such an analysis mistakes were likely to be repeated, but additionally as Lewis Coser pointed out, the most serious threat to socialism at the moment of writing came from Eastern European intellectuals who had suffered under state socialism and hence voiced a strong antipathy against all versions of socialism. However, *Dissent* also allowed for the expression of such opinions, giving voice even to those who thought that criticism of socialism should go much further and should be linked, in fact, to intellectual self-critique and the rethinking of core assumptions. Eugene Genovese who fought for this position in the journal argued that issues such as a belief in human goodness or malleability, the condemnation of hierarchy and authority, the secularisation of society as an emancipatory goal and anti-American self-hate as a disposition of intellectual minds had to be reassessed (cf. 1994: 375). In

response to to the many sceptical voices his intervention provoked, he added that concepts such as democracy, equality, and social justice also had to be fundamentally rethought. More generally, he urged intellectuals to spend some time considering what might follow from philosophical ideals once they had been accepted as guidelines for political practice. Though he did not become explicit, he seemed to imply that the uncompromising pursuit of such principles might provoke drives towards authoritarianism and despotism (cf. 1994a: 388). Despite such strong revisionist criticisms, such as Genovese's, most other authors chose to focus on reforming tasks and measures more commonly associated with the left.

Re-examinations had to be carried out not only on the national, but also on the global level. Paul Hirst demanded a "new theory of the distribution of power" for sites of governance which were to be found increasingly on the regional and the supra-national levels (1994: 242). Additionally, Michael Rustin maintained that such a theory of power distribution was important when he reviewed Ulrich Beck's *Risk Society*. Rustin accused him of idealism because Beck criticised ways of thinking, in this case "technological-scientific rationality", rather than the structures such thinking served – the powerful institutions of capital (1994: 398-9): "[s]ociety is seen as evolving toward a variety of networks, linked laterally as well as vertically, rather than as hierarchical chains of command" (ibid: 398). Rustin, an untypical contributor to *Dissent*, drew attention to the problem that it was certainly a helpful and necessary task to develop new theories of power distribution (ibid: 400).

While *Dissent* oscillated between idealism and materialism as bases on which to build theoretical work, explicit emphasis on the importance of utopian thinking was relatively scarce in its contributions. Even if Howe and Coser underlined the need to think about fresh versions of socialism and defined this as one of the future tasks of the journal, its focus seemed to lie more on discussing concrete political questions to be struggled with in the present situation than in the setting up of a new socialist project (cf. Howe 1990: 89-90; Howe 1990a: 301; Coser 1991: 102). However in a later article, Howe repeated the need of a certain type of utopianism and defined it as "utopian thinking qualified by democratic norms" (1992: 143). He considered this to be important because "if we don't bring up the basic economic issues and possible radical solutions, almost no one else will" (ibid: 143-4). This utopianism had to be different from traditional Marxist approaches not just in regards to its acceptance of democratic norms, but also in its avoidance of deterministic and mechanistic assumptions. It should "depict the features of democratic socialist society in workable detail – its structural arrangements, not just its envisioned qualities – without succumbing to excessively mechanical specifications" (ibid: 143).

More important than abstract considerations on utopianism was indubitably the participation in and organisation of concrete struggles. Many *Dissenters* regarded themselves as servants of a social democratic movement-to-form and subscribed to views such as that of Broadbent; social democratic leadership could convince people to modify their behaviour – without succumbing to the arrogance and condescension of vanguardism. It remained the task of intellectuals to defend people in trouble and *Dissenters* hoped that once they did, they would convince other middle-class people to do so too and thus facilitate the emergence of the middle class and poor people's alliance they intended to create. Walzer pointed out that the reason for siding with the weak and the poor lay more in ethical than in strategic reasons:

We can't cut our ties to people in trouble or to social groups in decline, for these are not merely the 'base' of the old left but the *raison d'etre* of any possible left. They can no longer be conceived, however, as a class apart, waiting for their historical moment. We must defend them, and help them defend themselves, as citizens of this society, not as the generative force of some ideal future. (1992: 468-9)

Left intellectuals, according to Walzer, were central for the coordination of the different special interests of marginalised groups – their professional training and independence enabled them to do this better than anyone else (cf. ibid: 468). Unlike the traditional ideals of universal intellectuals of the past, *Dissenters* knew that specialisation was required and that intellectuals should not shy away from becoming absorbed in intricate and detailed problems: "Because intelligent choices of public policies require both technical understanding and sensitivity to the values involved, in modern democratic countries a form of specialized intellectual activity has evolved that tends to combine both aspects of policy" (Dahl 1990: 227). In order to carry out these tasks, intellectuals had to direct a part of their activities towards themselves and develop a new culture of debate: "We must put an end to intellectual oscillation between unanimity and civil war. It's necessary to live with a democratic culture that at once entails compromise, concert, and the reality of conflict" (Rocard & Ricoeur 1991: 510).

Monthly Review

Agency

Among the contributors to *Monthly Review*, one found nearly-unanimous views on the continuing centrality of working-class agency. Beneath this overall consensus, however, there were differences in how exactly to define the working class and to consolidate its agency. A large group of authors stressed the importance of the metropolitan working classes even if they could hardly be described as revolutionary. Martin J. Morand, for example, argued that without a viable labour movement, no progressive legislation was possible and not even a meaningful democracy. He saw this thesis proven by the differences between the United States with its weak and Canada with its stronger labour movement (cf. 1990: 44). Similarly, Joel Kovel, in his obituary for Miliband, expressed the view that the labour movement remained central because it was the main antagonist of the ruling class – a perspective that he saw as one of Miliband's most important political legacies (cf. 1994: 57). However, despite their continuing faithfulness to the working classes, writers were realistic enough to identify working class political agency as to a great degree lying dormant. Consequently, they discussed the question of how to make it more active and more effective. One possible route consisted of the founding of new organisations. Istvan Mészáros criticised the defensive character of all working class organisations and envisaged a new type of unionism that should develop into an extra-parliamentary force – for him an alternative to their traditional reliance on reformist parties. Only extra-parliamentary pressure could make parliaments meaningful agents of change:

> There will be no advance whatsoever until the working class movement, the socialist movement is re-articulated in the form of becoming capable of offensive action, through its appropriate institutions and through its extra-parliamentary force. The parliament, if it is to become meaningful at all in the future, has to be revitalized, and can only be if it acquires an extra-parliamentary force in conjunction with the radical political movement that can also be active through parliament. (Monthly Review 1993: 22)

The question of whether the transformation of labour unions into such a force was a realistic option or else wishful thinking caused controversy. Most writers seemed to have few illusions about the leaderships of U.S. unions which, according to Morand, simply consisted of cynics (cf. 1991: 27-28). Kim Scipes similarly expressed reservations about unions' traditional forms of organisation and ideology and, reviewing an optimistic study by Brecher and Costello on the possibility of building bridges between labour unions and community groups, went as far as claiming: "[W]e cannot assume that what they [workers; S.B.] want today is something which all progressives are willing to fight for" (Scipes 1991: 42). Others, however, urged academics to regard unions neither as too monolithic nor as static. Mészáros founded his hopes on workers' likely disappointments with a toothless political and industrial leadership that could lead to radicalisation – as an example he pointed to direct action against the introduction of the Thatcher government's poll tax in Scotland (cf. Monthly Review 1993: 23). More generally, he observed the emergence of a surplus population marginalised by structural unemployment which might also become politicised and connect with third-world workers (cf. ibid: 23-24). Such scenarios required a view of the (American) working class that was more positive than the one presented by Scipes above. Jeremy Brecher and Tim Costello replied to such a negative characterisation by urging for a historicising, as opposed to an essentialist, perspective:

We suspect they [Scipe's criticisms; SB] result from a way of thinking in which unions, labor leaders, and workers are fixed entities with characteristics that can be known once and for all. [...] Scipes repeatedly presents social phenomena as if they possessed an essence that transcends time, place and specific historical context. (1991: 49-50)

Authors widely discussed this issue of linking or of building bridges in *Monthly Review* and suggested several types of coalitions and alliances. As in the other journals, a great deal was written about the possible linking of the labour movement and the social movements of the time. Most contributors believed that a focus on class struggle was an essential element within a radical rainbow coalition. Victor Wallis argued that the most stable forms of self-organisation developed along class lines, because they developed their political identities and goals from an analysis of the totality of the oppressive system – at least as long as they used a Marxist framework (and this was one of the tasks for which Marxism was still needed). In order to defend victories achieved in an endless cycle of anti-oppressive struggles, social movements had to unite a critical mass of the population behind them – otherwise each gain could easily be reversed. Only when the causal link between the different oppressive structures could be identified, it would allow the assemblage of such a critical mass and the emergence of an oppositional political culture (cf. Wallis 1991: 9-14).

While social movements thus needed a class-conscious labour movement, such dependence should be seen as a mutual. In order to be relevant, a labour movement had to open up itself and to coalesce with other groups. A long list of such groups was assembled in the journal's pages – among them youth associations. Michael Löwy argued that many youngsters, often with a working-class background themselves, aspired for a free and equal society, social and economic democracy, and self-administration (cf. 1991: 37). Apart from a general call for a trans-generational alliance, a number of more specific groups were proposed: the unemployed (existing just at the margins of traditional labour movements but in numbers that exceeded a mere 'reserve army of labour' and thus could become a threat to the existing order [cf. Monthly Review 1994: 2]), socialist ecologists (who were treated with suspicion by the discontented poor)(cf. Wallis 1992: 20-21), all those subscribing to the diverse utopian, anarchist, green traditions – who shared with Marxists the long-term goal of a stateless society (ibid: 21). Finally, the new social movements were also urged to open themselves up to people with disabilities and to sexual minorities (cf. Charlton 1994: 83). Such a broad network could develop into a radical U.S. civil society – and the belief that such a civil society could materialise under certain historical circumstances was not an illusion, but could be proven by historical precedence: Paul Sweezy claimed that American civil society would have blocked any brutal colonisation of Vietnam (which would have been possible in military terms) and, more recently – through keeping alive the memory of Vietnam – had forced U.S. governments to moderate their policy towards Nicaragua. This influence contributed to the ten-year survival of the country's revolution (cf. Watanabe & Wakima 1990: 7-8).

Up to this point, the selected reflections have mainly addressed political agency at the level of the United States. However, other writers focused on political agency at other levels. One of these was that of local grassroots activity. While lessons were often drawn from Third World countries, authors also presented insights into community activism in the United States. Since writers in *Monthly Review* were less likely to be university academics than those in the other journals, the journal published more hands-on coverage of such activity. It provided interesting examples of the problems of coalition building under conditions of diversity, but also its chances of setting up 'de-linked', democratically organised economies in, for example, old industrial communities such as rustbelt Detroit (cf. Boggs 1990: 12-13). Contributors disagreed in how far initiatives like these, reported from all parts of the world, were important for transformations on a global scale. Some, such as Samir Amin, boldly claimed that challenges to capitalism were more likely to come from the peripheries of the third and fourth worlds than from the capitalist West, or, for that matter, from the collapsing Eastern Bloc. He contended, however, that such agency – aimed at de-linking from the global economy – was necessarily anti-capitalist, but not automatically socialist (cf. 1990: 17-23). Elsewhere he justified his expectations in terms of the nature of capitalism: "In my view world expansion of capitalism is necessarily polarizing and by that fact it is inevitable that the people who are its principal victims – those who live at the periphery of the system – will revolt against it." (1993: 45) Sweezy also expressed the belief that, from a long-term perspective, revolutionary situations would develop in Third World countries which would weaken the capitalist centres and might eventually bring revolutions also to them. This was particularly likely to happen once revolutionary agency changed large countries such as Brazil (cf. Watanabe & Wakima 1990: 8-9). Others like Mészáros disagreed with the above opinions and took the more traditionally Marxist counter position against an over-reliance on Third World radicalism (and on all outcast radicalisms – as he emphasised in a late critique of Marcuse): while accepting that a great deal could be learned from political debates in Latin America, the future of socialism would be decided in the United States and the advanced capitalist countries in general (cf. Monthly Review 1993: 20-22). Finally, some authors expressed the view that only *international* solidarity by workers and cooperation among social movements could create a socialism that considered global justice and environmental sustainability (cf. Hermele 1993: 23-24). Arthur MacEwan emphasised that global – or at least transnational – solidarity was not an unreachable ideal but already political practice, despite the fact that workers were becoming competitors on a global scale: he hinted at the opposition to the establishment of NAFTA and suggested that the increasing feminisation of the workforce would strengthen the international dimension. At the same time it would also link labour and community struggles (cf. 1994: 3; 10-13).

The bulk of *Monthly Review*'s writing on agency was in a wide sense empirical but it also included some more theoretical considerations. A case in point was Ellen Meiksins Wood's article on E. P. Thompson. Referring to his best known quotation, on the principal intention of researching and writing *The Making of the English Working Class* – he wanted to save ordinary people from the 'condescension of posterity' – she explained that this passage "held a clear and immediate message about the agency of the working class in making its own history, a message that goes to the heart of the socialist project as the self-emancipation of the working class" (1994: 8). She summarised the essence of Thompson's work as showing the specificity, historicity and, thus, contestability of capitalism. He had illuminated the rationalities that had existed in late eighteenth and early nineteenth century England beyond market rationality and had chronicled examples which revealed that the people holding such alternative rationalities could win social and political struggles (cf. ibid: 10-12). These perceptions were in danger of being lost in newer trends in Marxist theorising. However, Wood remained convinced of their relevance for times to come: "[A]s the contradictions of capitalism become more and more evident in all parts of Europe and everywhere else, those hopes are likely to be justified again; and people will learn again not to think but to act, live, and struggle against capitalism" (ibid: 14).

Strategy
With the question of how to pursue this acting, living and struggling, the question of strategy became relevant. The most important recommendation to the readers was not to give up on socialism. The way forward was, in accordance with the Solidarnosc leader Lech Walesa, to keep and further develop what was good in socialism (cf. Marzani 1990: 25). Wood expressed this conviction most forcefully and directed it against a social democratisation of socialism:

At this moment in the 'long decline', capitalists themselves – in their increasingly desperate demands for 'flexibility' – seem closer than ever before to admitting that the imperatives of the capitalist market will not allow them to prosper without depressing the condition of workers and degrading the environment. In these circumstances, socialism may turn out to be less unrealistically utopian than is a 'social' capitalism. (1994a: 39-40)

The demand for socialism could only be expressed in class struggle – it remained, as Kovel put it, the conceptual linchpin of Marxism (cf. 1994: 52). Although they remained faithful to socialism, it seemed that authors also saw the socialist project in a phase between the struggles of the past and those – qualitatively different – of the future and hence in a process of self-reflection, renewal and reformulation:

This renewal will take time. The institutional forms of the old opposition – mass organizations, political parties, sovereign states – will mostly disappear and be replaced by new ones. The same will hold for ideas and ideologies, particularly the falsified and distorted versions of Marxism that acquired the status of orthodoxies in the Social Democratic and Communist movements of the late nineteenth and early twentieth centuries. (Sweezy 1994: 7)

Sweezy remained optimistic that this interim phase would eventually end. He based this belief on arguments similar to those presented by Wood – that capitalism was incapable of delivering what most people in the world needed and were lacking: decent jobs, security, and livelihood. To this end he claimed that "The human species is long suffering but it is not likely that it will tolerate forever what looks like a slide into ungovernability and chaos." (Sweezy 1994a: 11) As a first example of revolutionary activity of this new type, Sweezy identified the uprisings of the Zapatistas in Chiapas which were closely observed in the journal (ibid).

A large section of the space given to reflections on socialist strategy was dedicated to economic issues. Here, one perspective underlined the importance of small-scale socialist, or communitarian, economic experiments within capitalism. Grace Lee Boggs, herself involved in neighbourhood projects, saw such manoeuvres as a way of becoming independent of the world market. Independence constituted the only way forward for Third World countries as well as for the bitterly poor U.S. peripheries. Whereas her ideas stem from observations in Detroit, Amin claimed the attempt to delink from the world economy to be the most realistic strategy for socialists in the Third World. Once such delinking was in progress and guided by popular alliances rather than bourgeoisies, it could take a socialist direction. Amin explained the failure of third-world socialism of the past to take off with the cooptation of the bourgeois parts of popular alliances to the world system. Further, he proposed that the process of delinking had to take place not only in the economic sphere, but also in people's heads. This entailed "discovering the criteria of rationality in economic life different from those that govern world capitalism, freeing oneself from the constraints of world-capitalist value, and substituting a law of value of national popular reference." (1990: 23). Amin remained silent about the time frame of his delinking strategy. Did he see it as a revolutionary break or as a long process? His reference to post-independence third-world countries makes it probable that he preferred a rapid scenario. This would contradict the suggestions by Harry Magdoff who agreed that to work for socialism meant to "work toward opting out of the international network of capitalist trade and finance" (1991: 18). Unlike Amin, he considered this to be an incremental process.

Sticking to the goal of socialism meant continuing the fight against capitalism – something not to be confused with the fight against capitalists (cf. Marzani 1990: 10). Contributors considered this distinction indispensable for any attempts at finding suitable strategies. A redistributive and ecological politics could only really become effective once it addressed the problem of profit maximisation as the determining principle of capitalism. While this sounded 'fundamentalist', most agreed that social and environmental reforms within capitalism should be welcomed and supported at the same time. To do so was justified not just by the practical benefits of such policies, but also because in so doing they could cause incremental changes in the power structures of society – and thus pave the way for more radical change. Concretely, Marzani called for a Keynesian socialisation of investment and guaranteed employment, which he believed would not bring about the end of but would still radically alter capitalism (cf. 1990: 25). Another suggestion voiced in the journal was a conversion programme for U.S. industry which should support workers whose jobs were endangered by the end of the Cold War (cf. Plotkin et al. 1994).[1] The authors were

---

1 The editors of the journal declared a serious jobs programme in the political climate and of the time as illusory (cf. Editors of *Monthly Review* 1994: 57).

aware of the fact that raising taxes for such programmes would cause serious difficulties because of opposition from the wealthier sections of society. Therefore they pointed out that a concerted onslaught was needed against the basics and practices of American politics which granted the wealthier sections of the population privileged access to decision making processes: "financing short political campaigns from public funds, publicizing the issues and candidates' positions through the media and forbidding private contributions to political campaigns could contribute enormously to breaking the stranglehold of the super-rich" (ibid: 56).

Finding solutions to ecological problems was of paramount importance. In an interview, Sweezy voiced the opinion that capitalism had to disappear over the next one hundred years, otherwise the human species would not survive (cf. Watanabe & Wakima 1990: 10). As a role model, he pointed to the German Greens who – unlike U.S. environmentalists – had understood the close link between economic change and an end to rapidly progressing ecological destruction. For him, ecological sustainability was a non-negotiable goal and he called for

an attempt to achieve a movement which can educate people not only to the danger of the environment but also to the necessity for long-range planning and the ability to change the power-relations of human society in such a way as to make the preservation of the environment the first goal, the number one goal. (ibid: 10-11)

Activists should learn not only from environmentalists, but also from other sources beyond a narrowly defined socialism. In the same interview, Sweezy drew a surprising parallel between strands of Marxism, including even Maoism and liberation theology. He pointed out that liberation theologians strove for the establishment of the kingdom of heaven on earth. He conceded that while it was impossible to create an earthly paradise, liberation theology, just like Maoism, suggested a permanent revolutionary process for which the stage reached with the 'withering away of the state' (Marx's equivalent to paradise) should be seen as a sense of direction into which to move rather than a realistic final destination (ibid: 4). Closely linked to such appreciative evaluations of religiosity was a more general call for more sensitivity towards the spiritual aspects of human life. Kovel claimed the authority of Herbert Aptheker who defined Marxism as spirituality in action; in contrast to a religious spirituality it had nothing to do with mysticism, prayer and meditation but with struggle (cf. 1994: 40). This would give struggles a sense of purpose they otherwise lacked – to fight for something was only sensible as long as it was considered to be sacred, as Brentlinger explained. He diagnosed a permanent process through which people identified objects or values as sacred:

This is a profoundly self-creative aspiration which in its historical development leads to clarity and definition in the idea of the good society. The sacred lies within this aspiration to be which people in the past have tried to validate through a higher being. In this sense, the sacred has been illusory. But it records an important reality. The sacred is a monument to our highest moments of strength and purpose and self-affirmation. The higher being is our best self. (1992: 37)

For the sacred, humans would be willing to make sacrifices, to struggle and even to risk their lives: It would be a "necessary element of any community worth dying for" (ibid: 40).

Contributors tended to understand agency less as the result of objective conditions than of political will and political projects based on a socialist consciousness. Strengthening such consciousness constituted an important part of a socialist strategy. One of the relevant principles often mentioned was solidarity. Solidarity could become a tool for transcending the interests of specific groups, but any solidarity worth its name had to include the poorest and the weakest (cf. Hinkelammert 1993: 110). Such a form of unity was impossible to realise within capitalism and could become a driving force for overcoming it: "We must now help to regenerate the human dignity whose roots have been destroyed. We must stand up and cry out that capitalism without the possibility of solidarity is the negation of human dignity and we will not stand for that" (ibid: 112). Yet, the creation of such cohesion required Herculean efforts. As one contributor observed, the normal situation was rather the lack of solidarity among oppressed groups – for example, between Koreans and African Americans in the United States (cf. Kim 1993: 54). The most promising way out of such an impasse was to unite behind a demand shared by as many oppressed groups as possible. The same author suggested that such groups assemble in order to fight for universal access to health care. Once this common goal had been achieved, it would be easier to pursue more specific demands (ibid: 56-7). Alternatively, groups of activists could be encouraged to swap their projects and goals: women's groups could work towards AIDS awareness, African Americans towards reproductive choice, lesbian and gay groups against inner city gang violence. Learning from each other in this way could facilitate coalition building on a local and, in the long run, on a global scale. Though such aims could sound unrealistic, the author was able to point to certain historical precedents – for example, when African Americans on the West Coast of the United States protested against the imprisonment of Japanese during World War II, or when Japanese Americans demonstrated against the demonization of Arab Americans in the Gulf War (ibid: 54-5).

What could socialists do in the core countries of capitalism? In this context, authors debated the strategic functions of parties of the left. Some held the opinion that the third-party route to political influence – as it had been taken in Canada with the *New Democratic Party* – was less than promising in the United States (cf. Morand 1991: 27-28). Others, however, insisted on the need for the formation of a third party, especially as Oliver S. Land formulated it, since there were no single issues any longer – the human future in general was at a crossroads and survival needed coordinated socialist guidance (cf. 1991: 51-53). Alan Wald also proposed a clear and definite break with the Democratic Party and the formation of a new party based on "truly independent electoral formations that can become an arm of mass struggle, and democratically controlled from the bottom up" (1991: 60). He sympathised with an organisation that was in formation process during the time of writing – the *Labour Party Advocates* (ibid).

This seemed to be a reformist approach. Was revolution off the agenda in the core countries of capitalism? In these societies, it seemed likely that revolutions would occur only after a long preceding period of reforms. Hence the juxtaposition of reformism and revolution was misleading – reforms were revolution's precondition:

First, the initial region of socialist hegemony will already have had to free itself – as a precondition to its existence – from all externally based counterrevolutionary threat. Second, it will appear at a time when no capitalist country can any longer serve as a model to emulate, even in economic terms. Third, a greater number of appropriate changes in human attitudes and conduct will already have gained currency before the structural changes are introduced. This means, among other things, that both the taking and the exercise of power will be marked by a higher level of egalitarianism and democracy. Finally, the whole process of building up to any transition will have generated far more in the way of specific proposals for revolutionary change. (Wallis 1992: 9)

On the one hand, this was a clear farewell to vanguardism. On the other, it again echoed the widely-shared catastrophism – in the capitalist countries, things had to get worse in order to get better. Despite this perspective, the appropriate measure was not to criticise incremental changes for their insufficiency, but to initiate and support them. This course of action should include coalition building with all radical groups, even if they were non-Marxist (cf. ibid: 21). Critics looked again to Europe for hope; this time, however, not in the European Community but, quite to the contrary, in progressive resistance against a neo-liberal *European Union*. Singer pointed to the negative referenda results in France and Denmark on the Maastricht treaty and characterised them as signs of nationalist and social resistance (cf. 1994: 93). He anticipated further confrontations because of high unemployment figures, especially since joblessness now began to threaten the middle classes as well. For him, the struggles lying ahead in Europe were decisive:

This is why the coming confrontation in Europe is so vital. What is at stake is whether the working people of Europe will be more than ever appendices to the machine in a society based on profit or whether the associated producers, imposing a different logic, will start gaining mastery over their work and the organization of their society. (1994: 95)

It seemed that an effective political strategy had to be attuned to local conditions. There was no universal or global way forward, but situations changed fundamentally in the peripheries, in Europe and in North America. Contributors optimistically turned to parts of the world outside North America whose struggles and progressive moves would strengthen movements for change in North America.

Intellectuals
In *Monthly Review*, the tasks ascribed to the intellectuals were, broadly speaking, the same as in the other journals: they should formulate critiques,

conceptualize possible utopias, and educate the public. If socialists were supposed to lead history somewhere, they needed to know where to go. This sentiment implied a revaluation the status of moral discourse. According to this thinking, moral values were needed as guidance while scenarios of automatism and the development of revolutionary consciousness in the revolutionary process should be criticised as overly simplistic. This did not mean, as Cornel West clarified, that socialists should become moralist (cf. 1993: 59). The people associated with the journal were convinced that West's suggestions of a tactical and strategic essentialism appeared promising. They avoided two intellectual traps – moralist dogmatism as well as radical relativism. Both had to be criticised and *Reviewers* contended that intellectual work should not shy away from explaining why some moral positions were preferable over others. Leftwing thinkers had to take sides in the intellectual battle over the question of whether socialism as capitalism's other was dead or not. Calls for a socialist society had to be reiterated (cf. Sweezy 1993: 6-8). However, as mentioned above, it was not only capitalism that should be criticised according to *Review* contributors, but also Marxism (cf. Löwy 1991: 37-38). Nevertheless, central elements of the Marxist method of critique were still useful, as Sweezy explained – hence the tasks of *Monthly Review* and the thinkers around it would remain the same:

One of *Monthly Review*'s tasks in these years of counterrevolution has been to use Marxian methods to track and understand major developments on both sides of a polarized world. Another task was to chronicle, encourage, and where possible celebrate the successes of numerous Third World efforts to escape the confines of capitalism and start on a new road for all the tragically exploited and oppressed peoples of those unhappy lands. Whatever else happens, these tasks will remain. (1994: 5)

Nevertheless the contributors agreed that such chronicling and criticising functioned insufficiently to bring an end to capitalism. Just like writers in the other journals, they emphasised the need to start a creative process of utopian imagination – as an important step to move beyond the there-is-no-alternative discourse of the time (cf. Mészáros 1993: 35). Singer claimed that this discourse bore the danger of producing irrational, jingoistic, and reactionary solutions, especially in Eastern Europe, but also in the West (cf.

1994: 98). He called for pragmatism, the will to defend the bad against the worse, but also for the formulation of what he called a "realistic utopia" (ibid: 99). It required, among other things, to ask important questions: "growth? but which growth? for whose sake? for whose profit? for what purpose? for what kind of society and within which environment?" (ibid: 98) In other words, according to contributors these questions should become starting points for philosophies capable of overcoming what Grace Lee Boggs termed "scientific rationalism" – philosophies formulating changed relationships among human beings and between humans and nature (1990: 14-15). Such rethinking also required attempts at dealing with difference and diversity in order to create pluralistic and multicultural societies. Boggs expressed hope that impetus for such utopias would come from the margins of the world system. While Third World revolutionaries of the decolonisation period had mostly been trained in the West and internalised some aspects of Eurocentric perspectives, the next generation of Third World intellectuals and activists would not – they would stay free from both Eastern and Western Eurocentrism (cf. ibid: 17-18). Similarly, Buhle called for a "decolonisation" of the heads of Western people: they should investigate what could be learnt from Third World societies about the basics of a decent and humane society (1993: 56).

Finally, the educating role of intellectuals was mentioned in the pages of *Monthly Review* as well. Authors suggested that Marxism had still a great deal to impart and hence should be taught:

We have a theory, as old as Marx, which, without rejecting a concept of our species as producers capable of freedom, allows us to choose collectively to emancipate and realize ourselves in creative and free activity, to create ourselves in human history, and to change our natures through social transformation to become cooperative and supporting the biosphere and ourselves. (Weston 1990: 4)

According to Jack Weston, mass movements still needed to be informed about Marxist theories of social change, since only then could they identify the suitable time for revolutionary intervention – and without such intervention the power of industrial capital could not be weakened (ibid: 5-6). Singer saw another educational task with regard to the people in Eastern Europe. It was the duty of Western intellectuals to inform them about the less attractive sides of Western capitalism. They should explain, for example, the link between higher productivity and higher unemployment, social and gender inequalities, environmental degradation, the exploitation of the global South and the worldwide monopolisation processes within the media (cf. 1990: 90-91). Generally speaking, as academics, intellectuals should use their privileged positions (which they only relatively recently captured) in order to act as advisors to the public rather than as specialists working exclusively within the walls of higher education institutions (cf. McChesney 1994: 34). Their task was to decode hegemonic messages and ideologies (ibid: 32). The important educational responsibility of intellectuals at the historical conjuncture of the early 1990s was perhaps most aptly summarised by the journal's editor, Paul Sweezy, himself: "We can only do our best to explain what has happened up to now and help the new upcoming generations to understand what changes are needed if the human species is to survive into a decent future." (1994: 7)

Re-Starting History

A large majority of contributors still regarded the working class as an indispensable actor in any scenario of progressive political change. However, two modifications corrected traditionalist conceptions of working-class agency. Firstly, working class people did not constitute a monolithic whole with a collective political will, especially because social structures and people's identities were complex and contradictory. Some authors emphasised that working-class people legitimately pursued their personal interests in attempts at improving their individual material position. Others underlined that working people, when they became politically active, were guided by ethical considerations rather than simply their 'objective' class interests. Secondly, as indispensable as working-class agency for moves towards socialism was, this did not mean that the working class constituted the only or even the dominant actor. Instead, alliances with other groups of the population were required as well as with political movements. Especially the collaboration of working-class organisations and the new social movements was of crucial importance.

All writers were convinced that a trans-national cooperation of progressive political groups was essential in the late twentieth century. However, intellectuals largely understood such collaborations as consisting of simultaneous – and ideally, coordinated – struggles in different countries and regions of the world. The level of the national state remained the main site of struggle over political demands. Within all journals different opinions coexisted when it came to the questions as to whether third-world or metropolitan agents were the group more likely to initiate upheavals and which could contribute more to struggles for socialist change.

In any case, the cooperation of labour organisations and new social movements had to be organised. An effective strategy needed a reconciliation of pluralism and cohesion. Many intellectuals believed that Marxist theory could play an important role in this context – by revealing the interrelations and common roots of different forms of oppression. All journals bade farewell to traditional notions of revolution and – with the partial exception of *Dissent* – were at pains to explain the difference between a merely *re*formative and a transformative political strategy, and most agreed that they preferred the latter. At the same time, writers accepted to experience a historical conjuncture when socialists' struggles were often defensive. It was the left's task to defend welfare systems against neo-liberal cost-cutting policies and liberal democracy against hijacking by powerful, unaccountable 'interests'. Generally, the mood seemed to be one of qualified pessimism. All journals presented their version of the thesis that things had to go worse in order to wake people up. Then things might get better thanks to people's support for a revived left politics. Such strategies constituted the only realistic hope; with the demise of vanguardism, the notion that emancipation could only be understood as *self*-emancipation was taken more seriously than ever.

Contributors generally agreed as to the tasks of intellectuals in reconceptualised socialist movements. They should provide analytical critiques of social problems and political deficiencies, engage in what Wallerstein called 'utopistics' and act as spokespersons and educators of marginalised groups. This function, however, should not be interpreted as the task of speaking *for* other people. The only thing intellectuals could do was to speak *on behalf of* groups who could not otherwise make themselves heard in the public sphere . Finally, the function of critic entailed a sober – and self-reflexive – elaboration of the socialist struggles of the past and of the varieties of state socialism which had recently disintegrated.

New Left Review moved farthest from traditional ideas of working-class agency and tolerated opinions like Gorz's, who did not rule out the possibility that the working class could still play a political role but doubted its centrality in a post-industrial setting. All the other journals remained sceptical of the sustainability of political change without considerable working-class support. The American journals raised the topic in much more detail as to how important the role of organisations of civil society was to alliances for political change; the journals considered these players to be central in complementing the more volatile groups and informal collectives of the new social movements. Together with *Monthly Review*'s strong interest in grassroots activism, this emphasis seems to reflect the associational character of public life, including political life, in the United States and stands in marked contrast to the more centralist and party-centred organisation of political life in Britain.

Nevertheless *Dissenters* repeatedly pointed out that civil society should not become a substitute for an institutionalised political system. As a strategy, the left should try to contribute to debates on both levels – that of civil society and that of formal politics. Implicit in this call to action, was a command not to shy away from reaching out to organisations beyond the left, and indeed both *Dissent* and *New Left Review* called for broad centre-left alliances. The strategies suggested seemed to take note of the specific problems of marginalised people in Britain and the United States. While the British journals urged for a defence of the threatened welfare system of the United Kingdom, *Monthly Review* took into consideration the more drastic exclusion of poor people in North America. The proposed strategy of de-linking, recommended to communities in the U.S. rustbelt seemed adequate since inclusion into the slim welfare system would solve not even all of the most urgent problems.

Obviously, contributors measured the centrality of modified rationalities and well-founded ethics slightly differently. Although one should not overstate this point, the American journals published more deliberations on ethics, spirituality and the possibility – as well as the danger – of principled leadership successfully modifying people's opinions and behaviour. Perhaps the ethical dimension of American political discourse played a role in this context. Much more evidently, one of the specific features of U.S. politics provoked various statements: writers in the American journals reflected on how to deal strategically with the absence of a workers party in the country. *Dissent* treated Canada's *New Democratic Party* as an example for emulation while *Monthly Review* discussed the experiment of *Labour Party Advocates* and urged the left to cut their ties with the *Democratic Party*.

Despite the widespread agreement on the role of intellectuals, opinions differed as to the main task of intellectuals: whether theoretical practice, or the function of educator of the public or the capacity to act as specialist, serving either radical groups or state institutions. Apart from *Dissenters*' less hesitant approach to mainstream politics, these differences were minute, as were those on the level of modesty and self-restraint related to the functions of spokespersons. One obvious difference concerned the position of the 'individual'. The U.S. journals dedicated more space to reflections on human nature – from Genovese's critical statements on the negative consequences of good intentions to *Monthly Review*'s thoughts on the sacred. Echoing, as already stated, strands of American normative political discourse, these considerations might also reveal a higher level of confidence – and of fear – of what intellectuals could achieve in the political sphere. Still, intellectuals were needed among agents for socialist change, especially in their capacity as producers of strategically relevant analyses – this perception was universally agreed upon and served as a legitimisation for the existence of the journals themselves.

IV. Between Radical Critique and Moderate Recommendations?

This study has shown how the radical, Marxist-inspired intellectual left in Britain and the United States made sense of the collapse of the state-socialist systems of the Eastern Bloc. In a comprehensive contrastive comparison, the analogies, similarities and differences found in the journals as well as the specificities of the British and the U.S. reactions have been identified. The task of this final part of the study is to move one step further analytically. The first chapter deals with the question of whether the re-orientations with which socialist intellectuals concerned themselves after 1989/91 must be understood as self-adaptations to social democratic and post-Marxist positions, even if as perhaps reluctant ones.

The second chapter of this part offers a short tentative discussion of the problem as to whether the reactions analysed are divisively British or American, or whether they reveal the existence of a discursive community of the Anglo-American intellectual left. To a certain extent, reflections on this question must remain tentative as a definite answer would require cross-checking with further analyses based on different corpora of sources and using a variety of methodological designs. Finally, the last chapter completes this study with a short outlook on developments in the journals since the mid-1990s and on the state of the intellectual left in the early twenty-first century.

1. BETWEEN SOCIAL DEMOCRACY AND POST-MARXISM?

1.1. Democratic Socialism and Social Democracy

It is obvious that socialist intellectuals under the impact of the events of 1989/91 discussed varieties and developed models of democratic socialism which brought them close to central tenets of social democracy. A case in point was their acceptance of gradualism and reformism as the only possible roads towards 'more socialist' social and economic relations. This reorientation was accompanied by an acceptance of the norms and institutions of parliamentary democracy. They left behind the idea of revolution as a violent rupture or as abrupt comprehensive change affecting all dimensions of public life, but also the role of intellectuals as a revolutionary group; one which would follow a vanguardist strategy and lead society towards socialism. Ellen Meiksins Wood identified this idea of intellectual vanguardism or substitutionism as an important characteristic of the 'Second New Left', which became the core group in *New Left Review* from 1963 onwards. However, the same strategy was adopted by large sections of the 1968 and post-1968 New Left as well (cf. 1995: 33). In particular, it is the 'emotional' reactions in all the journals – in which writers deplore the loss of a generational project – which illustrate that this vanguardist self-image had run its cause. After accepting the inevitability of gradualism, socialist intellectuals tried to retain some distinction from social democracy by insisting on the transformative dimensions of their reformism. However, the distinction remained unconvincing because the boundary between merely reformist reforms of capitalism and transformative reform strategies was difficult to discern. Obviously the intellectuals assumed that transformative reforms, such as wage earners funds, would incrementally destabilise capitalism through changes in property relations, but no strategies existed for how to safeguard transformative reforms as long as they were in their early stages and hence could be easily overturned.

Socialist strategy, according to socialist intellectuals, still included the class struggle. However, this struggle was reduced to a working-class politics – to policies that considered and pursued the interests of working-class people via parliamentary work and were supported, backed-up, reinforced and radicalised by the extra-parliamentary activity of labour organisations.

It is true that socialist intellectuals demanded the extension of the principles of liberal-parliamentary democracy to all areas of public life. The problem was less that this constituted a gradualist, reformist approach than that they did not provide clear answers to the question of how to achieve this within the entrenched and self-protective power structures of capitalist democracies which they so lucidly analysed.

Several times intellectuals called for the preservation of the achievements of social democracy and reformist labour movements. The welfare states in particular were declared to be worth of protection. Practically, this amounted to a defence of Keynesian corporatism and of the link between economic growth – or increased efficiency – and 'functional socialism'. In this context, most intellectuals agreed on the importance of centre-left working-class parties. This sympathy for material working-class interests along the lines of the old labourist slogan 'a fair day's pay for a fair day's work', the declarations of empathy for social democratic parties and the emphasis on democratic rights and liberal principles again constitute examples of increasingly blurred boundaries between democratic socialism and social democracy: like the latter, the former had become a hybrid of liberalism and socialism. Fittingly, many intellectuals were now prepared to grant markets and even the profit principle a positive status and to accept relative equality or – to use Eric Olin Wright's phrase once more – 'less classness' as the goal of socialist policies. The retrieval and rehabilitation of thinkers such as Kautsky and Bernstein also testify to this reorientation. Similarly, the continuing insistence on the centrality of the national state as an arena of political struggle revealed an acceptance of existing institutions – even if it was slightly ironic that internationalists embraced the national state at a time when liberals and conservatives started speaking of the inevitability of globalisation and the consequences of declining state power. For the intellectuals, however, a strong state – all previous qualifications on the roles states play in the reproduction of capitalism formulated by Marxist-inspired state theory notwithstanding – remained an indispensable tool for redistribution. While this had been a position of left intellectuals long before 1989, many now followed the majorities in most social democratic parties of the time which changed their position on economic protectionism and backed the European unification project.

For most socialist intellectuals, a rhetorical and analytical commitment to socialism and Marxism remained. However, the study has presented numerous statements in which the intellectuals defined their socialist orientation as a point of reference or as a horizon rather than as a guide to political action. This abstract commitment often found expression in a critical perspective on the very welfare societies which should be defended and in a critique of the West's – and especially the United States' – geo-political strategies directed against the former Eastern Bloc as well as the global South. Furthermore, intellectuals claimed to have no illusions about the limits of parliamentarism. Despite these qualifications, they remained largely silent on those burning questions which social democracy had never been able to solve: how to organise redistribution – how to create opportunities for a 'good life' for everyone – without ecologically disastrous levels of economic growth; how to initiate redistribution on a global scale; and how to prepare and safeguard redistribution not just of wealth but also of political influence given the actual existing distribution of power in liberal or capitalist democracies. Altogether, socialist intellectuals became a functional 'keep left' tendency on the fringes of social democracy and liberalism at a time when Social Democracy and Liberalism moved rightward and – as 'New Realists' or 'New Democrats' – embraced many elements of Britain's and the United States' neo-liberal settlements of the 1980s.

1.2. Neo-Marxism and Post-Marxism

Despite controversial debates between those who called themselves Marxists or neo-Marxists on the one hand and post-Marxists on the other – debates which had started before 1989 – again a high level of conceptual overlap between both groups can be observed. While several post-Marxists such as Cornelius Castoriadis, André Gorz, Paul Hirst and Chantal Mouffe wrote for some of the journals, many others accepted post-Marxism's claim that the struggle for democracy should be the first order, even if the struggle for socialism played an important role within it. Socialist and post-Marxist intellectuals agreed on the irrelevance of traditional ideas of 'revolution' and emphasised the centrality of struggles over 'hegemony' in society, even if the latter subscribed to a discursive understanding of society and defined hegemony more restrictedly as a discursive concept. Still, both groups underlined that such struggles required the formation of coalitions and remained convinced that considerable degrees of variety and unpredictability would forbid prognoses on future progressive causes. They backed constitutionalism and emphasised the importance of constitutional change, they agreed on the necessity of accepting democratic principles, and propagated the idea of formal and informal governance at all levels of society and in all areas of public life. This notion of democratic struggles over hegemony tied in with an understanding of historical developments as contingent. Even if some intellectuals upheld the notion of history as the history of class struggles, these interpretations were pluralist and context-specific – as regulation theorists had already demonstrated the specificity of different types of capitalism and of the class struggles taking place within them. As a result, the shape and the outcome of future class struggles was unpredictable and depended on the formation of coalitions for potentially hegemonic projects.

Strategically, the acceptance of contingency required a focus on politics and on the forging of alliances at grassroots level and between existing organisations. The cooperation with and among the new social movements and non-governmental organisations was of central importance. In addition, neo- and post-Marxists called for a designing of concrete utopias with a modest character, taking on board ideas from concepts such as associative democracy, governance through institutions of civil society, and communitarianism. Just like social democracy, these models stressed the extension of democracy to the social and the economic spheres; unlike social democracy, they recommended various forms of de-linking from the capitalist economy.

Additionally and on a more theoretical level, socialist intellectuals appropriated many post-Marxist positions. Marxism had been 'cut to size' – and they applauded the diminution and welcomed the new climate of openness which fostered the search for new visions and sources of inspiration. In this context, normative debates moved centre-stage. Ethical reflections became even more necessary; the adoption of a weak form of historical materialism not only reinforced the principle of contingency but abandoned – or at least qualified – the dialectical principle. Historical openness called for the intention to 'make history' and thus lent legitimacy to vision, fantasy, creative thinking and open debate.

Again, a difference between the socialist intellectuals and post-Marxists lay in the former group's bleaker interpretation of international politics. In the late 1990s and after, this pessimism resulted in discussions on a 'new imperialism'. In terms of other problems, socialist intellectuals were no more inventive than post-Marxists: when it came to the question of how to realise grassroots self-emancipation within existing power relations, the former group's critiques of post-Marxists' belief that grassroots struggles could be replicated on the global level via existing institutions – from non-governmental organisations to the United Nations – was certainly justified. The same goes for vague ideas of global democratic governance. However, whereas socialist intellectuals criticised these ideas on the one hand, on the other they embraced them through their trust in transnational (for example, European) constitutionalism and the possibility of grassroots-level de-linking. Hence, just as in the case of social democracy, the disagreement between socialist and post-Marxist intellectuals concerned the field of interpretation, of how to perceive the political, social and economic world. These disagreements were concerned much less with which concrete strategies and policies followed from these interpretations.

2. British and American or Anglo-American Re-orientations?

The summaries which form the final sections of each of the analytical chapters (Part III) have tried to explain the differences between the British and the U.S. re-orientations and debates with specificities of the political cultures in Britain and the United States and of the respective political 'subcultures' to which left intellectuals in both societies belong. All of the political-academic journals analysed here published work from the opposite side (respectively) of the Atlantic, as well as from elsewhere. Furthermore, as many of the contributors had transnational professional careers, their publications necessarily reflect a blend of national and transnational influences. A comparison of sources within such a corpus can only yield tentative results and the following reflections are necessarily and correspondingly cautious. That being said, differences between British and U.S. reactions can, however, be deduced from the detailed analyses.

The re-orientations of the British intellectual left mirror a specific socialist tradition ranging from the socialist humanism of the 'first New Left' to the structural Marxism of the editorial core of *New Left Review*. For all of them, wherever they would position themselves in this field, the Cold-War experience was central. It proved extremely difficult to unsubscribe from a dichotomous East-West logic even if those intellectuals who had founded the journals deliberately engaged in attempts at finding a 'third' position. In political discourse among the British left, both the Soviet Union and the United States were closely associated with their international roles. The U.S.S.R. was evaluated positively for its contributions to the defeat of Fascism and to anti-colonial independence struggles. The United States was blamed for its imperialist postures and frequent acts of aggression against socialist or progressive states and movements beyond the Eastern Bloc. The fact that the society of the United States itself also constituted an arena of social struggles was certainly not ignored, but these struggles were seen as chanceless and regarded as playing only a minor role for socialist advance or retreat elsewhere. In other words, experiencing the omnipresence of the Cold War from a certain perspective and seeing it through British rather than U.S. eyes, encouraged the adoption of a quasi-Deutscherite position and forwarded the observation of the two 'superpowers' as relatively monolithic entities subjugating the world to their Manichaean logic – although one of the two, the United States, bore more responsibility than the other. Whereas this view was arguably less complex than the perspective presented by writers from within the United States, the British journals seemed to have a more familiar understanding of developments on the European continent. Their publications were more aware of the weaknesses of European Social Democracy as well as of the European unification project and they expressed a more profound pessimism about the social changes and reconfigurations of political power following the collapse of the Eastern Bloc.

On the one hand, reactions and re-orientations in the American journals seemed to reflect a radical U.S. tradition rather than just a more narrowly defined socialist one. Radicals in the United States had always had a more pluralist perception of popular struggles and put their emphasis less exclusively on the class conflict. On the other hand, the antagonism between former Trotskyist critics and former anti-Trotskyist supporters of the Soviet Union was still visible in the reactions to 1989/91, even if these positions had lost some of the immense relevance they had once had as a line of demarcation in the U.S. left. Considerations in the journals testified to the U.S. left's traditional weakness which made several European features – such as the existence of working-class parties – look very attractive. Additionally, reflections revealed a self-conscious perception among intellectuals that they lived 'at the heart of the beast'; a 'beast' which constituted one of the most powerful actors in world politics – if not the single most powerful one – but at the same time continued to be one of the most unequal societies in the rich and technologically advanced economies of the West. Hence authors were keenly interested in both social struggles in the United States but also in the country's role in international politics. In regard to the latter, the focus on the European arena of the Cold War was always complemented by observations on developments in other parts of the world, for example, in Latin America and in the Middle East.[1] It seems that writers in the United States also worked under the assumption that they lived in a post-revolutionary society which had developed valuable traditions and practices of participatory democracy, grassroots organisation and communitarianism. Obviously these characteristics had contributed to the dominance of identity politics in discussions of the U.S. left and to the importance of 'constitutional activism' in debates within the left.[2] At the same time, U.S. left intellectuals viewed the centrally-organised and comparatively effective Western European welfare systems with a mixture of admiration and envy and appreciated the strength of their labour movements and progressive parties.

The British and American journals did differ in terms of focus and reflection. However, these tendencies are in turn counterbalanced by a great degree of concurrence between British and U.S. intellectuals. Apart from many shared elements of British and U.S. political cultures and the close personal ties among contributors recruited from a global but even more from an English-speaking community of the intellectual left, some specific unifying elements need to be mentioned. Contributions to the British *Socialist Register* occasionally revealed the publication's proximity to the United States – many of the writers were Americans and wrote from a U.S

---

1   The point is not that the British journals did not cover these issues – they certainly did. However, coverage of these conflicts and developments had less of an impact on writings about the United States, the Cold War, or the collapse of the Eastern Bloc.

2   Constitutional activism, a term originally designed to define a certain approach used by some Supreme Courts when interpreting the U.S. constitution, stands for a perception that it is a continuing task of liberals and radicals in the United States to guarantee that the constitution's basic principles – freedom, equality, the pursuit of happiness – are not denied to any member or group of society.

perspective. *Dissent* evidenced a strong European influence, especially due to its roots in the originally Eastern European Jewish diaspora community in the United States, complemented by refugees from all over Europe in the mid-twentieth century. Finally, the English-speaking community of the intellectual left had its prestigious specialists who wrote on certain issues for more than one journal: the British Ralph Miliband's reflections on democratic socialism and the American Daniel Singer's articles on 'utopistics' could serve as examples. All this makes generalising comparative statements extremely difficult. Clearly, national political cultures and the narrower intellectual-political environments in which the contributors acted played a decisive role for their reactions to the events of 1989/91, but so did the Anglo-American dimension of intellectual-political discourse. Nevertheless, the findings in the analytical chapters suggest that, during the period investigated, the British intellectual left expressed a deeper sense of loss and mourning than the Americans.[3]

---

3 To say this with more authority would require another study which, on the basis of this one, would ask a representative sample of intellectuals about issues such as their relationships to British and U.S. political cultures, their understanding of Marxism, their interpretation of the Cold War, or their opinions on social democracy and post-Marxism. The study would be especially hindered by the problems that many representatives, particularly of the older generation – such as Howe, Magdoff, Miliband, Saville, Sweezy, or Thompson – have passed away since 1989; apart from a few exceptions, it is too late to ask the older generation. Still, tentatively one can observe generational differences: paradoxically, the younger generation of 1968 libertarian socialists seemed to feel more negatively affected than the older generation, many of whom had become members or sympathisers of Communist Parties in the 1930s and 1940s. An additional problem arises once one tries to draw a line between the two generations. To use the example of *New Left Review*, the first editor, Stuart Hall, is generally counted as a representative of the *first* New Left, whereas Tom Nairn, one of the central figures of the re-organised *New Left Review* as it existed from 1962 onwards as a representative of the *second* New Left – a New Left that was still pre-1968, but widely interpreted as the immediate forerunner of the 1968 movement. Both, however, were born in 1932.

3. Outlook and Conclusion

Almost immediately after 1989/91, radical and socialist intellectuals began to fear the consequences of a liberated and radicalised capitalism. This capitalism would not only increase the material and social polarisation in the relatively wealthy societies of Europe and North America; they also expected such a liberated capitalism to be incapable of dealing with existential tasks such as a global redistribution of wealth and the introduction of a mode of production that would end the destruction of the natural environment. These fears turned out to be well justified. The version of capitalism which political economists define as 'neo-liberal regime of accumulation' continued and intensified in Britain and the United States for most of the 1990s and 2000s, and the problems mentioned above were largely ignored. It was only towards the end of the decade of the 2000s that this accumulation regime ran into serious self-created difficulties. Thus the suspicion among left intellectuals that 1989 constituted a turning point in the history of capitalism has been vindicated.

The assumption that 1989/91 marked an ending for socialist intellectuals' self-image as a distinguishable group seems also correct. Intellectuals had to borrow concepts and ideas designed by others and in their self-perceptions this seemed to amount to a loss of distinction. To a certain extent, a two-generational project which united Western Marxism with 1968 libertarianism had come to an end. From now on, the socialist intellectuals in question could only formulate a certain political blend: a social democracy sensible to grassroots activities and struggles, and a post-Marxism aware of power structures, hierarchies and material inequalities in society. Additionally, such a blend could point to unresolved global problems. Still, one could argue, that giving a voice to such a perspective was politically of critical importance. Why for many doing this seemed to be not enough, especially since the re-thinking and modifying of traditional Marxism had started a long time before 1989, is a difficult question. Part of the answer is that the complicated character of Marxism as a system of thought – a hybrid of theory and eschatology – had exploded. Further, following discourse theoretical considerations, one could argue that the legitimacy of Marxist or Marxian-inspired systems of thought or social theories and their abilities to contribute a specific discursive perspective to interpretations of the political world had been put into question. Socialist intellectuals' materialist version of critical theory became increasingly incompatible with hegemonic discursive frames, which claimed that the events of 1989/91 had deconstructed the whole edifice of socialist theory. Socialist intellectuals were forced to note that the expressive modalities through which they interpreted the collapse – for example, their analyses of the Cold War – were declared illegitimate. The formation of discursive concepts changed: what hitherto seemed logical – for example, that realistic alternatives to capitalism existed – now appeared illogical. Of course, intellectuals could continue to express their perspectives. However, the chance to feed their specialist discourse into a politically relevant 'interdiscourse' had, as they had worried, declined. Radical intellectuals feared that 'capitalism's victory' constituted an epochal break not only in geo-political and political-economic terms, but further, that this break entailed dimensions of a paradigmatic shift in intellectual, political and popular thinking as well – which delegitimised the most important elements of socialist intellectuals' analytical approach. This rupture had dramatic biographical consequences for a generation of intellectuals who by 1989/91 looked back on at least two decades of political and intellectual activity. As a group, they suspected future isolation and anticipated that they would need to reinvent or re-orient themselves. Some did, over a considerable period of time.

All journals continued their work. They commented on, reacted to, and criticised the political developments and problems of the 1990s and 2000s. Some new phenomena promised hope – for example, the emergence of the anti-globalisation movement which the journals arguably had helped to found with their interventions in the globalisation debate and which seemed to re-start radical protest in the West from the mid-1990s onwards. Other phenomena were far from promising, such as the militarisation of international conflicts, heavily criticised by many contributors to the journals. However, this latter phenomenon opened up a new split among the socialist intellectuals because a minority began to defend interventions such as the U.N.-sanctioned war against Iraq in 1991. In this case, it was, surprisingly, Cold-War theorist Fred Halliday who lent his support (cf. Thompson 2007: 152). In later years, especially after 2001, many close to the journal *Dissent* but also some contributors to the other publications, such as Norman Geras, exchanged many of their former convictions and became 'left hawks' or – in analogy to the once leftist 'Cold-War intellectuals' – "War-on-Terror intellectuals".[1] They extended the notion of forming an intellectual 'rearguard' to a supporting role for the defence of Western democracy and secular enlightenment values against terrorist attacks and 'religious fundamentalism'. The majority, however, continued their critique of geo-politics and for some time engaged in analyses of a 'new imperialism'.

Organisationally, the British journals became increasingly 'Americanised'. Both *New Left Review* and *Socialist Register* often published more contributions from U.S. writers than from British or Canadians. To a certain extent, this shift has served to strengthen the trend towards 'aloofness', namely, the distance from political struggles in Britain, for which particularly *New Left Review* is frequently criticised. The American journals seemed to remain closer to developments in U.S. politics. While the British journals had once fulfilled important functions for the movements which emerged as a consequence of the moment and spirit of 1968, they have now become, to use the phrase of *Socialist Register*'s co-editor Colin Leys, "journals in search of a movement".[2]

Soon, another generational change will take place. It remains to be seen whether the journals will retain their characteristics. Currently, many writers – again with the partial exception of *Dissenters* – oscillate between analytical radicalism, accompanied by pessimism, and an embrace of centre-left positions in 'real politics' – a combination which occasionally seems contradictory. Obviously, socialist intellectuals have adopted a homeless left existentialism: they continue to produce analytically sound critiques, but doubt their immediate political effectiveness. This mood of subdued and isolated perseverance has probably been best summarised by Göran Therborn as early as 1993: "Reality is not necessarily as we think. That's why there is a need for empirical research. Society is not what it should be. That's why some of us continue to be on the left." (1993: 191)

---

1 I owe the term "War-on-Terror intellectuals" to Inderjeet Parmar.
2 This phrase was proposed by Leys in personal conversation.

V. Bibliography

Achcar, Gilbert (2000). "The 'Historical Pessimism' of Perry Anderson" *International Socialism* No. 88, 135-141.

Ahmad, Aijaz (1994). "Reconciling Derrida: 'Spectres of Marx' and Deconstructive Politics" *New Left Review*, No. 208, 88-106.

Albo, Gregory (1994). "'Competitive Austerity' and the Impasse of Capitalist Employment Policy" *Socialist Register 1994: Between Globalism and Nationalism*, 144-170.

Alexander, Jeffrey C. (1995). "Modern, Anti, Post and Neo" *New Left Review*, No. 211, 63-101.

Amin, Samir (1990). "The Future of Socialism" *Monthly Review*, Vol. 42 No. 3, 10-29.

Amin, Samir (1991). "The Real Stakes in the Gulf War" *Monthly Review*, Vol. 43 No. 3, 14-24.

Amin, Samir (1992). "Thirty Years of Critique of the Soviet Union" Monthly Review, Vol. 44 No. 1, 43-50.

Amin, Samir (1993). "Historical and Ethical Materialism" *Monthly Review*, Vol. 45 No. 2, 44-56.

Anderson, Perry (1976). *Considerations on Western Marxism*. London: New Left Books.

Anderson, Perry (1980). *Arguments Within English Marxism*. London: Verso.

Anderson, Perry (1992). *English Questions*. London: Verso.

Aronowitz, Stanley (1996). *The Death and Rebirth of American Radicalism*. New York: Routledge 1996.

Arrighi, Giovanni (1990). "Marxist Century, American Century: The Making and Remaking of the World Labour Movement" *New Left Review*, No. 179, 29-63.
Auerbach, Paul (1992). "On Socialist Optimism" *New Left Review*, No. 192, 5-35.
Avineri, Shlomo (1990). "Toward a Socialist Theory of Nationalism" *Dissent*, Fall, 447-457.
Avineri, Shlomo (1992). "Capitalism Has not Won. Socialism Is not Dead" *Dissent*, Winter, 7-11.
Barkan, Joan (1991). Contribution to "From Sweden to Socialism. A Small Symposium on Big Questions" *Dissent*, Winter, 97-98.
Bartholomew, Amy (1990). "Should a Marxist Believe in Marx on Rights?" *Socialist Register 1990: The Retreat of the Intellectuals*, 244-264.
Batstone, David (1991). "An Interview with Billy Bragg" *Monthly Review*, Vol. 42 No. 9, 20-29.
Bell, Daniel (1990). "As We Go into the Nineties" *Dissent*, Spring, 171-176.
Bell, Daniel (1991). "Socialism and Planning. Beyond the Soviet Economic Crisis" *Dissent*, Winter, 50-54.
Bell-Villada, Gene H. (1991)."Is the American Mind Getting Dumber?" *Monthly Review*, Vol. 43 No. 1, 41-55.
Benn, Tony & Eric Heffer (1986). "A Strategy for Labour. Four Documents" *New Left Review*, No. 158, 59-75.
Benton, Ted (1992). "Ecology, Socialism and the Mastery of Nature: A Reply to Reiner Grundmann" *New Left Review*, No. 194, 55-74.
Berman, Paul (1993). "The Future of the American Left. Part of a Continuing Discussion" *Dissent*, Winter, 97-104.
Berman, Paul (1994). Contribution to "A Symposium. The Left after Forty Years" *Dissent*, Winter, 9.
Bienefeld, Manfred (1994). "Capitalism and the Nation State in the Dog Days of the Twentieth Century" *Socialist Register 1994: Between Globalism and Nationalism*, 94-129.
Blackburn, Robin (1991). "Fin de Siècle: Socialism after the Crash" *New Left Review*, No. 185, 173-249.
Blackledge, Paul (2000). "Perry Anderson and the End of History" *Historical Materialism*, No. 7, 199-219.

Blackledge, Paul (2002). "'What Moves Is Only the Market': Perry Anderson's Historical Pessimism" in Colin Barker & Mike Tyldesley, eds. *Eighth International Conference on Alternative Futures and Popular Protest. Proceedings of a conference held at Manchester Metropolitan University, 2-4 April 2002.* Manchester: Faculty of Humanities and Social Science, Manchester Metropolitan University, no pagination.

Blackledge, Paul (2004). *Perry Anderson, Marxism and the New Left.* London: Merlin Press.

Bobbio, Norberto (1990). "Utopia Overturned" *Dissent,* Summer, 39-41.

Boggs, Grace Lee (1990). "Beyond Eurocentrism" *Monthly Review,* Vol. 41 No. 9, 12-18.

Bowie, Guillermo (1993). "Ethics and the Indigenization of Marxist Thought" *Monthly Review,* Vol. 45 No. 2, 37-43.

Brand, H. (1991). Contribution to "From Sweden to Socialism. A Small Symposium on Big Questions" *Dissent,* Winter, 99-100.

Brecher, Jeremy & Tim Costello (1991). "Reply to Kim Scipes" *Monthly Review,* Vol. 43 No. 7, 47-51.

Brenner, Robert & Mark Glick (1991). "The Regulation Approach. Theory and History" *New Left Review,* No. 188, 45-119.

Brentlinger, John (1992). "Socialism and the Sacred" *Monthly Review,* Vol. 44 No. 5, 27-43.

Broadbent, Edward (1991). "Thoughts of a Social Democrat. A View from Canada" *Dissent,* Winter, 82-85.

Brody, David (1994). "The Future of the Labour Movement in Historical Perspective" *Dissent,* Winter, 57-66.

Bromwich, David (2004). "Acting Alone" in: Nicholaus Mills & Michael Walzer, eds. *50 Years of Dissent.* New Haven: Yale University Press, 338-346.

Buhle, Paul (1990). "Marx and/or Freud: Joel Kovel and Psychoanalytic Theory" *Monthly Review,* Vol. 42 No. 1, 42-52.

Buhle, Paul (1991). *Marxism in the United States.* London: Verso.

Callaghan, John (1984). *British Trotskyism – Theory and Practice.* Oxford: Blackwell.

Callaghan, John (1987). *The Far Left in British Politics.* Oxford: Blackwell.

Cammack, Paul (1990). "Statism, New Institutionalism, and Marxism" *Socialist Register 1990: The Retreat of the Intellectuals,* 147-170.

Castoriadis, Cornelius (1992). "The Crisis of Marxism, the Crisis of Politics" *Dissent*, Spring, 221-225.
Charlton, James I. (1994). "The Disability Rights Movement and the Left" *Monthly Review*, Vol. 46 No. 3, 77-85.
Chun, Lin (1996). *Wortgewitter. Die britische Linke nach 1945*. Hamburg: Rotbuch.
Cloward, Richard A. & Frances Fox Piven (1993). "A Class Analysis of Welfare" *Monthly Review*, Vol. 44 No. 9, 25-31.
Cohen, G. A. (1991). "The Future of a Disillusion" *New Left Review*, No. 190, 5-20.
Cohen, G. A. (1994). "Back to Socialist Values" *New Left Review*, No. 207, 3-16.
Cohen, Mitchell (1991). Contribution to "From Sweden to Socialism. A Small Symposium on Big Questions" *Dissent*, Winter, 100-101.
Cohen, Mitchell (1992). "Theories of Stalinism. Revisiting a Historical Problem" *Dissent*, Spring, 176-191.
Cohen, Mitchell (1994). Contribution to "The Question" *Dissent*, Summer, 377-378.
Cohen, Mitchell (2004). "Introduction" in: Nicholaus Mills & Michael Walzer, eds. *50 Years of Dissent*. New Haven: Yale University Press, 1-8.
Cohen, Peter (1994). "Sweden: The Model that Never Was" *Monthly Review*, Vol. 46 No. 3, 41-59.
Collini, Stefan (2006). *Absent Minds. Intellectuals in Britain*. Oxford: Oxford University Press.
Coser, Lewis (1979). Contribution to "The First 25 Years", *Dissent*, Winter, 3-4.
Coser, Lewis (1991). Contribution to "From Sweden to Socialism. A Small Symposium on Big Questions" *Dissent*, Winter, 101-102.
Cox, Robert W. (1991). "'Real Socialism' in Historical Perspective" *Socialist Register 1991: Communist Regimes. The Aftermath*, 169-193.
Crosland, Anthony (1963 [1956]). *The Future of Socialism*. London: Jonathan Cape.
Cushman-Wood, Darren (1993). "Martin Luther King, Jr. and Malcolm X: Economic Insights and Influences" *Monthly Review*, Vol. 45 No. 1, 21-35.

Dahl, Robert (1990). "Social Reality and Free Markets. A Letter to Friends in Eastern Europe" *Dissent*, Spring, 224-228.
Daly, Glyn (1999). "Marxism and Postmodernity" in: Andrew Gamble, David Marsh & Tony Tant, eds. *Marxism and Social Science*. Basingstoke: Macmillan, 61-84.
Davidson, Neil (1999). "In Perspective: Tom Nairn" *International Socialism*, No. 82, 97-136.
Delahunty, Jim (1993). "New Zealand: The Welfare State Ploughed Under" *Monthly Review*, Vol. 45 No. 6, 28-39.
Denitch, Bogdan (1991). Contribution to "From Sweden to Socialism. A Small Symposium on Big Questions" *Dissent*, Winter, 103-105.
Derrida, Jacques (1994). "Spectres of Marx" *New Left Review*, No. 205, 31-58.
Deutscher, Isaac (1953). *Russia after Stalin*. London: Hamish Hamilton.
Diggins, John Patrick (1992). *The Rise and Fall of the American Left*. New York: Norton.
Dissent (1994). Introduction to "A Symposium. The Left after Forty Years" *Dissent*, Winter, 7.
Dworkin, Dennis (1997). *Cultural Marxism in Postwar Britain. History, the New Left, and the Origins of Cultural Studies*. Durham: Duke University Press.
Ehrlich, Avishai (1992). "The Gulf War and the New World Order" *Socialist Register 1992: New World Order?* 227-238.
Elliott, Gregory (1998). *Perry Anderson. The Merciless Laboratory of History*. Minneapolis: University of Minnesota Press.
Epstein, Joseph (1974). "The First Twenty Years" *Dissent*, Spring, 154-164.
Erber, Ernest (1990). "Virtues and Vices of the Market. Balanced Correctives to a Current Craze" *Dissent*, Summer, 353-360.
Fehèr, Ferenc & Agnes Heller (1991). Contribution to "From Sweden to Socialism. A Small Symposium on Big Questions" *Dissent*, Winter, 105-107.
Flacks, Dick (1991). "Making History and Making Theory. Notes on How Intellectuals Seek Relevance" in: Charles C. Lemert, ed. *Intellectuals and Politics. Social Theory in a Changing World*. Newbury Park: Sage, 3-18.

Foner, Eric (1994). Contribution to "The Question" *Dissent*, Summer, 378-379.
Foster, John Bellamy (1990). "Liberal Practicality and the U.S. Left" *Socialist Register 1990: The Retreat of the Intellectuals*, 265-289.
Foster, John Bellamy (1993). Introduction to a "Symposium on The Ethical Dimension of Marxist Thought" *Monthly Review*, Vol. 45 No. 2, 8-16.
Fukuyama, Francis (1992). *The End of History and the Last Man*. Harmondsworth: Penguin.
Galbraith, John Kenneth (1958). *The Affluent Society*. Boston: Houghton Mifflin.
Gamble, Andrew (1999). "Why Bother with Marxism?" in: Andrew Gamble, David Marsh & Tony Tant, eds. *Marxism and Social Science*. Basingstoke: Macmillan, 1-8.
Genovese, Eugene D. (1994). "The Question" *Dissent*, Summer, 371-376.
Genovese, Eugene D. (1994a). "The Riposte" *Dissent*, Summer, 386-388.
Geras, Norman (1987). "Post-Marxism?" *New Left Review*, No. 163, 40-82.
Geras, Norman (1990). "Seven Types of Obloquy: Travesties of Marxism" *Socialist Register 1990: The Retreat of the Intellectuals*, 1-34.
Geras, Norman (1992). "Bringing Marx to Justice: an Addendum and Rejoinder" *New Left Review*, No. 195, 37-69.
Geras, Norman (1994). "Democracy and the Ends of Marxism" *New Left Review*, No. 203, 92-106.
Gill, Stephen (1990). "Intellectuals and Transnational Capital" *Socialist Register 1990: The Retreat of the Intellectuals*, 290-310.
Gill, Stephen (1992). "The Emerging World Order and European Change: The Political Economy of European Union" *Socialist Register 1992: New World Order?* 157-196.
Gitlin, Todd (1993). *The Sixties. Years of Hope, Days of Rage*. Revised edition, New York: Bantam Books.
Gitlin, Todd (1993a). "The Rise of 'Identity Politics'. An Examination and a Critique" *Dissent*, Spring, 172-177.
Gordon, Linda (1990). "The Welfare State: Towards a Socialist-Feminist Perspective" *Socialist Register 1990: The Retreat of the Intellectuals*, 171-200.
Gorz, André (1990). *"The New Agenda"* *New Left Review*, No. 184, 37-46.
Gorz, André (1993). "Political Ecology: Expertocracy versus Self-Limitation" *New Left Review*, No. 202, 55-67.

Greenberg, Cheryl (2001). "Twentieth-Century Liberalisms: Transformations of an Ideology" in: Harvard Sitkoff, ed. *Perspectives on Modern America. Making Sense of the Twentieth Century.* New York: Oxford University Press, 55-79.

Griffith, John (1993). "The Rights Stuff" *Socialist Register 1993: Real Problems, False Solutions,* 106-124.

Grundmann, Reiner (1991). "The Ecological Challenge to Marxism" *New Left Review,* No. 187, 103-120.

Habermas, Jürgen (1990). "What Does Socialism Mean Today? The Rectifying Revolution and the Need for New Thinking on the Left" *New Left Review,* No. 183, 3-21.

Habermas, Jürgen & Adam Michnik (1994). "Overcoming the Past" *New Left Review,* No. 203, 3-16.

Hall, Stuart (1988). *The Hard Road to Renewal. Thatcherism and the Crisis of the Left.* London: Verso.

Hall, Stuart et al. (1978). *Policing the Crisis: Mugging, the State, and Law and Order.* Basingstoke: Macmillan.

Halliday, Fred (1990). "The Ends of Cold War" *New Left Review,* No. 180, 5-23.

Halliday, Fred (1990a). "A Reply to Edward Thompson" *New Left Review,* No. 182, 147-150.

Harrington, Mike (1963). *The Other America. Poverty in the United States.* Baltimore: Penguin.

Harvey, David (1993). "The Nature of Environment: Dialectics of Social and Evironmental Change" *Socialist Register 1993: Real Problems, False Solutions,* 1-51.

Hartz, Louis (1955). *The Liberal Tradition in America. An Interpretation of American Political Thought since the Revolution.* New York: Harcourt & Brace.

Heilbroner, Robert (1991). Introduction to "From Sweden to Socialism. A Small Symposium on Big Questions" *Dissent,* Winter, 96.

Hermele, Kenneth (1993). "The End of the Middle Road: What Happened to the Swedish Model?" *Monthly Review,* Vol. 44 No. 10, 14-24.

Hermele, Kenneth (1993a). "A Response to David Vail" *Monthly Review,* Vol. 45 No. 5, 32-37.

Hewitt, Marsha A. (1993). "Illusions of Freedom: The Regressive Implications of Postmodernism" *Socialist Register 1993: Real Problems, False Solutions*, 78-91.
Hinkelammert, Franz J. (1993). "The Crisis of Socialism and the Third World" *Monthly Review*, Vol. 45 No. 3, 105-114.
Hirst, Paul (1994). "Associative Democracy" *Dissent*, Spring, 241-247.
Hobsbawm, Eric (1978). "The Forward March of Labour Halted?" *Marxism Today*, September, 279-286.
Hobsbawm, Eric (1992). "The Crisis of Today's Ideologies" *New Left Review*, No. 192, 55-64.
Honderich, Ted (1994). "Hierarchic Democracy" *New Left Review*, No. 204, 48-66.
Hopfmann, Arndt (2000). "Monthly Review – im 51. Jahr" *Utopie kreativ*, No. 114, 395-9.
Horvat, Branko (1991). Contribution to "From Sweden to Socialism. A Small Symposium on Big Questions" *Dissent*, Winter, 107-108.
Howe, Irving (1985). *Socialism and America*. New York: Harcourt Brace Jovanovich.
Howe, Irving (1986). *The American Newness. Culture and Politics in the Age of Emerson*. Cambridge: Harvard University Press.
Howe, Irving (1990). "Notes from the Left" *Dissent*, Summer, 300-302.
Howe, Irving (1990a). "A New Political Situation" *Dissent*, Winter, 87-91.
Howe, Irving (1991). "Totalitarianism Reconsidered: Yesterday's Theories, Today's Realities" *Dissent*, Winter, 63-71.
Howe, Irving (1992). "Questions We Ask Ourselves and Can Sometimes Answer" *Dissent*, Spring, 143-145.
Inglis, Fred (1996). "The Figures of Dissent" *New Left Review*, No. 215, 83-92.
Isaac, Jeffrey C. (1994). "Civil Society and the Spirit of Revolt" *Dissent*, Summer, 356-361.
Isserman, Maurice (1993). *If I Had a Hammer. The Death of the Old Left and the Birth of the New Left*. Urbana: University of Illinois Press.
Jaggar, Allison (1993). "Moral Justification, Philosophy, and Critical Social Theory" *Monthly Review*, Vol. 45 No. 2, 17-27.
Jessop, Bob et al. (1988). *Thatcherism. A Tale of Two Nations*. Oxford: Blackwell, Polity Press.

Joseph, Paul (1990). "Political Changes after the Cold War" *Dissent*, Spring, 145-148.
Kaldor, Mary (1990). "After the Cold War" *New Left Review*, No. 180, 25-37.
Katsiaficas, George (1987). *The Imagination of the New Left. A Global Analysis of 1968*. Cambridge: South End Press.
Kenny, Michael (1995). *The First New Left. British Intellectuals after Stalin*. London: Lawrence & Wishart.
Kim, Elizabeth. C. (1993). "Toward a Cord of Solidarity: Progressive Social Change in the 1990s" *Monthly Review*, Vol. 45 No. 4, 52-57.
Kirchheimer, Otto (1990 [1966]). "The Catch-All Party" in: Peter Mair, ed. *The West European Party System*. Oxford: Oxford University Press, 50-60.
Kovel, Joel (1992). "Post-Communist Anticommunism: America's New Ideological Frontiers" *Socialist Register 1992: New World Order?* 254-269.
Kovel, Joel (1994). "The Spiritual Roots of Marxism" *Monthly Review*, Vol. 45 No. 9, 33-42.
Kovel, Joel (1994a). "Remembering Ralph Miliband" *Monthly Review*, Vol. 46 No. 4, 51-58.
Kowalik, Tadeusz (1991). "Oskar Lange's Market Socialism. The Story of an Intellectual-Political Career" *Dissent*, Winter, 86-95.
Kozak, Marion (2006 [1995]). "How It All Began: a Footnote to History" http://socialistregister.com/about/history.html (accessed 24.10.2006).
Krieger, Joel (1999). *British Politics in the Global Age. Can Social Democracy Survive?* New York: Oxford University Press.
Laclau, Ernesto & Chantal Mouffe (1986). *Hegemony and Socialist Strategy*. London: Verso.
Laclau, Ernesto & Chantal Mouffe (1987). "Post-Marxism Without Apologies" *New Left Review*, No. 166, 79-106.
Land, Oliver S. (1991). "Socialism in the 1990s. Where Do We Go from Here?" *Monthly Review*, Vol. 43 No. 2, 45-53.
Lansley, Stewart, Sue Goss & Christian Wolmar (1989). *Councils in Conflict. The Rise and Fall of the Municipal Left*. Basingstoke: Macmillan.
Lebowitz, Michael A. (1991). "The Socialist Fetter: A Cautionary Tale" *Socialist Register 1991: Communist Regimes. The Aftermath*, 348-374.

Levins, Richard (1990). "Eulogy Behind an Empty Grave: Reflections on the Future of Socialism" *Socialist Register 1990: The Retreat of the Intellectuals*, 328-345.
Livingstone, Ken (1983). "Why Labour Lost. Ken Livingstone Talks to Tariq Ali" *New Left Review*, No. 140, 23-49.
Löwy, Michel (1991). "Twelve Theses on the Crisis of 'Really Existing Socialism'" *Monthly Review*, Vol. 43 No. 1, 33-40.
Macdonald, Eleanor (1990). "Derrida and the Politics of Interpretation" *Socialist Register 1990: The Retreat of the Intellectuals*, 228-243.
MacEwan, Arthur (1990). "Why Are We Still Socialists and Marxists After All This?" *Socialist Register 1990: The Retreat of the Intellectuals*, 311-327.
MacEwan, Arthur (1994). "Review of the Month: Globalisation and Stagnation" *Monthly Review*, Vol. 45 No. 11, 1-16.
Magdoff, Harry (1991). "Are There Lessons to Be Learned?" *Monthly Review*, Vol 42 No. 9, 1-19.
Magri, Lucio (1991). "The European Left between Crisis and Refoundation" *New Left Review*, No. 189, 5-18.
Marable, Manning (1990). "Black Politics and the Challenges of the Left" *Monthly Review*, 41/11, 22-31.
Markovits, Andrei S. (2005). "The European and the American Left Since 1945" *Dissent*, Winter, www.dissentmagazine.org/article/?article=264 (accessed 13.03.2007)
Marquand, David (1994). "Reinventing Federalism: Europe and the Left" *New Left Review*, No. 203, 17-26.
Marzani, Carl (1990). "On Interring Communism and Exalting Capitalism" *Monthly Review*, Vol. 41 No. 8, Supplement, 1-30.
Mayer, Tom (1991). "Review of the Month: Imperialism and the Gulf War" *Monthly Review*, Vol. 42 No. 11, 1-11.
McCarney, Joseph (1991). "The True Realm of Freedom: Marxist Philosophy after Communism" *New Left Review*, No. 189, 19-38.
McChesney, Robert (1994). "Radical Scholarship in the Academy: the View from Communications" *Monthly Review*, Vol. 45 No. 8, 27-35.
Meidner, Rudolf (1993). "Why Did the Swedish Model Fail?" *Socialist Register 1993: Real Problems, False Solutions*, 211-228.

Meiksins, Peter (1994). "Labour and Monopoly Capital for the 1990s: A Review and Critique of the Labour Process Debate" *Monthly Review*, Vol. 46 No. 6, 45-59.

Meisenhelder, Tim (1993). "Amilcar Cabral's Theory of Class Suicide and Revolutionary Socialism" *Monthly Review*, Vol. 45 No. 6, 40-48.

Mészáros, István (1993). "Marxism – Politics – Morality" *Monthly Review*, Vol. 45 No. 2, 28-36.

Miliband, David, (1994) ed. *Reinventing the Left*. Cambridge: Polity Press.

Miliband, Ralph (1961). *Parliamentary Socialism. A Study in the Politics of Labour*. London: Allen & Unwin.

Miliband, Ralph (1970). "The Capitalist State. Reply to N. Poulantzas" *New Left Review*, No. 59, 53-60.

Miliband, Ralph (1973). "Poulantzas and the Capitalist State" *New Left Review*, No. 82, 83-92.

Miliband, Ralph (1990). "Counter-Hegemonic Struggles" *Socialist Register 1990: The Retreat of the Intellectuals*, 346-365.

Miliband, Ralph (1991). "Socialism in Question" *Monthly Review*, Vol. 42 No. 10, 16-26.

Miliband, Ralph (1991a). "What Comes After Socialist Regimes?" *Socialist Register 1991: Communist Regimes. The Aftermath*, 375-389.

Miliband, Ralph (1992). "Fukuyama and the Socialist Alternative" *New Left Review*, No. 193, 108-113.

Miliband, Ralph (1994). "The Plausibility of Socialism" *New Left Review*, No. 206, 3-14.

Miliband, Ralph (1994a). "Thirty Years of Socialist Register" *Socialist Register 1994: Between Globalism and Nationalism*, 1-19.

Miller, David (1991). "A Vision of Market Socialism. How It Might Work and Its Problems" *Dissent*, Summer, 406-414.

Monthly Review (1990). "Perestroika and the Future of Socialism – Part I" *Monthly Review*, Vol. 41 No. 10, 1-13.

Monthly Review (1990a). "Perestroika and the Future of Socialism – Part II" *Monthly Review*, Vol. 41 No. 11, 1-17.

Monthly Review (1991). "Review of the Month: Where Are We Going?" *Monthly Review*, Vol. 42 No. 10, 1-15.

Monthly Review (1993). "Marxism Today. An Interview With István Mészáros" *Monthly Review*, Vol. 44 No. 11, 9-24.

Monthly Review (1994). "Editors Comment" [on Plotkin et al. 1994] *Monthly Review*, Vol. 46 No. 7, 57-58.
Monthly Review (1994a). "Review of the Month: Unemployment: Capitalism's Achilles Heel" *Monthly Review*, Vol. 46 No. 7, 1-9.
Monthly Review (1999). "An Interview with Ellen Meiksins Wood" Monthly Review, Vol. 51 No 1, 74-93.
Morand, Martin J. (1990). "Canada: Our Model?" *Monthly Review*, Vol. 42 No. 2, 40-47.
Morand, Martin J. (1991). "U.S. and Canadian Labor: Convergence at Whose Expense? *Monthly Review*, Vol. 43 No. 2, 15-28.
Morgan, Kevin (2003). "Rummaging in Trotsky's Dustbin: or What Does the Left Need with History?" *Soundings*, No. 23, 132-141.
Mouffe, Chantal (1993). "Toward a Liberal Socialism?" *Dissent*, Winter, 81-87.
Mouzelis, Nicos (1993). "The Balance Sheet of the Left" *New Left Review*, No. 200, 182-185.
New Left Review (1960). "Editorial". *New Left Review*, No. 1, 1-3.
New Left Review (1982), ed. *Exterminism and Cold War*. London: New Left Review.
New Left Review (2002). "About NLR". http://www.newleftreview.net/AboutNLR.shtml (03.08.2006).
Newman, Michael (2002). *Ralph Miliband and the Politics of the New Left*. London: Merlin Press.
Norris, Christopher (1993). "Old Themes for New Times: Basildon Revisited" *Socialist Register 1993: Real Problems, False Solutions*, 52-77.
Nove, Alec (1990). "'Market Socialism' and 'Free Economy': A Discussion of Alternatives" *Dissent*, Fall, 443-446.
Ostendorf, Berndt & Paul Levine (1992). "Intellektuelle und die Krisen der amerikanischen Kultur" in: Willi Paul Adams et al., eds. *Länderbericht USA II. Gesellschaft, Außenpolitik, Kultur – Religion – Erziehung*. 2. Auflage. Bonn: Bundeszentrale für politische Bildung, 526-536.
Padgett, Stephen & William E. Paterson (1991). *A History of Social Democracy in Postwar Europe*. London: Longman.
Palmer, John (1992): "Europe in a Multipolar World" *Socialist Register 1992: New World Order?* 143-156.
Panitch, Leo (1988). "Socialist Renewal and the Labour Party" *Socialist Register 1988*, 319-365.

Panitch, Leo (1994). "Globalization and the State" *Socialist Register 1994: Between Globalism and Nationalism*, 60-93.
Panitch, Leo (1995). "Ralph Miliband, Socialist Intellectual, 1924-1994" *Socialist Register 1995: Why Not Capitalism?* 1-21.
Panitch, Leo (2001). *Renewing Socialism. Democracy, Strategy, and Imagination*. Boulder: Westview Press.
Panitch, Leo & Colin Leys (1997). *The End of Parliamentary Socialism. From New Left to New Labour*. London: Verso.
Panitch, Leo & Ralph Miliband (1992). "The New World Order and the Socialist Agenda" *Socialist Register 1992: New World Order?* 1-25.
Patnaik, Prabhat (1990). "Whatever Happened to Imperialism?" *Monthly Review*, Vol. 42 No. 6, 1-6.
Petras, James (1998). "A Marxist Critique of Post-Marxism" http://www.marxsite.com/Marxist%20Critique%20of%20Post-Marxism.html (accessed 27.11.2009).
Phelps, Christopher (1999). "Introduction: A Socialist Magazine in the American Century" *Monthly Review*, Vol. 51 No. 1, May, 1-30.
Phillips, Maxine (2004). "Foreword: Eighties" in: Nicholaus Mills & Michael Walzer (eds.). *50 Years of Dissent*. New Haven: Yale University Press, 169-171.
Plastrik, Stanley (1979). Contribution to "The First 25 Years", *Dissent*, Winter, 3.
Plotkin, Sheldon C. et al. (1994). "Is Economic Conversion and Jobs Really Possible?" *Monthly Review*, Vol. 46 No. 7, 45-56.
Poulantzas, Nicos (1969). "The Problem of the Capitalist State" *New Left Review*, No. 58, 67-78.
Poulantzas, Nicos (1976). "The Capitalist State. A Reply to Miliband and Laclau" *New Left Review*, No. 95, 63-83.
Prago, Alberto (1990). "On Marzani's Exaltation of Communism" *Monthly Review*, Vol. 42 No. 1, 53-54.
Przeworski, Adam (1985). Capitalism and Social Democracy. Cambridge: Cambridge University Press.
Przeworski, Adam (1993). "Socialism and Social Democracy" in: Joel Krieger, ed. *The Oxford Compendium to Politics of the World*. New York: Oxford University Press, 832-839.
Purdy, David (1994). "Citizenship, Basic Income and the State" *New Left Review*, No. 208, 30-48.

Rae, Bob (1991). "A Socialist Credo" *Dissent*, Winter, 42-45.

Rocard, Michel & Paul Ricoeur (1991). "Justice and the Market" *Dissent*, Fall, 505-510.

Roemer, John (1991). "Market Socialism. A Blueprint How Such an Economy Might Work" *Dissent*, Fall, 562-569.

Rorty, Richard (1982), Consequences of Pragmatism. Brighton: Harvester Press.

Rorty, Richard (1991). "Intellectuals in Politics. Too Far In? Too Far Out?" *Dissent*, Fall, 483-490.

Rorty, Richard (1992). "Richard Rorty Replies" [to Andrew Ross. "Intellectuals in Politics"] *Dissent*, Spring, 265-267.

Ross, George (1990). "Intellectuals Against the Left: the Case of France" *Socialist Register 1990: The Retreat of the Intellectuals*, 201-227.

Rosselli, Carlo (1994). "Liberal Socialism" *Dissent*, Winter, 117-123.

Rule, James B. & Dennis Wong (1990). "On Political Identities" *Dissent*, Fall, 478-485.

Rustin, Michael (1992). "No Exit from Capitalism?" *New Left Review*, No. 193, 96-107.

Rustin, Michael (1994). "Incomplete Modernity. Ulrich Beck's 'Risk Society'" *Dissent*, Summer, 394-400.

Ryan, Alan (1990). "Socialism for the Nineties. An Argument for this Time" *Dissent*, Fall, 436-442.

Samuel, Raphael (1989). "Born-Again Socialism" in: Oxford University Socialist Discussion Group, ed. *Out of Apathy. Voices of the New Left Thirty Years* On. London: Verso.

Sassoon, Donald (1981). "The Silences of New Left Review". *Politics & Power*, No. 3, 219-254.

Sassoon, Donald (1994). "Social Democracy and the Europe of Tomorrow" *Dissent*, Winter, 94-101.

Saville, John (1990). "Marxism Today: An Anatomy" *Socialist Register 1990: The Retreat of the Intellectuals*, 35-59.

Sayers, Sean (1994). "Moral Values and Progress" *New Left Review*, No. 204, 67-85.

Schumpeter, Joseph Alois (1967[1954]). *History of Economic Analysis.* London: Allen & Unwin.

Scipes, Kim (1991). "Labour Community Relations: Not All They're Cracked Up to Be" *Monthly Review*, Vol. 43 No. 7, 34-46.

Sedgwick, Peter (1976). "The Two New Lefts" in: David Widgery, ed. *The Left in Britain 1956-68*. Harmondsworth: Penguin, 131-153.
Segal, Lynne (1991). "Whose Left? Socialism, Feminism and the Future" *New Left Review*, No. 185, 81-91.
Sherman, Howard J. (1990). "The Second Soviet Revolution or the Transition from Statism to Socialism" *Monthly Review*, Vol. 41 No. 10, 14-22.
Sim, Stuart (2000). *Post-Marxism. An Intellectual History*. London: Routledge.
Singer, Daniel (1990). "Prometheus Rebound?" *Monthly Review*, Vol. 42 No. 3, 73-92.
Singer, Daniel (1993). "In Defence of Utopia" *Socialist Register 1993: Real Problems, False Solutions*, 249-256.
Singer, Daniel (1994). "Europe's Crises" *Monthly Review*, Vol. 46 No. 3, 86-100.
Snitow, Ann (1994). Contribution to "A Symposium. The Left after Forty Years" *Dissent*, Winter, 14.
Soper, Kate (1993). "A Theory of Human Need" *New Left Review*, No. 197, 113-128.
Sprinker, Michael (1993). "'Dancing in the Dark'. Perry Anderson on Socialism's Impasse" *Radical History Review*, No. 57, 98-115.
Sweezy, Paul M. (1990). "Nineteen Eighty-Nine" *Monthly Review*, Vol. 41 No. 11, 18-21.
Sweezy, Paul M. (1990a). "Preface for a New Edition of Post-Revolutionary Society" *Monthly Review*, Vol. 42 No. 3, 5-9.
Sweezy, Paul M. (1990b). "Cuba: A Left U.S. View" *Monthly Review*, Vol. 42 No. 4, 17-21.
Sweezy, Paul M. (1993). "Review of the Month: Socialism: Legacy and Renewal" *Monthly Review*, Vol. 44 No. 8, 1-9.
Sweezy, Paul M. (1994). "Review of the Month: Monthly Review in Historical Perspective" *Monthly Review*, Vol. 45 No. 8, 1-7.
Sweezy, Paul M. (1994a). "Review of the Month: The Triumph of Financial Capital" *Monthly Review*, Vol. 46 No. 2, 1-11.
Sweezy, Paul & Leo Huberman (1953). "A Challenge to the Book Burners" *Monthly Review*, Vol. 5, No 3, 159.
Therborn, Göran (1992). "The Life and Times of Socialism" *New Left Review*, No. 194, 17-32.

Therborn, Göran (1993). "Reply to Mouzelis" *New Left Review*, No. 200, 185-191.
Therborn, Göran (2000). *Die Gesellschaften Europas 1945-2000. Ein soziologischer Vergleich*. Frankfurt: Campus.
Therborn, Göran (2007). "After Dialectics. Radical Social Theory in a Post-Communist World" *New Left Review II*, No. 43, 63-114.
Thompson, Dorothy (1996). "On the Trail of the New Left" *New Left Review*, No. 215, 93-100.
Thompson, Duncan (2001). "Pessimism of the Intellect? The New Left Review and the 'Conjuncture of 1989'" *Socialist History*, No. 20, 19-39.
Thompson, Duncan (2007) *Pessimism of the Intellect? A History of New Left Review*. London: Merlin Press.
Thompson, Edward P. (1978). *The Poverty of Theory & Other Essays*. London: Merlin Press.
Thompson, Edward P. (1990). "The Ends of Cold War" *New Left Review*, No. 182, 139-146.
Trilling, Lionel (1950). *The Liberal Imagination*. New York: Viking.
Tyler, Gus (1991). Contribution to "From Sweden to Socialism. A Small Symposium on Big Questions" *Dissent*, Winter, 109-110.
Urbinati, Nadia (1994). "The Liberal Socialism of Carlo Rosselli" *Dissent*, Winter, 113-116.
Vail, David (1993). "The Past and the Future of Swedish Social Democracy: A Reply to Kenneth Hermele" *Monthly Review*, Vol. 45 No. 5, 24-31.
van der Linden, Marcel (2007). *Western Marxism and the Soviet Union. A Survey of Critical Theories and Debates Since 1917*. Leiden: Brill.
Vilas, Carlos M (1990). "Is Socialism Still an Alternative for the Third World?" *Monthly Review*, Vol. 42 No. 3, 93-109.
Wald, Alan M. (1987). *The New York Intellectuals. The Rise and Decline of the Anti-Stalinist Left from the 1930s to the 1980s*. Chapel Hill: The University of North Carolina Press.
Wald, Alan M. (1991). "Remaking American Marxism in the 1990s" *Monthly Review*, Vol. 43 No. 5, 58-63.
Walker, Alice (1994). "The Story of Why I am Here, or: a Woman Connects Oppressions" *Monthly Review*, Vol. 46 No. 2, 38-43.

Wallerstein, Immanuel (1992). "The Collapse of Liberalism" *Socialist Register 1992: New World Order?* 96-110.
Wallerstein, Immanuel (1994). "The Agonies of Liberalism: What Hope Progress" *New Left Review*, No. 204, 3-17.
Wallis, Victor (1991). "Marxism and the U.S. Left: Thoughts for the 1990s" *Monthly Review*, Vol. 43 No. 2, 5-14.
Wallis, Victor (1992). "Socialism, Ecology, and Democracy: Toward a Strategy of Conversion" *Monthly Review*, Vol. 44 No. 2, 1-22.
Walzer, Michael (1983). *Spheres of Justice: a Defence of Pluralism and Equality*. Oxford: Robertson.
Walzer, Michael (1992). "Scenarios for a Possible Left: Where Can We Go from Here?" *Dissent*, Fall, 466-469.
Walzer, Michael (2004). Can There Be a Decent Left?" in: Nicholaus Mills & Michael Walzer, eds. *50 Years of Dissent*. New Haven: Yale University Press, 314-322.
Wapner, Paul (1994). "Environmental Activism and Global Civil Society" *Dissent*, Summer, 389-393.
Watanabe, Yuzo & Yashiaki Wakima (1990). "Marxist Views. An Interview with Paul Sweezy" *Monthly Review*, Vol. 42 No. 5, 1-15.
Weinstein, James (2004). *The Long Detour: the History and Future of the American Left*. Cambridge: Westview Press.
Weisskopf, Thomas E. (1992). "Challenges to Market Socialism: A Response to Critics" *Dissent*, Spring, 250-261.
West, Cornel (1993). "The Author Replies" *Monthly Review*, Vol. 45 No. 2, 57-60.
Weston, Jack (1990). "For an Ecological Politics of Hope" *Monthly Review*, Vol. 41 No. 9, 1-11.
Wieviorka, Michel (1994). "French Intellectuals: End of an Era?" *Dissent*, Spring, 248-252.
Wilentz, Sean (1994). Contribution to "The Question" *Dissent*, Summer, 384-385.
Williams, Raymond (1979). *Politics and Letters. Interviews with New Left Review*. London: New Left Books.
Wollen, Peter (1993). "Our Post-Communism: The Legacy of Karl Kautsky" *New Left Review*, No. 202, 85-93.
Wood, Ellen Meiksins (1990). "The Uses and Abuses of Civil Society" *Socialist Register 1990: The Retreat of the Intellectuals*, 60-84.

Wood, Ellen Meiksins (1994). "E. P. Thompson: Historian and Socialist" *Monthly Review*, Vol. 45 No. 8, 8-14.
Wood, Ellen Meiksins (1994a). "From Opportunity to Imperative: the History of the Market" *Monthly Review*, Vol. 46 No. 3, 14-40.
Wood, Ellen Meiksins (1995). "A Chronology of the New Left and Its Successors, Or: Who's Old-Fashioned Now?" *Socialist Register 1995: Why Not Capitalism?* 22-49.
Woodhams, Stephen (2001). *History in the Making. Raymond Williams, Edward Thompson and Radical Intellectuals, 1936-1956.* London: Merlin Press.
Wright, Eric Olin (1993). "Class Analysis, History and Emancipation" *New Left Review*, No. 202, 15-35.
Yih, Katherine (1990). "The Red and the Green: Left Perspectives on Ecology" *Monthly Review*, Vol. 42 No. 5, 16-28.

VI. Acknowledgements

Many people in many places have, in many ways, contributed to the completion of this study. My gratitude goes to all of them, but especially to Gregory Albo, George Comninel, Leo Panitch, and the late Ellen Meiksins Wood in Canada; to Mitchell Cohen, Todd Gitlin, Joel Kovel, Wallace Bond Love, and Alethea Wait in the United States; to Claire Annesley, Heide Connell and the late Ron Connell, Karin Connell and John Taylor, Andrew Gamble, Peter Gattrell, Bob Jessop, Mike Kenny, Colin Leys, Kevin Morgan, Inderjeet Parmar, and Göran Therborn in Britain (as well as to the Sociology Department at Lancaster University and the School of Social Sciences at Manchester University); to Astrid Bungenstock, Hans Kastendiek, Jürgen Kramer, Petra Naumann, Ralf Schneider, Alfons Söllner, Gesa Stedman, Klaus Stolz, and Olaf Wahls in Germany (as well as to the John F. Kennedy Institute for North American Studies at the Free University of Berlin).

VII. Detailed Table of Contents

I. Introduction: the Paradox of 1989 | 7

II. Analysing the Impact of 1989 on the British and the American Intellectual Left | 21
1. 1989/91 and the Prospects of Socialism: Options for a Theoretical Debate of the Left on Strategies and Agencies | 21
1.1. The Intellectuals' Core Ideas of Democratic Socialism | 23
1.2. Social Democracy as a Model and Social Democratic Parties as Agents of Social and Political Change? | 26
1.3. Post-Marxism as a Re-formulation of, or a Departure from, Socialist Strategies for Change? | 36
2. A Short History of the British and the American Intellectual Left and the Journals Analysed | 45
2.1. The Many British New Lefts | 45
2.2. *New Left Review* and *Socialist Register* | 51
2.3. Two Generations of the American Intellectual Left | 60
2.4. *Dissent* and *Monthly Review* | 65
2.5. Similarites and Differences among the British and the American Lefts / 73

III. Crisis and Re-orientation: Evidence from the Journals | 77
1. The Moment of 1989: Emotional Responses to the Collapse of the Eastern Bloc | 77
   New Left Review | 78
   Socialist Register | 82
   Dissent | 84
   Monthly Review | 86
   Coming to Terms with the Crash | 88
2. Assessments of State Socialism | 90
   New Left Review | 91
   Socialist Register | 103
   Dissent | 110
   Monthly Review | 117

3. The State of Theory | 131
3.1. Marxism | 131
New Left Review | 132
Socialist Register | 145
Dissent | 155
Monthly Review | 160
3.2. The Retrieval of Classics from the Radical and Socialist Traditions | 172
New Left Review | 172
Socialist Register | 179
Dissent | 180
Monthly Review | 183
3.3. Marxism and Radicalism | 187
4. Out of the Impasse: the Search for Models | 190
4.1. Dimensions of Democratic Socialism | 190
New Left Review | 190
Socialist Register | 201
Dissent | 211
Monthly Review | 221
4.2. Market Socialism – a Promising Project? | 231
Dissent | 232
New Left Review | 238
Monthly Review | 240
Socialist Register | 241
4.3. Sweden and Other Dreamlands | 242
New Left Review | 243
Socialist Register | 244
Dissent | 246
Monthly Review | 248
4.4. Europe: Capitalist Club or Site of Struggle and Project for the Left? | 250
New Left Review | 251
Socialist Register | 253
Dissent | 256
Monthly Review | 258
4.5. Locating Socialism | 260

5.	Re-starting History: Agency and Strategy	263	
	New Left Review	264	
	Socialist Register	275	
	Dissent	284	
	Monthly Review	292	
	Re-starting History	305	

IV. Between Radical Critique and Moderate Recommendations? | 309

1. Between Social Democracy and post-Marxism? | 310
1.1. Democratic Socialism and Social Democracy | 310
1.2. Neo-Marxism and Post-Marxism | 312
2. British and American or Anglo-American Re-orientations? | 314
3. Outlook and Conclusion | 316

V. Bibliography | 321

VI. Acknowledgements | 339